Cagney & Lacey ...
and Me

Cagney & Lacey ... and Me

An Inside Hollywood Story

OR

How I Learned to Stop Worrying and Love the Blonde

Barney Rosenzweig

iUniverse, Inc.

New York Lincoln Shanghai

Cagney & Lacey ... and Me

An Inside Hollywood Story OR
How I Learned to Stop Worrying and Love the Blonde

iUniverse books may be ordered through booksellers or by contacting:

iUniverse
2021 Pine Lake Road, Suite 100
Lincoln, NE 68512
www.iuniverse.com
1-800-Authors (1-800-288-4677)

Because of the dynamic nature of the Internet, any Web addresses or links contained in this book may have changed since publication and may no longer be valid.

The views expressed herein are the sole responsibility of the author and do not necessarily reflect the views of iUniverse or its affiliates.

ISBN: 978-0-595-41193-1 (pbk)
ISBN: 978-0-595-67878-5 (cloth)
ISBN: 978-0-595-85549-0 (ebk)

Printed in the United States of America

To those (both friend and not) who didn't live long enough to be able to read this book (in no particular order): Dick Reilly, Barbara Avedon, Sidney Clute, Al Waxman, Judy Mann, Larry Hilford, Aaron Rosenberg, Aaron and Myrtle Rosenzweig, Grandma Fanny, Howard Strickling, John Patterson, Ray Danton, Ronald M. Cohen, Jack R. Guss, Doc Calvelli, Peter Stone, Lee Guber, Stan Margulies, Bill Hayes, Monique James, Leon Shamroy, Jack Priestley, John Newland, Merwin Gerard, Lou Gallo, Harrison Carroll, Gary Nardino, Joel Oliansky, Morgan Hudgins, Helen and Jerry Kushnick, Steve Bernhardt, Jo Corday, Helen Neufeld, Shelley List, Melvin Levy, Jimmy Starr, Donald March, Jack Atlas, Buddy Rich, Bill Golden, Phil Scheuer, Elisha Cook Jr., Mort Werner, Quinn Martin, Anthony J. Hope, Mike Piller, Susan Strasberg, Bill Traylor, Peggy Feury, Louella Parsons, Lou Rudolph, Ray Walston, Harvey Hart, Eddie Milkis, Hedda Hopper, Larry Tisch, Brandon Tartikoff, Bob Batscha, Arthur Knight, Bob Wood, Terry Southern, Dick O'Neill, Clark Ramsey, Meta and George Rosenberg, Emily Torchia, Dan Curtis, Jay Bernstein, Brian McKay, Aaron Spelling, Jeanette Nolan, Howard Duff, Jose Ferrar, Mercedes McCambridge, Aleene MacMinn, Jack Warden, Tony Malara ...

... and also to the very much alive Sharon Gless and Tyne Daly, without whom the whole thing might well have been pointless.

CONTENTS

ACKNOWLEDGMENTS

For creative and thoughtful help with this tome, my grateful thanks to Carole R. Smith, Alan Trustman, Debra Weiss Goodstone, David Halberstadter, and Diane Robison. For encouragement and cheerleading beyond the call to Bridget Gless, Allyn Rosenzweig, Judy Samelson, Michelle Urrey, Naomi Caryl, PK Candaux, Peter Falk, Sam Perlmutter, Tom Healy, Steven Bochco, Bill Robinson, Rosie O'Donnell, Stephen Booke, Linda Bloodworth and Harry Thomason, Susan Grode, Michael Plonsker, Torrie Rosenzweig, David and Erika Handman, Gregg Miller, Penny Sansevieri, Paul Gendreau, the editors and staff of iUniverse, and to the entire company, crew, and friends of *Cagney & Lacey*, many of whom did not get mentioned in this work, with a particular tip of the hat (in the category of under-credited and in no particular order) to Ron Ramin, Mitch Danton, Doug Burdinski, Ronni Chasen, Michael Dante, Jim Gross, Ben Hammer, Helaine Head, Jan Ambler, Bob Jermain, Stanley Kamel, Dana Kaproff, Brooke Kennedy, Roni McAfee, Terry Kingsley-Smith, Dan Lauria, Nancy Malone, Rachel McCallister, Randy Morgan, Gaye Ann Bruno, Lois Nettleton, Allison Hock, Sandra Oh, David Paymer, Nicholas Pryor, Nan Mishkin, Mary Dean Pulver, Gail Reese, Judy Sable, Paul Sand, Carolyn Seymour, Hope Slepak, Frank South, Dale Henry, Soon-Teck Oh, Diane Dimeo, Michael McLean, Todd Thaler, Rose Marie, Joe Viola, Marcy Vosburgh, Sandy Sprung, Joe Feury, Lee Grant, Claudia Weill, Leo Penn, Sam Weisman, Chip Zien, Ed Plante, Dinah Manoff, Harry Sherman, Bill Lanteau, Lori Slomka, Sharon Rhode, Dorothy Swanson, Ken Wales, Bill Conti, Chris Cooke, Shannon Litten, Carolyn Elias, Robert Foxworth, Terri Fricon, Gail Strickland, Kevin Sullivan, Bill Taub, Lynne Thigpen, John Valentine, Fredd Wayne, Gary Wood, Steve Robinette, Steve Rosenbloom, Austin Lander, Donna Garrett, George Putnam, Kathleen Long, Stacy Codikow, Jason Bernard, Tony La Torre, Troy Slaten, Barry Primus, Paul Mantee, Margo Feiden, Tamu Blackwell, Marvin Kaplan, Brian Shapiro, Jonelle Allen, Forest Whitaker, Kathy Bates, Judith Ivey, Brian Dennehy …

… and to Richard M. Rosenbloom, Stan Neufeld, and Mick McAfee, who contributed far more than these pages show.

INTRODUCTION

In the 1980s, the television series *Cagney & Lacey* was on the air for six seasons, becoming a part of the landscape and the language for the last twenty-five years. To many it was more than mere entertainment; to some it was the quintessential show for working women, a flagship for the women's movement and—at last—an opportunity for real women to relate, and to identify with, what they were seeing on their television screens. This was all amplified by blind luck and good timing, for it was in that pre-Internet era when "on the air" meant being part of the primary pastime of North America.

In those days Americans watched television the way God meant us to: on one of the three major television networks and without remote control. In the continental United States, there were then sixty-six hours of prime-time network television per week (prime time being from 8 PM to 11 PM six nights per week and 7 PM to 11 PM on Sunday, for a total of twenty-two hours multiplied by three networks). Discounting the hours and half hours devoted to news and magazine programs, such as *20/20* and *60 Minutes,* or television movies, miniseries, and specials, that left approximately forty-eight shows aired on a weekly basis: forty-eight shows with their forty-eight executive producers who, week after week, were "on the air."

Only forty-eight.

There are a hundred U.S. senators … fifty governors.

Being "on the air," with a show dealing with the lives of two contemporary, urban women, a constituency of thirty million American viewers every week, and a license from CBS to say and do just about whatever we wished was very heady stuff.

The show was not only groundbreaking; it was iconic. Regardless of genre, there is nary a history book dealing with television in the twentieth century that does not list *Cagney & Lacey* among the finest shows ever produced.

The series was honored throughout the world, setting new precedents in the United Kingdom via the BBC, while simultaneously becoming one of the most honored dramatic television series in the history of the CBS Network in America, garnering Emmys, citations from the Congress of the United States, the State of California, the cities of Los Angeles, Chicago, and New York, and the ACLU; the Humanitas, Scott Newman, and Christopher awards; a special Luminas from Women in Film; as well as citations and salutes from the Museum of Television & Radio, the National Commission of Working Women, the National Organization for Women (NOW), the National Women's Political Caucus, and National Abortion Rights Action League (NARAL), and other women's groups throughout the country.

Individual episodes were singled out for praise or condemnation, depending on subject or just whose ox was being gored. The title became a punch line for cartoonists, comedians, and newscasters alike, a common reference point in the language for strong women and the feminist movement.

In the 1980s, CBS charged $300,000 per minute to advertise on *Cagney & Lacey*. That same network paid us to fill forty-six minutes a week of airtime with our beliefs, hopes, and fears, our values and humor. Those minutes may not have been brilliant, but millions of people liked them, and, more often than not, they were even celebrated (surprise, surprise) as something socially and culturally significant.

We made 125 episodes and five television movies. We earned an impressive thirty-six Emmy nominations, winning fourteen of these awards with episodes ranging in subject from abortion, to racism, to substance abuse, to Western medicine's assault on the female mammary. There were comedic episodes and stories of great loss, of love, and of family and friendship—to the point where, twenty-five years later, *Cagney & Lacey* still ranks as one of the best dramatic television series of all time.

I was there at the very beginning. I was the producer of every one of the 135 hours delivered to the world via television broadcasters, cable, and satellite as series episodes or movies for television: the guy who could say, without fear of contradiction, "Christine Cagney wouldn't say that."

Every episode, every script, every music cue, every edit, and every piece of casting was under my personal supervision. I was the one who took on every network note, every fight with the television establishment, from breaking through the all-male bias of just how women relate to one another, to whether it was all right to hear the sound of a flushing toilet while one of our female leads visited the commode, to a woman's right to choose to terminate a pregnancy, to the tastelessness of sexual humor in the workplace. I won far more of these battles than not.

After years of penury, humiliation, and struggle to learn the craft of producing, those 125 episodes and five movies of *Cagney & Lacey* gave me all I ever wanted from a life in show business. I loved it, and you would have, too.

I loved it not only because it was great, but because while it was going on I was conscious of what was happening around me and to me. It was not just another job. I knew that those were very special years when they were occurring, and I lived them very much in the present. All that had gone before—all the miseries of my first twenty-five years in Hollywood—was repaired by *Cagney & Lacey,* and I was made whole. Those years of the very long ago may well become the basis for another tome, but *Cagney & Lacey* and the people who made it possible were responsible for most of the very best years of my life.

It was wonderful, and this is that story.

CHAPTER 1

OUT OF THE DARKNESS …

Cagney & Lacey production central, Lacy Street, Los Angeles, April, 1988:

The very last day of the very last episode of the very last season of my television series took place on the first Monday of the month of April 1988. I was in my office, very much alone and waiting for an emotional reaction that would not come. I stared at the phone. Moments before, I had slammed down the receiver, ending an awful argument with my oldest child. She was then twenty-eight. I was fifty. One of us should have known better.

Those were difficult times between Erika and me, and my anger at the phone call was rapidly turning to guilt as I continued to glare at that damned phone, wondering if I should call my child back, what I would say if she would even take the call, and why these conversations with us were (seemingly) always so awful.

The phone rang. Weird to be staring at a phone and have it just ring like that. It was Barbara Rosing calling from our production office:

"We're holding the last shot. They won't make it without you there."

My flesh and blood family would have to wait. I set down the phone's receiver and walked the hundred or so yards to the squad room set of my beloved series.

The final shot was a somewhat complicated set-up with the camera placed on a small, crane-like dolly. This facilitated a smooth camera move throughout the squad room, so as to capture various, specific moments with individual members of the cast who had been spotted in different places in the set by the director. The purpose of such a move is to guide the audience's attention to what is important in the scene, while adding a certain amount of cinematic fluidity to the filmmaking, while (not coincidentally) reducing or eliminating the need for additional individual shots or "coverage," saving money and time both on the set and in the editing bay.

On my arrival at the familiar set of the 14th Precinct, I was asked, for the first time in my career, to ride the dolly and look through the camera's lens as a final "rehearsal." When the less-than-a-minute move was complete, I nodded my "approval," thanked the dolly "grip" who had guided me through the whole process, and then dismounted the "best seat in the house" in order to fade into the background and watch my cast and crew do what they had done so well for over 125 episodes.

As the assistant director called for quiet, my mind drifted back to the argument with my daughter and how I might try explaining to her my poor temper during our not-so-long-ago fight by telephone. The thought entering my mind was to send her a note, referring to this very moment in the life of my show and the dark mood into which I was being enveloped, opening the missive with:

"One of my children died tonight."

Before I could even consider the possible tastelessness of that remark, my eyes began to well up. A moment later the final shot was complete. It was a "wrap," and all on stage began to applaud, shake hands, and hug each other. Within minutes I was alone in the room. Everyone had exited to pack up; to grab a drink, a piece of pizza, or a slice of cake; and then to go home. I took a bench seat along the wall and surveyed the now-empty room, not unlike Walter Payton at Chicago's Soldier Field at the end of his last football game. Like him, I just sat there, trying to soak it in, recognizing that—at least for me—it was the end of an epoch.

An electrician entered the squad room set, ignored me, and began his nightly chore of turning the overhead lights off, one by one. I wished I had hired a videotape camera person to record this moment, and then it was over. I was crying as Sharon Gless, and then a moment later Tyne Daly, entered the room. They flanked me and each gave me hugs, but in the seconds that elapsed before these two fabulous women joined me, my mind flashed back fourteen years to another darkened room, one with a flickering light behind me and a beaded screen in front as I viewed the movie *Scent of a Woman*—not the one with Al Pacino, but the original—a seventies Italian film starring Vittorio Gassman, which predated the American version by a generation. It was my second date with Barbara Corday, a woman then in her late twenties who was near the beginning of a promising career as a writer for television.

Ms. Corday was then the lesser half of the writing team of Avedon & Corday; her partner, Barbara Avedon, was at that time in her mid to late forties, a writer of several years' experience, with an impressive array of television writing credits. Relatively new to the game as a team, the Barbaras were having some success as comedy writers for hire when I picked them for their first dramatic writing assignment on a then-new hour series for CBS developed by former William Sackheim lieutenant, David Levinson.

Levinson would serve as executive producer for the Universal Studios project, and I was being asked to produce under his aegis. The series was alternately called *Sons and Daughters* or *Senior Year*. It was to be a continuing, or serial, drama, focusing on the lives of a group of suburban high school students. It was set up as a cross between *Peyton Place* and *American Graffiti*. Unfortunately, it had all the drama of the lighthearted *American Graffiti* and all the humor of the hyper-dramatic *Peyton Place*.

The setting was a medium-size American town. The heroes were ball players, sports editors, and cheerleaders. The heroines were pom-pom girls and gals from the wrong side of the tracks. I was, in most ways, perfect casting for this vehicle. I had been one of those kids; I had grown up in Montebello (a small, working-class town in the midst of southern California oil fields), and it was not so many years before that I had forgotten what that was like. I don't think the then-thirty-something David Levinson much appreciated my unique pedigree.

My supposition is that he was probably brought up as the overachieving, scholarly son of a well-to-do Chicago family, who spent much of his boyhood practicing the piano and attending concerts in the metropolitan environs of the Second City. Being asked to create a series about kids who grew up without his discipline (and who seemingly, in that long-ago time, were having a lot more fun than he) was now the task at hand. I'm guessing he never liked those kids. Worse than that, he didn't much like me.

I refer to it as my period of watching paint dry. Levinson would allow me to do little else. The show was the first cancellation of the season. I don't think the then-network chief Fred Silverman allowed CBS to air three episodes.

Not everything was bleak that summer.

Barbara Corday had recently separated from her second husband, and I was in the process of ending my five-year "thing" with the beautiful Jeannine from Malibu Beach. It was all business during the day, but vibrations of mutual availability were in the air when Corday phoned my office.

"I don't know what the proper protocol between writers and producers in a situation like this is," she began, "but I was wondering if you'd like to come over for dinner one night this week."

"Your protocol is fine," I said, then added, "Look, you work, I work, why not go out to dinner?"

From that moment, Barbara Corday knew she had found the man for her. My feelings were articulated then and years later in the "Choices" episode of *Cagney & Lacey*: Barbara was a cactus. Jeannine was a fern. Barbara didn't need any watering at all. That was OK with me.

Dinner was our first date, and that led to our second night out together and the movie *Scent of a Woman*. The theater was in Westwood Village, and the 400-seat house was at least half full. The movie was in black and white, and the story took place in southern Italy shortly after World War II. The laughs at this sexy comedy were audible and primarily based on the relationships (or lack of same) between the somewhat older, sometimes slightly vulgar Italian men and the objects that attracted their lusty attention: the beautiful Italian girls of that sunny climate, invariably dressed somewhat scantily in what seemed to me appropriate given the film's summer setting.

Most of that Westwood audience, including me, seemed to appreciate what they were watching; that is until I became aware that the film was having quite a different impact on my date. Ms. Corday was clutching the arm of her seat so tightly her knuckles had been drained of their color.

"Are you all right?" I whispered as I leaned closer to her.

Her answer was succinct: "This is the most degrading, the most sexist film I have ever seen," she said. She was, I thought, clearly upset.

"Do you want to leave?" I asked.

"No," she said. "You watch. Later we'll talk."

I am a heterosexual male and a product of the 1950s. The evening I am describing took place in the mid-1970s. Words such as *sexist* and *feminist* were not part of my everyday lexicon. I sat back to watch the movie with a clearly angry woman on my right.

Gloria Steinem talks about moments of epiphany: those all-too-rare occurrences where the proverbial lightbulb goes off and you have an insight, an ability to understand something in a way that heretofore you had not. Ms. Steinem calls them "clicks." *Epiphany* is too grand a word for anything having to do with me, but that night in a darkened movie house in the heart of Westwood Village, I had a click. It was, for me, a mini-miracle that changed my life from that evening on—a watershed moment that would heavily impact what would, ever after, become the bulk of my work as a Hollywood television producer.

That night—I am almost reluctant, embarrassed really, to explain—I was watching the film, and without any conscious thought on my part (and with no further comment from my date) I found the movie had been transformed. (Imagine a boy pulling the wings off of flies. Most would find that cruel and worthy of keeping an eye on the child's developmental processes. But take that same child's actions and have the victim be someone with whom it is easier to relate—a human being for instance—and the reaction to the perpetrator is very different indeed.) Just as it was in the metaphor about the child pulling wings off of flies, somehow, in my mind's eye, what I was looking at on that flickering Westwood screen took place not in Italy, but rather in Stuttgart, Germany. The time frame was not post–World War II, but the late 1930s. The women were not women, but male Chasidic Jews. By making this transference, I "saw" the sexist humor for what it was, something that only worked at the expense of someone less powerful and accomplished, only to the detriment of the object of the joke. The seemingly lighthearted movie playing on the screen had, as a result, become a truly anti-Semitic document.

It was a revelation.

It forever altered my perception. Corday would later comment: "Barney's not a feminist, but he gets it."

I got it all right.

What I "got" that evening has become an automatic response. It applies to automobile ads, to bachelor parties, and to what used to be one of my favorite pieces of musical theater, Leonard Bernstein's *Candide*. I can't watch it anymore without being offended. As for advertisements, for me, it is no longer a half-naked girl selling that product; it is a scantily clad Chasid. The empty, insincere smile sickens me. I know there is nothing short of force, or a desperate need for money, that would bring this person to do such a thing. It is degrading and—as a witness—I, too, am somehow demeaned.

Since that evening in the spring of 1974, I've walked out of more than a few stag parties, declined invitations to several others, and have been turned off to some previously enjoyable entertainments. On the other hand, it gave me an understanding of how it might feel to be accorded second-class citizenship status in a land where few acknowledged that bias, and it put me in touch with the sense of how it feels to be powerless in a world of the powerful. It made me uniquely qualified to advance these observations by making *Cagney & Lacey*. What a terrific trade-off.

CHAPTER 2

FUNNIER THAN CALIFORNIA?
WHAT ISN'T?

By the end of '74, Corday and I had become an item. By mid-1975, the Barbaras had expressed an interest in working with me on developing several ideas, including *The Malachite Kachina*, a treatment for a theatrical motion picture I had acquired from Cliff and Jean Hoelscher, a young, bright couple I had met at the Atlanta Film Festival in 1972 while screening *Who Fears the Devil*, my first independent feature motion picture.

Initially I had hoped to woo a major female film star to the title role. Once it became clear that was not going to happen, I pitched the character of the distaff private-eye, with its hoped-for filmic send-up of classic film noir, to Avedon & Corday. A development deal on the concept was made with NBC as a possible series to be called *This Girl for Hire*. It became the first of several properties I would develop with this writing team.

The two Barbaras, who needed to make a living and keep themselves current in the job market, would work for other producers as well during this period, but more and more the synergy of our troika was something we all acknowledged. Our lives began to intertwine, and, along with Avedon's then-husband, Dr. Mel Avedon, we would become a more than occasional social foursome.

My education from both Barbaras concerning the feminist movement had now escalated to reading on the subject, including Molly Haskell's *From Reverence to Rape: The Treatment of Women in the Movies*. In that work, which remains a fascinating textbook on Hollywood's on-screen view of women from its earliest days, Ms. Haskell made a statement that haunted me: never in the history of motion pictures or television had Hollywood made a film where two women related to each other as did Paul Newman and Robert Redford. In other words, there had never been a buddy movie featuring women. Why not make one? I approached Corday with the idea. She liked it. She presented it to her partner. I went to Ed Feldman, my old pal from my previous life as a motion picture publicist.

Since his days of publicizing Ray Stark and Company, Ed had become the head of Filmways, a small motion picture and television company that put up seed money for films. Though the company did not finance pictures, it could be effective in setting up a venture that would facilitate funding and, more importantly, was willing to put up highly speculative start-up dollars for a motion picture screenplay.

I pitched Ed the idea: a Newman and Redford movie, with and for women. Not much more needed to be said. A good "pitch" is most often given in what is referred to in the trade as a *TV Guide* log-line. In other words, you ought to be able to communicate your idea in a short sentence. We talked about genre. That meant Ed was interested. The ball was now in my court. I liked the cop arena and used the then-successful motion picture *Freebie and the Bean* (with James Caan and Alan Arkin) as a prototype. Because Filmways had just had *Fuzz*, a profitable film in release with Burt Reynolds and Raquel Welch playing police officers, there was no argument from Ed. We fought for New York as a locale despite the extra expense because, as Barbara Avedon explained, "it's funnier than California."

The Filmways legal department had informed us that our selection of the title *Newman and Redford* would not hold up in court should we be sued. We would have to come up with another and did, including such unfortunate choices as *Cross My Bra and Hope to Die. Fair Game* was tentatively agreed upon for reasons no one seems to recall, and a deal was struck. Including their fees as writers, my supervisory money, the dollars to send both of the writers to New York for a week of research with the NYPD, and script typing, Ed was committing a total of $27,500 of Filmways' money. It was the last time anyone would have to put up a speculative dollar on what would become *Cagney & Lacey*.

Avedon & Corday delivered the screenplay less than two months after taking off for that research trip to NYC. I thought it was a funny and raunchy theatrical motion picture screenplay. Ed was ecstatic with the results, and it was now his job to be about the business of getting a major motion picture studio interested in putting up the mega-bucks required to make a motion picture.

The Barbaras would keep writing for television, including several projects I had in development (a movie-for-television, an after-school special, a daytime soap, and a dramatic television series). We enjoyed working together more and more, despite our lack of success in actually getting anything made. We were in development hell in almost every section of the business to which a writer/producer team can gain access. No one was giving us a green light to production. A large part of this was the climate in the Hollywood community at that time, and that brings about this background information:

When I began in television in the 1960s, networks were run by broadcasters, men (there are still, nearly fifty years later, precious few women in the truly lofty upper echelons of network management) who came from radio. In those days the over-riding message from the New York broadcasting giants was "leave it on." A good show, it was believed, would find its audience; the network chiefs left the show-making to the show-makers. They were successful with this formula, and when corporations become successful they do the equivalent of what a successful indi-vidual might do … they buy something, not a new hat or a new car, but maybe a new building. And what they do with that new building is fill it up—with executives. In the late 1960s, and all through the early 1970s, that's just what the networks did.

Were these new executives broadcasters like their predecessors? People who wished to make a career working through the public airwaves? Not really. They were young MBAs, many from the Ivy League, interested in the glamour of show busi-ness. They might well have speculated that a brief sojourn at the network—in one of those new buildings in Hollywood, rubbing elbows and trading favors with show business royalty—could move them on to their ultimate goal of potential moguldom with a decided insider's advantage. *Variety*, the bible of show business, said it best: "Indy-prod with a multi pic-pac." Translation: independent produc-tion with a multiple picture contract.

Fresh out of graduate school, in their low-pay/high-profile positions, their pay-ment was in power; they could say no to men and women with great credentials, earning five to ten times per year their own meager compensation. Their pay-ment was in access to the super moguls with whom they might eventually ally. Why serve a long apprenticeship when all it might take is the "green lighting" of a certain project that could well feather some future nest of their own? Does this sound like a conflict of interest? In the 1980s, young men and women on Wall Street would lose their careers and some would go to jail for far less onerous activity. Generals at the Pentagon, who reaped far less compensation, would find themselves under congressional investigation. But in Hollywood it was business as usual—a great scandal, save for one key missing ingredient. No one cared. No reporter wrote about it; "Indy-Prod with a Multi Pic-Pac"—the headline announcing the whereabouts of the new about-to-be millionaire was the extent of journalistic exploration.

In the late 1960s, a seemingly unrelated event was taking place. Quinn Martin, one of Hollywood's finest producers, with such credits as *The Fugitive* and *Streets of San Francisco,* developed a way of keeping a core group of writers under his wing and exclusively his. He would pay them more than money. He would massage their vanity, allowing them to be called "producers."

Of course these writers weren't producers. Quinn Martin was the producer. Every show bore his individual stamp. It didn't matter. Quinn called these writers producers to keep them happy and on the job even if they were producers in credit only. Other companies followed suit, popularizing the concept of what would become known as "the hyphenates." A proliferation of credits followed, totally altering the role of the producer as I had known it.

The producer who fought this proliferation (and therefore diminution) of credit was labeled a troublemaker. I was not the only one-time prominent producer to be blacklisted by a Harvard MBA newly employed at a major network. In the late 1960s, as a result of creative differences over a TV movie project I had started under the supervision of then-freshman ABC exec Jerry Isenberg, I found myself marked "uncooperative" and therefore unemployable at that network. My blacklisting at ABC extended years past Isenberg's leaving the network—and his subsequent sojourn into indy-prod with his own multi pic-pac.

In fairness to Mr. Isenberg, I *was* uncooperative. I thought (and still think) that being uncooperative was a big part of my job; that being the producer meant fighting for what I believed was correct … that defending the original vision was the way to demonstrate my passion for the material. Isenberg wanted someone who would follow his instructions … to go along with his notes.

Into the 1970s and beyond, network executives more and more elected to deal with the writer directly, believing that they could always hire a production manager to care for whatever logistical functions might arise. The producer was, in their view, extraneous; besides, most writers in Hollywood were accustomed to "taking notes," having been conditioned for years by producers and directors in this collaborative process.

For some writers this new era was a boon. Being good at a meeting was the criterion. One's acumen at a typewriter became secondary. Some, it is true, excelled at both. But now, for the first time, the writer who stuttered, took time at his or her lonely desk to think out an idea or phrase, was too old to be considered hip by younger network types, or—just possibly—too temperamental or opinionated, that writer was at a distinct disadvantage.

"Giving good meeting" was a must. The era of the hyphenate saw the network executives take over the role of the project initiator. They took control of what would be said and by whom.

To be affable—agreeable to the "new" idea pitched *by* the network executive *for* the network executive—to be able to interpret and execute the story the MBA network executive wanted, *that* became primary. What would get on the nation's television screens became the province of the very few. Broadcasting was to become narrow casting.

The effects of the young MBAs and the newly anointed hyphenates in Hollywood cannot be overstated. Bright though many of these executives were, brilliant as some would prove to be, it was basically one person giving out ideas to writers instead of multiple producers pitching their diverse projects. The narrowness of vision, even from an ingenious source, was still only one view. The sameness of it would become all too abundantly clear, as television would—with the exception of a few bright, shining moments—become worse instead of better: less courageous, less innovative, less passionate.

It was also inefficient, for in the wake of this creative rough-shodding by networks came an era of fiscal irresponsibility of writers-turned-producers. The literary bent of many of these talents ill-prepared them for the visual, fiscal, mechanical, and temperamental realities of day-to-day production. Arguments about what a line of dialogue might mean were colored by the ego of the writer-producer himself, or, conversely, by his too-easy willingness to take yet another note and make a change.

Lacking someone with an overview with whom to communicate, the production manager would often find himself waiting outside the hyphenate's office for the pages to come out of the typewriter while the whole production team expended precious (and costly) time awaiting word of what to do next.

Because the hyphenate would now be on location scouts and occupied at preproduction or casting meetings rather than at the typewriter, there would no longer be ten scripts in hardcover to start a season. This created major economic and creative repercussions. It is not a coincidence that the most expensive *Cagney & Lacey* episodes ever made were the few I wrote.

Behind all of this was the new pseudo producer, the network executive. The power and money of his organization solidly behind him, the anonymity of his desk squarely in front of him, this executive was closest to having it all. Their names did not go on the screen to risk the wrath and ridicule of critic and public alike; their careers, contracts, and personal fortunes were not at stake. They were like grandparents who enjoy the child but never have to deal with the dirty diapers. They had it all, except for money; for the fact was (and is) they weren't very well paid in dollars. Never mind, indy-prod with a multi pic-pac would eventually take care of that.

It is a myth that talent, like cream, rises to the top. Too often, it is those fragile, talented individuals who are crushed by the system.

The erosion of the network audience has come about largely due to new technology, but partially, I believe, also because of the incestuous vision of the too few who became the storytellers. Ironically, that very erosion would, ultimately, force the networks to cut costs and reduce the size of their executive staffs, which had caused the problem in the first place. The proliferation of credits, which resulted in the loss of so many truly talented producers in this field, would eventually have to be confronted. It was.

A new title would be invented, one that has yet to be seen on any television screen: show runner. It is evidence of a desire to return to the way it was done in the beginning. A show runner, not necessarily a writer or a director, someone with an overall vision, someone who can handle the network or studio needs, who can communicate with the cast, hire the writers and the directors, supervise the editorial concept, and turn out, week after week, a consistent, promotable product. It sure sounds like a producer to me, but that credit, if it is ever to mean anything again, will have to be retrieved from an awful lot of production managers, staff writers, and assistants.

As originated by Barry Diller and his ABC minions—and subsequently by Fred Silverman and his subordinates first at CBS, then ABC, and NBC—this system could be very oppressive and wasteful. In the more than thirty years that have followed—with all their power and virtually unlimited funds—the networks have managed to create less than a half dozen superstar hyphenates. Enormous amounts of capital expended, a lot of talented, passionate, hardworking producers buried, to create—over an entire generation—a handful.

You cannot cut down rain forests in Brazil and not have it affect the weather in North America. You cannot build concrete canyons in areas that were once flat and not get wind. Swimming pools and golf courses in desert resorts have raised the humidity and caused rainy seasons and droughts, where heretofore they did not exist.

In the 1970s, Diller, Silverman, and a young group of network executives messed with the ecology of Hollywood. Their imprimatur is still being felt. Of more importance to this piece is that this is where I found myself all those years ago: an overqualified, true, non-writing producer in an awful rising tide, just trying to survive the onrushing tsunami.

CHAPTER 3

LIMBO WITH GRANDMA FANNY

Back at Filmways, Ed Feldman was not having any success in getting financing for a *Cagney & Lacey* motion picture. Every studio head then in Hollywood was male. Confronted with the *Cagney & Lacey* screenplay, they demurred. They simply didn't believe the script. They did not accept that women talked to each other or related to each other in the way we had indicated.

The men of Hollywood had their own mythology, reinforced by the films of their predecessors (also males):

"A woman isn't a woman until she's had a child."

"A woman might have a job but would give it all up in a minute for the 'right' man."

"Women can't, and don't, have friendships the way men do."

"Women are in constant competition for Mr. Right."

… And, the seemingly inevitable male fantasy of the Madonna/Bitch.

Is it any wonder Hollywood had never produced a buddy movie for women?

Sherry Lansing, the recently retired head of Paramount Studios and the producer of *Fatal Attraction*, among other films, was, in 1975, a youthful assistant to Dan Melnick, the MGM studio chief of the moment. She liked the Avedon & Corday screenplay and kept hounding her mentor to consider it for production. Her persistence outlasted his obstinacy. He finally condescended to make an "offer." He would fund the movie for $1.8 million contingent on getting Ann-Margret and Raquel Welch as the two women leads.

It was all pretty silly. In the mid-1970s it was barely possible to hire these two women for that price, let alone have enough left over to make a film. Furthermore, it should be remembered just who Ms. Margret and Ms. Welch were all those years ago. Neither had yet achieved the hard-won recognition they have today as talented actresses; in those days they were simply symbols of Hollywood's male fantasy of the super-endowed sex goddess. They were then the polar opposite of what we were trying to accomplish with *Cagney & Lacey* and, so as to keep the record straight, our prototypes for casting in those early days were Sally Kellerman and Paula Prentiss.

Things were also not going so well on my other project with a female lead. The written presentation for NBC by Avedon & Corday on *This Girl for Hire* is to this day one I use as a reference and an example for would-be pilot makers to follow. It is well-written, entertaining, and informative. The reader of those less than two dozen pages knows exactly what the show is about, what the film will look like, what the characters sound like, how they dress, and how they relate to each other. It made it very easy to visualize not only the eventual screenplay but the film itself. It was such a strong guide that it all but guaranteed a solid screenplay. All one had to do was follow the map of that presentation to pay dirt.

We had been operating under the guidance of network development executives Lou Hunter and Deanne Barkley. Now the project had stalled before going to the final stage of ordering a pilot script. Irwin Segelstein, then of NBC's upper echelon, had pulled the plug.

"A woman's place is in the kitchen and the bedroom," he said to his staff. What Deanne Barkley rejoined I do not know. What I do know is we were out of business at NBC and that Ms. Barkley didn't stay around at the network too much longer after that.

That spring, across town, the team of Aaron Spelling and Leonard Goldberg had struck some pay dirt of their own with a show featuring women. It was called *Charlie's Angels,* and it had made the ABC lineup for the fall of 1976. The good news was I was on the Spelling/Goldberg shortlist of producer-for-hire candidates. The bad news? Another Spelling/Goldberg series, *The Rookies,* had finally been canceled. Its writer/producer had been Rick Husky, who ten years before had been my protégé on *Daniel Boone* (my first producing job) and before that (in the early 1960s) at the MGM publicity department. It was on *Daniel Boone* that Rick had received his first writing assignment, launching his career. Now he was being asked to set up the company's new series with Farrah Fawcett, Kate Jackson, and Jaclyn Smith, who he was then dating.

Rick called me within a few days. "I hear I beat you out of a job. I'm sick about it," he said.

"Don't be silly," I countered. "They know you a lot better than me. You've been with them a long time and done a hell of a job. It's only natural they would want you."

"Listen Barney," Rick said, his tone almost conspiratorial. "I'm exhausted. I really wanted a major break after my series, but I couldn't turn these guys down. All I agreed to do was get 'em started. I'm only doing the first six episodes, so stay on top of this. Push your agent to get you in here. There'll be a job by fall."

Rick had heard me talk about how cold it had been on the outside. How, as a non-writing producer, trying to make a living on supervisory fees of $2,500 here and $1,750 there was a bad joke. I appreciated the tip. Meanwhile, development went on. So did the calendar. It was midway through 1976. In the four years since 1972, my name had appeared on only two productions: *Men of the Dragon* in release in 1974 and *One of My Wives Is Missing* in 1975. Things were bleak.

A couple of times a month, I'd drive across town to visit my grandmothers, Fanny and Minnie. They did not live together, but both resided on Los Angeles' east side. Minnie was my paternal grandmother. Fanny was on my mother's side. She was also one of my principal creditors.

Nether woman was rich. No one in my family was. Fanny had worked all her life, and her needs were small. During this period, she would loan me upwards of $8,000. Instead of interest, I showed up every other week at her place. I'd eat a little boiled chicken and bring her up to date with what was going on in my life. The meetings with Grandma Minnie were shorter. She didn't cook too much, and the conversations turned more on the Mexican American kids in the neighborhood who were making her life so unpleasant. Show business didn't interest Minnie. Fanny longed for the day when she would see my name on her television screen again.

One night, Fanny's impatience at my lack of screen credit had me on the very treacherous ground of trying to explain television development to a civilian. At best this is a trying and difficult conversation. With a woman in her eighties, not noted for her powers of concentration even as a youth, this was a formidable task.

"It's like the shmatte[1] business, Grandma."

I thought I might have a chance here by comparing my trade to the one industry Fanny really knew. For years she had labored as a seamstress in the garment district in Los Angeles.

"I go in with my dresses. Some are long, some are short. Some have patterns, some have bright colors."

Grandma Fanny was smiling. She was enjoying this. Am I a storyteller, or am I a storyteller?

"I go into Cole of California and to Martin, and I go into Catalina Casuals, but right now, no one is buying my dresses." There was a pause. I presumed the metaphor was sinking in.

"Maybe I could help," she said.

I put down my chicken leg. The napkin hid my supercilious grin. "Grandma, how could you help?"

Her tone indicated that the word *schmuck* might well have preceded her imperious statement. "I know about dresses."

"No, no, you misunderstand. It's an analogy." I said this last part very slowly, pedagogically. "They're not really dresses, Grandma. They're ideas, projects, potential television shows. And it's not really Cole, Martin, or Catalina. It's ABC, NBC, and CBS. See? I go in with my stuff, and nobody's buying."

I looked at her. Her eyes narrowed, focusing on me. I nodded slightly as if to say, "You get it?" Then limply added, "They're not buying my dresses."

Grandma Fanny nodded sagely. She drew in her breath through her nose, then slowly, thoughtfully, let it escape before speaking. "Maybe you should make men's suits."

God, I miss Grandma Fanny. I laughed more that night than I had in years. The tension of the past months, even years, came out of me as I literally rolled on the floor in glee, totally unable to control myself. Grandma Fanny was pleased I was having such a good time.

---

[1]   *Shmatte*, a show business yiddishism, literally meaning rag, but often referring to a dress or the clothing-making business. Rhymes with *lotta*.

CHAPTER 4

CHARLIE'S ANGELS

Spelling and Goldberg were not too pleased with the early work they were seeing on *Charlie's Angels*. Rick Husky's protestations of being tired were finally being listened to, and word went out for his replacement. My old Universal nemesis, David Levinson, had been brought in to produce at least a couple of episodes until it could be determined by Spelling, his partner, and the ABC network how to proceed. They would have to make a decision soon. The show was due to go on the air in a matter of weeks. I began to lean heavily on new-to-me-agent Bob Broder, regarding this "gun-for-hire" gig at Spelling/Goldberg.

"What's the big deal here, Barney?" Broder was quizzing me by phone. "We haven't discussed your going back to series television. You never push for any other show—what's so special about this one?"

I was not one of Broder's more important clients, and he obviously had no clue what it was like trying to make a living on scanty script supervisory fees. It had been months since I had had a real paying job.

"Because it's going to be a major success, and I need to be connected to a hit right now. Because if I'm right—and this show about women detectives *is* a hit—then it just might get *Cagney & Lacey* and *This Girl for Hire* made. And, finally, I taught Rick Husky everything he knows. He's a great act for me to follow!"

Broder got the picture. Within a few days I got a call from him with instructions to attend a 10 AM screening at projection room F at the 20th Century Fox facility leased by Spelling/Goldberg. I was to view nearly three hours of film, then proceed to Aaron Spelling's office for a meeting. What I was there to see was three and a half episodes of *Charlie's Angels*, Spelling/Goldberg's about-to-debut television series. It was pretty dreadful.

The format, as I recall, was to open with a scene of action, then to cut to Charlie's office. There, in that posh interior, a slide projector was put into operation, and, *Mission: Impossible*-like, the audience (and the Angels) would be brought up to speed on the necessary expository beats of that week's episode. Charlie's disembodied voice would come over the telephone speaker box, adding commentary to those projected images, explaining what the caper was and what each of the Angels was to do. Then, in varying degrees of harmony with their assignments, off they would go to complete the tasks outlined and assigned to them by their unseen boss.

The shows droned on, the flaws of each magnified by their—as yet—incomplete status. Sexist jokes were scattered throughout each one of the episodes. It didn't offend in the same way as did *Scent of a Woman*; these jokes were simply too lame to be measured on that scale. It didn't matter. I wanted this job; my mind raced as I walked the eighth of a mile across the Fox lot to Spelling's suite and my audition.

I was told to go right in. The offices were magnificent. It was the bungalow that had belonged to producer Jerry Wald during my earlier days at Fox. The suite had vaulted and beamed ceilings; there was a large fireplace and wet bar. Wald had been one of Hollywood's legendary producers, said to be the prototype for Budd Schulberg's *What Makes Sammy Run*. Now the office was Spelling's. I entered the sanctum to find the mogul alone in the vast room and on the phone, saying, "I know, Fred. I agree with you."

I learned later that the Fred on the other end of the line was ABC's then-president, Fred Pierce. Spelling looked up, saw me standing at the door, and beckoned me toward a seat opposite his fine antique desk.

"You're right, Fred," he said. "We feel the same way."

A long pause while he listened, then, referring to Fred Silverman, ABC programming chief, he continued. "Freddie's right, it is embarrassing. But, Fred, Barney Rosenzweig is here now to take over the show, and we feel he's going to turn this around." Spelling went on a minute or so more as I beamed. The job was mine.

Aaron and I adjourned to another table in the office, away from his desk, so that his manservant could serve up lunch. It was for one. That was OK with me. I had to do all the talking anyway.

I launched into my spiel. "First of all, I do believe the show can be an enormous hit. I still feel strongly about the concept and the casting. Having said that, I'd like to focus on where I think mistakes have been made."

Aaron busied himself with lunch but did motion me to go on.

"For openers," I said, "the show begins on five minutes of static exposition. It's cinematically uninteresting and all potentially boring. Worse, it violates one of the basic tenets of the private-eye genre, which is that the detective deals directly with the client—a character who is traditionally interesting, sometimes bizarre, and possibly dangerous. That doesn't happen here because Charlie—who is never seen—meets the client off-stage and merely tells the Angels about it."

I was revving up; Spelling continued his noontime repast.

"Remember those Bogart films where Sidney Greenstreet or whomever had to live in a refrigerated room or like an orchid in a hothouse?"

Aaron nodded. I went on. "By introducing such a character through our detectives, we not only make the exposition more interesting and visual, but we also give our detectives eye contact with the client. We give them a personal stake in all this. Our leads would no longer merely be mercenaries. The result is that we will like them better." I had not so subtly made this a mutual project with a lot of "we"s and "our"s, not wanting to trust my status on the project to Spelling's earlier pronouncement on the phone to the head of ABC.

"Finally," I said, "the women should be more in charge and less the minions of someone we never see and therefore care about very little."

I noticed Mr. Spelling's brow furrow slightly. I plunged forward. "Let me give you an example of what I'm talking about. We would open, as we do now, on an action scene. Then, instead of going to Charlie's speaker box, we cut to the home or office of the client. He or she has hired the Angels because of their reputation or a relationship with Charlie. After that scene (where the goals of the caper are now explained by an interesting character in a unique setting), we then cut to Charlie's office and the speaker phone. There the Angels will outline to Charlie (instead of the other way around) what they learned and what each of them will do on the case. Charlie will then say: 'Good thinking, Angels,' and we'll be off and running."

I was pleased as Aaron approved my changes. He seemed grateful that someone actually had an idea about what might be wrong. I knew what I was doing was a lot more visual and certainly better storytelling. I also believed I was accomplishing a service for all concerned, including the audience, by making these working women brighter and more independent than my predecessors had.

Spelling summoned Leonard Goldberg, we shook hands, and I was on board. I then went on to meet my new story editor, Ed Lakso, who, although picked for me by Messrs. Spelling and Goldberg, was someone with whom, after an hour or so of preliminary discussions, I felt I could work with happily. We were in full harness in less than a day.

Part of our routine was to take long walks around the Fox lot, kicking around story and character ideas. I would come up with a scene, taking time to illustrate to Lakso how it might be staged, lit, and photographed. I'd go into incredible detail over this particular vignette (which might be the beginning, the middle, or the end of a story).

"Now," I said to Lakso on the first of these strolls, "the interesting thing is how did they get there and how do they get out?"

That would become Lakso's job. Sometimes we'd work it out in tandem, sometimes we would alternate spinning webs for each other; mostly he did it on his own. He was extremely fast and facile.

The scripts started coming quickly, and they were good. The bosses thought they were great and sent memos (called Goldbergrams in those days) praising the work almost daily.

It was two weeks away from the production being turned over to our scripts when the first episode (completed by my predecessors) would air. I had volunteered my services to reedit what I had seen, but the offer was refused with thanks.

I wasn't being altruistic. I was plenty worried that once the audience viewed these early episodes we might never get them to return. My concern was also how any critic could ever be brought back to the show so that we might demonstrate the effective changes we were making.

My concerns aside, the opening night ratings for Rick Husky's version of the series were immense. The numbers were precedent setting. Hopefully, the drop off the following week would not kill us. There were some jokes from all quarters about the taste of the viewing public. The next week's numbers on Rick's second episode came out on the first day of production of the first episode under my aegis. They were higher than the previous week. *Charlie's Angels* was a bona fide, major hit.

Mr. Goldberg was not being facetious when he then reversed himself, saying, "Let's not make this show too good." He thought he was onto something, however accidental. I would argue that the show was a smash in spite of the fact that it was awful, not because of it, but more and more I was being tuned out.

Goldberg believed the audience to be masturbating adolescent males. I felt the majority of viewers were young girls delighted to see fantasy role models on the screen, just as girls of my generation had been all too happy to read the exploits of Nancy Drew. Of course the girls wanted their heroines to be good looking. Didn't Mr. Goldberg and I want Errol Flynn and Clark Gable to be handsome?

I had been in that Westwood movie theater a few years before when *Cotton Comes to Harlem* made its debut in 1970. It was the first of the so-called blacksploitation flicks, and I attended it with an audience primarily composed of people of color. They cheered the film. All their lives they had, along with me, applauded the exploits of John Wayne and Humphrey Bogart. Now, for the first time, someone who looked and sounded like them was doing all the star turns and getting the gal at the end. They loved it, and why shouldn't they? It made perfect sense to me then, and it made the same kind of sense to me when I conceived *Cagney & Lacey* as well as when I argued with Spelling and Goldberg as to who the audience was for *Charlie's Angels*.

The disputes were more than esoteric. My recollection is that they centered on the cheap, sexist jokes that my executive producers wanted inserted. I would fight and argue that it was a fundamental mistake to insult the very audience that was most loyally supporting the show. Kate Jackson, Jaclyn Smith, and Farrah Fawcett helped to make many of the arguments moot, as more and more they refused to say many of those double-entendre lines. Perhaps it was the critical comments they were reading about the show in the nation's press; perhaps we simply underestimated them. Whatever it was, their consciousnesses were obviously being raised as well.

The mail, and ultimately several key articles by psychologists and sociologists, would confirm that the primary core of the *Charlie's Angels'* audience were teenage girls and young women. It didn't matter. The arguments with my bosses continued to escalate. The honeymoon was definitely over.

There was more going on than was readily apparent. Despite protestations to the contrary and their allegiance to an ever-growing empire, Messrs. Spelling and Goldberg were having a tough time letting go of this project and, apparently, dealing with my popularity with the stars, saying at one point to Ms. Fawcett: "We don't need anyone telling us how to make a hit of our show." It was to get even pettier.

Editorial sessions were held on episodes, and I would not be notified. Projectionists would phone in sick and then appear at other parts of the lot to screen the show for either Mr. Spelling or Mr. Goldberg, excluding me from the process. These bosses could, of course, at any time squash me like a bug, but they actually appeared (at least from my perspective) to prefer this sort of psychological warfare to direct confrontation. Their operation was one where everyone was constantly off-balance. Chaos was the norm. I think the fact that they couldn't make me perspire drove them both a little crazy.

Thirty years ago with three of the most beautiful women in the solar system, making me the envy of all the guys at my weekly poker game.

Photo: Rosenzweig Personal Collection

Christmas had come. I received my corporate gift from the company. It was a large glass urn filled with walnuts—perhaps a hundred pounds' worth. I removed the card, replaced it with one of my own, and sent the vase to agent Broder. The new card read: "*Spelling and Goldberg have been chipping away at my nuts for the past four months; here's your commission.*"

My life there was a misery, yet now as I get older and have run a company of my own, I do understand Spelling and Goldberg a bit better than I did. It *is* difficult to let go, to give authority to someone else on a project you have created and nurtured. It wasn't entirely their fault. There is plenty of evidence that some men and women have had a real talent for working with these two. Many stayed with Spelling for years and profited substantially in the process. I was unable to make whatever adjustments were necessary. I do not say this proudly. It is simply a matter of fact. Neither Leonard nor Aaron were evil men. They had their eccentricities as I, in the years that have gone by, have developed mine. I didn't see that so clearly then. I *did* hate working there and regard it as one of the worst, if not *the* worst, experiences of my professional life in Hollywood.

I never wanted to be in that situation again. I needed to analyze what to do. I was honest, hardworking, and loyal—all good qualities for an employee, though not necessarily such a hot combo for an entrepreneur. I really didn't mind being a hired hand and felt I had few entrepreneurial skills. I had, however, recently discovered that the primary problem with being an employee is the possibility of getting a Leonard Goldberg for an employer. I needed help. I decided I would seek out a partner, someone with some muscle and clout who could run the business, keep a lot of administrative stuff off my back, and allow me to do what I do. That's when I met Mace Neufeld.

CHAPTER 5

"WE HAVE FOUND CHRISTINE CAGNEY ..."

Mace Neufeld wanted to expand into television production. His talent management company, BNB,[2] was a major success. With his partner, Sherwin Bash, BNB had been built into one of the premiere boutiques in the industry. Singers, rock groups, and other performers came under their protective wing. Now he was offering me the opportunity to lead this expansion into TV.

The doorway to the reception room of their impressive Beverly Hills suite of offices announced not only the housing of BNB, but of a record company, a music publishing house, a motion picture enterprise, and something called Buckmace Productions, a joint venture between writer-director-actor Buck Henry and Mr. Neufeld (this last resulting in *Quork*, an unsuccessful television series produced by David Gerber).

Bob Broder had received an offer for my services at Universal for a new series based on the comic book heroine Wonder Woman, so it was easy for my agent to voice disapproval of Mace's offer (at $40,000 per year it was less than half of what Universal would pay for my services). I overruled my agent, believing this was my opportunity to fulfill a dream.

We had little credibility and no talent under contract or projects on the shelves. There was no staff, only my secretary, Dorothy Blass, and myself. We were at

---

[2]   Initials were for Bash (Sherwin), Neufeld (Mace), and Bernard (Harvey). They managed such artists as the Captain and Tennille, the Carpenters, Kansas (the rock group not the state), Chaka Khan, Lou Rawls, Cheryl Ladd, Jim Croce, and others. In the past, they had represented even greater luminaries, including Neil Diamond and Frank Sinatra.

ground zero. I told Mace it would take two years to make BNB Productions a reality.

I hustled. I haunted libraries; I read incessantly. I wound up with something like thirty hours in various stages of development among the three networks. I was constantly meeting with someone in middle management at ABC, CBS, and NBC, or working with a writer on material for one of those companies. I had a miniseries in development, as well as several movies for television, a three-hour special, a daytime soap, one-hour dramatic shows, half-hour comedy shows, and an after-school special. My mandate was to get something made, to get some show on the air.

In those days, networks made very few of the shows they broadcast. Most were contracted for and licensed from studios or independent producers such as Spelling/Goldberg. This was all before the U.S. Congress abandoned the financial interest and syndication rules and the resultant vertical integration of the enter- tainment industry, which not so long ago led to Disney acquiring ABC, Viacom CBS, and GE taking over NBC and Universal. Unlike today, fortunes could then still be made by independent companies in the television business; Mace wanted a piece of that action. Our overhead was small, and we were one *Waltons* away from becoming a Lorimar.[3]

Despite his lofty ambitions, Mace was, in my view, a bit of a dilettante. He attended a total of three network meetings in the two and a half years we were together. At the last of these he arrived late; his avowed purpose was to take pic- tures of the auspicious moment when Brandon Stoddard gave us a go to film our miniseries of *John Steinbeck's East of Eden.*

The previous meeting had been in Jonathan Axelrod's office at a critical moment with our one-hour dramatic series pilot *American Dream.* There he made but one single statement.

I was in a battle royal for the life of my favorite project of all time. We were on our third major rewrite. While Avedon had taken a much-needed vacation, I had teamed Corday with comedy writer Ken Hecht to create this show when it was to be developed as a half-hour comedy. Now we were attempting to go forward as a dramatic series, which had brought about substantial changes in format, along

3   Lorimar was the brainchild of Lee Rich and Merv Adelson and had blossomed into a major television entity before being taken over by Warner Brothers in 1989. *The Waltons* was the company's first bona fide hit, followed by such shows as *Dallas*, *Eight is Enough*, *Falcon Crest*, and *Knot's Landing*.

with changes in the creative team. I had followed network executive Jonathan Axelrod's instructions, and now the pilot script was in deep trouble. I was determined to turn things around at this meeting, to go the way I wanted to go in the first place: to hire the writer I had initially fought for in vain. Finally, I wanted to undo yet another piece of Axelrod meddling by resetting the locale. The network executive had insisted on New York City as the backdrop, and I wanted to return the concept to its original locale: Los Angeles.

Axelrod had been through a rough afternoon. Our meeting with him, as luck would have it, had been scheduled right behind one with the irrepressible David Gerber. "The Gerb" was one of the best salesmen in the business. His vocabulary ranged from the colorful to the fanciful. (I think he actually made up words and phrases as he went along, but who could know? That would require actually being able to keep up, not only with the syntax of what was being said, but the manic delivery as well.) Axelrod, the network executive on the receiving end of this verbal onslaught, was a beaten man before I even entered the room. Thanks to Gerber wearing out the exec about some project of his own, I was winning point after point on *American Dream*.

OK, go back to the original concept. OK, get rid of the writer they had foisted on me. OK, hire Ronald M. Cohen to rewrite the fine original (but too soft) script by Barbara Corday and Ken Hecht. The only point that remained was locale. *American Dream* was my story. The kids were my kids. The hero of this piece was me. I wanted it set in Los Angeles. After all, it was conceived by me, an L.A. native, while trying to find an alternate route to the Coliseum to watch a USC football game. Axelrod wanted the same story set in the East—his place of origin. This was an urban tale, and to Axelrod urban meant the vertical landscape of an eastern city, not the low-profiled megalopolis that dominates the West Coast. It was the only issue unresolved between us; I had won everything else. I didn't want to give in on this. Not only did I have passion and creativity on my side, I had economics as well. Los Angeles is the capital of the entertainment industry. In those days, the show could be more economically produced there than in any other city in the country. Besides, it is where I lived and where my family lived. Why be on location for six months of the year when you could come home to your own bed every night?

Axelrod just might have been wavering. It was at this juncture that Mace decided to speak up. "Philadelphia's a nice town," he said.

If looks could kill, Mace's grave would now have more than a quarter century of overgrowth.

Axelrod gained strength from this division. The result was a compromise. *American Dream* would be set in Chicago. Unlike Philadelphia, Chicago at least had a semblance of a film production community. It was also (unlike Philadelphia) outside of the expensive New York unions' jurisdiction. Finally, it was the hometown of then-writer-elect Ronald M. Cohen.

Mace had attended just one other meeting, in the early days of our association, and it had involved *Cagney & Lacey*. Here, it helps to know that Mace is what I would term a twitcher. He is not unattractive, in sort of an older, Garry Shandling way, but he is, well, I think, sort of a nervous type. I remember him constantly pulling on his cheek, his cuticles, and his ears. He appeared to me to be uncomfortable in a chair. So it was not too great a surprise when, at a CBS pitch, in the first of the three meetings he attended during our association, Mace sat down on the couch and promptly spilled coffee all over himself.

It was all really OK, all except the line about Philadelphia, that is. What I must say, however, is that he did finance my passion. He did capitalize my dream. Furthermore, in the days of 1978 and 1979, when the Captain would tell Tennille that he no longer wanted to pay six figures in annual commissions and the rock group known as Kansas threatened to join the already-defected Carpenters, Mace held firm against his partners' wishes to further cut costs by adding television to their already abandoned or disbanded record and publishing companies.

Mace believed in his vision and ultimately broke off his partnership and the business that he knew to form BNB Productions. We would no longer be a part of the original BNB, nor would we be in the talent management business.

Cagney & Lacey, meanwhile, had been languishing on the shelves at Filmways for a couple of years. The last action had occurred with Leonard Goldberg some months before—before our relationship irreparably deteriorated. I had given the script by Avedon & Corday to Goldberg as an illustration of my position regarding the depiction of female relationships. He not only liked it but indicated he would be interested in acquiring an equity position to produce it as a motion picture. I had agent Broder pull the project as my relationship with Goldberg fell apart.

Now, with the forthcoming release of films such as *Julia* and *The Turning Point*, I feared my concept of making a female buddy movie might again be one of my too-little-too-late moments. Corday urged me to make the project for television before the women's movement totally passed us by.

My friend Ed Feldman had left Filmways. I inquired of the company about having the rights to *Cagney & Lacey* revert to me. They had no interest in that. Would they sell me the rights? They countered with the proposal that I develop the project and that, if I were successful in selling it, we could form a joint venture with my new alliance at BNB. That's what we did.

I now had control of the Avedon & Corday screenplay but had to face the TV industry conundrum that you can't submit a completed work to television development executives. To do so would give them little to "develop" and imply they were not very necessary. My solution was to turn what already existed as a theatrical screenplay into a television presentation. First, I excised the plot from the manuscript. Much of it was then too risqué for television or too expensive. Some of the jokes were now dated as well. Without the plot, I was left with some thirty plus pages of character relationship and some damn good dialogue. I turned those pages into a blueprint for a television series, bridging gaps where necessary with simple narrative devices such as, "Here's how they are at work," or "at home," or "Newman and Redford, watch out!" It began its rounds of submissions to each of the networks—twice (once to each network as a drama with comedy, then back again to each of the comedy development departments as a comedy with drama).

The partnership twixt Avedon & Corday was proving, at this time, to be less than stable. Avedon wanted to spend less time at the office, to approach the work on a more leisurely basis. Corday loved the action of being on staff of a television series and enjoyed the team play, the structure of the workplace, and its attendant camaraderie, including *Turnabout*, the Universal comedy starring John Schuck and Sharon Gless, created by Steven Bochco from a concept put forth by Michael Rhodes based on a Hal Roach 1940s comedy of the same name. It was from that studio, at that time, that the two Barbaras called to tell me, referring to Ms. Gless, "We have found Christine Cagney."

I was not all that impressed until some months later when, in Corday's Beverly Hills den, I saw a beautiful blonde playing Carole Lombard in the television mini-series *Moviola: The Scarlett O'Hara War* on NBC.

"*That's* Cagney!" I bellowed.

Corday nodded knowingly. "That's Sharon Gless."

Did someone say better late than never?

At this time I had nearly a dozen different projects in one stage or another in development at the various networks—all under serious consideration and all at little or no cost to my employer. I was working hard, and I was as prolific and creative as I have ever been in my life. The problem was nothing was getting made.

The two years I had told Mace it would take to become a viable production entity were coming to an end. We were very close, but, as yet, no cigar. Mace would prove to be patient.

Corday and I got married in the backyard of our new home in L.A.'s Hancock Park. Having begun this partnership, Corday decided to sever her old one. She would end the team of Avedon & Corday and do so in order to take a job as a comedy development executive at ABC. It was a major career change and one I advised against. Fortunately, Corday took her own counsel. She quickly moved to vice president in charge of comedy at ABC, parlayed that period in the spotlight to an indy-prod deal at Columbia Studios, which led to her being asked to move to the executive suite at that studio as president of their television division. She weathered the first of two major corporate mergers and then was terminated by Columbia, only to land on her feet once more as the executive vice president in charge of prime-time programming at the CBS network. She thrived in the spotlight and for a very short while was arguably the most powerful woman in the television industry.

I could have used some of that clout in 1979. By the time of our marriage, *Cagney & Lacey* had been turned down by every drama and comedy department in town.

Jeff Sagansky, then at NBC, liked it, but he and his assistant, Bob Singer, bowed to their boss, Fred Silverman, who ordered a different female cop show to be developed by another producer. By reading and liking *Cagney & Lacey* months before Silverman's brainstorm, Sagansky and Singer had me frozen in the marketplace. I could not risk offending them by going elsewhere; before proceeding with another producer-in-favor with their chief, Sagansky and Singer at least should have pointed out to Silverman that another female buddy cop show had been officially submitted to the network months before. By not doing that, it left open the possibility that our idea had been plagiarized.

Real damage had been done here. I threatened suit. Months later, in an NBC projection room—court order in hand—I viewed the film commissioned by Silverman.

"Gentlemen," I said to the audience of NBC attorneys as the lights slowly came up in the room, "I don't want to be associated with this project even by lawsuit."

The network's lawyers were relieved and candid. They had read *Cagney & Lacey* and frankly couldn't understand why their creative people chose to make the show they did—especially when they had this other choice.

Spelling/Goldberg had also made a two-woman cop pilot for ABC, complete with stiletto heels and plenty of cleavage. It was a spin-off of their private-eye show set in Vegas and also not worthy of a lawsuit. Goldberg may have read *Cagney & Lacey*, but he didn't get it.

In desperation,[4] I had sent it to the movie divisions of the networks. There was nowhere else left to go. "Too episodic," said the men at ABC. NBC was clearly not going to touch it now. In those days that left only CBS.

Finally, the Eye network responded: It was Peter Frankovich on the phone. "You should take this project to our series people, Barney. It's more a series than an M.O.W."[5]

"I'll be honest with you, Peter. It's damaged goods. I've already been to your series people, and they turned me down."

"Well, I won't turn you down," the TV movie exec went on. "I like it. Let's develop a script."

I never told him one already existed. Avedon was still on holiday, so Corday came in and together we pitched Frankovich our new story. Avedon returned, and the two women worked out all the story beats. It was given a go to screenplay, and Corday pulled out to begin her new career at ABC. She gave the best parting gift a writing partner can present to an erstwhile teammate: a job with a solo writing credit. With thirty to forty pages already written from their earlier collaboration and the rest thoroughly blocked out by the two of them, there is little doubt that, had Corday asked their guild to arbitrate, there would have been a shared credit on that script. Corday's was a generous act and, as is so often the case in these matters, not fully appreciated. I don't believe Avedon ever really forgave Corday for the split.

---

[4]   In desperation because even a successful M.O.W. makes its producer relatively little money. A theatrical motion picture or a television series has almost unlimited upside potential. A miniseries could then be (maybe) profitable but was mainly prestigious. Still, in the late seventies, we even believed that certain miniseries might generate big profits, although that rarely proved to be the case. M.O.W.s were a last resort for *Cagney & Lacey*, for it had potential as a theatrical film and, failing that, as a series. Unfortunately, we were, at that time, pretty much alone in that belief.

[5]   An acronym for Movie of the Week, invented by then-ABC chief, Barry Diller. Also sometimes referred to as Movie-for-Television or Made for TV movie.

CHAPTER 6

THE MAELSTROM

The Frankovich/CBS endorsement was nice, but more "development" was not what I needed. Somehow I had to get something into production. It was all incredibly frustrating. The industry is (and was then) like a series of concentric circles, the kind of design formed in a pool of water when disturbed by a small object falling therein. Those in the maelstrom, and closest to the inner circles, were people like Wolper, Spelling, Goldberg, Lee Rich, and Grant Tinker; *they* were in the business. The rest of us were "in development." (Today one would substitute JJ Abrams, David E. Kelley, John Wells, Jerry Bruckheimer, and maybe Steven Bochco; it is the same game now, only with different players.) We would joke then, only half kidding, that "development" was something invented by the networks to keep thousands of us believing we were in the business and therefore too preoccupied to go to the justice department.

My one-time USC pal Bernie Sandler had helped me get *Angel on My Shoulder* to then-ABC superstar Peter Strauss. It proved to be an easy sell to the actor. He had just done *Here Comes Mr. Jordan* on stage and was looking for something in that genre to combat his (he thought) too-serious TV image.

Even with this outstanding package, I could not get a commitment out of Leonard Hill at ABC. In frustration, after months of waiting for a green light from the network, I hired Bill Haber, cofounder of the powerful CAA agency, to represent the project. He brought back Hill's remark: "Yeah, yeah, we oughta make it. Is there any way to get Barney out of the picture?"

Now, I could restate my case here: how I found the property, discovered it was in the public domain, shepherded the screenplay through multiple drafts, and contacted—and interested—Peter Strauss in starring in the vehicle. I could point out how my last M.O.W. for the very same network had been *One of My Wives Is Missing*, a certified smash. What would be the point? It wasn't personal. Hill had a finite number of films to make and an almost equal number of commitments to those guys in the maelstrom. If he said yes to me, he would have to face their wrath and their well-aimed complaints to his bosses. If he said yes to me, there would be one less film commitment for a powerful pal with whom he might partner once he went indy-prod with a multi pic-pac.

The same thing was holding up *American Dream*. It was all those Spelling/Goldberg commitments and others like them. Rather than be candid about this, the network executives would try to get you into business with one of their open commitments. A secondary position was to stall, to keep having "problems" with the material, to continue demanding rewrites or other time-consuming changes; anything to keep from telling you that trade in this industry is indeed restrained and restricted to those in favor, those in the club, those closest to the center. I get it now. Eventually I got closer to that maelstrom; I got a peek at the Holy of Holies, but that was not what I was experiencing in those early days of development hell.

Corday and I would be at dinner, and I would be so nauseous from the beatings I was taking from Hill and Axelrod I could only consider ordering soup. I couldn't imagine swallowing anything solid. My wife was ebullient and cheerful, feeling chatty about her new job at ABC and all of her bright and hardworking fellow development executives.

Crazed into a hyperbolic state, I would interrupt, "Barbara, I am sitting here like someone trying to deal with the fact that they are sending Jews to death camps by rail, and you lounge across from me wearing your SS cap, asking me to look at how efficiently you are operating the trains!"

My new wife took it in stride. Later that night she would ask if I was coming to bed.

"I've already been fucked by the network once today," I growled.

Does this sound funny now? It wasn't then. It was that week that I awoke from an epic nightmare. I was in a cold sweat. Maybe I was only half awake. Anyway, I would share it with Corday. She was my spouse and could not testify against me in a California court.

The dream-scheme: *I enter the fifth floor at ABC's Century City offices. In my hand, held at my side, is a .357 Magnum revolver. I walk past Lana, the friendly receptionist, into Leonard Hill's office and blow him away: two, three shots maximum. His body parts are splattered against the walls and windows. Then I walk down the hallway, the short distance to Axelrod's office. I empty my revolver at point-blank range—more gore.*

I drop the gun and am taken into custody. My defense will be not guilty by reason of insanity. I can prove those two bastards drove me crazy. I will be revered throughout Hollywood for my good deed.

While I'm undergoing treatment during my brief incarceration, I'll write a book about the whole thing. It will be called The ABC Murders.

CHAPTER 7

A PRODUCER'S MEDIUM

Dramatic episodic television was my niche. Its pace uniquely suited me. It was life-defining. I knew that from my induction at the age of twenty-nine, as a freshman producer on *Daniel Boone*.

It was *Cagney & Lacey*, of course, that brought me industry-wide recognition. Besides the show itself, I received respect and admiration beyond my dreams for fending off the network's onslaught of threat, intimidation, and cancellation. It moved me to the forefront of my profession, ahead of many with longer, and perhaps more impressive, lists of credits.

None of this recognition would come my way until the mid-1980s. No matter. I believed—even without corroboration—the veracity of my self-serving statement that I was good at this from the mid-way point of my first season as the wunderkind producer on *Daniel Boone*. I knew I could do it better than anyone.

Television is a producer's medium. Episodic television is even more so. Many people are good producers and fine storytellers. Some are better than I. There are even those who can, and have, produced better individual episodes. That is not what this is about.

Week after week, show after show, week-in, show-out, twenty-two times a year— the maintenance of that qualitative control, the attention to character and to detail, the management of a series—that is where I always thought I was better than everyone else (although since leaving the business in 1995, the work on *West Wing* by John Wells and on *Alias*, as well as *LOST* by JJ Abrams, has me reconsidering that statement).

I was the daddy, the confessor-priest, the citizen-general, the final arbiter of taste and judgment, the decision maker, the diplomat, the cheerleader, the storyteller, the promoter, the press agent, the boss. It was only a partial list.

The company was in jail, and I was the light that came in through the bars. I loved it.

It wasn't just *Cagney & Lacey*. I felt that way about the work—my job.

It *is* a talent of sorts to convince oneself that what's being done not only has impact, but import—that doing it properly, both creatively and technically, counts for something.

This is where Mr. Neufeld and I differed. I felt he was more obsessed with his public persona and paying homage at the altar of success. Still, he was there for me at a critical time. In failure, he was supportive and downright paternal. It was in triumph that we had our problems.

The awful years of development began to turn into a production horror story. All at once—literally simultaneously—our tiny company got green-lighted on a movie-for-television to be shot in Los Angeles (*Angel On My Shoulder*, starring Peter Strauss, Barbara Hershey, and Richard Kiley); a pilot for an hour dramatic series filming in Chicago (*American Dream* with Stephen Macht and Karen Carlson); and the multi-million dollar miniseries presentation of *John Steinbeck's East of Eden* with an all-star cast, filming primarily in Savannah, Georgia, and in and around the Steinbeck Country of Salinas, California. All of this was in the early spring of 1979, and all of it overlapping. I was living in airports, while I imagined that Mace was alternately dreaming on the Mexican Riviera or scheming behind my back in Hollywood.

Our pilot film of *American Dream* made the ABC mid-season schedule. We were to have our first series on the air. Now, in success, my "Jewish renaissance man," as I had come to refer to Mace, began taking credit for my work in articles and paid advertisements in the trade press. We quarreled. I was infuriated at what I perceived as a power grab, and what I would characterize as his betrayals on *American Dream,* including broken promises made to me regarding creative control. Mace Neufeld's words resounded as I walked away from my dream show: "Barney, baby, it's payday. What do you care? It's only television."

I would not continue in the relationship. We agreed to meet to effectuate a divorce. My attorney and pal, Sam Perlmutter, was given instructions by me to "just get me out with my underwear." The meeting took place down the hall from Mace's office in an unassigned office cubicle with BNB production exec Tom Brodek, Sam, myself, Mace, and his attorney du jour, the powerful and connected Bruce Ramer. We were there to divide the knives and forks.

Negotiations were going better than I feared; perhaps, I thought, Mace was afraid of my bringing suit for what I characterized as his various earlier misrepresentations to me. Of course, Brodek could also be a calming influence.

Whatever the reason(s), I wound up in sole possession of several projects, Mace retained a few, and that left only *Cagney & Lacey* in dispute. It had by this time received a go to production as a CBS movie-for-television. Because it had been originally developed by me before my tenure at BNB, the terms of my contract with Mace vested me with 75% of the profits and Mace with 25%. This was proportionately diluted by the 50% of the profits held by Filmways and the 10% profit share held by Avedon & Corday, half of which was paid by Filmways and half by BNB. Thus, Filmways had 45%, I had 75% of 45%, and Mace had 25% of 45%.

In those days, the profits on an efficiently produced movie of the week normally ran between a quarter and a half million dollars. It was a nice little business in the days before network ownership of just about everything, but it never contained the upside potential of a television series or a theatrical motion picture. I had been turned down everywhere in my desire to make *Cagney & Lacey* a series. Making it as an M.O.W. was truly a last resort.

Several weeks before, after being rebuffed by Universal talent head Monique James when I had inquired about loan-out possibilities for the services of Sharon Gless, Peter Frankovich of CBS had suggested Loretta Swit as the actress to play Cagney. Swit was a CBS star in her role as Hot Lips on *M*A*S*H**, which was then still one of the network's premiere hits.

"Look, Swit's a great choice," I told Frankovich. "She's the right age, the right look, and has a good sense of comedy, but she's already committed to a series for you guys. You're blowing me out of the water here. You're killing any chance this has of becoming a back-door pilot."[6]

"Barney, Barney, Barney," came the head-shaking reply. "You've already tried to sell this project as a series, and you failed. What you did do is sell it to us as an M.O.W. That's what it is. That's all it will ever be. We want Loretta Swit. We have a commitment with Loretta Swit, and we're willing to turn that commitment over to you. Unless you can come up with a name we like better, then that's who we expect you to use."

---

[6]   Back-door, as the name might imply, refers to any kind of project that serves as a pilot for a new series without going through the traditional developmental process. It could be something begun as a movie, an episode, or a special.

Dealing the actress to me got CBS off the hook for a pay-or-play[7] commitment to Swit, and it gave them a recognizable star in an otherwise (to them) undistinguished movie project. There were not many chances that I would come up with a piece of casting they would like better.

I knew all of this, of course, while meeting with Sam, Mace, and Ramer. I was concentrating on regaining rights to projects with upside potential, including *This Girl for Hire*. Mace, typically, was looking for quick cash. In the course of the negotiating process, I picked up a couple of properties I thought had real prospects for the future and, in exchange, reversed positions with Mace, allowing him to gain the lion's share (2/3 of "our" end) of the (we all thought) limited profits, in what we all then believed was the soon-to-be one-shot appearance of a CBS M.O.W., *Cagney & Lacey*.

It was a small enough piece of change that at one point, growing exasperated with the process of having to have this meeting at all, Mace simply got up and stormed out of the room, saying, in reference to *Cagney & Lacey*, "Fuck it! Take the whole, damn thing. I don't give a shit."

There was only an instant of stunned silence, and then Bruce Ramer was running down the hall after his client, shouting back at us over his shoulder that what Mace had just "offered" was not on the table.

Ramer and his client were soon back in the room, and negotiations resumed. To this day, whenever I see Bruce Ramer, I think of the multi-millions that his hallway sprint cost me.

There were other niceties in our deal: despite the level of ownership now being skewed in Mace's favor, *Cagney & Lacey* would be my project to supervise, and, in remembrance of my experience with Mace's sabotage of *American Dream*, I had him contractually excluded from any and all creative discussions with either Filmways or CBS regarding this M.O.W.

Finally, I was to be released from all exclusivity to BNB (at this point called Mace Neufeld Productions) and set free to pursue the lucrative offer I had received from Paramount Studios. I was walking away with a lot more than my underwear.

What I didn't know was that Mace had been in negotiations with long-time acquaintance Marvin Davis about getting the Denver oil magnate involved in the entertainment business. Davis, I would later read in *Variety*, would commit

---

[7]   "Pay or play" is a guarantee, usually to an actor, that the talent will be paid regardless of the film being made or not.

something like five million dollars to Mace before deciding to move on and take 20ᵗʰ Century Fox private. I'm guessing Mace saw no reason to share this windfall, so, with all due respect to Sam's negotiating acumen against the more experienced and powerful Bruce Ramer, Mace was probably as anxious to be rid of me as I was of him. It would not surprise me if Mace had convinced Mr. Davis (then a newcomer to Hollywood) that it was he—and he alone—who had created "all this action" at BNB.

Anyway, I was out and happily so.

Golden Globe winners for *John Steinbeck's East of Eden:* Jane Seymour, who won for Best Actress in a miniseries, is flanked by Mace Neufeld and Ken Wales. My Globe is in my right hand and out of camera range. Lesson: hold such stuff close.

CHAPTER 8

SERENDIPITY IN CHINATOWN

The announcement that Corday had become the vice president of comedy development at ABC was made official, and I gave her a major party at our home to celebrate. My new deal at Paramount was a rich one, quadrupling my previous draw under Mace and assuring me big bucks in success. It also provided me with a suite of offices only slightly less ostentatious than those of Benito Mussolini.

The contract with Paramount was for my exclusive services with one exclusion: "*Cagney & Lacey*, a movie-for-television." The Writers Guild was about to declare one of its periodic strikes against management and my new offices needed painting; it seemed like a good time to suspend and extend my Paramount contract and make a movie for CBS.

We had a Cagney (Loretta Swit). Our search began for a Lacey. Ms. Swit had her choices, a not-so-long list of perhaps twelve names. CBS had its preferences as well, mostly stars of other series on their network (the most noteworthy among them being Michele Lee of *Knots Landing*).

We also had a license fee from CBS of $1,850,000 and a budget, based on what Filmways figured it would cost to shoot the entire film in New York, at $2,250,000. The potential deficit of $400,000 was way too much for a simple movie-for-television.

We re-budgeted for filming in Los Angeles with less than a week of establishing shots and second unit work in the Big Apple. The figure came down $200,000, but the bottom line was still too rich for Filmways' coffers. They asked me to rewrite, setting the show in Los Angeles. I refused.

During this minor impasse, Richard M. Rosenbloom, Filmways vice president and line producer, and I filled a day or so selecting director Ted Post and interviewing actresses for Lacey. One strong candidate emerged: Tyne Daly. She was also on Swit's list, but conspicuously absent from the network's.

At this juncture, Tom Brodek reminded me of the not-too-unpleasant experience I had had making *American Dream* in Chicago with a crew composed almost completely of local talent. His point was that you could do the same thing in Toronto, where there was an existing film community. Furthermore, in Canada, because of the monetary exchange rate in the early 1980s, when you arrived on a Monday with a million dollars, on Tuesday you had a million, two hundred thousand. We were talking about shooting Los Angeles to look like New York. Why not Toronto? It might even be easier; like New York, Toronto has bundled-against-the-cold citizens in the background and slate gray skies similar to New York. Better yet, there were no palm trees.

We sent production manager Stan Neufeld (no relation to Mace) off to Canada to scout out the situation and thus began the trend toward shooting in what has since become known as Hollywood North.

Cliff Alsberg, who had left ABC and was now a vice president at Filmways under Rosenbloom, was inadvertently a big help with his incredibly naive and chauvinistic notes on the screenplay. The young executive unwittingly served two valuable services: a reminder to be ever on the alert for that traditional male mentality that had stymied the project for so long, and secondly, by ignoring the comments and notes from Alsberg, and simply moving on, the tone was set for how I would deal with Filmways on creative issues. It was a course from which I never deviated.

The script that Avedon had finalized, loosely based on her earlier screenplay coauthored with Corday, had many of the Cagney/Lacey/Harvey and squad room moments millions of Americans came to appreciate in the ongoing series. Unlike the series, it was very heavily plotted. The primary cop story dealt with what appeared to be a serial killer of Chasidic Jews in New York's famed 47th Street Diamond District. In the story, much to the chagrin of the ambitious Christine Cagney, she and her partner find themselves excluded by the male cop elite from working on this prestigious case.

The killer, we eventually learn, is Schermer, a fugitive Nazi war criminal, who has effected his unlikely escape to the United States after the war by taking on the identity of a Chasidic Jew—complete with beard, peot, and tallis.

Midway through the drama, the female detectives overhear in the squad room that the serial killer just might be a regular procurer of prostitutes. Cagney and Lacey, having been relegated to the John detail, now have a lead of their own, directing them to a material witness in the Chasidic neighborhood, a prostitute who reveals that, unlike other émigrés of his age group, one suspect has no Nazi death camp tattoo. (In one draft the hooker also confirmed this particular customer [Schermer] is not circumcised and therefore, despite all other outward appearances, probably not Jewish). It was a not-unclever cop story, one that was plausible in the involvement of our novice, third-grade detectives, and one that fully exploited the relationships they maintained with each other, with their loved ones, with their jobs, and with the all-male bastion of conservatism with which they came into contact on a daily basis.

Rosenbloom and director Ted Post were preparing to leave for Toronto. I would stay behind until we had a Lacey. Before I let him get away, I wanted Post to meet with Barbara Avedon. I felt by spending a few hours with this talented and brilliant woman he might gain some insight into the feminist perspective, which was such an integral part of this project. Three or four hours with Barbara Avedon could not possibly hurt my then-sixty-something-year-old male director, I reasoned. I set the appointment and instructed Barbara to give him an earful. She called early that evening. "Barney, all he wanted to talk about was Schermer!"

Director Ted Post had spent the afternoon with one of Hollywood's foremost feminists, author of the first buddy film ever made with women leads, and what he wanted to glean from that encounter was a deeper understanding of the (male) villain's character. According to Avedon, he sloughed off any conversation regarding the attitudes of the two women leads, their relationship, their politics, or their history. Does it help the reader to understand my incredulity if I include the information that in the screenplay Schermer has no lines of dialogue?

I determined I had better finalize the Mary Beth Lacey casting and get to Toronto, pronto.

CBS was really pressing for Michele Lee. I was weakening. I liked her as well as CBS star-of-the-time Mimi Kennedy. Besides, I was anxious to get up to Toronto and see what damage was being done. Rosenbloom and Post were on the phone from Canada. Would I take one more fight with the network for Tyne Daly? I took two more. The first ended in their agreement to meet the actress.

The next morning Tyne Daly and I convened for breakfast at Dupar's, a coffee shop in the San Fernando Valley. Aside from some pleasantries at her interview a few weeks before, this was our first conversation. I tried to distract her from being nervous. A half hour later, we held hands as we walked across Ventura Boulevard to the offices of CBS movies for television chief William Self.

Tyne had to be tense. You could never tell. I've known her now over twenty-five years, and I still can't discern when she is acting off-stage and when she's not (maybe it's because she is always acting). Anyway, she was easy and charming in the interview. Self, Frankovich, and the rest were affable but noncommittal as Tyne and I left the office together at meeting's end.

It was later that afternoon I got the call from CBS. "Go ahead with your choice. Tyne Daly is approved."

We were Toronto-bound.

The first Cagney. Loretta Swit and me on the Toronto location in 1981.
Photo: Rosenzweig Personal Collection

The shoot was one of the most pleasant of my career. At that time, working with CBS as opposed to ABC was like trying to compare Tahiti with the Gulag. The writers' strike had development at a standstill. My Paramount offices would therefore be closed for the duration. For the first time in many years, I was allowed to focus on what was at hand. What a contrast to the way my life had been just months before.

John Steinbeck's East of Eden had aired on ABC just weeks prior to our production start. It garnered extremely high ratings and pretty good critical notices. The pilot of *American Dream* debuted while I was on location in Toronto to not such high numbers but universally enthusiastic praise. Both received a fair share of award nominations.[8]

Director Post got us through our twenty-day schedule with alacrity (especially noteworthy since he had a crew that in those days was not nearly as experienced or efficient as a Hollywood company). Ted may not have been the best casting for this type of material, but he listened and tried to give me what I asked for; I'm plenty grateful for that.

We finished in Toronto and moved on to Manhattan for two days of whirlwind photography in order to get as many of those typical New York settings with our principals in the foreground as possible.

Dick Rosenbloom had worked with award-winning director Joe Sargent on *Hustling.*[9] He passed on to me what the director had taught him about how and where to design the maximum amount of shots in order to effectively convince the viewer that the film they were seeing was entirely shot in the locale in which that story took place, despite having a very limited time at the site. Basically, it came down to concentrating the bulk of on-site filming at the very outset of the piece in places that were clearly identifiable, in order to firmly implant in the viewers' mind that what they were seeing had been shot in its entirety "on location." When *Cagney & Lacey* aired on CBS, friends of mine who lived in New York chastised

---

[8]   *American Dream* was Emmy nominated for Best Teleplay of an Hour Dramatic Show (Ronald M. Cohen, with story by Barbara Corday and Ken Hecht) while *East of Eden* was nominated for best miniseries (losing to *Shogun*). Jane Seymour was nominated for Best Dramatic Performance in a miniseries by the Hollywood Foreign Press. She and the show both collected Golden Globes.

[9]   1975 award-winning TV flick starring Lee Remick and Jill Clayburgh. Directed by Joe Sargent and written by Fay Kanin from the novel by Gail Sheehy. Lillian Gallo was the producer.

me for being in town for so long and not making contact. They were astonished when I told them the company was only in the city for two days.

One old New York friend I did contact while in the Big Apple was Michael Fuchs, a rising young executive with the then-burgeoning pay cable system HBO. Michael was a tennis-playing buddy of mine, and I phoned upon my arrival at LaGuardia to ask if he was free that evening for dinner. He wasn't. He had a date and was doubling with another couple. Then, after a beat, he asked, "Why don't you join us?"

I thanked him, but said I didn't want to be a fifth wheel.

"Nonsense," came the reply, "these are old friends of mine … you'll enjoy yourself."

I tagged along, positioned at the restaurant—as luck would have it—between the two women. Michael, having ordered the several course Chinese feast, became more and more engrossed in his conversation about the movie business with attorney-turned producer Bob Levine, who had just completed production on the film *That Championship Season*. I talked to my female tablemates.

Lois Lugar sat on my right. She was a sales executive with Embassy Pictures who had recently moved to Los Angeles. Like me, she was in town on business. The new CBS topper Harvey Shephard (whom I had yet to meet) was, it seems, a longtime pal of hers. She promised to set up a lunch so I could be properly introduced. I was already glad I had accepted Michael's invitation.

Suzanne Levine, on my left, was more than the spouse of the attorney-turned-film producer who was occupying my host. Ms. Levine was the managing editor of *Ms.* magazine, Gloria Steinem's famed feminist monthly. It was the publication that targeted the core of the audience I was trying to reach. Beyond that, it was known as a source of material for opinion makers, especially those in Washington and New York.

"Tell me about the project that brings you to the city," she said.

Be still my heart.

CHAPTER 9

THE MOVIE DOCTOR

I have stated that the experience of our production in Toronto was a pleasant one. That was generally, but not specifically, true. Rosenbloom's production ace, Stan Neufeld, brought new meaning to "lean and mean." Still, I learned a lot from both Stan and his boss and, for even more than the most part, respect their desire to place the dollars on the screen. As mentioned, Director Post just didn't get the "jokes," so that, too, was bothersome.

Mostly what was wrong is what is wrong on every film project. You start out with this pure idea and then enter into this unwieldy collaboration. It is your child. At birth you have hopes that the baby will grow and prosper and perhaps, after graduating cum laude from Harvard Medical School, go on to become a famous brain surgeon. Instead, your baby drops out of high school and opts to join a heavy metal band. The trick is finally to remember that, no matter what, it is your baby. You have to fall in love with it all over again, not because it has fulfilled your dreams, but because (no matter what) it is your child.

You have to remember why you wanted to do it in the first place. This is no easy assignment. The development process alone is so debilitating, so time-consuming, and so oppressive that oftentimes when you finally do get the order, there is no joy in it. The good news is you got the order; the bad news is now you've got to make this piece of dreck[10] (for, more often than not, that's what your idea has become as it has gone through the over-networking of a bunch of TV executives).

After development there is pre-production, location scouting, casting, and budgetary problems—more concessions. Then production, one compromise after another.

---

[10]   *Dreck* (rhymes with wreck): Yiddish for "crap" (as in junk, garbage, excrement; performances of grossly inferior quality).

"My character wouldn't say this," whines the actor, as if he or she were the author. The sun does not set as scripted, nor do the two dozen extras you can afford look like the throng described on paper. Finally, you see the film, assembled by an editor, operating on his or her own, perhaps thousands of miles away from the production itself. This person may be in the throes of some personal crisis or be merely a modest talent.

You look at their work—your work—and it is all you can do not to vomit. You wonder how the hell you can fall in love again with this. Somehow you must, but first there is putting a good face on it all. So what if the picture is twenty-one minutes too long and you have no faith in the director's editorial sensibilities? The director is entitled to a cut, and in this case there was mercifully no air date or deadline pressure.

"OK," I found myself saying as the lights went up on our silent and sober audience; the director had brought his wife (for moral support, I guessed). Also, in that West Los Angeles projection room, besides myself, were Rosenbloom, Avedon, and Corday. Despair was in the air.

"It's going to be good—pretty good," I went on: "Ted, I've never worked with you in editorial before, so I'll just say it's yours. You've got fourteen days of hard work ahead of you. (It was the minimum guarantee given to members of the Director's Guild.) In broad strokes, I'll just give you two notes: the picture needs pace, so try to give it that, and please don't lose any scenes. In other words, avoid the temptation to lop out big chunks and, instead, squeeze out the time."

Ted Post nodded. He "*knew*" just what I was talking about. Maybe not. Days later, film editor Gregory Prange informed me he hated the instructions he was being given by our director. He threatened to resign—more than once. I urged him to continue on, saying that if what we saw was not an improvement that he and I would have plenty of time together—after the director's departure—to work it out.

"Not an improvement" proved to be understatement. Two weeks after the initial screening, the film was now no longer twenty-plus minutes long, but a few minutes short; my request for pace had been interpreted as fast. Every line was butted right up next to its predecessor. There was no air, no breathing space, no reactive or reflective moments—just an onslaught of verbiage and information, and, well, it was awful.

The lights went up in the projection room. Avedon was not somber and silent this time. Her head was in her hands, and she was in tears. Mercifully, Corday missed this running. Rosenbloom merely mumbled something as he excused himself from the projection room. Ted Post was stoic. I do not recall his response to the solemnity of his audience in any way. I was in enough of a state of shock that I cannot remember if I thanked the director for his contribution or not. Prange and I went immediately to work.

What was most disturbing about the film was not the pace. Despite this disparity in length and editorial techniques, both Prange's cut and Post's had the same thing in common: the lead was unlikable. Christine Cagney came off too hard-edged, too strident. Since she was in nearly every scene, this was disastrous for the film and for what Avedon, Corday, and I had set out to prove all those years before: that a Newman and Redford film could be done with women. This version of the Avedon script not only lacked the charm of a typical "buddy movie," but confirmed the old saw that guys get angry while women get bitchy. The film, unfortunately, was an affirmation of much of the male mythology I had heard about women since beginning this project. That's what Avedon was in tears about, not some missed joke or some plot point gone awry.

Loretta Swit was the hero's foil in *M*A*S*H**, the gal no one really liked. It worked great there; it was a disaster in our film. Could she have been directed out of that? I think so, but hard to tell. Like me, Loretta was so conscious of the fact that her director did not understand the issues of the piece (and so totally into the persona that had made her a star) that she might not have trusted him to change her performance. Anyway, no one tried. She was a major TV star, and it takes a very special eye to discern that what may be OK in one vehicle might have a very different effect in another. I must confess, as is often the case, none of this appeared obvious to any of us until after the film had been assembled. The more I worked on the film, restoring "air" and modifying the pace at which it might play, the more I finally became aware of this systemic problem.

I began to experiment, eventually having Prange recut virtually every scene, playing—almost the entire film—with Loretta just off-stage or with the camera on her back or over her shoulder, forcing the audience to focus on the person with whom our leading lady was interacting and giving them less of a look at the harshness of our leading lady.

Without changing the continuity of the film itself, we had thus restructured the entire picture from inside each scene out. Prange and I worked at a good clip, and we completed our task several days ahead of my self-imposed three-week deadline. Rather than screen early, I took a few days and had Prange add a temporary music track to a number of scenes. It not only gave the film a lift but helped dictate a rhythm for editing several moments that heretofore had been rather lifeless in the movie.

We screened the film again. My sense was that, overall, Director Post was impressed, although somewhat distressed about a couple of shots I had used that were not designed to be shown without a cutaway to Swit. Trying not to be disloyal, Mrs. Post (I must say) still seemed pleased. More important to me were the reactions of Barbara Avedon and Dick Rosenbloom. The latter simply said, "It's a miracle," while Avedon threw her arms around my neck and declared me a genius.

As involved as I have always been in the development of ideas and screenplays, writing and writers are not my favorite part of the business. If I could make a living at the job of my choice, it would be "movie doctor." Among its many honors, the series *Cagney & Lacey* won both an Emmy award for editing and an ACE award,[11] always with young and previously unacknowledged editors. The two Best Director Emmys[12] the series garnered were on episodes handed over to me by their respective recipients at from six to nine minutes over length. I was the one who supervised every cut, who spotted every musical cue, and who approved every dub. I've rarely seen a film I didn't believe I could improve—in many cases make substantially better—with just a few days in the editing bay. If I am allowed to stake out only one claim, one singular talent, one area that I am good at and care about, this is it.

A film begins as a vision, a pure idea. One then enters into an unwieldy collaboration with a writer, a financier, a cast, a director, a staff, and a crew, with mechanical equipment, with electrical current, and with God (will the sun shine or will it rain?). Ultimately, each production would come to an end; what was left was me, the film, a machine, and a film editor. The compromises that were part of every day's routine were now interesting puzzles to be temporarily railed at and then worked out; the collaboration reduced and therefore simplified.

My executive acumen may leave much to be desired. I have limited patience with the pretensions of directors and the persistent bellyaching of a crew. My forbearance with actors might easily be questioned. I can, however, look at the same piece of film over and over again. I am tireless in this arena, remembering every

---

[11]   American Cinema Editors Award (Eddie) 1984–85, Geoffrey Rowland for the episode "Heat," and Academy of Television Arts and Sciences Award (Emmy) Jim Gross (1985) for the episode "Who Said It's Fair" Part II.

[12]   The episode "Heat," directed by Karen Arthur (1985), and the episode "Parting Shots," directed by Georg Stanford Brown (1986).

detail and every frame. I am constantly fascinated at how additions or subtractions (however subtle) will affect the overall impact of the drama itself.

I bring this film sense, as Eisenstein[13] called it, to story and script meetings as well. I can see the movie long before it is made. I argue and cajole the writer into doing the same—to come to a visual, instead of a literary, solution to a writing problem. Oftentimes, a look, a silent reaction, an insert of a specific part of the set or an actor's anatomy (a shoulder's shrug, a wince, the wringing of hands) can tell an audience much more than words could ever convey.

When practiced correctly, it brings about a subtle, or elliptical, aspect to certain scenes and to performances. "Less is more" was inscribed on the sweatshirt given me by the *Cagney & Lacey* writing staff, in acknowledgment of the constant lectures I would dispense on this subject.

My editorial (read visual) concepts, in other words, would impact writing, hence direction, and, therefore, performance. Left alone to practice these ideas fully in the mid-1980s, the results are there to be seen in nearly every episode of *Cagney & Lacey*.

The subtlety of performance in that series registers, not just because of good casting, good acting, and elliptical writing, but because we did not cut away. It should be noted that, from the inception of their six-year collaboration, Sharon Gless and Tyne Daly dominated their category at the annual Emmy Awards (Outstanding Performance by an Actress in a Drama Series). They both were nominated each and every year from the time of coming together as a duo, and one (or the other) won every year: Tyne in 1983, 1984, 1985, and 1988; Sharon in 1986 and 1987.

I often remember admonishing editors to hold on Tyne Daly or Sharon Gless for what seemed to the conventional television practitioner an interminable time.

"Just because you have an itch does not mean you have to scratch," I would lecture, referring to that initial anxious sensation when one might feel an audience will crave another angle, another piece of coverage to get them away from the intensity of this singular view. An argument from a film editor might ensue, and, often, at the very end of a scene, I might make such an accommodation, demonstrating that we did, in fact, have that other angle to go to, but, right now, I would caution, "I want the audience to know that this, and only this, is what we want them to see. That this is what is important. This is our choice."

---

[13]   Sergei Eisenstein, Russian film director of such classics as *Battleship Potemkin, Alexander Nevskiy*, and author of *The Film Sense*.

It's very "un-televisiony." It looks different from what audiences have been used to. It doesn't have that rocking, rhythmic, close-up, close-up, over shoulder, over shoulder, two shot, close-up, close-up, sing-songy approach that most TV shows—and every MGM and Ray Stark film ever supervised editorially by Margaret Booth—have. It helps, of course, to have the kind of performers who can hold the screen, who command your attention. It's nice when the script is conceived and designed with this approach in mind. It's always better when everyone is in sync and stylistically working toward the same goal. It's better, but not necessary. You can do an awful lot in that cutting room if you're a storyteller with patience and the film sense.

It is generally conceded that one such filmmaker was Darryl Zanuck, the legendary Papa Zanuck of 20th Century Fox and father to the terrific producer Richard Zanuck. Elia Kazan, in his fine autobiography, *A Life,* acknowledged his debt to Zanuck in this area on such films as *A Tree Grows in Brooklyn, Gentlemen's Agreement,* and *Viva Zapata.*

In each of these cases, the Academy Award–winning director was en route to his home in New York, within hours of wrapping those productions, leaving the entire editorial process to Zanuck. In that era, there was no stigma connected with this kind of abdication. (Just because you are good with actors and can stage and direct a scene, does not necessarily qualify a director for inclusion in Sergei Eisenstein's book.)

Great composers may be mediocre conductors; why should an artist be required to be both? The singularly lonely task of creating music on a page does not necessarily prepare one for leading a group of potentially temperamental fellow musicians, nor does it automatically imbue one with that physical grace that is aesthetically pleasing to the concert-goer. Because you can write a good song is not necessarily evidence that you should also perform it. Frank Sinatra and Barbra Streisand are pretty good proof that the opposite is also true, though I concede I rather liked "Evergreen."[14]

Meanwhile, back at the office, Rosenbloom wanted to have a public screening of our film. "We'll take over the DGA," he said. "Serve some wine and cheese—have a party."[15]

---

[14]   "Evergreen": (Love theme from *A Star Is Born*) Academy Award winner for Original Song in 1977. Music by Barbra Streisand. Lyric by Paul Williams.

[15]   Reference is to the DGA (Directors Guild of America), whose private theater facilities are regularly rented by filmmakers to show their work to Hollywood insiders. Seating capacity then was nearly five hundred.

I opposed this. I was "in like" with this film, not in love.

"But it's good," Rosenbloom argued.

"We've made a decent enough television film," I countered. "It's too flawed to play on the big screen. I don't want to be embarrassed."

Rosenbloom respected my wishes. Prange and I finalized the film, preparing it to be scored and dubbed. The WGA strike was ending. I would be moving back into my offices at Paramount. The urge to screen this picture, of which I was growing somewhat fonder on a daily basis, was increasing.

Swit saw the film with her manager and liked it but was concerned about how little we used her close-ups.

"Loretta," I began, "you're in every scene. "It's like being the star and host of a variety show. You've got to turn over the spotlight to your guests every now and then or risk the audience getting tired of you." That seemed to make sense to her.

I pressed my luck and set up another screening. This time we'd rent the small theater at 20ᵗʰ Century Fox Studios. It sat nearly a hundred. Swit came with pals, so did Tyne. I invited my mother and dad, my in-laws, and a few other friends. They laughed in all the right places. The women in the audience even let out an occasional cheer.

Women in Film was my next stop. In 1981 they were not the industry bastion of top women in the industry they would become, but rather a fledgling group … one whose understandable biases suited my needs. I screened *Cagney & Lacey* for fifty to sixty of their members. They cheered and applauded throughout.

I was learning something valuable. Although it was nice that people seemed to like the movie, what was of more interest to me was that even those who might be critical of a cut or two, of the camera work, of the story, of a performance, the pace, the music, or whatever—no matter what they might say of a positive or negative nature, no one ever said, "I don't believe it. I don't believe two women can do that."

That had been the fear from day one. That had been the prediction of all those studio heads so many years ago. That didn't happen. And that was the accomplishment.

So what if the picture had flaws? So what if it wasn't the Phi Beta Kappa of film-dom that I had hoped for? Cagney and Lacey were individually, and collectively, credible. That was the thing to be proud of—the thing that gave me the courage to send the cassette to Suzanne Levine at her *Ms.* office in Manhattan.

The film was worthy, and I was, once again, in love and proud to call it my own.

CHAPTER 10

OF THE ESSENCE

Oftentimes, when accepting a network's order for a television film, the producer is confronted with a good news/bad news situation. The bad news is the accompanying information that, along with the "go" to production, is a nearly impossible delivery schedule. After months, and sometimes years, of deliberation, the network suddenly has an air date open, and you are expected to fill it.

Hurry up and wait may be a commonplace characterization of the filming pace to a production crew, but its opposite is true in development. You wait, and wait, and then comes the dash for completion. It's no wonder so many projects fail—not only is there insufficient time to complete them properly, there is generally inadequate time to promote them.

This was not true for *Cagney & Lacey*. A confluence of events created a unique opportunity: First of all, there was the license fee negotiating process. With our high New York costs on the one hand and our lack of prestige on the other, a lot of time was spent finalizing the economic package before either the network or Filmways was assured that a film would actually be made. That took us into late January of 1980. At that juncture, an upcoming writers' strike loomed. It distracted the network executives in development, as they were kept busy trying to get scripts on their many projects completed before the labor walkout. As a by-product, the threatened strike also created a need for having movie programming stockpiled for the fall, in the event the strike delayed series production for the start of the new season. Finally, there was the decision to cast Loretta Swit. She would not finish the then-current season of *M*A*S*H** until March. Since the network doesn't buy expensive original programming for the summer, that left *Cagney & Lacey* with one of those spots for the fall, with the attendant luxurious post-production period in which to complete and promote the show.

It gave me time to send a cassette to Suzanne Levine, time for her to screen it with Gloria Steinem and others on her *Ms.* staff, time, so that their far-in-advance publication date and our air date might coincide. And so it did.

There, in the magazine's October 1981 issue, in full color and in their cop uniforms, were Tyne Daly and Loretta Swit—right on the cover. It was the first time in the magazine's history that a television project was so honored.

"The new TV show that asks the question: CAN WOMEN BE BUDDIES—UNDER PRESSURE?" That was the headline that introduced a four-page article by Marjorie Rosen, noted feminist film historian and author of *Popcorn Venus*.

Weeks before the *Ms.* publication date, I received my advance copy. Inside the magazine were pictures of our two stars and an even larger photo of the female writing team of Avedon & Corday. There was plenty of credit for me, too, and finally a special addendum to the article by Ms. Steinem herself: "If you would like to see *Cagney & Lacey* expanded into a television series …" followed by instructions on whom to write and where. This was very heady stuff.

CBS had made our air date in October official, which brought publicist Tom Brocato with his partner, Deborah Kelman, to Rosenbloom's office for a meeting. They had their usual list of proposals for screenings, theme parties, and star interviews, ad nauseam. The length of these lists is determined by the depth of your pocketbook. It's a typical shotgun approach: splatter a bunch of stuff on the wall and see what sticks.

I was getting impatient.

"Let me tell you what the campaign is," I interrupted. "It's the *Ms.* magazine article and cover—that's the campaign."

"That's all very nice," Brocato began his retort, "but their circulation is only about 500,000 …"

"That doesn't negate what I'm saying. *Ms.* is the sell. What you do is get four hundred advance copies and mail them with an FYI note to every important TV editor and women's page editor in the country. Let them discover the project themselves. *Ms.* is a super prestigious publication—an opinion maker—and the TV editors will easily pick up on the fact that something unusual has happened here, and they'll write about it. You don't need a press kit or anything. All the information you want to get out is in that article. Focus your time, energy, and budget on getting those magazines into the right hands and servicing the questions that come out of it."

OCTOBER 1981
$1.25

Ms.

The New TV Show That
Asks the Question:

CAN WOMEN BE BUDDIES—UNDER PRESSURE?

There Is To Know (So Far)
out Justice Sandra O'Connor

uples: Happy Women
d Gay Men

ne Electronics to the Rescue?

s: Fiction by Alice Walker
d Herbert Gold

The 1981 cover of *Ms.* magazine featuring Tyne Daly and Loretta Swit.

And that's what we did.

Cagney & Lacey aired on October 8, 1981, on CBS at 9 PM. A performance norm for that time period on a movie-for-television would be around a 28 share. *Cagney & Lacey* captured a 42, meaning that 42% of the people in America who were watching television were tuned to that one program. It was a major hit.

Within thirty-six hours I was summoned to Harvey Shephard's office. We knew each other slightly from the lunch that Lois Lugar had set up as promised all those months before at the New York Chinese dinner party hosted by Michael Fuchs. Filmways' president Sal Iannucci and the company's head of TV production Dick Rosenbloom were with me in Shephard's office.

"Can you turn this into a series?" Mr. Shephard wanted to know. We had no cast, no scripts, no staff, and no series concept or series bible. This is the stuff mothers raise their children on in the USA—the opportunity to be a wunderkind for corporate America.

"Watch me," I said with a smile.

"I want six episodes," Shephard said to the three of us. "How fast can you deliver?"

The president of Filmways and his TV production chief turned to me for an answer. I knew Shephard would be in New York for the fall scheduling meetings on May 1. It was then that the season would be over and the following year's schedule would be announced. If this was to be more than an exercise, I had to get episodes on the air before that May date so that Shephard would have something on which to base his decision. All I had to do now was arithmetic, subtracting six weeks from May 1.

"March 15," I said. "I'll deliver in time for a mid-March opening."

To do that we'd have to start shooting no later than early January; even then it would be nearly impossible to make dates on episodes four through six. I'd worry about that later. Shephard was smiling—one of those grins you hate to see across a poker table.

"You've got a commitment based on that," he said.

"Understand," I chimed in quickly (so much so that I'm sure all expected me to fudge on my promise of delivery). "I don't have Loretta Swit, unless you want to get her out of *M*A*S*H** for me."

Shephard smirked. He knew that I knew that he wasn't about to do that. He acknowledged my Swit-less state with a nod, paused, then said, "Recast. Re-sign Tyne Daly if you can, otherwise it's OK to recast that as well. This man," he was now pointing at me so that all in the room might clearly understand, "is of the essence to the deal."

It wasn't friendship (Lois Lugar's lovely lunch aside); I was the one who said I would deliver, and Harvey Shephard was allowing me to put my reputation, my relationship with the then-most successful network in the business, and, for that matter, probably my whole career, on the line.

This meeting took place on October 10. In just over two months we had to be in production on not one show but six. To shut down production, once we began, would not only be costly, it would preclude making air dates. The Thanksgiving, Christmas, and year-end holidays would take precious days out of this already too-short time frame. The best writers and directors were already under contract on existing shows or were preparing pilots to be shot in January and February. We would just have to face that—just as in so many other aspects of life—in the world of television series, the rich stay that way because successful series get the large orders, the early pickups, and the votes of confidence from networks, which not only allow life on a series to be pleasant but actually improve the work and make it easier to accomplish.

The best directors and writers are more readily available to a twenty-two-show order than to a show having a contract of thirteen, six, or seven. It's all economics. That fully ordered series will no doubt have reruns and foreign sales and therefore residuals for its creative staff. The short-order show may never be heard from again. It is, as a consequence, impossible for the new show to compete with that kind of reward system, and so the novice program takes the leavings—the writers and directors that the successful shows don't want or need.

Regardless of all that, we still had to find a staff, writers, directors, actors, and a crew, and we needed to find a place to photograph all this. We had no sets, and Filmways had no studio real estate, let alone sound stages. The abandoned building we had used for a precinct in Toronto had been torn down soon after we completed production. Besides, I did not believe that we could make a show on this kind of schedule in those days anywhere but Los Angeles.

Finally, there were legal problems. I was under exclusive contract in television to Paramount Pictures Corporation. My contract's only exclusion was for "*Cagney & Lacey*, a movie-for-television." It was not for *Cagney & Lacey*, a television series.

In addition, Mace and I were in the throes of trying one of our multiple and various settlements, and none of them anticipated the eventuality of *Cagney & Lacey* becoming a series.

Immediately after the conference with Shephard, I attended a meeting at Filmways. I quickly let my partners in on our legal complications. The men of Filmways thought they were witnessing the evaporation of their only foreseeable hope for getting on the air. The gloom in the room was palpable.

I then made my proposal in very take-it-or-leave-it fashion. I, too, wanted to make the show and was therefore too generous. Agents wait all their careers for this kind of opportunity: a weak and vulnerable production entity, a series order, and a client who is "of the essence to the deal." Stupidly, I did not consult my agent or lawyer. I was a team player, trying to work out a mutual problem with teammates Iannucci and Rosenbloom. This could have been one of the great business errors of my life, for there is no telling what—at that moment—I might have extracted from these anxious executives.

"I'm already making good money at Paramount," I began, "so figure I'll do this for half of my fee structure under that deal."

"How much is that?" The question was characteristic of Filmways' poor-boy mentality.

"I'm in at Paramount for $20,000 per episode for hour shows. I'll do this for ten, as long as my Paramount deal stays intact."

My in-place and outmoded deal at BNB called for me to get something like $2,500 per episode on any hour-long show. My proposal obviously represented a substantial increase to the penurious Filmways corps. They did not quibble.

"I'm doing this so cheap," I went on, "because, due to my situation at Paramount, I'm going to need a lot of help. You're going to have to figure on spending a whole lot of money on staff. We can't fool around here if you expect me to deliver as promised." There were nods of agreement all around.

"One more thing," I added. "Mace Neufeld stays out. I don't want him near me or the project. No meetings with you guys; none with the network."

"Barney, the guy's a partner in the project," pleaded Rosenbloom.

"Only financially," I shot back. "He's entitled to whatever he can negotiate with you guys, but I will not let him do to me on this what he did on *American Dream*.

To allow that to happen a second time would make me more of a fool than I am now for negotiating this deal without counsel."

The reference to an attorney cooled the room. I went on: "It must be clear in the deal that I have complete creative control and that Mace Neufeld is to be restrained from any conversations with CBS or you guys in this area. I will not allow him to stab me in the back again."

"Barney, how are we going to do that?" Iannucci asked.

I snapped back, "Your problem. Work it out."

That was probably a great mistake on my part as well. From my vantage point, the business affairs department of Filmways was to sophisticated negotiations in the television industry what the Keystone Kops were to law enforcement. They wasted little time before naively asking my former employer the equivalent of: What do we have to pay you to go away? Filmways was holding out a golden platter and saying, in effect, "Take it."

He pretty much did. Mace Neufeld retained his lion's share of profits and took a per episode fee. His company would be granted an "In Association With" credit, and he agreed to do nothing in return. He also understood he was to stay clear of me. He only made one mistake. He assumed I was smarter than I was, so he tied his fee structure into mine. Whatever they paid me for busting my hump, he would take half that amount for doing nothing. He probably assumed I would make a better deal for myself. If nothing else—based on his own experience with me—he should have known better.

CHAPTER 11

DO YOU WANT IT GOOD OR DO YOU WANT IT TUESDAY?

I had a show to produce. Corday was ensconced at ABC and therefore unavailable. I got Avedon on board. She would serve as my associate producer/story editor. Tyne Daly was convinced to try out starring in a TV series—something she professed she never wanted. As long as she was going to do it, she did want top billing. After all, she reasoned, she now had seniority. I couldn't promise that. We had no idea who Cagney would be, and what if it were someone who was clearly a bigger name? The woman who held my hand on the walk from Dupar's to the CBS office of William Self, and subsequently every evening at dailies in Toronto, understood. At Tyne's request, written into the deal, was that "billing shall be at the sole discretion of executive producer Barney Rosenzweig."[16]

My old writer pal from *Daniel Boone*, Jack Guss, came to work, bringing with him story maven Fred Freiberger. Both were questionable casting on my part, but I could find no one else whom I knew—or could trust—that was available and interested.

---

[16]   An interesting sidebar is that, since leaving Mace, I now called myself executive producer instead of the title I've always preferred, which is simply producer. To me, the executive producer was the guy, a la Mace, who put the deal together. The producer, on the other hand, is the creative force who makes the film. This is still true to a great extent in theatrical features. Sometime in the early eighties, this changed in television. I became aware of it the hard way when the Television Academy initially only invited the executive producer of *East of Eden* to be honored by them. They changed the invite that year for me, but I wised up in terms of future billing for myself.

The search for a Cagney began. As on the film that preceded this series work, inquiry was made as to the availability of Sharon Gless, the Avedon and Corday discovery of years before. Gless was unavailable, still under contract to Universal and, in fact, about to replace Lynn Redgrave in that studio's series *House Calls*.

We began to set up meetings for actresses who might play the lead. The first actress interviewed was Meg Foster. After she left the room I said, "As far as I'm concerned, we can stop looking. She's terrific." Avedon concurred. Rosenbloom and Iannucci were nervous about ending the process so soon.

"We can keep looking if you want," I said, "but let's not lose her. She's got something."

My new boss at Paramount, Gary Nardino, was trying to figure out a way to take over this series. After all, he "owned" me, and I was "of the essence." I pleaded with him to look the other way, saying that playing the kind of hardball he was contemplating might jeopardize his studio's position with CBS. Furthermore, I argued, if I could pull this off, he was going to have a much more valuable producer under exclusive contract. I offered to suspend and extend. Gary did not want to lose me for the pilot season. I assured him I could get properly staffed up and only moonlight the *Cagney & Lacey* job.

Guss, Freiberger, and Avedon were in place, but not a lot was being accomplished. I kept pressing Avedon for progress reports, for some kind of material. I was being "shined on."

More and more women, numbering in the hundreds, were lining up to play Christine Cagney. Actresses would tell us they had been the female lead in such and such a film, and we would screen it to see their work. They were on screen for all of eight minutes. It wasn't that they were lying; they *were* the female lead. What that invariably meant was they were the nurse, or the wife, or the secretary. The dearth of good roles for women made it clear why we were being bombarded with applicants. Besides the hundreds of unknown or relatively obscure players, Sally Kellerman, Susan Anspach, and Jennifer Warren were vying for the role.

The estimated cost of building our squad room on a rented sound stage in Hollywood was no less than $250,000. Amortized over six episodes, that's over $40,000 per episode for sets—and we still didn't have a Cagney loft or a Lacey apartment.

I suggested we do what we did in Toronto and find an old brick building in downtown or industrial Los Angeles and use that. The search was on. Ron Hawkins, a New York actor who had played Harvey Lacey in the Toronto movie, was holding out for more money. We decided to recast. Carl Lumbly, who played Petrie, Al Waxman, who was Samuels, and Harvey Atkin, who played the desk sergeant, all returned for the series from the Toronto production. We elected to look for a new Isbecki and create a character for my friend—and Avedon pal as well—Sidney Clute. The other change was that Cagney's father, who had only been referred to in dialogue in the movie, would now become at least a recurring character, if not a regular.[17]

We assigned my old *Senior Year* pal Brian McKay the job of writing the script that introduced Charlie Cagney on screen. Dick O'Neill was cast—our first and only choice. We had two guys we liked for Isbecki. Martin Kove was by far the least expensive. He had the job.

The location manager made a find: near Dodger Stadium, a 50,000-squarefoot, all-brick erstwhile furniture/mattress factory, now abandoned and five minutes away from those parts of Los Angeles we would use to double New York. The clincher: it was on Lacy Street.

Instead of the $250,000 estimated cost for the squad room set, we got that, the Cagney loft, the Lacey apartment, miscellaneous looks (interiors and exteriors), and office space for a grand total of $70,000, less than $12,000 per episode. It was a huge savings, even if the city fathers had misspelled Lacey.

Avedon was still hanging out with me in casting meetings and still not getting the job done with "her" writing staff. We would be shooting in a matter of weeks. Our sets were being painted and decorated; we were virtually cast—waiting only final network approval on a Cagney. We did not have page one of anything.

Avedon was to write at least the first script. Over two months had passed since her deal had been made, and all I had was three pages of an incomplete outline. I began to push very hard. My story maven was not in very good shape; her mother was dying, and none too gracefully at that. Corday's one-time partner could not cope with the pressure, and, without consulting me, she would attempt a solution of her own. Ms. Avedon phoned Harvey Shephard to tell him the delivery date was ludicrous and asked, "Do you want it good or do you want it Tuesday?" We would deliver in June, she told him.

---

[17]   A recurring character is just that—one who occasionally (or even often) returns to the series in the same role, but unlike a regular, there is not the same employment guarantee of a minimum number of episodes.

This was a kind of naive madness. There is no first-run network television in June. Our whole project was happening because of my promise to deliver. Rosenbloom was furious that Avedon would make such a call. We had to go on without her. I fired her, dug out the original theatrical movie script by Avedon & Corday, and—with Corday's help—cut and pasted a new script from the old with new material by me bridging the narrative gaps. It took a weekend.

I brought it to the office and declared it a model of what we were doing and a fix on where we should be going with the series. I felt like Moses bringing down the Tablets from Mount Sinai. Basically it was a direction, a formula, to be broken only for a better idea. We had to get started somewhere, and I was now prepared to say we start with this:

(A)   *A cop story with a beginning, middle, and an end.*

(B)   *A personal story of nearly equal length with the cop story and (ideally) tying in with the cop story in some thematic way. This story should feature either Lacey or Cagney.*

(C)   *A personal story of perhaps half the length and importance of the other personal story featuring the lead not featured in the longer personal story.*

(D)   *Comic runners, or running gags, involving the squad room, the other detectives, the booking area, or the Lacey household.*

We had been narrowing our choice of actresses down to under a dozen. Tyne Daly was now being included in the process. We would have her sit and chat with the candidate and see how the chemistry worked. We did readings with Tyne and the Cagney wannabes. We did the same with our two finalists for Harvey Lacey. Tyne and I wanted John Karlen (whom I had featured in *American Dream*); Iannucci and Rosenbloom wanted the other guy. To Shephard it was a toss-up until I told him Karlen was Tyne's preference.

"Well, then, no question. It should be the man she prefers. They've a lot of work to do together." Harvey Shephard had spoken, and so John Karlen was cast.

It wasn't so smooth with Cagney. We had reduced our selections to seven women, including Meg Foster. She won the roll on merit. It was unanimous, although everyone did wait for Shephard to speak first. "Who do you prefer?" he asked, turning to me.

"Meg Foster," I said. I knew she was the least known of our candidates, but I had liked her from the first. Shephard nodded, and then everyone concurred.

It wasn't until the next day that Shephard had second thoughts. He had learned that Emmy Award–winning actress Susan Clark was available and just might be interested in doing what then would have been her first television series. I was determined to be open-minded. Susan Clark was, after all, a major television name. She had, at that time, never before done a television series. Signing her would be a coup.

Ms. Clark had refused to read for the part. Shephard acknowledged this was to her detriment, especially in light of the obvious chemistry of Meg Foster's reading with Tyne Daly. Nevertheless, the network chief asked me to consider the insurance of some kind of name to replace the not-insubstantial loss of Loretta Swit.

A meeting was set for Rosenbloom, Daly, and me at the home of Ms. Clark and her then-husband Alex Karras. As the producer of *Daniel Boone* I had, some years before, given Mr. Karras his first acting role in Hollywood (first, in that all he had done on screen before that was to play a cameo as himself—a Detroit Lions footballer in the filmization of the George Plimpton tome *Paper Lion*). The evening was therefore off to a warm and nostalgic start.

Without trying to be too obvious about it, we worked out the seating arrangement so that Ms. Clark and Ms. Daly sat next to each other on the couch. We were all affable and friendly, but I concentrated on watching and listening to the two women rather than making, or contributing to, the conversation myself.

Clark and Daly seemed to get on famously and, so far as I could tell, had a fair amount of respect for each other. The conversations were pretty much of a general nature, primarily centering on their craft but not focusing at all specifically on our series or our production plan. A little over an hour later, the conference was over, and we bid Ms. Clark and Mr. Karras goodnight.

I was in Shephard's office the next morning. "It's OK with me," I said, and then added, "Provided we set the show in Kansas instead of New York and change the title to *Lacey & Lacey*."

The CBS chief was not big on sarcasm. I clarified my *Lacey & Lacey* remark by telling him my feeling that Tyne Daly and Susan Clark might be a viable duo as sisters, but that there wasn't enough contrast between the two of them to make for an interesting team. I also ventured the opinion that no one would believe Ms. Clark as the hard-bitten New Yorker we had written for Cagney. Harvey Shephard wasn't used to being disagreed with, and he did not take to my being cute about it. We argued. He pointed out the virtue of a star and the fine creative credentials of his candidate. I countered with my nominee's chemistry, sex appeal, and physical imagery. We were at a standstill. Neither was convincing the other. Shephard was adamant, and I wasn't blinking.

There was what seemed an inordinately long period of time where he simply stared at me. I stared back. Finally, I asked, "So what do we do now?"

He punched a button on his intercom. The voice of CBS casting director Jean Guest came over the speaker. Over the phone, and in as even-handed a fashion as he could, Shephard asked for Ms. Guest to choose between Meg Foster and Susan Clark for the role of Christine Cagney.

This blatantly self-serving setup had my eyes midway in their roll heavenward when the disembodied voice of Ms. Guest most unequivocally stated, "Meg Foster." I ceased my upward glance and smiled.

Ms. Guest received a cursory thank-you from her employer, who then punched some more buttons. CBS executive Bob Silberling's voice came over the speaker. Shephard's tone had somewhat changed, I thought. This time he indicated I was with him in the room and that we were having a "discussion" about the merits of who would be the best choice between the *known* Ms. Clark and the relatively un-famous Ms. Foster. Silberling equivocated and took a long time in doing so. Too many "on the other hands" later, Shephard bid farewell and punched the intercom again, summoning the new callee to his office. In less than ninety seconds, junior executive Gary Barton was there.

"Mr. Rosenzweig here and I are having a disagreement," Shephard began. I thought his bias was showing, but I said nothing. Shephard, at last, posed his question.

Barton did not hesitate. "Meg Foster." He then added, "Without a doubt."

Shephard turned to me. "All right, I guess we're cast." That was it. I quickly flashed to those days at ABC and the awful experiences and endless waiting for executive decisions: Tahiti versus the Gulag.

Tony Barr was the CBS vice president in charge of current programming. I invited him and his assistants to my office at Paramount. Anyone who visited me there had to be impressed. It was very grand. I moved to the club chair nearer the couch Mr. Barr occupied. The distance from my desk to the chair was substantive. It allowed me time to notice the number of dog-eared pages on the scripts held by the CBS trio. These turned-down corners presumably indicated the pages con-taining notes on ways to improve what I was breaking my hump to produce.

I had been here before. These were the experts. Their message was always heady and seductive:

"Listen to us, and you will be successful."

"Follow our instructions, and you will please us."

"We are your network; we know what we are doing."

"You should have seen (name any one of a half dozen hits on the network in question) before we fixed it."

There were other items on their agenda but not always so clearly stated, such as: non-compliance could mean a weak promotion campaign, a poor time slot, costly delays to the production schedule, or labeling the non-complier as a troublemaker.

"Before we begin," I said to the small gathering, "I would like to make a few opening remarks."

It took me several minutes. I talked of what I knew about television, what I felt about my work, what over-networking meant to me, and what I had endured on *American Dream*. I discoursed on what I had learned from that experience and was emphatic as to how I would not allow such a thing to recur.

I may never again be that eloquent. My monologue was heartfelt. My passion and zeal were unquestionably authentic, and my pain all too recent.

To his credit, Tony Barr got it. When I was done, he quickly passed through the first fifty-five pages or so of his note-laden script and simply made a request for clarity in the final sequence. I'm sure I said that I would try to accommodate.

There were other note sessions, of course. The path was not always smooth, but the tenor for the next six-plus years had been set that afternoon. I stated my position with clarity and with feeling. Barr, a fundamentally decent and caring man, understood it.

Did it help that Tony Barr was not after my job? That he was older than I? That he had already been a producer years before and was on this job as a step toward retirement? It couldn't have hurt.

Years later, Norman Lear and I compared notes. We had each had this same seminal moment with the CBS network. We had both taken this same tack. They were at different times, with different executives, but with similar results. My series became one of the most esteemed dramas in the history of television. His was *All in the Family*, possibly the most honored show of all time.

What Norman and I discovered we had in common at that uniquely pressure-filled time was simple: each of us had another job. We were each to get a lot of commendations for our foresight, our integrity, our raised consciousness, and our courage, but what we really had was a case ace.

Had I not had that two-year, no-cut contract with Paramount, had everything I wanted and needed been tied up in that one six-show order (with CBS working their seductive wiles, their pledges of support, their promises of understanding), I cannot say I could have—would have—been nearly the man I am credited with being today.

Early and happy days at a new CBS series publicity shoot. That is Richard M. Rosenbloom being given the lovely smile by Meg Foster. Tyne and I are to the left and higher, resulting in the optical illusion that I might be balding.

Photo: Rosenzweig Personal Collection

CHAPTER 12

BREAKING THE RULES

Jack Guss was at my home on a Saturday afternoon to discuss his rewrite of Claudia Adams's teleplay on the *Cagney & Lacey* episode we were to call "Street Scene," to be directed by Ray Danton.

The story predated the Bernard Goetz case in New York but was similar in that a seemingly normal citizen-civilian gets a gun and shoots a neighborhood teenage hoodlum. We were only weeks away from principal photography. Early in the story, Cagney and Lacey return to the apartment building that was not only the scene of the crime but the home of both the victim and the aging gunman.

In the script, there was a scene where our two detectives interrogated the wife of the man they arrested for the killing. She was described as a seventy-year-old woman in a wheelchair. Our heroines listened and took notes as the woman told them of how, years before, she and her husband had come to America with great hope of building a new and better life and how, ultimately, for them, the American dream had failed. The neighborhood they lived in continued to deteriorate, until finally it had fallen into its current state of disrepair.

Gangs of hoodlums ruled the streets and dominated the hallways; their intimidating graffiti was everywhere. The street toughs had taken to breaking into apartments and stealing social security checks from mailboxes. Finally, the woman related, her husband could not take it anymore. He bought a gun, and, when he was once again harassed by these gangsters, he shot the ringleader. The woman's pain was palpable. Even the hard-bitten Cagney, the screenwriter had added, was moved by her story.

You don't have to be as good a writer as Jack Guss to make this kind of scene an emotional read. Many could write it, and the proof of that is that probably hundreds have. I know that I've viewed some version of this scene certainly dozens of times.

We were in the kitchen at my house. Jack sat across from me, sharing a sandwich. Corday stood at the sink. The moment was curiously domestic. I was very critical, but not as specific as I like to be. I felt the scene was predictable and ordinary.

"Worse than that," I said, "it's a waste. Our two best actresses are standing there with notepads saying an occasional uh-huh," I exaggerated, "while this seventy-year-old day player sits in her wheelchair and does a monologue. The scene is a cinematic disaster waiting to happen—not only that, it's a bore!"

"It's necessary exposition, Barney." Jack was a friend and a pro. He was not overly defensive and was probably right to be somewhat frustrated at my only being critical and not giving direction on how to fix this thing. We were creating a series here. Few rules had been laid down. The two-hour movie had given us some guidelines, but that had been a very different format and pace than we would be exploring from now on.

Movies, after all, have a beginning, middle, and end; series, the creators hope, will never end. The former are usually plot driven, while the best of the latter are motivated by character.

Guss continued. "Somewhere in this section of the story, Cagney and Lacey have to learn what kind of a man the guy they've arrested is and how he got that way. You tell me a better way to do it."

There have been only a few major creative moments in my life. This was to become one of them. To accomplish it, I would have to break a cardinal rule of picture-making. In only a few sentences, I was going to create a scene that would be a stylistic benchmark for our series. It was a moment that would dictate a phi-losophy, a way of telling a story that would be unique to our show; that would put the emphasis of the series where I believed it should be; and one that would underline what I perceived to be our primary strength—the acting acumen of our two leads.

"Put the camera in the hallway," I began, "the door to the apartment opens, reveal-ing a little old lady in the background. She is in a wheelchair. She says nothing as Cagney and Lacey come out of the apartment and into the hall. (We've just saved a thousand dollars 'cause the lady's now an extra and not an actress.)" I paren-thetically digressed before resuming. "The door closes. Our leads are alone in the hallway. Cagney turns to Lacey and snaps, 'Did you learn any more from her by bringing her a quart of Harvey's chicken soup?'"

I went on, describing our camera following the two women down the hallway as they walked and talked and argued over what they heard the little old lady say and how they felt about it.

Jack Guss and Barbara Corday were both listening carefully as I proceeded. "What you now have is a scene of conflict that provides information instead of a straight expository scene. Further, the scene of conflict is between your two best actresses (and coincidentally our leads) instead of a monologue by—what at best—will be a very dicey piece of casting." I pointed out that this new scene also provided us with some great character stuff about our principals.

"It tells me, for one thing," I said, "that Lacey has a husband who makes chicken soup and that Cagney is embarrassed that her partner resorts to this kind of mothering/social work!" I manically continued. "It indicates, clearly, that Cagney and Lacey perceive the world from two disparate points of view and thereby sets up the ongoing possibility of always providing us with the necessary ingredient of any good drama: conflict; better yet—conflict between principals!"

Jack was now taking notes. The cinematic rule we were breaking was one learned in every freshman cinema class in the country: "Show don't tell." We were about to do just the opposite. We had actresses who could talk with the best of them. That was our strength. I was not so sure we could compete with other cop shows for cinematic pyrotechnics. Besides, ever since *The French Connection,* the car chase is the time when I went out to get popcorn.

"Let's do stories of revelation," I said.

What I meant by that was that the plots would be revealed to the audience only through the eyes of our leads. We would deny ourselves the legitimate cinematic device of parallel editing (an editorial concept best defined conceptually as "meanwhile, back at the ranch").

I expanded on my thesis. "Cagney and Lacey will be at their desks. The phone rings. 'A burglary is in progress at 53rd and Lexington.' By the time they get there the break-in is over. The perpetrator is gone. Cagney and Lacey deal with the aftermath, with the victims, with each other. How does the work impact them, their families? How do they relate to the men with whom they work?"

Corday had joined us at the kitchen table. She quietly added what was to become my favorite phrase: "It's a show about two women who happen to be cops, not two cops who happen to be women."

"That's right," I said. "Who gives a crap about all that cop shit anyhow? I've seen it."

Jack would not give us an argument.

It reminded me of comedian Henny Youngman, who would raise his left arm, the one holding the violin, over his head. "Doctor, doctor, it hurts when I do this!" The medical man's admonishing response? "Don't do that."

It's the same logic I was enforcing on *Cagney & Lacey*. I saw what we did well, and I emphasized it. What we weren't good at, I eliminated. I knew we had two great actresses to work with and a new concept in two women as co-equal leads and partners. What I didn't have was time or money for great action scenes. I was sure that what I was asking for would become our "signature."

More often than not, when confronted with one of those so-called obligatory scenes, we would trash the predictable moment and play it after the fact, with Cagney relating the tale to Lacey or vice versa in the precinct's ladies toilet (we called it the jane).

Why film Cagney's date of the week when we could have so much more fun watching the two gals dish about it afterward? Why dramatize that boring trial scene when Lacey could enact the parts of judge, DA, and jury for an impatient Cagney? Occasionally we even played the by-the-numbers job assignment scene in advance of it taking place, as Cagney would mimic an all-too-predictable Lt. Samuels, allowing Lacey to do a less-than-kind imitation of her partner in response.

Our directors for those first six episodes were Georg Stanford Brown, Reza Badiyi, and Ray Danton. Along with cinematographer Hector Figueroa, they set a visual style for the series—pretty much dictated by the practical interiors (complete with real windows and low ceilings) they were forced to use. It imposed a sort of gritty, natural look as opposed to the studio lighting on other shows that usually came via electrical equipment, strung from grids suspended from a sound stage's high rafters.

The fundamental style was simple and best stated by Director Danton: "You put the camera at the eye level of the women, say action, and get the hell out of the way."

Danton's admonition was mostly a compliment to our actors, but it also reflected the kind of material we were delivering and my own penchant for simple stories, simply told.

Although I admired what Bob Butler and Steven Bochco had created stylistically in *Hill Street Blues* (complete with intricate camera moves, a large canvas replete with a huge speaking cast and even greater numbers of atmosphere players, plus multiple action scenes), I remembered Henny Youngman, with his outstretched violin, and in no way tried to compete with that. We would concentrate on what it was we did best. Not-so-coincidentally, this was costing hundreds of thousands of dollars less per episode than what Mr. Bochco and Mr. Butler were spending.

We had a few broadcast standards problems, but they were minimal. I had pretty much fought and won those battles while prepping the original TV movie.

In that film, the Lacey marriage was under a great strain. Harvey had been unemployed for several months, resulting in a loss of confidence and self-esteem. This manifested itself in his disinterest and inability to have sexual relations with his wife. Tension and irritability were the consequences.

In one scene from that pilot M.O.W., Harvey dropped Lacey off at work just as Cagney was arriving. The two women exchanged pleasant enough greetings, and Cagney expanded hers to include Harvey. Not only did Harvey fail to reciprocate, but he then stomped on the car's accelerator to speed away in a manner that amplified the insult. Both women were a little embarrassed. Then, in an effort at making light of the whole thing, Cagney quipped, "His time of the month or what?"

"Absolutely not!" said the CBS censors for the movie. Jokes about the menstrual cycle had never been allowed at the network.

"You don't understand something," I countered. "This is essential to the character of the picture we are making. Women—especially in the workplace—have to put up with this kind of demeaning sexist slander all the time. We are debunking that kind of mythology with humor throughout the picture. If you attack that, then there is no reason to make the film."

I won a lot of arguments, but this was the toughest. The CBS West Coast standards executives simply would not break their code on this subject. I took it all the way to the top New York executive in the department: Alice Henderson, vice president, CBS broadcast standards.

Ms. Henderson was adamant. So was I.

"Without that line, I simply will not make the film." I said it sans blink. Ms. Henderson looked at me for the longest time. She was somewhat incredulous but saw I was serious and backed down.

There was the previously mentioned scene involving the prostitute, who because of her profession was able to help identify Schermer as a non-Jew by the simple fact that he was not circumcised. I won this argument as well but later, in a moment of self-censorship, removed the reference. I felt it called attention to itself and stopped the scene in which it was included rather than having it progress naturally.

The standards people were duly impressed that I could fight so hard for something—be given the license to do it—and then not do it because, in my view, the line called such attention to itself that it damaged the scene.

I was to have these second thoughts several times during the life of the series, and I believe we reaped many benefits in the process. I felt that as the network saw our concerns were sometimes the same as theirs (albeit for different reasons) things could only get easier. It cost me very little. I was much more interested in fighting for concepts and the right to explore them than to be granted permission to expand the allowable TV series vocabulary of off-color remarks.

Sometimes they co-mingled. We were always getting the standard request to reduce (by 10–50%) the number of *hells* and *damns* in a script. We would comply, but only as long as it was understood that Cagney could say all the *hells* and *damns* she needed—and even an occasional *crap, ass, butt,* or *bastard*. Although it was language, our point was conceptual. These were women trying to succeed and be accepted in an all-male arena. No one wanted to be more accepted than Christine Cagney, and so, even though her father might tell her to watch her mouth or her partner might wince, talking tough was an important aspect of the Cagney character. The network agreed.

The Lacey marriage was my idealized version of how I think a marriage ought to be. Harvey's culinary accomplishments, especially with spaghetti sauce, were my father's; his more intelligent wife, my mother. Harvey had political conspiracy theories because I do. Cagney hated the ballet and loved to drink, and so do I. She also had an overdeveloped sense of the romantic and was a workaholic. (Guess who?)

We were making my show, and I was generally pleased. I liked the look, and the scripts were solid, if not terrific. They were certainly well above the television series norm. I brought in comedy writer Gloria Banta to "female-ize" what it was we were doing. I was very nervous that my now Avedon-less staff was all middle-aged, white, and male.

Tyne Daly became our leader on the stage. She set the standard of excellence and attention to detail. The best writer I ever knew, Joel Oliansky,[18] became a devoted fan of the series and once told me that the best line of dialogue he had ever been exposed to on television was in those first six episodes. They were the words *thank you* spoken by Tyne's Mary Beth Lacey in straightforward fashion as she unhappily learned from ballistics that it was her gun that had fired the shot that had killed a fleeing bank robber. Simple stories, simply told.

---

[18]   The Academy Award–winning writer of *Bird* (the Charlie Parker story), *The Competition* with Richard Dreyfuss, the groundbreaking TV series *The Law*, and the very successful TV miniseries *Masada*, to name some of his very prestigious projects.

CHAPTER 13

SCHEDULING HITS/ SCHEDULING FAILURES

In the midst of this incredibly chaotic time, *Modesty Blaise*, my new pilot for ABC, was about to go into production at Paramount. I had sold this idea, based on the international comic strip heroine created by Peter O'Donnell, as sort of an *Avengers* in reverse—a bright, sophisticated, female James Bond, with her action-oriented male sidekick; it was to be a sexy, adult, action-adventure that should play at 10 PM. Mr. O'Donnell was (you should excuse the expression) gun-shy. Director Joseph Losey had made a theatrical film of his creation in the sixties starring Monica Vitti, Terrence Stamp, and Dirk Bogarde from a screenplay by Stanley Dubens. O'Donnell hated this bastardization of his work to such an extent that he repurchased the rights from the film's distributor. In order to win over this caring writer, I had, some months before, gone to London at the behest of Paramount boss Nardino. My mission was successful then, but, more and more, I found myself failing the gentlemanly author through compromise.

I had sold a ten o'clock show. ABC now wanted a program for eight o'clock. We were rapidly moving away from the *Avengers* and James Bond and more toward a camp cartoon. My ideas for casting and writing seemed all wrong to the network, and—out of gratitude to Nardino for looking the other way while I launched Cagney & Lacey—I went along, believing this would please my beneficent Paramount employer.

We went from some very sophisticated actresses I had met to casting Ann Turkel, a fashion model of limited acting experience and, in my view, questionable dedication to the actor's craft. When I would try to speak to her (as one would to Tyne Daly) about her character's arc and background, she would talk to me about her hairdresser. When I would speculate on the pain suffered by the character of

Modesty Blaise in childhood, she would respond with something like "my skin is very tawny in the sunlight." I went to Nardino. I felt this was impossible and said so. Gary made it clear that this was who he and Tony Thomopolis (then head of the ABC network programming and development) wanted. And that's who they got.

The March air date for *Cagney & Lacey* was drawing near. Harvey Shephard gave us what was then the most coveted time period in network television: 9 PM Thursday night.

We were to follow *Magnum, P.I.* on the CBS network, thus inheriting a 38 share of audience from this established monster hit. We were all ecstatic. The word throughout Hollywood and Madison Avenue was that here was a major success story about to happen. Imagine: a movie-for-television garners a 42 share, and, within months of that airing, it becomes a series and is scheduled to follow the biggest ratings winner on the number-one network. It couldn't possibly miss.

A pretty fair schedule of on-air promos[19] was ordered. For my taste they were too action-oriented and not indicative of what the show was about. "You're selling this like *Starsky and Hutch* in drag," I would complain. I would for the nth time paraphrase my spouse: "It's about two women who happen to be cops, not two cops who happen to be women." The CBS promotion department was confident of the rightness of its path. I was not making friends here.

We opened on March 25 against *Nine to Five*, a new ABC comedy based on the Jane Fonda-Dolly Parton-Lily Tomlin movie of the same name. It used the same hit song for its TV opening as it had on the successful theatrical feature.

True to predictions, we did inherit *Magnum's* 38 share; we then promptly dropped to a 24 share. Millions of folks—fully 14 percent of the people watching television in America—simultaneously rose from their chairs and changed channels. It was a movement of seismic proportions.

It had to be a mistake, an aberration. No one at CBS panicked. It would correct itself the following week. Perhaps some Nielsen home in Detroit had a power outage. No one could explain it.

The next week we inherited a 38 share again. We immediately fell to a 25. It was not an aberration after all. Harvey Shephard was on the phone. It was Friday morning. "You are canceled," he said.

---

[19]   The television equivalent of point-of-sale advertising.

I was not surprised. The news was devastating but not unexpected.

Shephard went on. Next week's episode (our third of the six) would air as scheduled, but only because he could get nothing else on fast enough. (For the record, number three did no better than its predecessors.) Shephard was bitterly disappointed at all this but showed little emotion. It was like talking to a very stern parent after handing in a failing report card.

I wanted to know when he would broadcast the final three episodes. He speculated that it would be sometime during the summer.

"Jesus, Harvey, by then your fall schedule is set. Can't I get on before the May meetings to have a shot for fall?"

Shephard was understandably incredulous. "Barney, you are canceled!"

"Let me tell you something, Harvey." I felt my adrenalin pumping even as I formulated my argument. "I started in this business at MGM nearly twenty years ago. My boss was the very venerable Howard Strickling, and he used to say something about the movie business that also applies to television and this conversation: 'If a picture opens and dies,' he would say, 'then it's the picture's fault. If it doesn't open, then it's the campaign's fault.' Harvey," I went on, "we never opened! Over ten million Americans turned us off without even sampling the show. You owe me an opening." Before he could acknowledge or counter this argument, I forged ahead. "Have you seen the demographics?"

"What demographics?" he wanted to know.

"For God's sake, Harvey. ABC has demographics. What the hell's going on over there at CBS?"

Shephard knew, of course, that my wife was an executive at ABC, that I might well have access to the kind of data to which I referred. I had, in fact, worked on some audience breakdowns, gleaned from Corday's office, in the hope of tracking some kind of pattern over the six-show life of our series. I had hoped to be prepared with a potential sales argument for the May meetings. I hadn't learned much, and what I had was, to say the least, incomplete. Despite my lack of preparation with these statistics, I grasped at anything to make my argument work.

"The goddamn demographics show that we shouldn't be on at 9 PM," I stated with authority. "We're 120th among kids and 116th with teenagers, but with adult women we're 24th—and we're 28th among adults of both sexes. Clearly we should not be following a teen heartthrob like Tom Selleck, nor should we be on before 10 PM. We're an adult show for God's sake!"

I was losing him. TV executives do not like to be told their business by producers any more than the other way around. He did promise he would think about all this and that we would talk again later that afternoon. For now, he had a bigger problem. The numbers on *Cagney & Lacey* were so low that he was being heavily pressured by Universal Studios to resurrect one of their earlier-in-the-season cancellation casualties by allowing them to play out their heretofore unbroadcast episodes in the failed time slot now occupied by my show.

"They can't do any worse," Shephard shared.

"It sounds like a good audience flow from *Magnum*," I conceded. "Good luck with it."

The Universal series was *Simon and Simon*. Given the lead-in by *Magnum, P. I.*, *Simon and Simon* became one of the major hits of the decade for the CBS network. It was exactly the same show with the same cast on the same network that had failed so dismally in the fall on Tuesday nights. Now, on Thursdays in the spring, it would prove to be a smash. This was far from the first time such a thing had occurred.

In fact, this sort of thing happens frequently enough to be almost commonplace. Scheduling hits are almost as numerous as scheduling failures. Why, in the face of this recurring phenomena, network executives continue to prematurely truncate series before they are given an opportunity to find their audience is one of the great mysteries of the medium. No one benefits. It is not only costly for both network and supplier to develop and launch a new show, but this hair-trigger mania curtails creativity and benefits neither the advertiser nor the audience.

Back at Lacy Street, we were in production on our last of the six episodes. I saw no need to share the news of our cancellation with the cast. They had been working night and day and were, quite understandably, exhausted. I let Rosenbloom know, of course, and told him I was scheduled to speak to Harvey Shephard again that same afternoon. I finally returned Mike Piller's call. He was then working under Tony Barr as our current programming liaison with CBS and years away from becoming the successful producer of some of the *Star Trek* adventures on UPN. It was in that Friday morning conversation that Piller gave me some information about the CBS plans for April that became the thrust of my afternoon confrontation with Shephard.

I was possessed by more than the desire to win. I knew that the cancellation of *Cagney & Lacey* would be perceived differently than the earlier demise of, say, *Simon and Simon*. There a cop show, featuring two private eyes, had failed. In the case of *Cagney & Lacey*, a police drama featuring two women had collapsed. That was the distinction. No one would consider not making another male-bonding show just because of the failure of one, but *Cagney & Lacey* would somehow be pointed to as demonstrable proof that a dramatic show with women as buddies could not succeed.

I was overwhelmed by the irony that my work would serve as yet another nail in the coffin of the women's movement. The very group I had hoped to aid—to be a spokesperson for—was now about to suffer even greater indignity, and I would be the cause.

I wanted the opportunity to prove that *Cagney & Lacey* could work in a proper time period—and to be given that chance before the May scheduling meetings in New York. Shephard was in disbelief at my temerity and tenacity. I was undaunted.

"On Sunday, April 25, and on Monday, April 26, you are playing reruns of *Trapper John* and *Lou Grant*," I began (using my notes from the day's earlier phone conversation with CBS liaison Piller). "Give me those two 10 PM time periods, and I will send Meg and Tyne on the road and spend $25,000 of my own money on the campaign: *Cagney & Lacey* are back … to back!"

"Save your money," was the terse response.

"Harvey," I entreated, "what have you got to lose here? I can't do worse than a rerun."

Shephard replied in classic "read my lips" fashion. "Barney, you are canceled. Why are we having this conversation?"

"This is not a conversation," I countered, "it's an argument. I want to know why you won't give this campaign a chance, and you're not telling me."

"I'm not going to give you two nights," he said.

I took it as an opening. "All right, if I can only have the one, I'd prefer Sunday at ten. I believe that's where we belong anyway."

My hubris was undeniable. Shephard agreed to think about it.

"Don't think too long," I said. "I need time to get into *TV Guide* and to plan out the promotion tour."

Rosenbloom consented to the expenditure of funds. Tyne and Meg agreed to go. Brocato began plotting out a tour of something more than a dozen key cities. With so little time before April 25, we would split up the two women and have them visit different cities simultaneously. Tyne would take the northern route east, Meg the southern. Both would leave immediately upon completion of photography of episode six. Harvey Shephard would make me wait until the following Tuesday for his essential permission.

"OK," he said at last. "You will replace a *Trapper John* rerun on April 25." I don't think he stayed on the phone long enough to hear me say thank you.

Rosenbloom and I divided up the country as well. Each of us began calling CBS station managers in the cities Meg or Tyne would be visiting. In essence we said that our star was coming to town on such and such a date and for "x" amount of time; that she would be available for local promos or any publicity or promotion they might see fit. All were cooperative to one degree or another. I'm sure Tyne and Meg could write books of their own about this journey. They did "on-air" conversations, phone interviews, and promos for the stations. They met with print journalists and did everything but open supermarkets. The whole thing went off without too many hitches, despite the reticence of some newspaper editors to meet with either of them and Meg's falling asleep in an airport phone booth from exhaustion, which resulted in her missing one of her flights. The whole thing from plan to air date was three weeks.

Then the show: April 25, 1982, CBS from 10 to 11 PM. The episode got a 34 share and came in seventh of all programs broadcast for the week. The ratings came out late the following Tuesday.

On Wednesday morning Dick Rosenbloom and I were in Harvey Shephard's office at his invitation. It was just the two of us with Shephard this time. Sal Iannucci was no longer part of the team. In the midst of our six-show order, Filmways had been taken over by the motion picture entity known as Orion Pictures Corporation, headed by the venerable Arthur Krim and his partners, Eric Pleskow, Robert Benjamin, and Mike Medavoy. None of them knew much, if anything, about television, but Iannucci, who had made a play to acquire the television division, was out. The management team at Orion decided—for the moment—to do nothing about selling off assets until they could get a better feel for the operation they now controlled.

None of that mattered much to me as Rosenbloom sat on the couch opposite Shephard's desk. I sat closer to Shephard and to the side. Typical of these meetings, it was me that Harvey Shephard addressed. It had been that way from the day he had declared me "of the essence." It remained true through cancellations and pickups, through good days and bad. Traditionally, it is the production company and its executives who are addressed or notified by a network, not the artist. Shephard made an exception in my case. Invariably his attitude permeated his network, the television company for whom I worked, and ultimately the industry itself. It made me somewhat unique among employee producers.

"There will be naysayers here who will say you did this against reruns on a dead Nielsen week.[20] I am not one of them. You took on a challenge, and you pulled it off." Harvey Shephard barely took a breath before adding, "I'm going back to New York with the recommendation you be on the fall schedule."

Dozens of CBS executives would be at those meetings—only three counted: William S. Paley, Bud Grant, and the man in whose office Dick Rosenbloom and I then sat. Three men would set the schedule for the CBS network, and I had one of them. I was focused on every word. This was one of the great moments of my life, and I didn't want to miss a syllable.

The naysayers to whom the CBS chief had referred were his own employees. *Cagney & Lacey* had not gone through the normal developmental process at the network. In fact, it had been passed on by the series development people at CBS not once, but twice (first as a drama with comedy, then as a comedy with drama). *Cagney & Lacey* was made as a movie-for-television. In those days at CBS, these department executives—from those disparate divisions—not only occupied different buildings, but the buildings themselves were located in totally different parts of the city. They did not get together to compare notes.

Cagney & Lacey, as a series failure, validated the system. The series people could always say: "Sure the M.O.W. was a hit; that's where it belonged. But we always knew there was no series there; that's why we turned it down." Besides, if Harvey Shephard could simply stake out a movie and declare it a television series, then maybe—just maybe—someone in power might ask why they needed all those junior development executives and their six-figure salaries. Maybe television would return to that simpler time of broadcaster and producer-supplier. Few in middle management at the networks would welcome that. Finally, there was the embarrassment. Not only were those development executives about to be proved

---

[20]   Just as there are Sweep Weeks of hyper importance to the purveyors and subscribers of the television rating system, so, too, are there times when the ratings don't count. Of course, like all absolutes, this is only partially true. Ratings are still taken, still read, and still used and abused. They are just not supposed to count in terms of advertising rates during the dead weeks, and the opposite is true during sweeps … that's where the amounts to be charged advertisers are most often set.

wrong, they would vividly remember for some time having to call the supplier(s) they were then working with and being forced to cancel a development deal or two because their boss had just plucked *Cagney & Lacey* out of the M.O.W. files. They would be embarrassed, for when you are in the power game, it always hurts to admit to those over whom you have power that you are not as powerful as you have led them to believe.

I asked if there was anything I could do to assist, referring to Shephard's scheduling meetings in New York in one week. Would it be helpful, for instance, for me to put together a list of potential staff for next year's season: different directors, story lines?

Shephard shook his head. "I trust you to make a good show," he said, then adding, "but I could use some ammunition."

I didn't have to say anything for him to understand I was prepared to cooperate.

"Will you take a short order?" he queried. (Our contract provided that, following the six episodes we had just produced, CBS was obligated to order no less than thirteen new episodes, should they wish to renew. What Shephard wanted to know was, would we take an order for less—say four or six? It was a major economic consideration for us and clearly of no small importance to Shephard.) I glanced at Rosenbloom, he nodded, and so I agreed.

The network chief spoke again: "Will you recast?"

"Who?" I sounded even more surprised than I was, but I was plenty surprised.

"Meg Foster."

"Why?" It was the only response I could think of.

"Barney," he said, "the two women are too similar. They're both blue-collar and too street. Believe me, this is not a throwback to our old casting discussion. I bought your argument about contrast then, but Meg Foster is not delivering that."

"I could dye her hair" was met by a disparaging look from the CBS chief. "Maybe it's my fault," I rattled on. "I could write her differently."

"She's written the same way that character was written when Loretta Swit played her. That time she popped off the screen. Face it, this gal simply isn't working!"

It was not the first time I had heard this. Corday had been concerned, if not downright critical, with Meg's portrayal from the first cast reading in our living room nearly three months before. My then-friend, producer-director Michael

Zinberg, after viewing the first episode some weeks before, had said that I had "bet on the wrong horse."

As my mother would say: "If enough people tell you you're drunk, lie down."

There was some silence in the room now. Creatively, Meg had been a pleasure to work with. This was tough, painful stuff. The decision was mine to make. Harvey Shephard was my only ace. He liked me and my show and had plucked me out of relative obscurity to make it. Now he had a problem, and he needed ammunition. I rationalized: it wasn't as if he were asking me to do something like cast a nineteen-year-old with a forty-four-inch chest; the name Suzanne Somers had not come up as a casting alternative. What he was asking for was what my wife, the co-creator of the series, had urged from practically the outset: "Get the right Cagney."

"Should I put together a list of possible candidates for the role?" I murmured. Shephard shook his head. The attitude in the room had changed to one of solemnity, worthy of the pain to which I was about to subject a fine actress and a loyal employee.

"No," he said, "that will only get the word out all over town and damage someone who's worked hard for us. It's all premature, anyway. I will only play that card if I have to."

CHAPTER 14

CPR AND HOT FUDGE SUNDAES

Harvey Shephard was scheduled to depart for New York the following Sunday. He said there was nothing more Rosenbloom or I could do; still, we both resolved to leave that weekend for New York to be close at hand should the need arise.

On the Friday before our weekend departure for the Big Apple, Corday and I attended the fortieth birthday party for actor Stephen Macht, the leading man on *American Dream*, my one-time *succes d'estime*.

At that party was Monique James, a woman I had heard about for many years but had never met. For more than a decade she had been the executive in charge of talent at Universal Studios, the person who championed the contract players and headed up a one-time considerable stable of new and not-so-new actors and actresses who were in business with that major monolith.

Ms. James had only recently left Universal to personally manage the career of the studio's very last contract player, Sharon Gless. It was a small conversation point between the two of us as we both recalled how the blonde actress had been offered the "Meg Foster role" (referred to as such, for that is what it still was at the time of Macht's birthday bash) for the TV movie as well as the series—and that each time the actress had been unable to consider the proposition because of her exclusive commitment to Universal—a circumstance that still existed, as Ms. Gless had replaced Lynn Redgrave as the female lead in the studio's ongoing TV series *House Calls*. In return for committing to this project for the life of the series, the actress would be granted freedom from exclusivity at Universal once the series ended. That clarified for me the career choice for Ms. James, making it one with a future. I wished her luck and Mr. Macht a happy birthday, excusing myself from the party to go home to pack for my trek to New York. Monique James and her client were a footnote in my history of this project; I had to get on and into the future. The next day, Barbara and I were off to New York.

I hung out with Dick Rosenbloom less than half the time I was in New York. The rest of the week and a half I mixed with my Paramount buddies at Gary Nardino's elaborate Waldorf-Astoria suite while we awaited word on *Modesty Blaise* and other Paramount projects. Barbara attended her own corporate meetings at ABC. Nearly everyone believed that, despite the ratings of the previous Sunday, *Cagney & Lacey* had been canceled. As if to confirm this, the final two episodes of our six had, at that time, not been given scheduled air dates on the network. I was sure my ABC *Blaise* pilot had no chance; nevertheless, both the information as to what was going on at the networks and the food were better at Gary's.

In addition to a grand piano, Nardino had a large easel in the middle of his Waldorf-Astoria living room. It held a board with movable strips containing the names of various on-air shows and the season's contenders. The strips were multicolored to reflect the network in question. The board was further divided into prime-time hours and nights of the week. Besides those slotted strips on the board itself, there were others for shows currently rumored to be in disfavor or in downright trouble—these were at the easel's base, strewn about on the floor. *Modesty Blaise* was prominent on the carpet; no one had much confidence in my Ann Turkel vehicle.

I wanted to be subtle about it, but try as I might I could not find a colored strip anywhere representing *Cagney & Lacey*. Nardino was positioned across the room at the bar as I hollered out: "Gary, where's my show? Where's *Cagney & Lacey*?"

"Forget it, you bum. You've been canceled!" It was good-natured in tone but also illustrative of the current scuttlebutt; *Cagney & Lacey* was not worthy of having a strip made for it, even if only to be discarded.

All of us hung out: 21 at cocktail time, Nardino's suite post-theater, various in-spots at lunch, and the Helmsley, the St. Regis, or the Regency for the *power* breakfast. We were all in the rumor game, and everyone was trying to pick up some hint as to what was going on. To even get a couple of minutes with Lou Ehrlich at ABC or Bud Grant at CBS would be a major coup. It's the closest thing the Hollywood creative community has to an old-fashioned political convention, replete with smoke-filled rooms. Television makers were all over the big town, and no one had anything to do but sit and wait.

The tradition goes back several years when, at one time, a producer might be called into the New York network meetings to explain how he was going to update or change his ongoing show, or how his series would differ from the pilot film he had made for their executive screening rooms. That rarely happens today. The West Coast network leaders already have that information in their pockets. They aren't anxious to let their New York counterparts have a confront with "their" suppliers. That's what Harvey Shephard did with me. When he felt the time was right to play the card he had, he did so.

I wasn't there, but here is my version of what might have happened: *A board is up on the wall of the CBS executive suite. Like Nardino's prototype, it has movable strips containing the names of CBS shows and those of their opponents. The subject is Monday night. Although only Messrs. Paley, Grant, and Shephard have the final say, the room is filled with perhaps a dozen or so executives representing research, sales, affiliates, corporate, development, and so forth. Everyone has an opinion, but now a decision must be made. What will replace the now-to-be-canceled* Lou Grant? *No consensus.*

Shephard ventures forth an idea: "What about Cagney & Lacey? *I was impressed with its showing last Sunday evening." Perhaps research and sales nod, acknowledging the possible wisdom here. Too many others disagree. The idea is put aside. Most in the room disregard the last showing as a promotional aberration. Some dislike the series outright. They are left without a replacement for* Lou Grant. *They leave this impasse and move on to discuss Tuesday night's schedule. So it goes, covering each night through the week. Time passes. Hours become days. They are back to the subject of Monday and the need to replace* Lou Grant *with something.*

Again, Harvey Shephard brings up Cagney & Lacey. *It's old news; it's all but being booed down, when Shephard plays his card: "They will recast!"*

Ah, the romance of the unknown. Suddenly, this is hot. There are assurances made by Shephard that the new show will have all the virtues of the 34 shared last outing. Add to that the glamour of a new, important piece of casting, and it is all the ammunition it takes for Mr. Shephard to have his way.

I wasn't there. I have fantasized the scene so many times it has become real to me, but it is fantasy. Harvey Shephard never shared with me what actually occurred.

While this was going on, I was at a bar in the Village with my cohorts from Paramount when a hysterical man entered, yelling for help and for someone who knew CPR. I raised my hand.

As head of the studio at Paramount in the early eighties, Michael Eisner had instituted a program on the lot where all employees had to be certified at this basic emergency skill. I had completed the course only days before. The hysterical man was the son-in-law of the victim. She was a woman in her fifties and a tourist from England. She had arrived in New York that afternoon, had a meal with her family, and then collapsed. Her coloring was light blue as she lay on a New York sidewalk, unconscious and not breathing. I did what I had been taught to do, and the woman began to gasp and finally to breathe normally. Within minutes she was on her feet and seemingly fine. Everyone was excited, especially me.

I never learned her name. She forgot to say thank you, but it was all OK.

It made me quite the hero of our little clique, and that night at Nardino's I was in demand to tell once again just how this event had evolved.

Everyone was in attendance that night, mostly because Bud Grant had RSVP'd that he would be there. I could tell by the pallor of Harris Katleman's complexion that the CBS boss had given the 20ᵗʰ Century Fox TV chief a not-so-happy private preview of Fox's failure to crack the CBS schedule. Grant only gave those previews to the elite of his peer group, the studio heads and a very few top independent suppliers.

Now Grant was in my sphere. He wanted to leave the party, but his companion, Linda Fernandez, had just requested hearing the story everyone was talking about. She wanted every detail on how one of their group had saved a life on the streets of New York.

That sound in the background was the gnashing of teeth by every producer in the room, the guys and gals who hadn't been lucky enough to be there at the bar when the cry "Anybody know CPR?" had been raised.

My story was over. Linda gave me a hug, Bud shook my hand.

"How much CPR does my series need?" I whispered as I leaned in close on the handshake.

"I'd call you if it was in trouble." He smiled. Then he added, "You haven't heard anything from me, have you?"

"No," I said innocently.

"Well then," he said, "everything must be all right."

It was a few days later at 11:10 in the morning. I had just emerged from the shower at the Sherry Netherland Hotel when the phone began to ring. I was alone because my wife, having completed her own meetings at ABC-NY, had elected to return to Los Angeles that very morning. She had to go back to work, and there was no telling when CBS would announce.

I answered the phone and heard CBS executive Kim LeMasters. "You have a pickup for thirteen for the fall, contingent on the recasting of Meg Foster."

My nowhere near over-the-top response? "Fan-fucking-tastic!" I all but screamed.

"Congratulations," said Kim. He went on to inform me that the schedule itself for the entire CBS lineup would be released to the press the following day and that I should attend the announcement.

I had only one question. "Has *House Calls* been renewed?" It was not unusual to inquire about another show. One might have a friend or family connected with that project.

"No," came the reply.

I said thank you again, hung up, and called Corday at Kennedy Airport. They got her off the plane to take the call. Asked by fellow first-class passenger Bud Grant why she was all aglow upon her return to the aircraft, Corday told him of the pickup.

"Oh, hell," he said. "I could have told you that."

I next called my mother, then Tyne. Finally, I phoned Ronnie Meyer at Creative Artists Agency in Los Angeles.

"I am inquiring about the availability of your client, Sharon Gless, to play the role of Christine Cagney in the CBS series *Cagney & Lacey*," I said. "We have a firm order of thirteen for the fall."

"She's not available," was the reply. It was early morning in Los Angeles as Ronnie Meyer went on, "She's doing *House Calls*."

"You can bet me she's doing *House Calls*," I chimed back. "That show has been *canceled!*"

That afternoon, having shared at 21 what would prove—over the years—to be the first of many ceremonial hot fudge sundaes, Rosenbloom and I began working out our strategy for getting back into production. We needed to properly staff our new thirteen-show order. Recasting Meg Foster was only one of our problems. Rosenbloom did not know who Sharon Gless was. A larger issue was Ronnie Meyer's belief that his client would not want to replace yet another actress in a television series.

There was also the problem of Gary Nardino. He would look the other way no longer. It was time to spend some real money and properly staff this series so that I could let it go. I had promised my Paramount employer that I would now become a coupon clipper; that *Cagney & Lacey* would be set up in such a way so that little or no work would be required of me.

Our first thought was to go after the staff of the then-newly canceled *Lou Grant*. Only April Smith, who was the least experienced of that crew, was available and interested in hiring out on yet another series. We signed her as writer/producer. She found Bob Crais, of *Quincy* and other such shows, to be her right arm. April also went after the comedy writing team of Patt Shea and Harriet Weiss. This selection made Tony Barr nervous. He would not approve the choice. At April's request, I went directly to Shephard and got the OK to get them on board. It was nice to have an early win for Ms. Smith. She was grateful, but it was all for naught. Ms. Weiss hated working in the hour form, didn't feel comfortable with doing a drama, and, rather than watch an award-winning comedy duo split up, Ms. Shea joined her partner in asking for—and getting—a release from their contract. Frank Abatemarco then joined the staff, followed by Jeffrey Lane. The writing corps was complete.

Joe Stern was put in place at Lacy Street, and he functioned as sort of a producer, liaising with April and her staff who were working out of the Westside offices of Orion, nearly an hour drive from our downtown production site.

Stern's credit deserves qualification only because April was really his superior in money and power, and he had little support from Rosenbloom. He was therefore forced to try to function without much of a portfolio. It was years before he would earn his stripes as executive producer on *Judging Amy*, teaming up (again) with Tyne Daly and for the first time with star/coproducer Amy Brenneman.

Within days of my return to Los Angeles from those New York meetings, Meg Foster came to my office at Paramount. She wanted to fight for her job. I listened sympathetically but told her there was nothing I could do to help. Clearly I could not stop her from doing whatever she felt was in her best interest, but my counsel was that this was a juggernaut that was now in motion and that she would be alone in trying to stop it. Even her friend Tyne Daly, who was outraged and eager to defend her fellow thespian, was powerless. Ms. Daly had stormed into my office and announced her resignation, which I did not accept. She ranted and raved. It was to no avail. Tyne, as Harvey Shephard would tell her, had a simple choice: she could either spend the remainder of the year making *Cagney & Lacey* or spend the time in court. Meg was calmer. She wanted to fight, but she needed allies. There were no effective ones to be had. For me to join arms with this one-time comrade would quite conceivably end the series. I believed that what we had accomplished and what potentially we might achieve far outweighed this issue. I stated that simply, and I believe Meg understood, although there is no question that she must have suffered a lot of pain from this so-public rejection.[21]

A day or two later, I was in Shephard's office with the CBS casting head, Jean Guest. We were joined in the meeting by Tony Barr, as well as several members of Ms. Guest's staff. They were poring over all the possible names that could play this part: a veritable who's who of "B" television actresses.

I sat quietly apart from the group facing Shephard. He, as usual, remained seated behind his desk. Finally, Guest completed her tally. Shephard turned to me. "What do you think, Barney?"

"I have only one candidate to play the role," I said, taking a dramatic pause. "Sharon Gless."

"You can't get her," said Guest, complementing her ominous prediction with an authoritarian tone.

"I'll get her," I said.

Shephard broke the ice beginning to form in his office by saying, "If you can get Sharon Gless, then this meeting is over."

With that I got up, thanked everyone, and left. What was to follow was several weeks of the toughest negotiations I have ever witnessed.

---

[21]   Years later Ms. Foster was to play a recurring role for me, opposite Sharon Gless, in our television series *The Trials of Rosie O'Neill*, with the most interesting aspect of that being we never spoke of that time in the long-ago.

The familiar cast is in the background of this company photo of our first half dozen episodes. That is Meg Foster, our then Cagney, way in the back between Tyne Daly and Marty Kove. Sid Clute can be seen between Meg and Tyne, in front of Al Waxman and to the side of John Karlen, and that is Ken Wales right behind Tyne's left shoulder and next to Sgt. Coleman (Harvey Atkin). And the guy whose head can barely be seen behind Atkin is director Ray Danton. Richard M. Rosenbloom holds the *C&L* banner with me, and the infamous Stan Neufeld (no relation to Mace) is to the far left, third row back. Hector Figueroa is on the far right in the second row, transportation chief Dale Henry is right behind him, and that is Barbara Rosing, wearing a cop uniform four rows back and to the right of center. Too many others to mention. A hardworking bunch.

Photo: Rosenzweig Personal Collection

CHAPTER 15

FINDING A WAY TO DELIVER THE GOODS

It seems agent Ronnie Meyer was right when he predicted that Sharon Gless really didn't want to replace yet another actress in a television series. It was only days after the meeting at Harvey Shephard's CBS office where I had told Jean Guest that I would deliver La Gless. The actress now sat across from me in a large booth at Musso & Frank's, Hollywood's oldest restaurant. It was the first time we had ever met. Monique James sat beside her client. I was flanked by Corday on my left and Rosenbloom on my right.

"You're not replacing another actress," I countered. "Another actress was temporarily holding what has always been your part."

I reminded her of how Avedon and Corday had discovered her on the set of *Turnabout* and how they had phoned me in my office six years earlier to announce: "We have found Christine Cagney."

Monique verified to Ms. Gless that the role had been offered her not once but twice.

I was good, I thought. It was years before I would find out, in front of an audience at the Museum of Television & Radio's salute to *Cagney & Lacey*, that Sharon left that luncheon, turned to Monique, and said, "I don't like the one with the beard." That would be me.

Facial hair or no, our negotiations were getting closer. Gless was apparently weakening on her opposition to doing another television series. She may not have liked "the one with the beard," but she did find Corday agreeable, and she was impressed with Rosenbloom. Monique James and Ronnie Meyer were helpful. They believed this was an important opportunity for their client. Billing, of course, was an issue.

It was brought out that Ms. Gless was then the bigger television name and that it should be duly noted in the only place that mattered: right there on screen.

The Gless camp was correct. Sharon had starred in two TV series and been featured in a third. *Cagney & Lacey* was Tyne's first. Sharon's established price was also thousands more per episode than was Ms. Daly's.

It is difficult to explain to a lay person just why billing is so important. It represents status in the industry, one's power relative to one's peers. It can be worth real money.

That it is, in fact, more than merely ego is best demonstrated by the case involving billing credit on the television series *Executive Suite*.[22] MGM assigned actor William Smithers fourth billing on that one-time series, despite the performer having a contract stating his credit would be no less than in third position. The actor sued and won, collecting damages in the millions of dollars.

I was fighting for equality for Tyne Daly. After all, she had seniority on this series, and I felt that equal treatment in all things should be the order of the day. I believed it was the only way to ensure a happy set. I was also up against a rapidly approaching deadline, albeit admittedly self-imposed. On May 25 the CBS affiliates were having their annual convention. It would be in San Francisco. Our cast had been invited, along with the stars of all the other CBS shows. It was a gala affair and would be well covered by the nation's press corps. I envisioned Tyne Daly being introduced, taking Sharon Gless by the hand as she walked toward the stage, and presenting her new partner, the third—and final—Christine Cagney. I felt it was a terrific forum for this announcement.

Merritt Blake, Tyne Daly's agent, was attempting to keep up with the pace. He was no match for the sophisticated Ronnie Meyer and the latter's powerful Creative Artists Agency. He also didn't have much with which to bargain. His client's contract read: "Billing shall be at the sole discretion of executive producer Barney Rosenzweig."

I assured Merritt I was doing my best for his client and that he was in a windfall situation here in that Ms. Daly's salary would be raised to be equal to that of her new costar, even though we were not contractually obligated to do so. Ms. Daly

---

[22]   William Smithers v. Metro-Goldwyn-Mayer Studios, Inc., 139 Cal. App.3d 643, 189 Cal. Rptr. 20 [1983] and also Smithers v. Metro-Goldwyn-Mayer Studios, Inc., 696 P.2d 82, 211 Cal. Rptr. 690 (1985).

would benefit to the tune of several thousands of dollars per week. Merritt agreed to put himself in my hands.

We were getting closer. There was little doubt this was going to work. Ronnie, Monique, and I came up with some formula for sharing the billing that was about as equal as you could get: Sharon to the left and Tyne to the right; Ms. Gless's name to be slightly lower than Ms. Daly's.[23]

"How are you going to work it out with Tyne Daly?" the Orion business affairs negotiator queried. I reminded him of the special billing clause, negotiated many months before, giving me discretion. Then came the bad news: it seems that when Meg Foster was signed I was asked, per the contract, which one was to get top billing? I used my "sole discretion" and gave it to Tyne. In a subsequent redrafting and finalization of the contract, the "sole discretion" clause was then deemed moot by the Orion lawyer, and he simply wrote in that Tyne Daly would receive top billing.

I called Merritt. Now it was I who needed help.

"Barney, read your contract. You have control. It's at your discretion, although I can tell you, Tyne is going to be pissed."

"You read the contract, Merritt. It's not the way either of us remember it."

What amounted to a scrivener's error had totally altered my situation and laid waste literally weeks of difficult negotiations for the services of Sharon Gless. Ronnie Meyer and Monique James could be effective with their client, but there was no way they would entertain any offer that had her billed in second position to Tyne Daly. Merritt was amused for a few seconds, then, having referred to the actual contract, assured me he understood the problem.

"It doesn't matter what is typed here," he began. "We'll honor the spirit of our agreement. You have sole discretion as to billing, Barney, but you've got to tell Tyne what you're doing, and I'm warning you she's not going to be happy about it."

Tyne and I had not met since her futile pleas for Meg Foster some weeks before. She would now use her new leverage to urge me to go back with her to CBS and fight for Meg. I tried to bring the conversation back to a realistic plane.

---

[23]   "To the left and lower" is considered slightly better billing than "to the right and higher," since most people read from left to right. Still, the higher position is coveted as well, hence the fairly even status this method of billing enjoys.

"To hell with Merritt and the spirit of the agreement," she railed. "I've got a contract that says I get top billing, and I'm not giving it up."

There was no reasoning with her. There was no appeal I could make that would soften her position.

She was, it seemed to me, that archetypical downtrodden soul who at last had power. She would use it even to the point of abuse. She was playing a heroine of the Irish Revolution right in my office. To get Sharon Gless, I was empowered by CBS to replace Tyne Daly if necessary. It would have been counterproductive for me to share that with Ms. Daly. At that moment in the drama, martyrdom, I speculated, would probably have been welcomed by my Irish heroine.

It was a remarkable scene. On any normal day, Tyne Daly is as moral, ethical, and as fair-spirited as you could ask. This was not a normal day; an emotional button had apparently been touched. What I believed was happening was that Tyne now saw an opportunity to get back at the bosses for years of any number of real and imagined wrongs. The balistraria were manned. It was up the Irish, and all I could do was hang on and try to get to the end of the ride.

The affiliates' meeting in San Francisco would begin the following day. Tyne, John Karlen, Al Waxman, Sid Clute, Carl Lumbly, and Marty Kove were all en route to the Bay Area. We did not have a Cagney. It was more than three weeks since I had assured Jean Guest I would deliver Madame Gless. The adversaries on both sides seemed to relax. It was over, they thought. The deadline had come and no resolution. Next case.

Not so. The deadline was mine. It was imposed to get maximum press coverage of our announcement. We still had nearly a month before we had to be in production. Few, if any, of the antagonists realized this. They had taken me at my word that May 25 was as long as I could wait.

Sharon Gless phoned. She wanted to thank me for my interest in her and to say she was sorry it couldn't be worked out. It was probably for the best, she appended. I asked if she would meet with Tyne Daly if I could arrange it. Gless demurred. I was just so sure, I quickly added, that once these two talented people met one another they would find a way past all the silliness that had been part of the negotiating process.

My "wish she were our" Cagney wasn't so sure of the efficacy of this idea. She did not, I suspect, want to weaken her own bargaining position but finally conceded that if Tyne were to call she would certainly talk to her.

I phoned Tyne in her suite at San Francisco's Fairmont Hotel. I woke her from an afternoon nap and urged my grumpy star to phone Sharon Gless to make an appointment to get together for a chat, now that the pressures of a negotiating deadline were past. Tyne resented that I believed Sharon Gless, an actress of whom she "had never heard," was of such importance to me and to CBS.

"Get another blonde" was Tyne's simplistic instruction. I was emphatic but still held back the ultimate killer piece of information: that if anyone was going to be replaced it was *not* going to be Sharon Gless.

Tyne agreed to call. She took Sharon's number. I was grateful. In less than fifteen minutes Tyne was calling me back. "Well, I did what you asked and nothing. Your candidate couldn't have been colder or more aloof, and she had absolutely no desire to get together and chat. She doesn't even know who I am." The whole conversation, according to Tyne, lasted only a matter of minutes.

I was surprised. I was sure I had read Gless better than that. Still I didn't really know her, and if Tyne said she frosted her, well then maybe it was better I find out about this kind of duplicitous behavior now. Maybe we weren't so close to making that deal work after all. I thanked Tyne for making the effort. I said I knew it was a lot to ask and she was a real champion for doing it. "Sorry I woke you. Have fun up there." Tyne accepted all my apologies and thanks with the clear implication that I still owed her.

Within minutes the phone rang again. This time it was Sharon Gless. Her report of the phone conversation with Tyne was substantially different, saying Tyne could not have been less courtly. Her opening statement, which, according to Gless, left little room for a continuing dialogue, was that she (Tyne) was only calling because her boss had insisted she do so. Beyond that, the short-lived phone conversation was confused by the fact that Ms. Gless did not recognize Tyne's voice. (Sharon had recently viewed the tapes of the six *Cagney & Lacey* episodes we had made and had not realized that the accent used by Mary Beth Lacey sounded not at all like the everyday voice of Tyne Daly.) I thanked Sharon for the call and apologized for what I characterized as the rudeness of my star.

Monique James phoned. "Well, Barney, I guess it was just not meant to be."

"Let me tell you what's meant to be, Monique," I interrupted in my most forceful tone. "What's meant to be is for your client and my actress to stop this shit and get on with the very important business of getting this series going. This is going to work, and you can bank on it."

Al Waxman and Sidney Clute were on the phone from San Francisco. "What's going on?" they wanted to know. Did we have a Cagney or not? I told them it had all fallen apart, and I let them know in no uncertain terms of Tyne's part in the ruin of the negotiations. Then I lied. "You know, we have a pickup contingent upon recasting Meg Foster. It has now come down to get Sharon Gless or the pickup is null and void. We are merely penciled in on the fall schedule. The commitment is not in cement. I just can't get Tyne to understand that she's winning a battle here and losing the war, and, if I can't get her to compromise on the billing thing, we're simply not going to have a series."

The guys were stunned. I knew they would find a way to bend Tyne's arm in old Baghdad by the Bay. To an actor, billing is important, but a job is crucial.

Next I was on the phone to Merritt Blake. "Your client's behavior is inexcusable, Merritt. I will not have her scuttle these negotiations or my series." I told him I did not wish to discuss it with Tyne any further and that he better get her out of this self-destructive mode. I then gave him the final word. "I will replace her if this does not work out. It will be easier," I said, "to find a new Lacey in this climate than to get a better Cagney than Sharon Gless."

Merritt Blake got the message and was back on the phone with me within the hour asking for Sharon's address. Somehow, someway, Tyne was going to do something. I gave out the information and instructed all principals to back away from the process. The long Memorial Day weekend was at hand.

"Let's all have a good holiday and talk about this next week," I said. Still, just in case, I gave the phone number of my rented Palm Springs condo to Rosenbloom, Ronnie Meyer, and Monique James.

By some means Tyne had learned that May 31 was Sharon's birthday. Balloons were followed by a visit in which the two agreed to talk about men, babies, or any subject at all except their most recent dispute.

Tyne showed up at Sharon's tiny Studio City home with two bottles of champagne. The rest, as they say, is history. Not quite. Tyne's latest solution was to alternate billing. It was movement, but the Gless camp needed more. Surprisingly it came from Merritt Blake. He suggested that there was something more to give Gless that, in fact, had never before been on the table.

All the conversations concerning billing—and all the contracts on this issue— were all about position on screen on the show's titles. Nothing had been said about publicity and advertising. Often times this comes into play in the movie business where, besides newspapers and magazines, advertising includes the lobby displays and marquees of the theater. There are no lobby displays or marquees in television and precious few print ads. Still, it was enough.

Then—a significant sin of omission: Tyne was not told. Her contract was revised upward to receive equal money with her costar. She was given assurance of equal treatment in accommodations and whatever other perks had been granted Ms. Gless, and she was to receive top billing on screen in every other episode. Her final concession was that she would take top billing on the even-numbered episodes, thus assuring Ms. Gless top billing on the first show, an odd number and, coincidentally, our opening night. This is usually the show reviewers across the country see, comment on, and write about. It is this episode from which they invariably record the billing of the series.

This is where Tyne, managing her own affairs, didn't get as much for herself as I had offered her in the first place. Her contract, unlike Sharon's, simply neglected to say anything about publicity and advertising. Had Tyne accepted to the right and higher, everyone in the industry would have understood that this was the closest thing to equality there is in Hollywood billing disputes. By negotiating for herself and angering me (her primary ally) in the process, she wound up with second billing in all publicity and advertising and second position on the only episode that really mattered: the one that opened the season.

None of that was of any import at the end of the first week in June 1982. I had delivered on my pledge to supply Sharon Gless; Corday was supervising the clothes shopping for the Cagney look; April Smith and her cohorts were writing; and our production staff was busily making preparations to commence principal photography. The first of our thirteen-show order would be before the cameras in a matter of weeks.

Monique James and her beautiful client, Sharon Gless, in my favorite picture of this duo.
Photo: Rosenzweig Personal Collection

CHAPTER 16

LETTING GO … AND OTHER FAILURES

I could now turn my attention to fulfilling my obligations to Gary Nardino and Paramount by actually trying to earn the right to the splendid offices in which I was ensconced.

Modesty Blaise was now in the past: "toast" as some say in Hollywood. I began to develop new projects under my Paramount deal. I went to work with Gil Grant on a couple of scripts, with Ronald Cohen on a third, with award-winning writer Sidney Carroll on a possible miniseries, and with a relatively new writing team, Steve Brown & Terry Louise Fisher, on my old favorite, *This Girl for Hire*. I was determined to redevelop this as a movie-for-television, emulate *Cagney & Lacey*, and have it serve as a back-door pilot. This new-to-me writing team would work from the very succinct Avedon & Corday treatment.

I knew it was a possible series, so did Nardino, and so did our writers. I elected to tip off Shephard as well, saying I'd rather develop through my friends in his movie department—and then deal directly with him—instead of the naysayers in charge of series. Harvey Shephard understood.

At night I would make the 30–45 minute drive from Paramount Studios in Hollywood to L.A.'s west side to check in with April and her gang. I would even make an occasional late night appearance at our production center at Lacy Street, another drive of nearly an hour, depending on traffic. On the night of a Dodger game? Fuggetaboutit.

Most of the crew from the Meg Foster era was intact, but the place had changed. In order to make certain camera moves possible and to increase our efficiency, aspects of the set itself were altered. April had requested that Samuels be given an office with a view of the squad room instead of a desk right in the middle of everything as he had had in the first six shows. This request followed TV writing convention and made it somewhat easier for separate confrontations to be written and staged. It was also closer to that with which she was familiar from *Lou Grant.*

April also brought some further attention to detail that I thought was valuable and that became an integral part of our series. It was she who insisted on the conceit of having the dramas appear to take place at the same season of the year they would air. Thus, even though it was summer in Los Angeles as we filmed, if the episode would be broadcast in November, then it called for heavy coats and scarves to be issued. It did more than add verisimilitude; it also brought something to the show I had not anticipated—a continuity of character. Now one episode would follow its predecessor just as the spring follows the winter. I had never done this, really never considered it before. It was April's idea and one that our cast took full advantage of as they "strung their beads."

We were not a serial, but the characters were to become more and more serialized. It's true each episode had a beginning, middle, and end and could stand on its own, but now the actors could treat their work as evolving characters in a novel. Cagney and Lacey would unfold, and change, as events impacted on their lives.

In my previous series experience, 90 percent of the episodes could be run in any order. What April was proposing made it a bit more complicated to produce but infinitely more satisfying to watch.

She also moved the Laceys from Manhattan to Queens (much more plausible given the Laceys' economic status) and altered the decor of Cagney's loft. She encouraged me to try a different style of music for the underscore, and, although we didn't agree on the result, the music certainly changed and, I believe, for the better. She also wrote "Recreational Use," which, in my judgment, was the single best script ever delivered on our series.[24]

Of all the writers I worked with on this show, April Smith had the greatest impact and made the finest creative contribution. What then went wrong?

It wasn't just the lack of humor in the episodes; for years I continued to try getting more and better jokes into the show no matter who was on the writing staff. It

---

[24]   The negative aspect of praising Ms. Smith, with whom I had no rapport, is that inevitably it must be done at the expense of others who were more loyal and with whom I had a better working relationship.

wasn't the lack of political commitment, although this was a problem for me. April not only didn't seem interested in feminism, she appeared downright opposed to it. (One early episode, "Affirmative Action," was, on paper, one of the most flagrant examples of Queen Bee-ism I have ever read, and only the sympathetic performances by Sharon and Tyne—and the former's comedy instincts—elevated that negative piece of material to the point where its anti-feminism tack was pretty much neutralized.)

It wasn't April's lack of experience in production or post-production, for she quickly acknowledged my superiority in post and gradually began to defer to our production manager on most matters in that arena.

What it came down to was our inability to work together on any kind of a collaborative basis. I had promised her I would be an absentee boss—that the show would be hers to run. After giving her relative autonomy on a few episodes and seeing what I felt were opportunities squandered, I found I could no longer stand by while my views and offers of help were scarcely heeded.

April was talented. Many of her ideas were unique and top drawer, but the episodes themselves were not working, not living up to their potential at all. Further, Ms. Smith was not, in my judgment, showing signs of maturing in the job or giving any indication that she would listen to anyone's suggestions. Corday had given up. So had Rosenbloom, whose solution was to try to find a replacement for Joe Stern, to find a producer he could respect who could get control over this series, and to put a rein on Ms. Smith and her writing gang. For this he was prepared to pay top dollar. It was not the sort of thing you heard from Rosenbloom or Orion, and it certainly indicated just how desperate he had become.

I was spending more and more time on *Cagney & Lacey*, trying to undo what I perceived as the damage being done during the day by reediting the film material at night. I also was indefatigable in my attempts to impose my views on the scripts.

Meanwhile, I did put a good face on our troubles with the network and with Tyne and Sharon. Ms. Gless was quite good on film I thought, but, in the first week or so of filming, Corday and April were less than sanguine. They took the actress to lunch, women to woman, to discuss their feelings and to suggest ways Sharon might change her performance. The actress listened but basically ignored their instructions.

I was not unpleased. On the contrary, I felt Ms. Gless was asserting herself and demonstrating an amazing contrast to her predecessor, finding humor on the page even where it was not written. The actress was now in fast company with better material and more of it than had been part of her previous series experience. She had an instinctive kind of timing that was working, and yet she remained insecure. Tyne was the vaunted dramatic actress. Sharon, on the other hand, had no such reputation. One TV reporter smirked in print that Gless came from the Copacabana School of Acting.

I believed, and Joe Stern agreed, that what we were getting was quite special. Meg Foster was a fine actress but somehow never claimed the role as her own. The show with Meg was more *Lacey & Cagney* than the other way round. Now the screen was being vested with behaviorisms (many invented by the actresses themselves) that defined who these people were and how they were different: Cagney was always first through the door. Lacey drank coffee from a pottery mug; Cagney from a Styrofoam cup (the nester/the transient). Cagney could never look at her watch without winding it, and so on.

We began to do things to augment this, not only in the writing, but in the way things were photographed. The Lacey character, like so many working women, was not only being asked to do her full-time job, but to be a full partner at home and mother to her children. She could best be described in one word: tired. Still, as if it were *The Enchanted Cottage*, we photographed her more tenderly, more lovingly, at home. With the addition of Gless, Lacey's partnership with Cagney fell into proper balance. We could, therefore, more effectively deal with the characters' differences in terms of expressions of ambition, social and moral responsibility, and their individual attitudes toward their profession.

They didn't always catch the bad guy. That was just not done in television twenty-five years ago. We almost snuck this by CBS, but Tony Barr wouldn't have it. April begged me to take this fight. I did, and we won.

But these things aside, the show itself left a great deal to be desired. Nardino wasn't happy either.

"Barney, this really is unfair," he said. "Either give up that series and come to work here full-time or give me relief on my deal."

Leaving Paramount had me sacrificing six figures of guaranteed compensation, my lovely, pretentious office, and—should one of my various projects there ever get off the ground—a lot of upside potential. Nonetheless, Nardino was right. I phoned Rosenbloom.

"I found the producer you're looking for," I said. Rosenbloom was ecstatic when he heard it was me. I was only going to do it until we got on track. There was no way they would pay me what I could get in the marketplace, but I wanted this show to be launched properly. The money problem was not only their penury, but that other factor that would dog me and this series for years, Mace Neufeld.

"I'll work for the non-exclusive executive producer fees you're already paying me," I said, "but I want several things in return." I asked for Rosenbloom to take on the payroll my assistant, PK Knelman, and my secretary, Adam Chuck. I wanted him to bear the costs of my move down to Lacy Street and, finally, I wanted everyone who was in the West Los Angeles office and who was connected with the show to be moved down there as well: editors and their equipment, along with April and her staff. I did not want to spend my life on the freeway. Rosenbloom agreed to every point without a whimper. Joe Stern's office would be quickly cleaned out for my arrival, and construction crews would appear over the weekend to build the cubicles inside the Lacy Street edifice that would house writers and editors. It would take weeks to even partially work out the kinks of inadequate air-conditioning, heating, plumbing, and soundproofing in that nearly one hundred-year-old structure. It would not take nearly so long for April and me to come into direct conflict with one another.

I thought I could be a coupon clipper, a grandfather to this project I had conceived. If that was ever possible, it was not to be with April Smith. She had been reared in the MTM[25] school that traditionally allowed great freedom to its writer-producers. April had basked in the reflected creative light of Gene Reynolds and Jim Brooks on *Lou Grant*. She had apprenticed under Seth Freeman on that same show. She had, in reality, produced little, if anything. The opportunity to do more would have been in her future on that MTM series, if only the Ed Asner vehicle had remained on the air another season or two. That hadn't happened, and so the chance was denied her. Now she was getting her break on *Cagney & Lacey*. Well, not exactly. She had to deal with me.

I like to feel I am a reasonable, even benevolent, despot. I engage in debate with my staff. I like to create the impression of a non-totalitarian environment. I might say, for instance, "If I cannot convince you of the efficacy of my argument with my argument, well then, I will reexamine my argument." But that is not necessarily as democratic as it appears.

---

[25]   The company formed by Mary Tyler Moore and her then-husband Grant Tinker. Besides *The Mary Tyler Moore Show*, their writers delivered such series as *Rhoda, Lou Grant, Hill Street Blues, St. Elsewhere, White Shadow,* and *Remington Steele.*

First of all, I am glib. I have a gift of gab. Few, particularly those in less powerful positions, can stand up to my verbal blitzkrieg. Second, there was passion; I cared deeply about what it was I did, and I approached the work with nearly religious fervor. Third, most of the time I had more experience than the person I was confronting. I'd just been at it longer and, invariably, on a day-to-day basis, put in more hours doing it. It was, therefore, tough to beat me in an argument on my subject unless you do what April did.

April would appear to listen, then do basically what she wanted in the first place. Not completely. She did defer to me in editorial. On the first filmed episode, she had spent twice the allotted (and budgeted) time closeted with our film editor, second-guessing herself so many times that the inordinate number of splice marks made it almost impossible to run the film through our projectors. She remained unhappy with the results. She then consented to viewing the film with me and watching how I might reedit the work. She was impressed, and when her loyal lieutenant Bob Crais viewed this latest version, she heeded his urging to turn over the supervising of the film editors to me.

By the time of our second episode, Corday had lost whatever consulting voice she might have had. Barbara's few notes were disregarded, sometimes ridiculed. My spouse became so offended and was made to feel so impotent that she simply gave up and stopped contributing.

It was one thing for them to treat my friend, and Orion TV topper, Dick Rosenbloom as if he were some sort of cretin, but Corday was a fellow writer—the co-creator of this series. It was no small thanks to her that these people had jobs. Barbara Corday and her erstwhile partner, Barbara Avedon, saw to it that none of us, ever again, had to face the proverbial blank page. The hardest part of the writing had been done; the creation of the characters, the finding of their voices, the venue in which they operated, all that—plus a thirteen-show order with Sharon Gless and Tyne Daly—had been handed these writers. All of that seemed not to matter to the gang of four (as I had come to refer to them). They patronized me by relinquishing post-production. On everything else, it seemed, I was only to be paid lip service.

I tried, having impressed Ms. Smith and Mr. Crais with my editorial acumen on episode one, to push my luck by getting them to visualize, prior to editorial, how what they were writing was actually going to play—what the realistic constraints of time and budget might do to their creative vision. There was a scene with Tyne Daly and an octogenarian in a wheelchair (yes, we were back to that). I would point out how static this nearly six-page sequence would appear on film.

April would tell me how the moves with the wheelchair would be "choreographed."

I knew how little money we had for sets. I knew our budget called for shooting eight to nine pages of dialogue per day. This woman was defending giving a five-and-a-half-page scene to an actor well past his professional prime (especially in terms of memorization of reams of material), keeping one of the finest actresses on television in a passive, reactive mode, and then had the hubris to talk to me about *choreography!* I threw up my hands. It was our third episode.

"Shoot it your way," I said. "Maybe you'll learn something."

The less-than-six-page scene took an entire day of production. It was all the actor could do to remember two sentences back to back, let alone any wheelchair choreography. It's just as well, for by the time we partially furnished the set and added two actors and a camera, not even Evel Knievel could have maneuvered that wheelchair through the clutter in any way other than the basic forward and back.

If Ms. Smith learned anything, she kept it to herself. The work went on. The gang of four kept me involved to some extent because they needed me to fight their battles with the network and Orion. They felt director Reza Badiyi was not in tune with their literary efforts; they needed me to dismiss him and get Orion to pay off his multiple-episode guarantee.

What, one might well ask, was I doing? Why was I pussyfooting? Initially, it was because I was still at Paramount. I was an absentee executive producer. I came to hate that. More and more I heard myself sounding like Leonard Goldberg from my bad old days on *Charlie's Angels.*

My notes on scripts continued to be largely ignored. I was getting angry. The irregular hours of the writing staff, their seeming reticence to listen to anyone but themselves, and their penchant for assigning themselves scripts or sharing credit with freelance writers who came to work on the show only increased my frustration.

I had worked too hard, and come too far, for this. By episode six I was in there with both feet. My agreement to leave Paramount had me, along with all other personnel, moving to Lacy Street by episode seven.

This, of course, was not April's understanding of the way things would be, but at first she seemed to almost welcome the help. She waited nearly three weeks before having her ultimatum delivered to CBS: "It's either him or me."

I knew nothing of this when I appeared in the office of Kim LeMasters, who was then the CBS VP in charge of drama and one heartbeat away from Harvey Shephard's job. He innocently asked me how things were going between April and myself.

I elected to be candid. I told him how talented I thought she was, but that working with her was difficult. I added that I understood how she might have trouble with me since she had originally been given to believe (by me) that I would serve in a merely advisory role. I added that I was cautiously optimistic that now that we were all physically together at the same plant, things might get better. That's when Mr. LeMasters told me of Ms. Smith's ultimatum. Before I could fully react, Kim added, "Harvey laughed."

Of course. There was no way in the world CBS, or any company, would have responded favorably to such a threat. She had been on the job only a few months. I had conceived the project, produced a super-successful M.O.W., designed a series almost overnight, delivered those first episodes as promised (on what many believed to be an impossible schedule), taken a cancellation then turned it into victory, brought them Sharon Gless, as pledged, and given up a lucrative major studio deal to come to the aid of this series. In opposition was this producer-come-lately saying, "It's him or me."

It *was* funny. It was also pathetic and foolish.

Ultimately, had she been a little patient, it would all have been hers. I wasn't going to stay. I couldn't afford to. Orion was not prepared to meet the economic terms that I could get almost anywhere else in town. Not only was this a problem for them psychologically (for they knew me when …), it was a real fiscal barrier. The entertainment explosion of the early eighties was in high gear everywhere, save for this fledgling company. Fees for top creative personnel were growing geometrically.

My fee of $2,500 per episode (worked out in 1978–79 for my deal with Mace) was, at Paramount in 1981, $20,000 per episode and escalating each subsequent year. This was a reflection of the burgeoning economics of the syndication marketplace for one-time network programs then in reruns. Prices for these episodes were skyrocketing with no end in sight. As a result, major television companies would pay whatever they had to in order to assure themselves of more units for future syndication and to have the talent under contract to create and produce those units.

Orion was not a major television company; its new management team wasn't even sure it wanted to be in television. They had already gotten rid of Iannucci and would keep Rosenbloom and his division only so long as he delivered on his guarantee of little or no deficits. That meant a lean and mean production plan, no fancy offices, and no highly paid creative personnel.

I liked my fancy offices at Paramount, the luxurious frills that accompanied any major studio deal, and my high fees. There was more. When Orion paid me one dollar, they had to pay Mace Neufeld fifty cents. Because of the settlement with Mace, I was actually more expensive than anyone else they might hire.

There was no way they were going to match what I could get elsewhere. I knew it and didn't even ask. I would move into Lacy Street on a very temporary basis, exercise my contractual creative control, get this series on the right track, and then turn it over to April Smith. All this I would do for my $10,000 per episode non-exclusive executive producer's fee—money Orion was contracted to pay for the life of the series even if I elected to move to Hawaii and sit on the beach leisurely reading scripts and commenting on them by trans-Pacific telephone. My offer to do the hands-on work for no additional compensation, even on a temporary basis, was thus most welcomed by all parties—save, of course, for the gang of four.

In my office at Lacy Street with my favorite photo of Sharon and Tyne in the background.
Photo: Rosenzweig Personal Collection

CHAPTER 17

COMINGS AND GOINGS

The crisis over April's ultimatum was, as far as I was concerned, nonexistent. I continued on in a "business as usual" fashion, never mentioning the incident or acknowledging that I had even been told about it.

We were in production on episode eight, preparing and casting episode nine, cutting episode seven, spotting and dubbing episode six, and beginning our script meetings on episode ten.

The show had debuted with episode five to good reviews and not bad ratings. I would do my best to bury episodes two and three. "Stringing beads" or no, I was not going to open with weak material. Where necessary, we re-shot scenes to accommodate the new continuity imposed by this release pattern.

Despite industry-wide predictions that the show would fail—that Harvey Shephard had been victimized by his own hype—the ratings were more than acceptable, performing from 15% to 20% better than the previous inhabiter of the time period, *Lou Grant*. There was reason for optimism. I believed that at any time Harvey Shephard would phone and increase our order by nine additional episodes to the full season complement of twenty-two.

April's original script for episode ten—the aforementioned "Recreational Use"—was excellent, tough, and sophisticated: Cagney romantically involved with a fellow officer from another precinct, a cop who used drugs "recreationally." It was bold and uncompromising. Even the network asked for very few concessions, and, although I had yet to earn the kind of power I would eventually have, what fights I did have with the network for this material were largely and comparatively easily won.

Meanwhile, I had script notes of my own. My concerns were mostly for purposes of clarity. April's writing style was sparser than I was used to. Ninety percent of my notes addressed the issue of this minimalist approach. I met with the gang of four in a small brick building we called the schoolhouse. It was adjacent to our Lacy Street factory complex and was used almost exclusively by the writers for their gang-bang approach to material.

I believe I'm good with script. It's a subjective call, but one that I feel comfortable in making. Too many fine writers have endorsed this view for me to feel very modest about it. I have written, and do write. Basically, however, I do not consider myself a writer. I *am* a storyteller. I also feel I'm a friend of writers. I invariably (sometimes to the project's detriment) work within the universe they have created. I do not generally throw out material and start speculating with a litany of what-ifs. My job, at least this part of it, was to try to get on the page the things that would help the reader, the director, the actor, the staff, and the crew visualize and realize the concept for which the writer is striving.

In addition to feeling I'm good at it, I also believe I am a benign and friendly force. Not only am I noncompetitive, I am supportive. That's my immodest belief. That's my view of how I operate with writers. Imagine then my reaction when one or the other of April's staff would, in support of their leader and in reaction to my notes, scoff or even titter at my comments.

Scoff and *titter* are not commonplace verbs in my vocabulary. They are the only terms I can conjure to portray the behavior to which I felt I was being exposed. My not understanding something or asking for clarity somehow seemed to make me a fool in their eyes. They had what appeared to be a sense of their own personal power (individually and cumulatively) that must have been somehow intoxicating. It was as if they were all "on" something, and April's smiling, somewhat-girlish demeanor only served to encourage her minions.

We were midway through my comments and the writing staff's titterings on "Recreational Use" when I excused myself from the schoolhouse and phoned April's secretary, requesting that she tell her superior that I wished to see her in my office as soon as possible.

"It is to my eternal discredit," I began my spiel to Ms. Smith, "that I allowed you to deride Barbara Corday, who, by the way, was instrumental in the creation of this series, and that in reaction to your behavior in this matter, I never said a word." April was now in my office, sitting opposite my desk as I continued on, with deadly calm, giving no indication by action or inflection of my emotional state. I would leave it to my words to convey my sense of outrage.

"It is also reprehensible that I did, and said, nothing when you so trivialized Richard Rosenbloom that he will no longer even visit this plant. That I again did, and said, little when you drove Reza Badiyi (one of the sweetest men I know) to tears, is unforgivable. But now you have gone too far. You have finally insulted me, and I tell you, lady, that does not happen. Not in my store. Not on my show. Not from one of my employees."

I left no room for a rejoinder. I don't think she had one. I went on. "If you are operating from the illusory position that you have some kind of power around here, let me disabuse you of that. This is my schul,[26] and only at my pleasure are you allowed to worship here. Now, I want changes in this script. My notes are simple. If you cannot—or will not—do them, then I have a very fine writer standing by who will execute them this weekend. The choice is yours."

Before she could speak I made an addendum. "Understand something: for however long you remain in my employ, you and I will meet privately in my office one-on-one. I will never again attend a meeting with your staff. They are unworthy of my time or patience, and I will expect drastic changes in that department in the very near future."

"Can I take the weekend to think about this?" April wanted to know.

"No," I responded. "I will need this weekend to have the script reworked if you are not going to do it."

"Even if I agree, I can't be finished by the weekend," she said.

"Can you have the first two acts by Friday?"

She nodded.

"That's OK with me," I said. "I can make a judgment from that just how seriously you are addressing my concerns."

Two days later, Harvey Shephard called. We would be picked up for the full season. He was giving us an order for nine more episodes.

I had April and her staff join me in the squad room set, as I had the company hold up work on this first day of episode nine to inform them of the happy news: four

---

[26]   Or *shul*. Yiddishism, rhymes with tool, and means the same as synagogue ... a place of worship and learning.

more months of employment on a good-paying job for everyone. Good reason to celebrate. I then called the attention of all gathered to April Smith and her "fine staff," who had done so much to bring us this far. Everyone applauded. I don't believe I have talked to Frank Abatemarco or Jeffrey Lane since.

Back in the producer's wing, we celebrated the pickup. April had her arm around my waist. I held her close and offered her champagne. She declined. She had a lot of work to do by Friday.

The threat that I had another writer in position to rewrite over the weekend was not an idle one. Ronald M. Cohen had agreed to work with me on the assignment should I need help. We had become quite good friends since our sojourn together on *American Dream*. I had been instrumental in getting him his new deal at Paramount, and, just prior to my decision to leave the studio, we were to work together on a project of his. Ronald had showed a friendly interest in *Cagney & Lacey* almost from the beginning, and we often talked of it. He was the one who had encouraged me to exhort the writers to search for, and explore, the moral dilemmas that would become a cornerstone of our series.

He was now a gun I did not have to use. April did the rewrite, addressed herself to all my notes, and easily accomplished 80 percent of them on her first go-round. Naturally, I was pleased. April was happy enough with the results on paper but not with our relationship. She tried different variations on her original ultimatum, first going to Rosenbloom with a proposal he would not even discuss. Then, with nowhere else to go, she elected to come directly to me.

She had a plan that called for a sort of production troika. She would be in charge of script with little or no input from anyone else. I was to supervise post-production, while the physical plan for the series itself, including casting, would be divided between April and Orion's designee, as long as that person was not me.

My counter was that things go on as they had been with one important change. I would insist that Abatemarco and Lane not be renewed at the end of the first thirteen episodes and that April replace them for the back nine. I would be happy to continue with Crais, but that was her decision. This was unacceptable to April. Whatever we negotiated between us, her staff would have to remain intact. I was not negotiating. The gang of four was toast.

My adamancy about two of the foursome was multifaceted. It was necessary, in my view, to break up this offensive (to me, for openers) quartet. Still, I had hoped not to throw the proverbial baby out with the bathwater. Abatemarco and Lane were the most recent additions to the staff, the two I respected (by far) the least and—in my view—the most easily replaced. The fact that Abatemarco had a harder time altering one of his scripts to my notes, or those of the network, than any writer I have ever dealt with, and that Mr. Lane had involved us in a plagiarism suit over his most recent teleplay, might also have added to my equation.

The conversations went on for days. April and I were immutable on this one issue. She was loyal to her staff, and I simply would not put up with that group any longer.

Finally, a new element: April said if she could not control who was on her staff then she would ask that she be allowed to resign and that the option on her contract not be exercised for the back nine. I accepted her resignation with genuine regret.

Bob Crais was in my office minutes later. He, too, asked to be relieved of his contractual responsibilities. I tried to talk him out of it and even went so far as to offer him a directing assignment, which I knew he dearly coveted. He held firm. It's possible these two thought they had me in a box. I like to think it was more than the old "nobody can write this show but me" syndrome. I felt these were principled people who believed in their duty to be loyal to their troops. I wanted Abatemarco and Lane out, and they did not. They were protesting this decision with the only power they had: the will to withhold services and give up their jobs.

Within an hour of all this, Frank Abatemarco's agent was on the phone. She had heard that April and Bob would be leaving the series and wanted me to know of her client's interest in continuing—provided he be given April's position as writer-producer. The body wasn't even cold. Loyalty among the gang of four, I observed, was very one-way.

I could not resist. I told April of the call and that I felt she was a fool to go to the mat for these guys who would not do the same for her. She refused to believe that I had not made up the whole thing.

The grave news of April's departure went through our little company. "One by one, the actors—then Dick Rosenbloom and even April's husband, who came by to introduce himself—asked me to reconsider." I was clear with them all. April was welcome to stay. I wanted her to stay, but there was, and could be, only one boss on this show. That boss would be me.

Finally, Tyne and Sharon came in tandem to see me, requesting my rapprochement with Ms. Smith.

"Writers will come, and writers will go," I began. "The same is true of directors, of crew and staff—even members of our acting ensemble. The only constants," I went on, "are you and me. We are here for the duration. You have contracts, and

I have a vested interest unlike that of any mere employee. Get used to it, and get used to dealing with me, year in and year out. I will be here for you as you will be for me. That's our deal. I will never say to you, 'It's only television,' and you must never unfairly exploit your power over me by refusing to do your work. As long as that remains true, I will continue to use every possible moment and every bit of power I have, right up to the final edit, to make what we do deeper, richer, fuller, better."[27]

The war was over.

The next day at lunch, Harvey Shephard told Dick Rosenbloom and me of his pleasure at the success of the series thus far. We had averaged a 28 share against Monday Night Football and the NBC movies, and that was fine. I was learning to appreciate the value of being in a slot where the expectation level was not too high; I'll take that any day and leave the inheritance of a 38 share to the other guys.

"You'll get clobbered during February sweeps," Shephard went on, "but if the show comes back in March and April to these kinds of numbers, I can guarantee a pickup for the fall."

That afternoon, I met with the writing team of Steve Brown and Terry Louise Fisher. They had done a good job on *This Girl for Hire* and, now, for the first time, were considering doing episodic television. I had explored this with them several months before but had been turned down. Now they were ready. The deal was in place for them to join the *Cagney & Lacey* company with only the issue of credit still being open; they wanted to be called producers.

I pleaded with them not to press this issue. They had never done episodic television before, had never produced before. I told them how I felt personally about the proliferation of credits issue, how I would never go after their credit as writers and how multiple producers on a show leads to confusion on a production and, ultimately, hurt feelings (witness my very recent debacle with Ms. Smith).

"We know we're not producers," said Mr. Brown. "We acknowledge that you're the boss and the defacto producer, but the credit is a deal breaker for us. We want to be in the club."

I felt I was up against it. The gang of four had left the cupboards bare. I needed scripts fast, and I had no other strong candidates who were immediately available

---

27   These four words, *deeper, richer, fuller, better,* came to me by way of Tyne Daly, who quoted her mother, Hope Newell Daly, as the source. It became our slogan on the show.

or interested. All I had to oppose this was my belief system and principle. Hoping the producer gods would forgive me (and knowing I would never forgive myself), I caved on this issue, and Steve and Terry went to work.

They did not have April's experience, but Mr. Brown had an extraordinary story mind and Ms. Fisher was extremely fast and facile. They were also a comparative joy to work with. They complemented the staff with their very good choice of Chris Abbott, and we were off and running. Like Jack Guss, and unlike the gang of four, these writers understood my vision and worked with it. Terry was interested in politics, and Steve had us so well organized we could concentrate more on content and the Ronald M. Cohen school of moral dilemmas. The show began, really for the first time, to look and sound like the grown-up *Cagney & Lacey* it would become.

CHAPTER 18

DEEPER, RICHER, FULLER, BETTER

Harvey Shephard was pleased when I first gave him the news of my departure from Paramount and my plan to move downtown to the Lacy Street factory, which housed the production of our beleaguered series. I made him aware that this entailed no small financial sacrifice on my part, but that I could be made whole with a "go to picture" on *This Girl for Hire*. He said he understood and would look into it.

Negotiations with Paramount, settling out my contract, would be ongoing for months. Several properties were in dispute, and the question was which would come with me and what would remain at the studio. I was to get the TV movie rights to *This Girl for Hire*, but the series rights to that project were to stay at Paramount, with me locked in as a profit participant.

One project that continued in dispute for some time was the pilot script of *Feel the Heat*, on which I had worked with Ronald M. Cohen for ABC. Ann Daniel, the selfsame ABC junior executive from the days of *American Dream*, had by now been promoted to head of drama development at the network. She seemed pleased to be, once again, working with the team she so respected on that long ago, ill-fated venture. When word came through that *Feel the Heat* would receive an order as a pilot film, it naturally intensified the negotiation process between Paramount and me.

In the interim I had also been told that *This Girl for Hire* would be given a go-ahead at CBS. Suddenly, with a series on the air, an M.O.W. green-lighted, *and* a pilot commitment, I was one very hot producer. ABC let Nardino know that I was "of the essence" on *Heat,* and the blustery Italian went berserk. No one told

Nardino whom to hire, especially if it was someone he'd just released from an exclusive studio contract.

Cohen was hysterical as well. He felt the steamy melodrama he had written and set in Miami and the Florida Keys could be his *Cagney & Lacey*. While it was true that in the past he always wanted my involvement on this venture, he now believed that his interests would be best served by my withdrawal from the project. I quietly assured him that I would not stand in the way of his getting an order, but that he must allow me to use the opportunity this afforded me to finalize my extradition from Nardino's domain. Ronald was hardly mollified.

Things got stickier and stickier as ABC and Paramount fought for over a week as to whether Barney Rosenzweig would, or would not, serve as executive producer on the pilot.

Ann Daniel had bought a team; now the disposition of that team was in doubt. She had reason to believe Nardino was merely involved in a macho maneuver. Cohen didn't seem to understand that; with or without me, he alone was simply not acceptable to the network.

I wanted out, wanted to help Ronald, and wanted to get something for my efforts and for putting a good face on all this with ABC. Nardino's position was the most graphic of all; he was the powerful head of a major television operation, and he wanted "his" executive producer to devote 100 percent of his time to the project or withdraw. (It should be pointed out that had *Cagney & Lacey* been a Paramount show, Gary would have accepted something substantially less than 100 percent of my time on *Feel the Heat*.)

I maneuvered among all parties and, with the aid of attorney Stu Glickman, got a decent settlement from Paramount on my overall contract, assured Ann Daniel that I believed a good picture could be achieved without my services, and I further agreed that, if the parties wished, I would function as a non-exclusive creative consultant, which I did. It turns out I would earn that stipend over a long, rainy weekend in the Florida Keys, brokering one of many misunderstandings between director Ray Danton, producer Eddie Milkis, and my friend, Ronald—the writer and wannabe executive producer.

I worked on budgets for *This Girl for Hire* (too high at $2,250,000), assisted Glickman on the negotiations for a license fee on that project (too low at $1,800,000), finalized the production and editorial on what I will call the "April Smith initial order" of thirteen *Cagney & Lacey* episodes, all while supervising the script work from Terry and Steve on the nine scripts for the back end of the season. It was a rare day that ended before 2 AM or started after eight in the morning.

I would meet with publicists on *Cagney & Lacey,* or lawyers on the TV movie, or the Paramount negotiations in the morning, with the *Cagney & Lacey* writing staff and production team during the afternoons, and with the *Cagney & Lacey* editors at night. I would generally meet with Ronald M. Cohen on the weekends.

One Friday night, while working on finalizing an episode in editorial, I got a call from the production manager, Bob Birnbaum. It was nearly 9 PM, and work on our location was drawing to a close. The production schedule called for the company to return to Lacy Street for one more scene in order to finalize the week's work, but Ms. Gless, I was told, "refuses to go on."

Birnbaum went on to report that the actress said she was exhausted and wanted the shoot called off at the end of the location sequence we were then finalizing, rather than continue on with the planned company move back to Lacy Street for the week's final scene. This final scene not only finished the episode but filled out our guaranteed daily crew minimum of a twelve-hour shooting day.

The crew was guaranteed—*and paid*—for a twelve-hour day, five days a week: a sixty-hour work week, which included twenty hours of certain overtime pay. Tyne and Sharon were carrying the primary weight of our entire hour-long dramatic series. No other women in our industry were asked to do that. It merits comment.

Our stories of revelation concept had the plots of our shows being revealed to the audience through the eyes of at least one of the principals. This meant that Tyne, Sharon, or both were in virtually every scene. We did not enjoy the luxury of being able to parallel edit to some six-to-ten-page sequence featuring actors other than the two leads.

There was very little work, at all, in which at least one of our two leads was not present. Furthermore, we—me, the network, and the American viewing public—required them, as women and as stars, to look a certain way. Paul Michael Glaser or David Soul might stroll on the set of *Starsky & Hutch* fifteen minutes after waking and, having shaved and towel-dried their hair, be ready for camera. These women—as do most females over thirty in our business (or, if you will, Donald Trump)—required two hours of hairdressing and makeup. Then there were the wardrobe fittings, the publicity demands, transportation time, and so on. They came to work that much sooner than the bulk of the crew and got that much less sleep in order to work what was, at least, a fourteen- to sixteen-hour day.

Under Aaron "Rosy" Rosenberg at 20th Century Fox, I served as an associate producer on two Doris Day films (*Do Not Disturb*, with costar Rod Taylor, and *Caprice,* costarring Richard Harris); on both of them, our cinematographer was the revered Leon Shamroy. Though he has been dead over twenty years, no other cinematographer to this day can match the number of awards Shamroy accrued during his career. His work on *Wilson, The Agony and the Ecstasy*, and *South Pacific* alone assured him of more Academy recognition than most cinematographers receive in a lifetime. This venerable and talented cinematographer would refuse to photograph Ms. Day in close-up after 4:30 in the afternoon. By then, gravity had taken its toll, and Shammy would say, in his own ruthless and inimitable style, "Her face looks like a pan full of worms."

Sharon Gless was then approaching forty, the same age Doris Day had been at the time of my apprenticeship. The cinematographers we gave Sharon were several rungs below the artistry of Leon Shamroy, and every day we worked many hours past Shammy's 4:30 PM deadline.

Who said any of this was going to be fair? It is series television, with its unreasonable hours and its impossible deadlines, and that is what we had all signed on to do.

It had been less than a half hour since Birnbaum's call, and I was on the location. My sartorial ensemble distinguished me from the six dozen crew members who stood around awaiting the arrival of the boss as if it were a scene from *On the Waterfront.*

I smiled at those flanking the route to the motor home of La Gless and entered the sanctuary. To my surprise, Tyne Daly and Martin Kove were there, along with Sharon. To Sharon's eventual surprise, neither was to lend their (apparent) promised support.

"What is going on?" I asked, not too sternly. Tyne did not speak, nor did Marty. They each looked up from their seated positions to the blonde actress who was standing in the rear.

"I'm tired." The actress then added, "We're all exhausted." Sharon looked to her co-workers for some show of solidarity. None was forthcoming.

"It's tiring work," I acknowledged. I was very calm, almost soft-spoken. I then referenced our first conversation at Musso & Frank's restaurant, recalling I had forewarned her of how debilitating the work would be and reminding her of how she had ridiculed my then-stated thesis that whatever she had done before could not possibly be as difficult as this.

I would not give in to her demand. To print the expletives she then directed at me would be unfair. You have to know Ms. Gless to appreciate that she has a mouth on her that men in a naval transportation unit might envy. I didn't know her that well at the time and apparently blanched at the verbal onslaught. Tyne and Marty kept their eyes on each other's shoelaces.

Sharon then continued with a litany of mistakes she felt had been made in the production plan and various other inefficiencies that could be laid at my managerial doorstep. She looked again to Tyne and Marty for support—no help there.

"Look," I said, "let's cut to the chase. We are not lovers, we are not even friends. We are in business together. That means negotiation. Sometimes you will win, sometimes I will win. That is what negotiations are all about. This one—I can tell you up front—you will not win. Forget the fact that your specific argument is subject to dispute—you just did it badly. You gave me an ultimatum in front of my crew, and that was a mistake from which your argument cannot recover. By definition you lose this one because I'm the boss. You know it, and you know how important it is that they know it."

My gesture indicated that the "they" to which I referred was the throng outside the motor home. "Unless," I smiled, "you want to be the boss."

Sharon shook her head.

"Are we straight?" I queried. She nodded. So did Tyne. So did Marty. I exited the motor home.

"We go," I said to Birnbaum with a thumbs-up gesture. The crew restrained itself from cheering.

As much as they would have liked getting off early, a film crew likes even better knowing who's in charge. The danger of having the actor win this one was that next time the big bosses might send someone in to run things that might be even worse. Besides, no one wants the inmates running the asylum.

An hour later the company was at Lacy Street and setting the lights for our final sequence of the week. I was moving among the crew, providing—I hoped—moral support for what had, in fact, been a difficult day. Gless passed me on the way to the set without saying a word.

Wanting things to be friendly, I stopped her to inquire if she was OK. The next thing I knew we were into the argument again, and this time not far from the set itself. The area quickly cleared as the discussion grew in intensity, Sharon finally saying something to the effect that the long hours were going to make her and Tyne sick.

"It's OK if you get sick," I countered. "I'm insured for that."

Sharon's eyes widened. What she said was, "You are a fucking shit." From her it sounded no worse than "You are despicable." She then made a perfect exit toward her motor home. I stood there for a long beat. I, too, was working long hours, and nobody was writing my dialogue. I seriously considered letting her stew and then made one of the wiser decisions of my life. I went after her.

Only seconds had passed. As she heard me approach her motor home, she took the only refuge she could find, locking herself in the bathroom of the vehicle. The motor homes we supplied our stars were of pretty good size, but, even allowing for that, a head in one of these trailers is not particularly spacious. I stayed in the front room portion and announced my determination to remain and see this conflict to its conclusion.

I was midway through delivering (to a closed bathroom door) my apology for the thoughtless comment concerning the status of our insurance, when she emerged. It was hard for her to be angry. She was too caught up in the ridiculous image of the granddaughter of Neil McCarthy[28] hiding out in the toilet of a motor home, and speculating on the odds of being able to escape by way of a porthole-like window.

"Well," she said, groping for some semblance of dignity, "this is silly."

It was only a little after that when I told her what I had said to Tyne Daly—perhaps a year before. "You may add salt to my tomato juice. You may add pepper, or Tabasco, or vodka to my tomato juice; but you may not piss in my tomato juice. That's what went wrong tonight." In case the point was missed, I quickly added, "You were pissing in my tomato juice."

My leading lady understood. It was territorial. Sharon is a child of the Hollywood community and knows better than most what is required of a pro. She apologized for the whole scene, and I promised to try to be more attentive to her requests.

"Provided I don't make them in front of the crew," she said, filling in the obvious blank.

---

[28]   Neil McCarthy, the one-time ultimate entertainment lawyer, had been the attorney for Cecil B. DeMille, Howard Hughes, and Spencer Tracey to name a few. He was one of Hollywood's major luminaries when Hollywood was really Hollywood, and he was Sharon's maternal grandfather, partially responsible for making her a fifth-generation Angelino and, therefore, among Southern California's blue bloods.

"You got it," I replied.

I too had learned something that night. Play out these confrontations to their conclusion. Do not put them on hold. Deal with them frontally, and immediately, for they do not get better by themselves. Unfortunately, something I had put on hold with Tyne Daly, in the days before this learned lesson, would now come to the fore.

For Christmas I had gifted each of the women with an 18-karat gold police whistle and chain from Tiffany. Tyne returned hers to me with a note written on the back of a title page from one of our scripts, as if the whole thing was unworthy of stationery. I had, she wrote, betrayed her, and so she could not accept my "token of friendship."

The deal over billing continued to fester, and Tyne remained volatile. One day she was demeaned by the work, the poor quality of directors, her "honor gone"; later that same afternoon she might stop by my office, overflowing with enthusiasm for what it was we were attempting to do, the journey, our art. This was not a crazy person, far from it. She was exhausted from a near-impossible schedule at work, the everyday demands of family, and—let us not forget—she is an actress.

Being the star of a television series was, I believe, never Tyne's dream. I had seduced her into that life. In fact, I think, being the star of anything was fairly antithetical to who Tyne Daly is and/or wants to be, on the one hand. On the other hand, she can be a pure diva of operatic proportions.

Within days of the returned-whistle incident, Tyne mentioned that she and Sharon wished I would reinstate the practice of calling them at home after the network airing of the show each Monday night. I had stopped phoning the two women when I finally tired of getting beaten up by their lack of acceptance of the work, hating me, or missing their close-ups.

"Deeper, richer, fuller, better never stops. It is a constant war against time and limited funds and the mediocrity of most of us," I wrote in my diary about that time. I went on with the entry: *"Tyne and I made an agreement: When we finally make a good episode, we will all quit. I tell her it will probably take several years of practice to accomplish this."*

Another note from my diary, referring to Sharon and Tyne, sums it up: *"January 28, 1983: They are tough and demanding … I love them."*

To the men on *Cagney & Lacey*, I had gifted sterling silver police whistles. It prompted my friend, Sidney Clute, to ask what he could possibly give me in return. It seemed, to him, I had everything. I told him that what I really wanted was for him to take care of himself and to remain healthy and happy on our series for years to come. He began to weep as we hugged each other. We both feared that the backaches he had been experiencing were the return of his cancer. My once-robust tennis pal was now becoming very frail.

Next it was Steve Brown and Terry Louise Fisher presenting me with a problem. When I met them on *This Girl for Hire,* they had been living together. That phase of their lives had ended, and now, with *Cagney & Lacey,* they were attempting to work together for the first time without personal involvement. To hear them tell it, it was not going well; still, they were determined to finish the season and fulfill their contractual obligations. They just wanted me to be aware of it, lest things got testy. This information was given to me quite gratuitously (as if I might give a shit), and there was also some reference to the possibility of my occasionally serving them as padre, to which, if memory serves, I reluctantly agreed. And to think people wonder what a producer does.

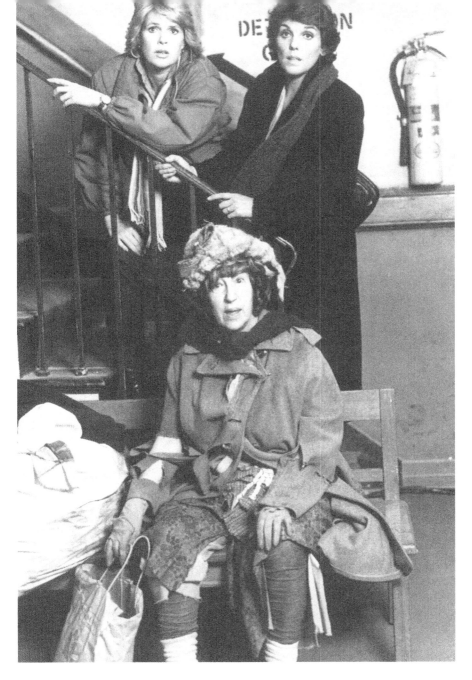

A photo taken by then-*C&L* PA (production assistant) Stacy Codikow. This picture, in which Sharon and Tyne share the spotlight with Barbara's mother (Jo Corday, in character as the bag lady Josie on the set at Lacy Street), wound up in *People* magazine: A nice coup for Ms. Codikow, as well as our show. Barbara's mom was pleased, too.

Photo: Carole R. Smith Personal Collection

On the set of the 14th Precinct at Lacy Street.

Photo: Rosenzweig Personal Collection

CHAPTER 19

WHAT CAGNEY REALLY WANTS …

I have never known Sharon to do a crossword puzzle, although both she and Tyne are regular answers in the *New York Times* and other such publications. This must have been her "in character." It certainly is on the set. Her desk and the holding pen in the background. Note the cup in the foreground. Cagney used hers for a pencil holder, preferring to have her coffee from a Styrofoam cup. Tyne's Mary Beth Lacey drank from hers.

Photo: Courtesy of MGM

The pressure on Brown & Fisher and their first script for *Cagney & Lacey* was considerable. It would be the first work from the new team we would see, and it would be scrutinized as few others.[29] In it, the team went to their strength: Brown's excellent sense of story structure and Ms. Fisher's understanding of the legal bureaucracy (something she would eventually exploit to its fullest by co-creating, with Steven Bochco, *L.A. Law*). Terry had been a lawyer with the district attorney's office in Los Angeles a few years before. We all were to benefit from this period of civil service.

The day after this episode aired, Harvey Shephard told me that, like everyone else, he was concerned about the departure of April Smith and Bob Crais, but that "… last night's episode was top drawer … one of the season's best." It was a most welcome congratulations. He added, at a lunch a few days later, that while watching the episode, his wife, Dale, stated that if he canceled *Cagney & Lacey* the marriage was over. That Harvey and Dale Shephard have one of the more stable relationships in all of Hollywood gave me reason to smile.

"Open and Shut Case" was quickly followed by another Brown & Fisher teleplay, "Date Rape." Here, too, there was nearly a unanimous reaction: almost everyone hated it. Corday began the criticism, followed quickly by Tony Barr's office, then the broadcast standards department at CBS, then Dick Rosenbloom, and, finally, Tyne Daly, who had been beating on the writing staff for weeks until they were punchy. At the end of our cast's initial table reading of this latest tome, Tyne tossed the script across the room saying, "This is garbage."

I did not agree. I liked the script, and so did director John Patterson. We were joined in supporting Steve and Terry's effort by Sharon Gless, but I suspected her endorsement was more because of the material's raunchy quality than because of the very nice political statement the piece made in its thematic presentation of the tastelessness of sexual humor in the workplace. The police drama on which all of this was hung was an acquaintance rape, which brought its share of insensitive, deprecating snickers from the men in the squad room.

That all the naysayers were successfully confronted and that the episode became one of our better ones is not as significant as a particular moment on the set of this specific production.

The scene to which I refer took place in the squad room. A discussion was heating up between the Lacey character and the men of the 14th regarding what does, and

---

[29]   "Open and Shut Case," written by Terry Louise Fisher & Steve Brown; directed by Nicholas Sgarro.

does not, constitute rape. Samuels, the commanding officer, enters the fray with the observation that his wife's favorite movie is *Gone with the Wind*.

"'So romantic,' Thelma used to say." And then Samuels adds, "so how come when Rhett Butler carries Scarlett O'Hara upstairs it's romance, and with some other poor slob it's rape?"

Lacey's rejoinder is swift and to the point, and she states it in front of everyone. "Begging your pardon, Lieutenant, but if you don't know the difference between rape and romance, you've got a serious problem." With that she exits the squad room.

Samuels is taken aback, and Desk Sergeant Coleman refers to Lacey with the thematically proper sexist tension reliever: "Her time of the month, or what?"

This was not the Cagney character, turning a sexist comment on its head the way it was used in the original Avedon teleplay; this was the all-too-typical male "explanation" for anything to do with a female that a guy may find inexplicable.

At any rate, at this point Sharon spoke up. She wanted her character to say something. To her, Cagney was John Wayne in a skirt, and she felt she should come to the defense of her partner.

It should probably be pointed out that up to this juncture the entire action of the three-plus-page sequence had taken place around the desks of the two women, with the blonde detective not contributing to the debate.

This was in the early days in the overall history of the series; we were still all getting to know each other. By example, it provides an opportunity to make several points, not the least of which is who does what, along with some potential responses during such a crisis moment.

The scene in question had been lit and rehearsed; hours had passed in the process. The sequence was about to be committed to film, and the star wanted a change.

"Get me a writer down here," the director might shout, believing it's all working beautifully, and, if he can just get this scene, along with its necessary coverage in the can, there's a shot at maintaining the day's schedule of eight to ten pages.

The writer (in this case, God help me, writer-producer) is summoned. "Think fast," she, he, or they, might say to themselves. "Don't be defensive; it's only one line. The problem is, it's got to be a beaut, a real Clint Eastwood-topper …"

The crew stands around and waits.

That's the setup, and that's the cast of characters—all well-intentioned, hard-working people. The actor-star who wants something to say, the director who thinks it's a good idea (but just come up with it fast so we can shoot), and the writer who is so conditioned to taking notes he or she is automatically doing what is requested, for to refuse might:

(a) Delay production—the consequences of which are usually foreign to this person of strong literary bent, but known to be undesirable.

(b) Bring stinging accusations concerning their egotistic unwillingness to change anything from the way they wrote it in the first place, precipitating, yet again, an unfavorable comparison to William Shakespeare.

Besides—it's not a bad idea. The star should have a topper—right?

And that is why you need a producer: a real one; someone who understands the actor, the material, the characters, the production schedule, and the editorial concept of how the scene will ultimately be put together.

I disagreed with Gless and leaned in close, excluding those around us, to explain my point of view. "Let me tell you what Christine Cagney wants," I began, gaining her undivided attention.

"What Cagney wants—more than anything—is to be in the club, to be one of the guys. It's much more important to her than saying or doing the right thing, or even coming to the defense of her partner. So, not only do I not want you to say anything here, but after Coleman's line about her time of the month, I'm going to cut to a reactive close-up of you to emphasize the fact that you, indeed, say nothing."

Sharon's eyes lit up as if she were a child on Christmas morning as she referred to the character about whom she still was learning. "Boy," Sharon nodded, "she's a real cooze[30], isn't she?"

"Well, let's say she's flawed." I smiled in reply. It was an important moment for us all. Only weeks before, in our episode "Jane Doe #37," Sharon was unable to relate to—and refused to play—what she perceived as weakness in her character. Now she got it; the epiphany was fundamental to so much of what we would do in the future.

It would be the cornerstone of what Sharon would bring to the series. Her willingness to henceforth play a character with real flaws rather than a conventional TV heroine, plus her unmatched likability, gave us a license few in television had

---

[30] The ultimate "C" word. A vulgarism referring to female genitalia.

ever had before. Cagney could be ruthless, self-serving, ambitious. She could lie or cheat, flirt for gain, or be insensitive to others and—as Sharon would play it—we would forgive her.

For a picture maker, it was a remarkable asset. Four and three-quarter reels of Cagney pushing, manipulating, and generally being a shit. In one episode, her machinations even resulted in an informant's death. One silent moment at the end: Sharon's Cagney with a tear in her eye. Our hearts would be broken, and all would be forgiven. She didn't even say, "I'm sorry." It didn't matter. It was a very fun thing to watch.

Sharon would never concede our point about Peter Lefcourt's script of "Jane Doe" (even after the script itself received our first Writers Guild award nomination), but she never again hesitated to play full tilt what we would give her in the way of a social or psychological handicap.

Tyne meanwhile had come back from a two-day holiday with a complaint. The workload at home, with two adolescent daughters and a husband, was as great as it was at Lacy Street—only at home no one looked after her as our comfort squad[31] did for her at our factory. The discussion led to our episode "Burnout," and to Ms. Daly's first Emmy Award.

---

[31]   The term *comfort squad* is generally applied to those members of the crew most closely associated with the actors: makeup, hair dressing, wardrobe. Added to this group, in our case, were fan mail coordinator Toni Graphia and general helper/assistant to the stars, Ms. Beverley Faverty.

CHAPTER 20

FILM NOIR, MARY POPPINS, AND THE U.S. POSTAL OFFICE

Peter Lefcourt, with whom I had happily worked on *American Dream*, actively pursued work on *Cagney & Lacey*. He did not ordinarily hire out as a freelance writer of episodes but made an exception as an avowed fan of the show. "Jane Doe #37" was the first script he created for us and could well have been the last, as he was driven almost as crazy as I over Sharon's not getting the empathic possibilities between a character such as Cagney and a common bag lady. No amount of "there but for the grace of God" arguments could win this one. Ultimately, Sharon bit the bullet and did it, but totally without conviction. I remember putting the picture and the performance together frames at a time.

Lefcourt's next script, "Let Them Eat Pretzels," was an even worse experience. Everyone loved it; hardly a note from the network, and nary a reason to suspect a problem with this tongue-in-cheek effort. It wasn't the fact that once it aired we would offend millions of Arab Americans with our descent to stereotype, but rather that days before the commencement of production, Tyne would announce, vis-à-vis the subplot of the piece (which made up perhaps 30 percent of the script), that she would not do mother-in-law jokes, as she found them cheap, sexist, and offensive. Neither Chris Abbott, Terry Louise Fisher, nor Barbara Corday had prepared me for that one, but I felt Tyne might be right, so Lefcourt was brought back for yet another eleventh-hour rewrite.

It's a comment about something that, despite all this Sturm und Drang, Lefcourt leaped at the opportunity to head up development of six scripts, commissioned in the hope of a pickup for the following fall season. I had been told Steve and Terry did not want to work together in the future, so my thought was to keep the present team working on the back nine, while Peter prepared for the hoped-for fall pickup.

Chris and Terry indicated they wished to stay on, working under Lefcourt. Scripts, being worked on by Peter Lefcourt for a season that might never happen, were the least of my problems.

The Nielsen numbers on *Cagney & Lacey* were now worse than ever. Football season was over, and, to replace their Monday night game and as if to go after what remained of the *Cagney & Lacey* audience, ABC delivered more and more strong exploitation films aimed at the female viewer.

February sweeps saw us battered by a made-for-TV film showing Ann-Margret giving away her children from her deathbed (the ultimate "crip" movie),[32] as well as an ABC exploitation film dramatizing the sweeps scare of the year: herpes. I was quoted as criticizing the viewing public, who, when given a choice between this film and *Cagney & Lacey*, chose to watch a running sore.

The specter of the show dying hovered over all of us. I had come to love this project more than anything I'd ever done—Tyne and Sharon more than anyone I've ever worked with. And why was that? What was it about my two stars? They were constantly challenging, brilliant beyond my experience, talented, and magical together and separately. I had often said, before meeting them, that one of the frustrations for a filmmaker is that you never get to hear the words as good as you did in your head. No matter how good the actor—even if it were Laurence Olivier—the words on the page were somehow clearer and better when you first read them and imagined their sound and delivery. In my experience that had always been true. That is until I met Tyne Daly and Sharon Gless. For the first time in my life, they said the words in a way that was better than I had imagined.

The closeness of the company was palpable. There were still some minor kinks to work out, but, by early March, everyone was proud of what they were doing and aware of what was expected of them. It was truly a great gig, and the very real prospect of its premature demise was devastating to us all.

On *This Girl for Hire,* the financial news was getting worse. I had, at my request, gotten approved as being fiscally responsible for this project, meaning that all dollars spent over the license fee came out of my personal pocket and not some studio or major corporate entity. Of course, the opposite was also true; any profits or

---

[32]   "Crip" movie: slang for cripple, aka, "Disease of the Week."

production savings would be mine to keep. Being "at risk" is the only way to make any real money in this business, but it can also be frightening.

Lee Rosenberg was now, once again, my agent. I had come to have a personal affection for attorney Stu Glickman, and an old intern of mine, Tom Kane, was functioning as production manager on the M.O.W. I liked all these men, yet I found myself second-guessing the choices and alliances I had made. I used to accuse one-time father-in-law and mentor "Rosy" Rosenberg of misguided loyalties; now I began to wonder if I, too, was guilty of hiring people I liked rather than those who might be best for the job.

Despite the gloom-and-doom prognosis on *Cagney & Lacey*, we kept fighting. Rosenbloom and I took Sharon and Tyne to a convention of CBS affiliates in Vegas and put them on the road to plead our case through the regional media. Shephard was getting plenty of support mail when he called to say, "Don't convince me. Convince the audience." Our ratings picked up a bit, but they were so dismal against the *Thorn Birds* and other major ABC blockbusters that we were all feeling buffeted.

Now, a blast from the past: Farrah Fawcett responded to my sending her the script on *This Girl for Hire*. She liked it and wanted to play the role. There were, of course, problems, such as availability and money. The latter was being spent by me as if we were going into production in a matter of weeks. Farrah was talking about waiting months.

Meanwhile, not one of the town's A directors would agree to, or was available for, the film. The turndowns had me in a funk. I was now down to such ordinary choices that I considered directing myself but realized I was too tired, too otherwise occupied, and (truth to tell) too cowardly to do so. I had to face that it was a lot easier saving these films in the editing room (while cursing the silly SOB who actually did the directing) than taking on the responsibility myself.

Nardino and I journeyed to Farrah Fawcett's hilltop home for an incredible meeting. Nardino couldn't help himself; he was salivating at the prospect of tying up Fawcett for the series of *This Girl for Hire*. He described the meeting as a "ten." Well, the house certainly was; the California ranch-style manse included, among other amenities, a built-in, sunken racquetball court and a studio for her rather extraordinary work as a sculptress. Farrah's live-in fella, Ryan O'Neal, joined us and was exuberant in his support of the material. He was pushing (along with us) for Farrah to close. She asked for twenty-four more hours to think it over.

The next day Gary called to tell me super agent Sue Mengers was now negotiating for Farrah. This was the agent who represented many major stars, from Jane Fonda to Barbra Streisand. None of us could recall if Ms. Mengers had ever negotiated anything as puny as a star deal for a mere television series.

Mengers gave Nardino the news that the star's availability might be delayed another six months or more. I told Gary I couldn't afford to postpone, and he countered that he just might pay me to do so. This, I speculated, could be my dream come true: being paid to do nothing.

In the days that followed, Farrah was in and out of the project so many times it became silly. Ms. Mengers was driving everyone crazy, as she inappropriately tried to apply her motion picture style of negotiating to television. They really are very different businesses. In the 1980s, that was even truer than it is now.

First Nardino, then Shephard, gave up on her. Mengers, having no luck negotiating with anyone else, then came after me.

"Look, Sue. The picture starts in a matter of weeks. You keep telling us Farrah is not available for six months. Why are we having this conversation?"

"You will wait for the star," said Mengers, sounding like something out of Billy Wilder's *Sunset Boulevard*.

"Sue, I don't know who you think you're talking to, but I'm not Ray Fucking Stark, and this is not one of your multi-million dollar features. This is a movie-for-television, and I will hit the ignition switch and it will start on schedule if I have to shave, put on a wig, and play the part myself."

More than once I've felt we would have been better off if I'd done just that.

For over a decade I had, with irregularity, nurtured *This Girl for Hire* from its beginnings as the Cliff and Jean Hoelscher project, *The Malachite Kachina*.

Their script became a treatment for a television series by Barbara Avedon & Barbara Corday at least a year before I would challenge the distaff writing team to create Hollywood's first female buddy movie. It would then serve as my introduction to the writing talents of Steve Brown & Terry Louise Fisher, who came on board to adapt the Avedon & Corday treatment to screenplay form. This treatment (or presentation) did more than break down the plot. It carefully illustrated, in both stage directions and dialogue, how the characters talked, how they related to one another, how they dressed, what the key sets were to look like, and the cinematic style of the piece in terms of art design and photography. It even gave a strong indication of the humor to come in the two or three short scenes that

Avedon & Corday had included. I mean no disparagement at all of Steve and Terry's considerable talents when I say that never could any writer(s) have had an easier assignment than to follow this blueprint.

This Girl for Hire provided me the opportunity to jump-start cinematographer Robbie Greenberg's career in Hollywood. He went on to do excellent photographic work in films and television, including Robert Redford's *The Milagro Beanfield War* and *Free Willy*. It also afforded me the opportunity to work with a cast of prestigious performers, many of whom I had admired most of my life, including Jose Ferrar, Howard Duff, Celeste Holm, Elisha Cook Jr., and Ray Walston. Jerry Jameson's directing was uninspired, but, well, acceptable; Robbie Greenberg's work, outstanding. The script worked beautifully, and the sets, costumes, and music were near perfection. Why then is the movie such a colossal bore?

The girl for hire is Barbara Brady, a private-eye who is a child of Hollywood. Brady lives with her mother (played perfectly by Celeste Holm), a former Hollywood bit actress, and her mother's live-in lover, who runs a film memorabilia shop on Hollywood Boulevard (Howard Duff).

Though the action takes place in modern day, Barbara Brady dresses in the style of the forties, because it goes with her hairdo and the cherry 1948 Chrysler convertible she drives. She carries a snub-nose .38 revolver, which, when coupled with all those capers with which she gets involved, makes her mother very nervous. Mother Brady blames herself:

"I knew I should never have let you go to all those Humphrey Bogart movies," she laments.

It's a vehicle for a star.

As Barbara Brady, Bess Armstrong acted the part nicely. She comported herself like the pro she is. If she is a star, however, it's from the fairly antiseptic school that Julie Andrews attended. Following my meeting with Ms. Armstrong for the first time, I remember noting in my diary: *"What's Mary Poppins doing in* The Maltese Falcon?"

It was too late for such a lamentation; she was already mine. The battle to get CBS to approve someone, especially someone with some individuality and star power, was long and arduous. Ultimately, I failed.

I continued to have Harvey Shephard's ear; it wasn't enough. Farrah Fawcett would have done the project; she needed a commitment to series from CBS. Shephard would commit to a fortune in holding money for Ms. Fawcett (to keep her off the market until he could see the film), but Farrah felt she was being asked to audition, and neither she nor Ms. Mengers would, understandably, allow that.

My original choice was Bernadette Peters, who, I was told at the time by her agent, was at that place in her career where this vehicle would be most welcome. I could not persuade Shephard, and, throughout the four months this debilitating process took, he remained adamantly opposed to my choice. By the time we settled on someone, I believe Ms. Peters was cast as the lead in Stephen Sondheim's then-new Broadway smash, *Sunday in the Park with George*. Next case.

I sold relative unknown Madolyn Smith to Shephard three weeks after I first auditioned her in my office. I convinced Shephard of the efficacy of the idea of going with a relative unknown and assured him that the money saved would go into a supporting cast, actors with TVQ.[33]

CBS casting head Jean Guest once again pronounced that I couldn't get her for a series. I had, of course, heard that before from Ms. Guest in reference to Sharon Gless, and so I am sure I demonstrated some impatience in relating that young Ms. Smith had read for the role in my office only weeks before. I had only waited this long because the mandate from Ms. Guest's office was for a recognizable name.

Shephard ended the budding confrontation by sending me out to sign the actress. Too late. In the intervening days since coming to my office, Ms. Smith had accepted the sought-after role of Madame Sadat in the prestigious miniseries *Sadat*, starring Louis Gossett Jr. I was now guilty of selling something to a network that I could not deliver.

Harvey Shephard had more important things to do than help me cast this movie, even if it was a possible back-door pilot. Of course, it wasn't that to Ms. Guest. It said M.O.W. on the interoffice business affairs memo, and—as far as she was concerned—that's what it was. She suggested I go after Teri Garr, and that I do so the same week Ms. Garr learned she was one of five nominees for filmdom's Oscar as Best Supporting Actress for Sidney Pollack's *Tootsie*. It took nearly two weeks to get an official turndown from Ms. Garr, who was then in Europe promoting her latest film and, I presume, celebrating her Oscar nomination.

---

[33]   For more than a generation, so-called Q scores have provided the clients of Madison Avenue advertising agencies with data to aid in their marketing, advertising, and media efforts. TVQ references the industry standard for measuring familiarity and appeal of a particular performer or fictional character or a program that one or both might be on. It can also be used to summarize the perceptions and feelings that consumers have over such things as familiarity or likability.

All the while money was being spent. *My* money, for I was on the line as being financially responsible on this project. It was a first for me, making me an owner, not an employee, and giving me (in 1983) investment tax credits worth nearly $100,000 and the potential for up to a half million dollars in ultimate profits. It was a great opportunity but required my mortgaging my home as security to demonstrate my financial stability to the network. It is all about delivery. The network wanted to be assured that when their air date arrived, I would be there with a film—and not with a tin cup.

Anything the film might cost over the agreed-upon license fee would be my responsibility. I would be required to personally pay the difference. The casting delays were forcing postponement, thus increasing costs. These delays would escalate into other departments, as wardrobe, for instance, would have to be created at overtime rates due to the scheduling problems brought about by our inability to have an actress available in a timely fashion for costume fittings.

If Jean Guest wanted a recognizable television name, Paramount's Gary Nardino (who still had some control over my fate since his studio owned the series rights) demanded an actress who would also agree to a series should the M.O.W. be successful. This was a major complication and added to my conflict with Guest.

I tried to remind Gary of my success with *Cagney & Lacey* despite the necessity of recasting Loretta Swit. He was not interested in taking that kind of chance. He threatened to enjoin me from making the film and argued that I was damaging his negotiated-for rights to *This Girl for Hire* as a series. Attorney Stu Glickman said not to worry, but Gary is formidable. More than once he brought forth the specter of the full weight of the Gulf & Western Corporation.[34]

Karen Allen, who, long before she was the girlfriend of *Indiana Jones*, I sort of discovered for my miniseries *John Steinbeck's East of Eden*, turned me down. She was exhausted from the play she'd been doing off-Broadway. It was the same play Farrah Fawcett was going into (*Extremities*), thereby replacing Ms. Allen. Each of these firm offers took an average of nearly a week to transmit and to get rejected. Each week was costing thousands.

Production manager Tom Kane was beside himself. So, too, were my business manager and my agent. They combined, along with my lawyer, to convince me to give up ownership for a smart distribution deal with Orion. I was still trying to save *Cagney & Lacey* from its all-but-certain demise, and the whole process had

---

[34]   In those days, the parent company of Paramount Pictures Corporation.

me exhausted. I gave in to my representatives and made the Orion deal at just about the same time I agreed to make my ninth offer for the lead in this movie.

CBS had finally given assent to Barbara Hershey, who I believed to be perfect for the part, but she was in the tenth spot. First I was required to go to number nine, Ms. Guest's choice, Bess Armstrong. I capitulated; and that's what Mary Poppins was doing in my loving but light tribute to film noir.

All of this came to its conclusion during the week of network scheduling meetings in New York. I was in the Big Apple at Rosenbloom's request to help with the all important sell on *Cagney & Lacey*. We had put together a brochure, at the last minute, consisting of reviews and whatever research data we could come up with that gave our cause any credibility at all. It was not a strong case. Still, NBC and ABC's schedules were so unimaginative, and really unchallenging to CBS in 1983, that Rosenbloom and I began to believe that CBS (and Shephard in particular) would renew *Cagney & Lacey* simply because it could afford to do so.

It was late in the afternoon when I received a call at Orion's New York office from Harvey Shephard. He was calling personally to tell me of his decision to cancel my series. I had been passing time, looking at a preview copy of Rick Rosner's *Lottery* pilot, which had just been given a go at ABC. Shephard talked. I listened. Rick's successful pilot droned on in the background. Shephard told me what a difficult decision this had been.

"I know," he began, "that you know how much I love the show." He didn't feel it could be made any better (or quite obviously that it should be given another chance).

I had felt for some time his personal disappointment in the ratings performance of the show. Somehow, in some way, despite the acclaim, the reviews, and the genuine affection for the series in the Hollywood community, I believe Harvey Shephard had been embarrassed by the (to him) one-sidedness of this love affair.

I remained low-key, telling him I understood. I thanked him for the opportunity of making twenty-eight episodes of a show of which I was quite proud. I turned off Rick's pilot, informed Rosenbloom, and went to my Orion-provided cubby-hole to begin notifying all concerned.

First Corday, then Tyne, a message to Sharon to return my call when she got back to her hotel from her then-current location shoot in New Orleans (on *Hobson's Choice*, a CBS M.O.W.), the office, the remaining cast, the writers, and my mother. The conversations with the cast members were moving, albeit brief. I also took the time to phone a few of our most vocal fans, the ones with whom I had previously struck up some correspondence. I had quite a list.

"I'm OK," I told Rosenbloom. "I was steeled for this." I went on to say that I felt good about the work, that I was very proud of what had been done, and that I had no bad feelings or regrets. Mamma always said, "Leave 'em wanting more," and that was what I was doing. At the hotel I received my first condolences.

"My God," I thought, "people already know." I felt a twinge of pain. I decided to escape, to go to the theater. A musical would be a good idea, I theorized. Why did I pick *Nine* (the musical play based on Fellini's *8 ½*—the great Italian filmmaker's free-wheeling homage to *Death of a Salesman*)?

Early in Act II, I was depressed and walked out midway through the performance. From the bar at Frankie and Johnny's 45th Street bistro, I phoned Sharon Gless in New Orleans. She was alone in her hotel room and matching me drink for drink. We both were in tears, and, well, it was just sad, that's all. I finished the call and ate alone.

The next day I was a bit hung over but resolved to resurrect *Cagney & Lacey*. I began to formulate a pitch: "The show that would not die."

This Girl for Hire needed attention, but I kept flashing on *Cagney & Lacey*. I realized then, the day after cancellation, why all of us (or at least why I) felt so close to this. Just as in *M*A*S*H**, *Barney Miller,* or *All in the Family*, our characters were honest and true to themselves. Most things in movies and TV are not. Archetypes and melodramas are the hot commodities. It is, after all, easier to sell James Bond than *On Golden Pond*; easier, yes, but it is the Golden Ponds that people remember and about which they get emotional.

In eight months, Sharon, Tyne—all of us—revealed more about ourselves to each other than the folks on *Dallas* or *Dynasty* might in eight years. I really believed we could have caught on with one more chance. But who would give it to us? ABC? NBC? HBO? The last two had already said no.

I returned to Los Angeles. I had major work to do on *This Girl for Hire*. Production was really only days away, and I hated the wardrobe and sets. I did some yelling and some last-minute fixes, but I remained in a funk. Corday said I was always like this when in pre-production. It wasn't that. It was the movie of the week business as opposed to the series game. As if I didn't miss *Cagney & Lacey* enough, the process on this M.O.W. only exacerbated the problem.

Starting up any production is difficult, but with a M.O.W. you're going through this whole crank-up only to dismantle it all within a matter of weeks. At least with a series, things finally smooth out and one gets to do the job one really knows how to do. Series television is the closest thing to the old studio system we have in Hollywood today: crews who know each other, know how to work together, and understand the project on which they are working. A family emerges, a camaraderie, a shorthand. None of that occurs on these twenty-day one-shots. It was all just start-up: one crisis, one disappointment, one compromise after another, then time to strike the sets and wrap.

I busied myself with revamping Bess Armstrong's wardrobe and pressing for some additional work on our sets. I also had to begin to pack up my office at Lacy Street with still no clear idea of where I would go.

Judy Mann of the *Washington Post* called. She had been the first big-time newspaper columnist to give *Cagney & Lacey* a major boost. She had understood and appreciated what we had attempted. Now she wanted to know what I was doing to save the series. I explained there was little to be done, but that if I thought of anything I'd let her know.

Corday had recently left her post at ABC and had taken a spot as a producer at Columbia. Herman Rush, Columbia's top guy in television, had given her an outstanding deal and was offering me the same contract to join his studio. Things had recently been so difficult with Nardino that I questioned whether any studio would be the right idea for me. One option was to stay in the M.O.W. game as an indy. Considering what I was going through on *This Girl for Hire,* that was also a less-than-happy prospect.

I turned my attention to the mail. There were perhaps two dozen letters awaiting my return from New York. They concerned themselves with *Cagney & Lacey.* It was fan mail, but not of the usual sort; it was not written with a crayon, nor did it say anything about the author kissing their pillow every night while asking for a photo.

These fan letters were typewritten and on personalized stationery. They were well thought out and articulate. The senders were clearly educated and in that upwardly mobile group Madison Avenue likes to reach out and touch. Their letters were primarily missives of thanks. Their authors were, at the time of writing, unaware of the network's cancellation of the series. They had simply seen something that affected them and had begun to watch. They were pleased to discover that it was not a one-time thing and hoped that this series, and its quality, might continue.

It took me a little over a week, but I eventually responded to each of those letters, answering whatever specific questions the correspondent might have asked, and generally responding with thanks for his or her support. I then went on to inform them of the cancellation and to let them know that my next project, which also had series potential, was a M.O.W. called *This Girl for Hire*. As Grandma Fanny would say, "It shouldn't be a total loss."

About the time I finished the last of these nearly two dozen letters, a man arrived at my office. He was a messenger carrying three boxes. Each box was big enough to contain a case of wine. What these boxes contained was much more heady than wine—it was more fan letters: conservatively, more than a thousand.

The messenger had come from CBS. Apparently their policy on a canceled show was not to burn the mail but to forward it on to the producer. The messenger put down his burden and left.

I took a handful of envelopes at random from each box. They, too, were typewritten and on personalized stationery. There was, however, a difference from the earlier letters; these people were angry. They were writing to protest the recent CBS cancellation (something that had yet to occur when the letters I had just answered had been composed).

There was no way I could write to each of these people individually. I made the decision to construct a form letter. Adam would take the addresses off each of the envelopes, and we would respond. It was going to cost more than a few hundred dollars in postage. I decided not to inform Orion, who I knew would not approve the expense. We used up the stamps we had in the office, and I bought the rest myself.

I drafted the letter in longhand on a legal pad. I began by apologizing for the fact that what they were receiving was a form letter, then went on to explain that there was simply too much mail for me to answer individually. I thanked them for their interest and did the best I could to point out that a cancellation by a network was very final and not something an executive producer could do an awful lot about.

I then began the final paragraph. I can, to this day, see myself as if by way of an out-of-body experience. I prepared to reapply pen to paper to close out this correspondence, when I grinned mischievously, then wrote: *"It is my perception that no one in power at CBS even read your letter. My suggestion, should you still be agitated about this matter, is to write your local newspaper as well as* The Los Angeles Times *and* The New York Times, *on the theory that network executives may not read their mail, but they do read their newspapers."*

That was pretty much it. It took Adam over a week to get all the envelopes addressed and out. By mid-July, Lee Margulies in *The Los Angeles Times* and John J. O'Connor of *The New York Times* wrote individual articles about the incredible volume of mail they had received on the cancellation of *Cagney & Lacey.*

New York's O'Connor was quick to observe that this "was clearly orchestrated by executive producer Barney Rosenzweig" but went on to write that this fact did not negate the grassroots essence of the campaign, in that letters came from all over the country, and that in most cases the authors had to have written at least two separate letters. The campaign to save *Cagney & Lacey* was unofficially launched.

The gang is gathered on the Lacy Street squad room set. From left, in the rear, Carl Lumbly, Sidney Clute, Al Waxman, John Karlen, and Martin Kove. Sharon and Tyne flank their grateful producer.

Photo: Rosenzweig Personal Collection

CHAPTER 21

WHO WOULDA THUNK IT?

Weeks before John J. O'Connor's story in the *New York Times*, at the very beginning of the summer of 1983, Lee Rosenberg convinced me to make a studio deal. My fantasy of just stopping work for an extended period of time would have to wait. There was a substantial offer in place from Herman Rush at Columbia, and it would be criminal, in Lee's eyes, to watch me dissipate the heat from *Cagney & Lacey* and *This Girl for Hire*.

Before accepting the Columbia deal, I insisted that Orion be given the opportunity to match the offer. They had been fair with me and pleasant to work with throughout *Cagney & Lacey*. They had been there for me when I (incorrectly) thought I needed help on *This Girl for Hire*.

Lee did not believe that Orion, basically a small motion picture company uncommitted to television, would step up to such a heavyweight deal. I agreed and assured him he would not have to waste time in negotiations. "Just give them the Columbia deal and say, if you can match it comma for comma, point for point, dollar for dollar, then Barney would prefer to be in business with you. Let them know there will be no negotiating down from that deal." Lee did just that, and Dick Rosenbloom asked for three days to respond. That gave him time to fly to New York to pitch the proposal to his management.

That was in June of 1983. To our amazement, Orion did step up, and I was now theirs, exclusive in television for two years, commencing September 6, immediately after finalizing and delivery of *This Girl for Hire* and my well-earned summer vacation. The deal was for megabucks in advance of fees I might earn on future productions and made me a major participant in profits and a hefty partner in gross receipts.

Meanwhile, as the letters from the *Cagney & Lacey* fans generated more publicity and, as a consequence, more letters, another predictable phenomenon was taking place.

It was summer, and the networks launched their rerun-dominated schedule. *Cagney & Lacey*, no longer confronting first-run movies on ABC and competing against a particularly dull baseball season on NBC, began to soar in the summer Nielsen's.

To this day, summer ratings do not count for much with the networks; that was even truer in the early eighties. Still, it did give TV editors and their newspapers something to speculate about during those slow news days of July and August 1983.

I went to Shephard with the latest Nielsen's and a plea to make a *Cagney & Lacey* M.O.W. He turned me down. When ABC's Stu Samuels passed, I considered it the final nail in the coffin. NBC's Steve White had rejected the idea earlier with a not-so-nice note. I think it was W.C. Fields who said, "If at first you don't succeed, try, try again … then give up. After all, nobody should think you're crazy."

The mail continued to pour in, and the Nielsen's on our summer reruns had us consistently among the top five rated shows in the country. No one of importance cared.

I had moved from my Lacy Street office and, with Corday, had taken a house for the summer in the Malibu Colony (the home of the estranged wife of Tyne Daly's agent, Merritt Blake). Three days a week, I drove to a West Los Angeles cutting room, where I worked on the final edit of *This Girl for Hire*. That was where Judy Mann, Liz Smith, Marilyn Beck, and other columnists and reporters found me. My phone was beginning to ring a lot. Everyone wanted to know what I had heard from CBS. I, of course, had heard nothing. What's more, I didn't expect that I would.

I stated this fact for publication and announced my plan to make *Cagney & Lacey: The Movie*. I told the newspaper folk that I expected to begin photography the following spring in New York; that Sharon Gless and Tyne Daly would, of course, play the title roles; and that I had a script by Ronald M. Cohen that was too hot for the network and that would now be expanded to feature length. All this, I went on, was of course contingent on getting the executives at Orion to agree. I was, I said, optimistic about that.

The truth was that Mike Medavoy of Orion had turned the idea down cold, that Dick Rosenbloom had denied my request to spend $5,000[35] on a press agent to handle this burgeoning campaign, and that Jamie Kellner—Orion's then-

---

[35]   Press agent pals Gene Schwam and Julian Myers volunteered to help out, even after Rosenbloom had turned down my request for some sort of payment for them.

syndication maven—had said an emphatic no to my suggestion that we take the series to Metromedia in the same way MGM had with the then-newly canceled series *Fame*. The Orion sales chief simply did not believe *Cagney & Lacey* had the same demographic appeal to local stations as the MGM musical series.

I was keeping the whole thing alive, single-handedly, from a one-line phone (without a hold button) in an editing cubicle and from my vacation house in Malibu.

I had a theory at work here that was not unlike what I sent out in that, now somewhat celebrated, form letter; Mike Medavoy might not believe me that there was a movie in *Cagney & Lacey*, but maybe he would if he read it enough in the newspapers.

The mail, including petitions, continued to flow in support of *Cagney & Lacey*. I was not ecstatic over *This Girl for Hire* but was finally convinced it was about as good as it was going to get. It seemed to me to lack style, which was doubly damning when one considered it had always lacked content.

I just could not get enthused over this picture. My view must have been colored by the demise of *Cagney & Lacey* and the fact that we had come in at least $50,000 under the license fee on *This Girl*. It meant my decision to lay off the project with Orion was a lousy one. The only reason for making this film was money, and now I had come up with substantially less than I might have. Hindsight is 20/20. Still, it did have me a bit dysphoric as I ruminated over the various and many sour business decisions I'd made in my life.

In late August, the final day of editing on *This Girl for Hire*, I got yet another phone call. It was from my friend, Julian Myers: *Cagney & Lacey* had received four Emmy nominations from the Academy of Television Arts and Sciences (Sharon and Tyne, the show for Best Dramatic Series, and Mo Harris, et al., for sound mixing). Although less than I had hoped for, it represented 80 percent of the nominations garnered by the entire CBS network. The press was having a field day with this. There is nothing the print media enjoy more than tweaking the noses of the networks.

Let's face it: the newspaper business has never been quite the same since the invention of the phrase "film at eleven," and, as a consequence, there really is very little love lost between the two media forms.

About this time, Tyne came out to Malibu Colony Beach for a visit. She brought two bottles of champagne and a toast for Corday and me. "For regular people, you two are extraordinary."

We got a third bottle delivered and, save for one ounce that the teetotalling Corday took for the salute, Tyne and I drank the rest. Very drunk and very sentimental about *Cagney & Lacey*, we had a lot of fun.

Calls, mail, visits continued, and all heaped praise on my defunct series.

I was on a dubbing stage a few weeks later, supervising this nearly final process on my less-than-spectacular M.O.W., when Corday called with more news: the latest Nielsen's showed *Cagney & Lacey* to be number one in the country. More nose tweaking from the nation's print media.

USA Today came out with a front-page headline, including a color picture of Tyne and Sharon: "**CBS Canceled Cops Number One**," it said in very bold type. Kim LeMasters called with congratulations. What the hell does that mean? ABC's *Good Morning America* wanted Tyne and Sharon to appear on their show. What irony. We couldn't get them this coveted spot before we were canceled. Rosenbloom reluctantly paid for the women to fly back to New York.

"What are we trying to accomplish here?" he wanted to know.

My position was that from this point until September 26 (the day after they would give out the Emmys), we were news, and we would be fools not to take advantage of the heat.

Perhaps, I speculated to Rosenbloom, we'll get Medavoy to reconsider, possibly Metromedia will come through, maybe—if nothing else—we'll get one of the networks to rethink picking up an M.O.W. or two based on the show. Meanwhile, I began putting together a pitch on *Lacey & Lacey,* a half-hour sitcom idea for Tyne Daly and John Karlen. They would play the same characters they had in the original series, but all the action would take place in their Queens apartment as Mary Beth, a New York City detective, returned home nightly to her blue-collar husband and family.

Barbara Boyle, then a feature film development executive at Orion, was sympathetic to the idea of *Cagney & Lacey: The Movie.* We met to effectuate a strategy to win over her colleagues. I believed I was on to something here. Even as a failure, *Cagney & Lacey* had over twenty million hard-core enthusiasts. These fans were activists; they were not merely passive or nonselective observers of entertainment. I felt these fans could be appealed to and convinced to pay to see their favorite show on the big screen.

Other television shows had made this transition. I believed I could make the film for a reasonable price (five million dollars in 1983 was well below the mean), and with all the recent publicity, we certainly had that sought-after merchandising tool: the pre-sold title.

Despite all this, Medavoy and his colleagues at Orion remained unconvinced. I speculated that if I could get Harvey Shephard at CBS to guarantee that he would purchase the theatrical film for his network, say, two years hence in a pre-buy arrangement, that might help tip the scale for Medavoy.

It occurred to me that my longtime friend Michael Fuchs, then head of HBO, also could be of assistance here. He could not only agree to license the film for his pay cable service, I reasoned, he could put in a good word with Medavoy, with whom he had great influence. It would, I felt, be most helpful for the head of HBO to say to his counterpart at Orion that he would look with favor on such a film as *Cagney & Lacey: The Movie*. Fuchs was less than enthusiastic.

I got an appointment with Harvey Shephard, hopefully to convince him to agree to a pre-buy on *Cagney & Lacey: The Movie*. It was a major long shot.

The morning of the Shephard appointment, I decided there was no way I could browbeat him into this. Still, the meeting had been set, so rather than cancel I took a new tack. As it was the week of Rosh Hashanah, the time of the Jewish New Year, I pointed out to Shephard that I only came by to thank him for the year of *Cagney & Lacey* and for *This Girl for Hire*. I told him how grateful I was for the opportunity. He seemed to relax as I was not selling. He was quite nice about complimenting me and the show. Finally, at a quiet and pleasantly warm moment in our conversation, he leaned into me and said, "What do you think are the chances of *Cagney & Lacey* coming back?"

Are you ready for this? This was the head of programming for CBS! This was the guy who went back to New York City with a schedule in hand that excluded *Cagney & Lacey* in the first place. This was the guy who kept telling every journalist in America that summer ratings didn't count! I was flabbergasted.

"Harvey," I said, "you're asking me?" I will always remember the look on his face (and yet still another time I would wish for a video—this time of my own [had to be incredulous] expression).

What he meant, Shephard quickly explained, was that if he had some fallout (which he anticipated) in his new schedule, could I, in fact, put the show together again? I told him I thought so. He went on to explain that because of troubles with finances with New York, his budget for development had been cut. He had, as a result, few scripts for mid-season. It might pay to bring back something with which he and America were already familiar.

"I think we could put together a good campaign," he said.

"America wins!" I countered.

"I like that," he said.

At one point in the meeting, Shephard told me how upset he had been with the way women were being portrayed on television. It's why he cared so much for *Cagney & Lacey* and was so disappointed when the bulk of the audience rejected the concept. He talked about being a villain in his own home—how not only his wife, Dale, was upset with him, but his daughter was constantly after him: "Daddy, how could you cancel that series?"

It was some rare meeting.

I reported all this to Rosenbloom. He, too, was in disbelief. We agreed to keep all this to ourselves and to play out the hand to see what would happen.

The following Monday we were contacted by Metromedia, the station group that was responsible for keeping *Fame* alive after network cancellation. Orion's Jamie Kellner, Dick Rosenbloom, and I were in their offices the day after that. Their first question was where had we been? They loved the show and were most anxious to put it on their stations. I glared across the room at Kellner. It was a terrific meeting, and the only question was would we be able to produce the show for the smaller dollars Metromedia had to offer? We promised to look into that and get back.

At 4:04 PM the following afternoon, Wednesday, September 21, 1983, Alan Levin, the senior VP in charge of business affairs for CBS, was on the phone. "Can you put it all back together again?"

I told him I believed it was possible. Levin was a business man, and this was a no-nonsense corporate kind of conversation. Six minutes later Harvey Shephard called. He was happy for me and gave me a sense of what was being talked about. An order of six or seven episodes, to be ready by spring, a protected time period, then—if all went well—on to the fall of 1984 with an order for twenty-two and success.

The summer of 1983 was over. For two weeks I had been operating under my new overall deal with Orion Pictures Corporation. My new deal, which did not anticipate the renewal of *Cagney & Lacey* as a series—a series, that two months earlier I could have purchased for maybe a dollar and a half. Had I had a single notion that such a renewal was possible, I certainly could have had Lee Rosenberg address it in my new deal—but who would have thought of such a thing?

I would not rain on my own parade as I focused back to that incredible call from CBS: "We have made a mistake; can you put it back together again?"

I drove over to Rosenbloom's office in Century City. We would plunge immediately into the work. No time to celebrate. On arrival, I was told Bud Grant, Shephard's boss from CBS, was on the telephone. He wanted this all finalized by the Emmy broadcast that Sunday. He believed we were going to win Best Series, and he had an image of me, "Rocky-like," holding that statue aloft and making the announcement to the world that Cagney and Lacey were back. I told him I appreciated the imagery, but there was a lot to be done between now and then.

Rosenbloom and I huddled. Our presumption was that Sharon would be the stumbling block; after all, she was the one who hadn't stopped working since the show's demise. She would give up the most by returning to our series.

I wanted to get everyone in a room around a large conference table and hammer this out as if this were an international peace parlay. I was optimistic that there was a lot of goodwill here and that this nontraditional approach would work better than the conventional "us versus them" negotiating stance so common to labor/management talks. Rosenbloom turned me down. I backed off of this position but insisted on bringing in the agents for Tyne and Sharon.

At 5:30, Merritt Blake, Tyne's agent, was there. He wanted to make it work but did not want to be stupid. I assured him that he and his client would be treated equally with Sharon and her agent, Ronnie Meyer. Meyer came in at 6:40. He's a lot tougher than Merritt, though he conceded he wanted it to happen. That night I talked to both of the women, and it was clear to me that they were excited, happy, and wanted this to work out. Could it be done by Sunday?

The next day, Thursday morning, Tyne and I talked on the phone. "Barney," she said, "it'll work out, but it can't happen by week's end. There's too much for me to think about." I went to the office and called Rosenbloom.

"I don't think we can settle this before the Emmys," I said.

"You're telling me!" he exclaimed, and then he read me Ronnie Meyer's demands for Ms. Gless: a long list and very expensive. CBS was dismayed and Levin suggested pulling the offer, but Rosenbloom mollified him. We continued strategy meetings, trying to ascertain what we wanted, what the actresses would settle for, and what we could get from CBS. Those questions were put on the back burner that Friday morning when Army Archerd's column in *Daily Variety* revealed the whole story as his lead item.

We had pleaded with everyone for secrecy. We did not want this out prematurely because it effectively now let CBS off the hook. I had been quoted extensively in the press urging CBS to ask us back. Well, they had, and now the world knew it. The shoe was on the other foot—the ball, very much, in our court.

I did several phone interviews that day. We appeared nationally and locally on television with the news. I was attempting to sound encouraged while committing us to nothing and, at the same time, trying to maintain public support and not have us appear greedy.

I had a lovely lunch break with Tyne, complete with champagne, then on to a meeting at CBS to pitch a new project to drama VP Carla Singer, set up over a week before the *Cagney & Lacey* news. What a reception at the network! From Harvey Shephard, Carla Singer, and Tony Barr. The secretaries and assistants applauded as I walked down the hall.

The next morning I received a phone call from Mace. "I have to read about this in the papers? You couldn't call?"

I smiled as I paraphrased his comment to me of nearly two years before. "Mace, baby. It's payday. What do you care? It's only television."

Halloween at Lacy Street. Everyone showed up with a Rosenzweig mask, including the award winner, who had earrings and lipstick added and was called Mary Beth Rosenzweig. This all led to editor Chris Cooke's invention of "Barney, the Stick;" it was sort of a fly-swatter topped off with my picture and accompanied by the legend that one could take it to network meetings or battles with an in-law or whomever and be assured of ... oh, I don't know ... something.

Photo: Rosenzweig Personal Collection

The gang in an attempt at humor. That is Sidney Clute in front, flanked by Sharon and Tyne with (from left) Marty Kove, Al Waxman, John Karlen, and Carl Lumbly. No one remembers now, but I am betting this was Kove's idea.

Photo: Rosenzweig Personal Collection

CHAPTER 22

BACK BY POPULAR DEMAND

What was happening to me, or more precisely, to *Cagney & Lacey*, had never happened before. Sponsors had, in the fifties and sixties, brought back TV shows because some member of their board of directors liked what he or his spouse had seen. Bill Paley had resurrected a show every now and then because it was a personal favorite. One network had licensed another's reject, in some desperate ploy to get out of the ratings cellar, or brought back one of its own out of an elongated hiatus, but this was different.

The sets for *Cagney & Lacey* had been dismantled or sold; its actors, writers, crew, and staff were no longer under any kind of contractual obligation. The show was over—except it wasn't. *Cagney & Lacey* was brought back by popular demand.

Other forces were at work; CBS had lost over seventy million dollars that year in the cable business, forcing economies throughout the corporation, including program development. That made Mr. Shephard and his staff a lot needier in 1983 than they had ever been before. There was Gloria Steinem, who would publicly chastise Messrs. Paley and Wyman at CBS for their short-sightedness in prematurely ending the only dramatic show on television to feature women. There were those incredible ratings for the summer—all that press, the reviews, the nominations, and the letters. Harvey Shephard called it an avalanche of mail.

Now the monolith had been brought to its knees in the best David and Goliath tradition. It was a great story, and it has been retold many times. It took everything mentioned heretofore to pull it off, plus eleven weeks of the most grueling, emotional negotiations in which I have ever been involved.

Needless to say we did not get our announcement at the Emmys. First of all, Bud Grant's fantasy required that the series win. It did not (*Hill Street Blues* won for the second year in a row), though Tyne Daly did for Best Actress in a Dramatic

Series. Everyone around us at the ceremonies that Sunday was buzzing about the story published the previous Friday. Was it true? Would *Cagney & Lacey* be back on the air and, if so, when? Mostly we answered with knowing smiles.

I mentioned that all contracts with the artists were void; all save one: mine. My old deal on *Cagney & Lacey* was in place in perpetuity; my old deal, calling for me to work for $10,000 per episode (less than one half of my newly negotiated fees on any upcoming show, now memorialized in my new contract at Orion at $25,000 per episode); my old deal, with its measly share of profits and no mention of gross. My old deal, which called for my former associate and eternal nemesis, Mace Neufeld, to be tied to my fee structure and owning three times my share of the profits. My old deal, which no one seemed to remember, was only created in the first place to allow me just enough time to get the series up and running.

Now we had an "opportunity" at CBS to audition yet again. I was, as far as anyone knew, still "of the essence." I was the key to getting Tyne and Sharon to re-up. I was the guy who everyone acknowledged knew how to handle this show, and I was the guy now being asked to suspend his new deal (with all that terrific upside potential) at a time in his career when he had the most heat, in order to what? Take a chance? To possibly sully that memory with a very minimal seven show order?

CBS had said they had made a mistake; they were not saying, "Come on, we're going to make you rich."

Cagney & Lacey was the greatest come to me/go from me act in the history of network television. We had been rejected on a national scale, and now we—the actors and me—were being asked to forgive all that and come back and try out once again. Not only that, I was being asked to do it under an antiquated deal. I balked. I submitted that this new circumstance with CBS should fall under the terms of my new arrangements with Orion.

"What about Mace Neufeld?" they wanted to know. There was no way they felt they could accommodate my current pact plus his.

"Put *Cagney & Lacey* under my new deal, and I'll take care of Mace out of my end," I said.

They wouldn't do it. That should give some indication of the disparity in the two contracts.

All this put a pall on what should have been the happiest time of my life. I kept on trusting something would work out, while laboring at bringing together again the things needed to make our series.

Rosenbloom and I attended a meeting in the CBS conference room with Shephard, Levin, Shephard's lieutenant, Kim LeMasters, and Levin's second in command, Bill Klein.

It was sort of an official start to negotiations, and it was here we would learn the parameters of what we needed to know to begin the real work of putting everything together again.

What was actually going on was celebratory. Something rare had happened, and we were the participants. It wasn't a question of who won and who lost; maybe we all won. It was just that it was kind of an historical moment, which had everyone smiling and enjoying the afterglow.

Then LeMasters spoke up: "Since the show obviously failed in its last incarnation, what changes do you anticipate making in these next seven episodes to fix the series?"

Talk about your wet blanket. I said something about us being invited to come back and that I was not aware any fixes would be required. Shephard stifled his lieutenant, and we got on with the business at hand.

That meeting took place on September 28: three days after the Emmys, one week after the CBS capitulation. Up to this point, the women and their representatives had been relatively patient, awaiting Orion's response to their opening salvo.

I had urged Rosenbloom to have open negotiations with the talent (Sharon, Tyne, and their representatives) and to rent a large table for the event (treating it all like the IA-AMPTP contract talks[36]), but I did not insist or fight for this idea hard enough. If I had been adamant, it probably would have happened; Rosenbloom rarely turned me down when I got that forceful. I was not adamant.

Rosenbloom's plan was to prepare carefully, to negotiate first with the CBS network, and then, empowered by the network to do so, he would negotiate individually with Tyne and Sharon, treating them as equally as possible. This plan was supported by Rosenbloom's management completely. I was the lone dissenter.

I felt the women needed to voice their frustrations to people in power. I felt they wanted—and needed—their day in court. I felt there were certain items (mostly billing) that could only be worked out between the women in a face-to-face

---

36   The IA (International Alliance of Theatrical and Stage Employees) and the AMPTP (The Association of Motion Picture and Television Producers) are two of the primary adversaries in Hollywood's labor-management disputes. The IA represents motion picture and television crews; the Association speaks for the major companies in the industry.

situation. I also worried that the time consumed by Rosenbloom's plan would only feed the women's anxieties and lead us closer to Tyne's departure date for the film she had committed to do in Europe: *The Aviator*, produced, as luck would have it, by none other than Mace Neufeld, which, despite the title similarity, was *not* the movie made famous by Martin Scorsese and Leonardo DiCaprio.

Three weeks passed; three agonizing weeks in which Sharon's and Tyne's ambivalence, paranoia, and fantasies flourished. Tyne's departure date for Yugoslavia and her role in the Neufeld film drew near.

Three weeks. Rosenbloom finally called me to tell me the offer: "$50,000 per episode, per woman. Double their previous salary. What," he asked proudly, "do you think of that?"

"It's only money," I countered. I did not think it would solve the problem.

Rosenbloom and I argued over this for a time, but it was now his ball, and he was playing this his way.

Why not, I asked, offer Tyne $35,000 per episode (a savings of $15,000 per episode) plus—through Orion—a $250,000 development fund for her and Georg's company? It would be cheaper in the long run, and Orion might benefit from the association with Tyne and her husband. What about offering Sharon less cash per episode and deal with her primary fantasy of a beach house? I quickly invented a free rental and ultimate (after 100 episodes) free deed to Ms. Gless for this. Why not, in other words, find out what these people believed might make them feel good about the perpetual come to me/go from me commitment they were about to make and deal with what they really wanted?

Rosenbloom did not want to be bothered. He did not believe they could turn down this kind of money, and indeed he was right; they did not turn it down. In fact, the Orion economic package was immediately gobbled up. But, to Rosenbloom's dismay, negotiations were far from over.

"Now," said the two agents, "let's talk about our other needs."

Rosenbloom had operated from his own sensibilities and those of his management. He had shot his bolt in the first round. I had lived with these gals for months—for twelve to fourteen hours a day—I knew better. I should have been more adamant.

CHAPTER 23

COME TO ME/GO FROM ME

Some things do not change: me, for instance. It has been somewhere between twenty and thirty years since much of all of this has happened, and I keep looking for the lesson, searching for the growth. Aside from my waistline, much of it is not readily apparent (at least to this reader). The emotional scar tissue is still, somehow, fresh, and, even where it is not, I do not seem to be able to recount these ancient moments or stories without falling back on my feelings of that time, sans anything resembling perspective.

This can be a good thing in terms of verisimilitude, but overall it is a weakness, especially when (pedagogically) I wish to face the class with the query: "What have we learned?" Not too much, apparently.

I make this digression for more reasons than self-effacement. Richard M. Rosenbloom is one of the kindest, smartest, and most decent human beings I have ever met in my life. He doesn't come out that way in much of what is to follow. There were times when we were adversaries—maybe only for an afternoon—but the story of that time I only know how to tell with the zeal I felt at that time. Dick Rosenbloom comes out the worst for it, and I am sorry about that.

There are some galley readers who have said some similar things about my treatment of Tyne Daly. I have never loved anyone I have not sired or slept with more than I love Tyne Daly. But, in the early days of our relationship on Cagney & Lacey, *before we had totally learned to trust one another, she was a piece of work and, on occasion, could be a very major pain in the ass. I just could not effectively alter what I remember, nor do I possess the will to sugarcoat. The brilliant and talented Ms. Daly is, therefore, presented by me warts and all, and I hope she either never reads this book or, if she does, rises above it to forgive me. In my mind, she will always be my star, as she is, very much, the star of this book.*

As for everyone else, I am (I fear) at times a bit tough on people I rather liked and a bit too easy on some whom I could barely abide. It is, I concede, an odd sort of attempt at even-handedness and may have occurred because, even though I may have failed, I tried very hard not to write one of those Hollywood books in which no one wants their name mentioned.

Meanwhile, back at those Century City negotiations for the resurrection of *Cagney & Lacey*, Orion had done nothing to address my deal. Sharon Gless pronounced she would not do the show without me, but so much money was at stake that I did not feel comfortable relying on that pledge. Shephard had not reiterated his demand that I be "of the essence," nor had he withdrawn it.

Orion felt, I suppose, that they could finesse this. After all, I was committed to the show, at least on a non-exclusive basis, for $10,000 per episode; they knew I could no longer threaten to do this from a beach in Hawaii, because they had me under a separate, exclusive televisioncontract for the next two years, requiring my presence in Los Angeles, as opposed to the South Pacific. Since, however, their strategy relied on the existence of both deals, they would, of course, have to pay me under the terms of both deals. I was, therefore, making plenty of up-front money. What I wanted negotiated was justice, in the form of a back-end reward for success.

There was no way I could do the series and devote enough time to properly developing new material. I was, therefore, being asked to give up the opportunity of tremendous upside potential on any new projects I might develop because Orion, the network, and the stars wanted me to devote my full and exclusive time to making *Cagney & Lacey*.

The idea was to get us beyond this seven-show order to the next season, and the next after that, and so on. I wanted to do it. I simply wanted to share in the reward if I was successful. Medavoy said he understood. He had already removed Rosenbloom from the negotiations with me, believing his TV president was too sympathetic to my position. The youngest Orion partner said he would pressure Mace to give me something from his deal, since Mace, after all, wanted to be in the movie business with Orion. It was clear Medavoy was not averse to using his leverage to accomplish this.

"Leave Mace alone." I glared at Medavoy to emphasize my adamancy. "Regardless of my personal opinion of Mace Neufeld," I continued, "he negotiated a deal in good faith, and as far as I'm concerned it's final." I leaned into the West Coast Orion topper. "I am your responsibility. I'm not interested in Mace's profit points, which may or may not be worth a quarter. I want the same definition of gross and the same guaranteed dollars that I have in my current deal with your very own company. I am giving up the possibility of having enormous personal success and am doing so for you and for this series. What I am asking you to do is acknowledge that and give me some of your end, without going near Mace. I want it as a settlement—compensation for what I am sacrificing on my new deal."

Medavoy heard me. He said he would take my plea under advisement, but the result was a stone wall. It was clear that they felt they could rely on my emotional commitment to the show.

Meanwhile, the air date for *This Girl for Hire* drew near. I now had a constituency of thousands of hard-core *Cagney & Lacey* buffs who had proven to be an effective force. I composed a letter on *This Girl for Hire* letterhead to the fans of *Cagney & Lacey*. I explained that the stationery was in reference to a new project brought to them by the same team that had made *Cagney & Lacey* (creators Barbara Avedon & Barbara Corday, writers Steve Brown & Terry Louise Fisher and, of course, yours truly). I wrote that I welcomed their views (as I was sure the network would) as to the project's suitability as a series.

To make all this a less-than-blatant commercial spiel, I integrated a lot of update information on the progress of the putting together of *Cagney & Lacey*. That's what I knew they were interested in, that's what we had in common, and that was what provided a legitimate segue from the results of one lesson in TV democracy to my suggestion of expanding the process to my next project.

You think this lacks subtlety? Paramount didn't. Gary Nardino had left his post as studio chief, and the team that replaced his refused to pay the less than $1,000 postage bill. "Too much *Cagney & Lacey*," they exclaimed.

I was in the midst of being crowned the reigning monarch of public opinion manipulation in the television marketplace, and these assholes were giving me a hard time over chump change. I was distracted by my *Cagney & Lacey* problems, disheartened by Paramount's myopia, and generally tired of fighting. The effort died. *This Girl for Hire* went on the air to very good reviews and reaped a 19 share of audience. It was one of the lowest-rated made for television movies in history.

How I missed Gary Nardino.[37] With all of his bluster, he was always a terrific salesman and a marvelous showman.

A skinnier me with *This Girl for Hire* star Bess Armstrong. Harry Langdon took the photo, used for an ad in the *Daily Variety*, where I apologized for the lousy ratings.

Photo: Rosenzweig Personal Collection

---

[37]   Nardino had left his presidency at Paramount Television in 1983 to become an independent producer on that lot. His biggest success was as executive producer of the Showtime series *Brothers*. Ironically, years later, he went on to become chairman and CEO of Orion Television, a welcome addition to that organization, but too late an arrival to really help *Cagney & Lacey*. He died at far too young an age, just after the turn of the century.

Meanwhile, on the *Cagney & Lacey* front, agents Merritt Blake and Ronnie Meyer had worked out a new compromise on billing for their respective clients, only to have it renounced by long distance. In a phone call, from her film location in Yugoslavia, Tyne Daly instructed Merritt to "Tell Barney, 'Barbara was right!'"

(Some weeks before, when we were all flushed with excitement over the CBS call to put it all together again, Corday had facetiously predicted that the whole deal would probably fall apart over billing. Tyne was now saying just that.)

I didn't know what to do. To wait until Tyne returned from Yugoslavia would surely result in CBS pulling out. I considered flying to the Mace Neufeld location to attempt to talk her into it but thought better of that major piece of aggravation. From my view, the ultimate blow up was near. I felt Tyne was wrong. What was more important was that she believed she was right. No amount of money or concessions would rectify her emotional feelings of righteous indignation.

That very same week, Warner Bros. worked out billing on a Burt Reynolds, Richard Pryor, and Clint Eastwood film. That could be worked out; this could not. It was crazy.

To be fair, though she was being very uncompromising and difficult, Tyne, as usual, had a point of view—something to the effect that *"I saved the show last time by compromising my billing; now it's Sharon's turn."* The flaw in that logic was that it was never "her billing," but rather a scrivener's error that, in an unhappier time (the firing of her partner, Meg Foster) had been a wedge she had tried to use (I would guess), to either have us bring back Meg or to release her from her contract.

I focused my energy on trying to convince Sharon to be big about this and give in, pointing out that each of us has a dark side, a part of us that is unreasonable; Sharon has hers, and indeed so do I. The billing thing was Tyne's. Meanwhile, the really hard work was propping up Dick Rosenbloom and his meager staff at Orion.

They were not a high-powered or sophisticated gang. They were simply not used to playing for these kinds of stakes. Rosenbloom was fatigued. He incorrectly believed that if deals were not wrapped up in a matter of days, CBS would rescind the order. The pressure, the time consumption, the millions at stake, his limited staff, and his own lack of experience in this area were conspiring to inundate him. Orion Television had practically come to a halt. The morning of October 25, we *lost* our Detective Petrie, Carl Lumbly, and that same afternoon the deal for John Karlen's Harvey Lacey was almost blown. (The Lumbly loss was later rectified, and our Detective Petrie came back to the show.)

The bottleneck created by *Cagney & Lacey* at Rosenbloom's office jeopardized at least one of my other projects, and I could only imagine what other Orion contract producers with less access to Rosenbloom were going through. Coupled with this were the normal difficulties of trying to put any project together, plus the emotional and historical complications of this particular project, as well as the ambivalence we all shared about walking away while we were still a hit. Finally, there was my own situation with Orion and how *Cagney & Lacey* complicated my ongoing relationship with them.

It was truly a pressure-packed period, and all the while the press looked on, the letters from fans kept pouring in, and we—quite naturally—had to continue to smile and put a good face on the whole thing.

Leadership was what was required. Orion had plenty of legitimate contenders for the post—Krim, Pleskow, Medavoy—but they were not forthcoming. All those high-priced, high-powered merchants of diplomacy and not a word from any of them. Rosenbloom's stance, therefore, was to stonewall.

It was left to Tyne's pal and publicist Marilyn Reese and her friend Monique James from Sharon's team to try to do something. All I could do was to assure Monique that Rosenbloom was serious; that as little as Orion had contributed in this whole process, they would do no more.

Mmes. Reese and James put Tyne and Sharon together by transatlantic telephone, and the next day I was to learn that the two principals laughed and cried for forty-plus minutes with a compromise being affected.

"It's all going to work out," said Monique.

Not quite. Four days later, Tyne told Sharon, via phone from Yugoslavia, that she could not live with herself or digest her earlier agreement to share billing. She apparently went on and on with Sharon about a myriad of other offenses perpetrated against her, most of them by me (including a meant-to-be warm and humorous congratulatory wire I sent regarding "the compromise." A simple thank-you from me would have sufficed, and I should have known better than to do any more than that).

The next morning I arrived at my office to find a very long telex from Tyne, addressed to me, in which she used her selective memory to recount the offense (my "betrayal" of her vis-à-vis her billing) that she had to live with and how, under the circumstances, she could not participate in the show. Mike Medavoy and Harvey Shephard were copied. The fact that the telex came from the production site where she was working on a Mace Neufeld film did not go unnoticed.

I took the position with Rosenbloom, Shephard, and Monique that basically I had all of the previous week: for better or for worse, right or wrong, this is the issue on which Tyne Daly would not compromise. I didn't ask her to—Sharon did (and that was done without soliciting my advice). I was pleased to be proved wrong, although I wasn't wrong for very long. After some argument, Rosenbloom agreed on my approach; he and I would meet with Ronnie Meyer, Sharon, and Monique to discuss our three options:

(1) Sharon capitulates on this

(2) We recast Tyne

(3) We drop the project

It would be Sharon's decision, and I felt that compromising her billing was the least distasteful of the solutions for Ms. Gless.

I believed this billing thing would end Tyne's contractual demands (provided it was settled her way so that her "honour"—as she spelled it in her infamous telegram—was unsullied). If I was wrong on this, it could be disastrous. This was a volatile woman we were in business with. I thought that, for her, a lifetime of "us versus them" was being challenged by the possibility of her becoming a "them." I could only guess to what extent she might go to sabotage herself, and us along with her.

Another concern at that time, assuming Sharon did capitulate, was the secondary negotiations with CBS and what that network would give Tyne (and Georg's) production team. I believed that in this area, Tyne had totally unrealistic expectations of what she could get. But it didn't matter. She was not only angry but believed she now had the bosses at her mercy.

Weighed against all that anger was an interesting gig, a forum, a platform for her—and a lot of money. It would, I speculated at the time, be interesting to see what road she'd choose. Me? I was a bit depressed and uptight but trying to keep cool.

Rosenbloom and I met with Sharon, Ronnie Meyer, and Monique. We stated our case well, pointing out our three basic alternatives in light of what we believed to be Tyne's irrational but firm stand. Tyne was no longer interested in sharing billing as we had come to know it—what she demanded was for billing to continue to alternate week after week, including publicity and advertising, and, in addition, she now insisted she be the first billed on all future odd-number shows, believing this would give her the opening night in perpetuity. (This came back to haunt her for the life of the show, for if she had stopped to do her arithmetic, she would have known that in success—due to our short order in 1984 being only for seven episodes—every subsequent season would now begin with an even-number episode.)

Sharon was genuinely pissed and disillusioned. On matters political, Sharon had always looked up to Tyne. Now she had perceived a crack in the Tyne Daly egg (vis-à-vis Tyne's public stance on partnership, feminism, sharing, and the work being all important).

"Add to that, the billing," snorted Sharon. Ms. Gless would go home to think on her answer.

The next day, I awaited word. Sid Clute came by for lunch. He looked good, despite his then-two-year battle with cancer. He asked me to tell the girls that if they really wanted to know what was important (as opposed to billing), they should talk to him.

That same day, Farrah Fawcett called to tell me that she saw, and liked, *This Girl for Hire*. We both agreed we would both have liked it a lot better if she had played the lead. I then heard from Monique.

"Confidentially," she wanted to know, "would Orion—not CBS, not Barney Rosenzweig—make a gesture, a new Jaguar sedan for Sharon?" I passed this on to Rosenbloom. He was concerned how this bribe would be interpreted by Tyne. I relayed that to Monique, who shrilled at me; their worst fears had been realized: Tyne was now in control of the show! I quickly backpedaled. (If only my deal were settled, I'd put up the damn car.) Rosenbloom felt he was wallowing in rot, then added he did not have my talent for duplicity. (Talk about your left-handed compliments!) I, too, had become tired of all of this. I called Monique and told her, "No dice," and to do whatever she had to do. I capped off the afternoon with a day's-end argument with Rosenbloom over the as-yet-still-unresolved status of my own deal.

At home that night, Corday and I discussed it. She pointed out that virtually whatever I got from Orion would be a gift; that they didn't have to give me anything. I had heard that before from Rosenbloom but had tended to discount this, for I had "leverage." I did not have to do the show! Not so, Corday pointed out. "You do have to do it: emotionally, egotistically, and pragmatically. If you don't," she said, "what credibility will you ever have again in a network meeting? What, in fact, will your passionate commitment to a show mean if you walk from this series, which has brought you more of the things you went into this business for in the first place than anything you have ever done?"

She was right. I had to do it. Corday was terrific at this stuff. How I wish I'd had her talking to Tyne and Sharon. I informed Lee the next morning to make my deal.

Corday kiddingly reminisced with me about Leo Corday, her songwriter father who, in 1949, sold "See the USA in Your Chevrolet" for $750 and no royalties. Bad deals seemed to run in the family.[38]

Late in the day, Merritt called me to tell me he had heard from Dick Rosenbloom that Sharon had given in on the billing crisis. My momentary relief was stymied by Merritt's question: What could he tell Tyne? Could he express our sincere feelings that we all felt the right thing had finally been done? He said he believed this was essential to getting Tyne to accept.

I told him he might be able to get people to eat shit, but I doubted if he could get them to say they liked it.

I passed this newest wrinkle on to Rosenbloom, who asked me to handle things with Tyne's agent. First, I called Sharon. "Thank you," I said. Sharon wanted to know why I sounded so sad. I fibbed. "It's been a difficult week, and I know how hard this has been for you."

"Don't shit me, Barney," she said as she laughed. We had a nice talk. She had spent the night alternating between disenchantment and anger over Tyne's latest position. I warned her to steel herself for a call from Tyne over the weekend, and she said she was not ready for that. She did assure me that all would be OK when shooting rolled around. I remember thinking how much I liked her. I called Merritt back. He was still searching for what to tell Tyne of an upbeat nature.

I told him I'd just gotten off the phone with Sharon, who had been in tears for six hours, and I suggested he merely say to his client that Tyne got what she wanted and that Sharon obviously wanted to do the show enough to let it happen.

Merritt wanted to know if anyone had acknowledged the efficacy of Tyne's position. I coldly let him know that in all of our opinions, Tyne's position was "bullshit." I reminded him of his earlier statements: "Just give in on this, and that's it." Now he wanted more. I warned him, in my most menacing tone, that if this didn't work, "I will bury you and your client!"

---

[38]   Leo Corday was a lyricist of such modest hits as "There's No Tomorrow," "How Many Stars Have to Shine," and "Take a Little Off the Top." His most famous work was the Chevrolet theme, made famous by singer Dinah Shore.

Calmer, having said that, I suggested he simply tell his client to send Sharon champagne and a simple thank-you—not to call, blaming the difficulties of time changes and long-distance telephone wires.

The deals with Sharon and Tyne were finally closed with Orion, but there was still no authorization for me to move forward with plans for production because both women still had negotiations to complete with CBS (separate and apart from their dealings with Orion). That process dragged on.

We were supposed to start shooting in six weeks, and I had neither staff nor crew, nor sets, nor finished scripts. Rosenbloom just might have been the unhappiest man in America.

CHAPTER 24

THE AUDITION

Richard Rosenbloom's despair during the negotiating process had turned to anger and to prognosis of gloom and doom. His negativity impacted all of us. It was so debilitating, and all so false. Everyone in America, save for Rosenbloom, knew this was going to work. No matter, he would not authorize any expenditure, and so we waited, wasting time and (eventually) paying crews for an inordinate amount of overtime for last minute, hurried preparations. It was all so silly.

"Maybe not so silly after all," I noted in my diary. Sharon Gless finally ended her CBS negotiations by telling them to forget their offer of a guaranteed movie of the week. She would stick with her Orion deal and didn't "need CBS's charity." Each day I was more and more impressed with this gal. Tyne Daly, on the other hand, having just arrived in New York from Yugoslavia, told her agent she would sleep on the final CBS offer.

Tyne Daly's previous M.O.W. price had been, perhaps, $40,000. CBS had offered her a guaranteed $200,000—plus everything Orion had pledged—and she had to *sleep* on it!? My diary note was: *"How outrageous."* Even allowing for a price increase because of her Emmy, one had to concede this was inflationary beyond reason. I was growing so sick of this whole process; I found myself hoping she would turn us down, longing for the press conference that would surely follow: "Lacey says no to Cagney." I was looking forward to "going public" with this entire mess, but then I would jog myself back to the realization that I must root for this all to come together—or must I?

I was not at all sure how Tyne and I would work together in the future. In addition, I was feeling like a jerk on the subject of my own deal. We had wasted so much time on this negotiating business that I was increasingly pessimistic as to what kind of staff I could put together, especially with Rosenbloom persisting with his anti-actor, anti-writer, anti-money spending approach. I just didn't want to root for this anymore—*que sera, sera.*

My agent, Lee Rosenberg, believed I should walk away from the whole thing; attorney Stu Glickman agreed with Corday that I really couldn't do that. I didn't know what to do, but it depressed me when, on top of my not knowing, my advisors couldn't agree. The real reason for doing the show was "I enjoyed it so much." The reality was that, save for a few weeks the previous spring, the whole production phase had been pure torture.

Rosenbloom called to tell me that CBS promised a second M.O.W. to Tyne after the 1985–86 season for $250,000, and, as a result, Monique was on a rampage. Sharon's camp had turned down CBS's "charity" (believing it was only one film at $200,000). Now, discovering they could have had a second film at $250,000 had, as far as Monique was concerned, blown the deal with Gless.

I talked to Monique. She was beside herself, believing she had badly advised her client. It would not, she said, be out of line for Sharon to fire both her and Ronnie Meyer. She had forgotten, she went on, the lesson of twenty-eight years under Lew Wasserman. She should have been tougher.

"What is the moral here?" she railed. "The bad side won." I told Monique I believed that she and her client took the high road, that they had a good deal and had gained the respect of all parties. Monique appreciated many of my comments, but she wasn't buying.

Ronnie Meyer and Monique James rightfully (I thought) believed that Tyne and Merritt Blake had used them for all their negotiations. Tyne had used Sharon to escalate her deal in every way, basing both her episodic and M.O.W. fees not on what she had received in the past, but, rather, what the, in those days, "more in demand" Ms. Gless had been paid. That's OK, they said, but now Tyne had played extra tough and gotten even more—that was what was driving the Gless corps insane.

Merritt Blake had used Ronnie Meyer and had come out the more successful agent. For a time, I was bogged down in having to deal with the managers' bent egos, but this was short-lived, as Sharon finally heard from Monique about the situation and couldn't care less about what Tyne got or didn't get from CBS.

The deal was finally set!

A week later, I chaired a publicity luncheon at Yamato's restaurant for our stars and their publicists, which is only noteworthy because of Tyne. She acted as if nothing had ever happened, as if the last several pages in this history did not exist. She seemed full of enthusiasm and raring to go. It was often thus with Ms. Daly, as I remembered then that it was she who got me into the diary-keeping business in the first place. So much with her was all illusion—except when it wasn't.

One month later, 1983 was drawing to a close. It had taken all of the fall's three months to make this deal, but now commencement of production on our seven-show order was only days away. I did some interviews, planned to do some more. The scripts—the ones originally developed by Lefcourt in the hopes of a pickup nearly a year before—were coming along nicely, praised by most, save for Tyne and Sharon, which was the norm. There had been a few minor references to the difficult weeks of negotiations but nothing too serious. Sharon had refused to accept any of the motor homes we'd shown her; Tyne continued to push for an unneeded full-time stunt coordinator. Stan persistently manifested his penurious ways (regarding furniture, phone lines, or any of the necessities of life at Lacy Street); Rosenbloom still headed up the cheapest operation in all of show business (as witness the company's Christmas gifts, usually consisting of some chintzy paperweight with the Orion logo, or attitudes toward minimal increases for long-time loyal employees). In other words, business as usual. I was focusing on the things that made 1983 one of the best years of my life, made even more so by the realization that 1984 could be even better.

"I feel like Warren Beatty," I would say to the press early in 1984. "I feel like I died, and Mr. Jordan let me come back to Earth to play quarterback for the Los Angeles Rams."[39]

There was another side to this. I also felt like a fool. Upton Sinclair wrote at length about the nature of big business and big money interests. The essence of Sinclair's point is that these capitalistic elements care for one thing and one thing alone: the maintenance of the status quo. It is that status quo, he wrote, that keeps big business and big money where they are and where they want to be.

Applying this to my industry in 1984, there were three major entities: the television networks, the A.C. Nielsen Company, and Madison Avenue. Then, as now, the networks broadcast programs, Nielsen rated them, and then—based on those figures—Madison Avenue placed its clients' advertising dollars at the networks. The networks each made hundreds of millions of dollars per year, Nielsen made

---

[39]   Reference is to the then-current feature film *Heaven Can Wait*, starring Beatty and based on the earlier Robert Montgomery vehicle *Here Comes Mr. Jordan*.

tens of millions, and Madison Avenue made hundreds of millions. Everybody won (and continues to win).

Into this perfect symmetry came this intrepid producer—corresponding with fans, contacting the press, and generally stirring things up to such a point that a network called and said, "We have made a mistake; can you put it back together again?"

They wanted seven episodes in the spring. I had demurred. I objected to being asked to audition. I asked for a full commitment, saying we would do the seven if they would also contract for twenty-two more for the following fall.

"Out of the question," they said.

"All right," I countered in those early days of September. "What about thirteen? I could be ready for air in January."

At that point Harvey Shephard took me aside. "Barney, don't be a schmuck," his tone was conspiratorial. "If you go on in January, you will be murdered by the February sweeps and the Winter Olympics. By doing seven, I can put you on in March after all that is past. You will be on in March and April against weak competition, and (with all the attendant promotion and publicity) your success will be assured."

Later, in a meeting with Harvey Shephard and Alan Levin, it was further avowed that CBS was not in this for the short haul. We would be given all the help possible, including a protected time slot. I bought it. I bought it, and I sold it. I sold it to my lawyer, to Sharon, to Tyne, and to their representatives. I gave upbeat interviews: CBS was, no doubt, completely sincere.

Our protected time period turned out to be our old failed slot of 10 PM Monday night, replacing our replacement, *Emerald Point*, which had proved to be a dismal failure.[40] Then we learned we would be preempted two weeks after our debut in March. It meant we would only get four shows on the air before CBS would make its decision. Four chances—not seven—and half of them after a hurtful preemption, in the weakest spot of the CBS schedule (a slot that just before our debut received a 14 share of audience). Then I learned from Shephard that only the dates in March would count. After that the season would be over, and the competition was insignificant, he said. Now our seven shots were two.

---

[40]   It was doing worse than we had done and, in this new year of 1984, was averaging less than a 20 share of audience.

Next I heard from Mort Pollack,[41] who told me of the great promo plans he had authorized. He couldn't imagine that I'd remember the figures from the past, and that this great promotion campaign was actually 20 percent below what we had had for our 1982 debut. Then I read in the trades that Harvey Shephard would experiment with *Emerald Point*, placing it after *Dallas* on Friday. It was the spot I had wanted. What could I conclude?

Harvey Shephard had positioned himself and CBS in the best win-win position possible. If, by some miracle, *Cagney & Lacey* was a success, CBS had a hit, which it could always use. In the more likely event that it were to fail, well then, you see, that would be proof that the system was correct, that it all works. Nielsen would be right. CBS would be right. And America should stop sending letters to networks and messing with this very perfect order of things.

The only way this could be better is if it didn't cost much. And it didn't. Five million dollars for seven hours of prime-time programming, a chance at a hit without development costs and included in the package (win or lose), was the greatest public relations campaign a major corporation could have. A chance to prove to their customers that they were not a mere monolith but a company with a responsive ear to the public will.

All of this I finally pieced together as my company naively went before the cameras that January on the first of seven episodes. There was nothing I could do about any of this, of course. No one I could "confront" or "expose." It was simply the game of capitalism, as played by the big boys, and, as stated earlier, they call it "win-win" (for them).

Back at Lacy Street, the tension was palpable. I joked that it was so thick one needed a machete to move from room to room. Emotional outbursts occurred on a daily basis, as each episode took on the magnitude of a pilot.

We were far from hitting the ground with alacrity. The timing between Sharon and Tyne was off just enough to be troublesome. The pressures of the "audition" were mounting; the scar tissue from the brutal negotiating process far from healed.

At one point, I pulled Tyne aside. "You are carrying the importance of your Emmy in one hand and the weight of the series in the other," I said. She understood. She had been pressing, working too hard. She promised to relax and enjoy.

Our staff now consisted of Peter Lefcourt and Terry Louise Fisher. The scripts were basically those developed by Peter in the fallacious expectation of a pickup nearly

---

[41]   Then in charge of networks on-air promo and advertising campaigns.

a year before. Chris Abbott was now no longer available. She had, in the time since our cancellation, accepted the offer to be writer-producer of Tom Selleck's Hawaii-based series, *Magnum, P.I.*

I brought writer Joel Oliansky into the mix to direct an episode, hoping I could induce him to write for us in the future. He was critical of the script I gave him to direct ("Partners," written by Patricia Green). He did not feel it was as good as the stuff from last season. He was right, and he was wrong. What he knew of last season's product was the end result that he had seen on television, inclusive of my work in editorial, the late-night script sessions with the women during production, and—more importantly—the efforts on stage of Sharon and Tyne. He had never before had to read one of our scripts in the raw.

Despite those points and my affection for both Peter and Terry (who were fabulous to work with), I had to agree with Joel that the level of writing was not up to the standard deserved by Sharon or Tyne's considerable talents.

Writers I had worked with, such as Oliansky and Ronald M. Cohen, I theorized, could eat Peter and Terry for breakfast and not gain weight. I worried that this duo of mine could certainly not be measured favorably against our competition of Bochco, Milch, and Kozell on *Hill Street Blues*, Fontana on *St. Elsewhere*, Holtzman on *thirtysomething*, Caron and Hall on *Moonlighting,* or David Kelley on just about anything. I continued to consider Steve and Terry a qualitative drop off, even from their *Cagney & Lacey* predecessors, Smith and Crais (though this judgment may, quite possibly, be unfair).

On my writing duo's plus side was their indefatigability, affability, work ethic, and desire to please. It counted for much. Nevertheless, I still continued my search for deeper, richer, fuller, better, believing that the writing would provide the key to that. I forced myself to get back in the swing of things, to realize that, yes, after all I'd been through, I still had to make a show. I spent more and more time with the writers, the film editors, and late at night with Sharon and Tyne. An interesting pattern developed that impacted heavily on our writing style.

At the end of our minimum twelve-hour shooting day, Sharon and Tyne would sign off the clock and repair to their respective dressing rooms to shower and remove their makeup. They would then convene in one or the other's motor home for a hug as a demonstration of solidarity, a quick drink to celebrate the day's work, a joke or two, and they would then address themselves to the next day's eight-plus pages of dialogue.

Somewhere in the middle of the second drink, I would be summoned from my office to join them. They were, of course, critical of the writing or occasionally confused by the intent of a scene. I would ask to hear it once, as written. They would try to get through "this shit," but invariably got hung up on a phrase, a speech, or an attitude that was bothering them.

I would hear all of this, make whatever points I felt were necessary for the meaning of the piece, and then begin to make minor adjustments in the scenes themselves. With each successive pass through, they became more familiar with the essence of what was there on the page and therefore more and more able to communicate an idea with less and less verbiage.

I have been quoted as saying that on *Cagney & Lacey* our best writing was done with an eraser. It was to this process that I referred. That is what was transpiring in those motor home meetings. Cutting, erasing, and making the scenes less and less verbal and more and more elliptical by using fewer words as the actors became more immersed in, and familiar with, the material.

You could never begin by writing this way, for the actors, or any other reader for that matter, wouldn't have a clue as to what the scene was about. But now, by making our two stars part of the process, it became their own. And in the hands of two such talented performers as Sharon Gless and Tyne Daly, the results were something to watch indeed.

These sessions would generally end between midnight and one AM. I would leave the rewritten pages for Peter to put through in the morning when he got in, usually attaching a note telling him what an extraordinary experience he had missed. It was what I imagine the theater to be at its best. It was stimulating, exhilarating, and inspiring.

Departing Lacy Street was like leaving home and family. Every night I would have to adjust to my real-life relations, who seemed almost like acquaintances compared to the kith and kin of *Cagney & Lacey*. The good news at my "real" home was that Corday basically understood.... She not only knew the demands of the job, but there was also the very real fact that she was at least as busy at her own job as I was at mine.

At the same time, I lived in dread of our first episode airing and the nation's press wondering—in print—just what all the fuss was about. How embarrassing all this would be if, after all the hoopla (with which I was so personally identified), it all came out to be just another show.

At the Beverly Hills Hotel where the announcement was made by CBS chief Harvey Shephard that a mistake had been made and that *Cagney & Lacey* would be back.

Photo: Rosenzweig Personal Collection

CHAPTER 25

AGAIN WITH THE LIGHTS AND SIRENS

The subject of pressure brings this narrative to Cedars-Sinai Hospital in Los Angeles. I was taken there by ambulance in late February 1984, midway through production of our fifth episode[42] and only weeks before our March 19 premiere on CBS.

Somehow I had herniated a disc in my fifth lumbar in the lower part of my back, a stress-related incident if ever there was one. I wound up being in traction and receiving physical therapy from the hospital for twelve full days.

Video equipment was installed in my hospital room, along with an extra phone line. From my hospital bed I continued my work, complete with writer consultations, casting conferences, editorial notes, and network meetings.

By the third day in traction at the hospital, most of the people on *Cagney & Lacey* had called, save for Sharon, who had sent a sweet note and flower (a simple yellow rose), and Tyne, who, to my surprise, sent a note via my worthy assistant, PK Knelman. It was a lovely, and loving, note. It was hard to keep up with Tyne's moods; the swings were enormous. I did appreciate the pressure she must have felt. Lord knows I felt it.

Several nights a week, I would work in the hospital on our video equipment with PK from 6 to 11 PM. I would give her my notes to pass on to the editors on three

---

42   "Bounty Hunter" was one of the best episodes we made and featured a terrific (and rare for us) guest star appearance, in this case from Brian Dennehy. Bill Duke directed with some help from James Frawley. Script was written by Steve Brown. Mr. Dennehy, with his appearance on Broadway in *Death of a Salesman*, became one of the many Tony Award-winning performers connected with our show.

episodes ("Matinee," written by Chris Abbott, directed by Karen Arthur; "Partners," written by Patricia Green and directed by Joel Oliansky; and "Baby Broker," written by Terry Louise Fisher and directed by John Patterson). They were all good shows, but "Baby Broker" was a stunner. I wanted it to open our season.

By the end of my first week in the hospital, CBS began filling the void. They admitted "Baby Broker" was a good episode, but they didn't think it was commercial enough to be first to air. We were back to talking lights and sirens again. They could not—would not—heed what this show was about.

It was difficult, if not impossible, for me to make this fight from my hospital bed. No one was at those screenings who could tackle Shephard. He and Tony Barr wanted "Matinee" to go first (not so terrible, it was a solid episode). What was disturbing was that they couldn't see the sell in "Baby Broker."

It had all the elements of those ABC exploitation M.O.W.s that knocked us off the air in the first place. I was concerned, and the staff was now getting nervous, about the network's reaction to our script for episode seven. It was good but *very* light on lights and sirens.

We were all getting a bit paranoid that CBS was still looking for a cop show here. I could win this fight, I thought, if I could just get out of traction and on my feet.

Episode seven, "Choices," written by Terry Louise Fisher and directed by Karen Arthur, is my personal favorite episode of the 125 we made. It was our biological clock show and came about as a result of conversations with Corday and her best friend, Ann Daniel, who was then approaching her fortieth birthday. Ms. Daniel was childless and confronting that very same timing issue in her own life. I decided that if, indeed, these seven audition episodes were to be our last, we were not going to have a body of work of nearly thirty hours of prime-time programming—featuring a single, childless, working woman in her late thirties—without exploring this issue.

Weeks before my hospitalization, I had talked with Peter and Terry about this, and, at my insistence, Terry agreed to write the episode herself. Should *Cagney & Lacey* be renewed for the following year, we most definitely did not want Cagney to have a child. Marriage was out of the question for the same reason. We wanted to continue to explore the relationship of contrasts we had already begun to enjoy with Christine and Mary Beth. It would be counterproductive, we felt, to have them lead similar lives.

If she was not going to have a child, what would happen vis-à-vis her pregnancy, as dictated by the biological clock idea? We felt abortion was too big an issue for us to handle in one episode, and one—we thought—was, quite possibly, all we had left. It was also doubtful that at the time we could have won network approval for a Cagney decision to abort, which is what we felt she would have done, despite her upbringing as a Catholic.

Having her do what Hollywood heroines had done for years (fall down a flight of stairs and miscarry) was something we longed to avoid. What then? Well, initially, I had a glib solution.

Carl Lumbly, who was the actor who played Detective Marcus Petrie, had, as mentioned earlier, been "lost" to the series during the negotiating process. His feelings had been hurt at what he considered a slight, which, in fact, was really only Orion's typically poor attention to the artist's psyche. I was eventually able to woo him back, but only on one condition: his return would be for these seven episodes only and that it would be his option alone as to whether he would return beyond that. My sell to Lumbly had been that rather than simply have Petrie disappear, why not work a few weeks more, continue in the ensemble he had been part of from the beginning, and assure himself of an episode that would deal with his leaving the show—maybe even complete with a terrific death scene? What actor could resist that?

So, my solution to Terry was simple: "Let's find a way, an excuse, for Cagney to be temporarily teamed with Petrie on a particular case. It should be a real simple case with easily recognizable bad guys. In the third or fourth act, there's a terrific chase. Petrie drives, and Cagney rides shotgun. Our detectives' car goes out of control. Petrie is killed; Cagney is injured. A by-product of that injury is that Cagney miscarries. But the obvious melodrama is masked by the tragedy that has occurred to a fellow officer and one of our regulars."

Terry bought it. So did Peter. She went off to work out all the story beats, and a week later was back in my office in dismay. First off, Carl Lumbly had exercised his option in an unexpected way; he had decided to return with us should the show be picked up. He did not want Petrie to die. That would be the least of it. The network would be yet another, more powerful, county heard from.

Tony Barr had unequivocally turned down the idea that Cagney be pregnant. This was network television in the 1980s, and, if CBS had yet to allow us to have the sound of a toilet flush in the women's room. They were (at least) being consistent in making this demand.

Cagney's pregnancy was totally unacceptable to Mr. Barr, and, as head of current programming for CBS and an important spokesperson for that network, he would not be moved. Barr had reluctantly accepted the fact that Cagney (in a pre-AIDS era) was a healthy, aggressive, heterosexual female with many sleepover boyfriends, but, quite obviously, he was not the least bit interested in dealing with the potential consequences of that kind of behavior.

I called Tony myself. I listened and, while disagreeing, understood the depth of his feeling on this issue. I believed it would be counterproductive to attempt an end run here by going directly to Shephard as I had occasionally done in the past.

(Every CBS executive knew of the relationship I had developed with their chief and the entree I had to him. It was a gun I generally kept holstered, but a weapon nonetheless. For Tony to confront me so solidly on this indicated that to go over his head would quite possibly bring an end to our working relationship.)

I suggested a compromise. "What if Cagney only thinks she's pregnant?"

Barr was a bit nonplussed. "Not even for most of the play," I continued, "only Act One and a small part of Act Two." I went on to briefly indicate how I thought it was morally wrong for us to have this franchise and not deal with an issue that women—especially working women—were forced to face every day.

Barr graciously accepted the offer. Call it compromise, call it face-saving— whatever, we had a "deal." Terry Louise was apprehensive, inquiring, "What am I supposed to do with this?"

I was on my game. First of all, we had to change the story anyway, since Lumbly had opted to breathe life back into Marcus Petrie. What we should go for now, I urged, was one of our real, moral dilemma/emotional shows.

Experience had taught us that in doing that it was best to keep the cop story simple. I referred to April Smith's script on "Recreational Use." "Use that caper!"

Both Peter and Terry looked at a loss.

"It's a year and a half later. The case from that show is finally coming to trial. Do the courtroom stuff you did so well in "Open and Shut Case.""

The very pragmatic Ms. Fisher had a question: "What about Cagney's pregnancy?"

My rejoinder was rapid fire: "Act One, maybe even part of Act Two, is the same as you had, all the same beats, all the same concerns. Cagney and the audience believe she is pregnant. Should she, should she not have the child? Does she want to marry? Her anger at being forced to decide now, her fear of what it does to her career, of the men at the precinct finding out, her embarrassment at the drugstore where she purchases the pregnancy test, all of that remains for us."

"Then she finds out she's not pregnant," Terry said without enthusiasm.

"Right!" I cheer-led, "And she speculates on what might have been and how she *feels* about all that."

"Hardly a page-turner," was the response from my distaff writer.

"Let me tell you something, Terry. That's where you're wrong. This is the stuff that makes episodic television great. You can't do what I'm talking about in a movie or a movie of the week, but here, in this forum, the audience is vested. They *care* about Christine Cagney. We've got 'em. They'll watch her ruminate on the vagaries of life for an entire episode if we told them to, but here we're also giving them a story—not to placate them 'cause they don't need it. We give them a story to show that in the middle of all this, Cagney still has a job. She still has to go to work, and that's the way it goes for a woman in the workplace in this society."

"What about Act Four? What's my finish?"

Ms. Fisher, it would appear, wanted it all. I didn't miss a beat. "Cagney is not pregnant, and she knows it and has dealt with it. The caper is over, and Cagney and Lacey have carried the day in court. The bad guy is gonna go to jail. They decide to celebrate. They go to a bar and get drunk as they talk about life, love, and babies. We'll shoot it the last day of our schedule. We'll use real booze; we'll use multiple cameras and shoot the shit out of the scene while those two gals get plastered." (This last detail, arguably, was one of the worst ideas I have *ever* had.)

Terry saw I was not to be denied; her pad was now open, and she was taking notes. I was drawing on the overlapping period involving my last days with old Malibu girlfriend Jeannine, and my early times with Corday.

"'Neil called,' says Cagney." I now had begun doing imitations of Cagney or Lacey, as the scene called for, employing a modest falsetto and slightly drunken slur as I interpolated both parts.

Terry's note-taking would get more furious. Lefcourt was the audience.

"'What did he say?' Lacey wants to know.

"'That I'm a cactus.'

"'I beg your pardon,' says the very drunk Mary Beth.

"Cagney answers, 'She's a fern. I'm a cactus. He says that's why he loves me. I don't need any watering at all.'

"'That bastard,' slurs Mary Beth."

"Cagney argues, 'No, no, he's right. It's me. I'm all mixed up on …' whatever. You know, Terry. All the stuff we want to hear her say about her life."

"Then what?" asked my reluctant author.

"When she starts to get down about her ambivalence," I continued, "Lacey chimes in—ever the optimist." (Again I did my vocal imitation of the drunken duo as Terry scribbled her notes).

"'No, no, Chris. Don't you see you've given the thoughts sound—sound and air. Now you'll be able to deal with it all!'

"There's a long silence." I took a grand pause, let it all sink in. "No one says anything," I continued. "Lacey can't stand it. 'So whaddaya gonna do?'

"'Huh?' asks Cagney."

"'Whaddaya gonna do?' Lacey demands."

"Cagney takes a long beat, takes a swig from her drink, and then, with a twinkle in her eyes, says, 'I'm gonna do just what Scarlett O'Hara would do. I'm gonna think about it tomorrow.'

"Cagney smiles, Lacey smiles, they clink glasses, freeze frame, end of episode."

Terry put down her pencil. I wanted to relax, but I didn't know if I'd made a sale.

Lefcourt spoke up: "Do you understand what Barney's giving you the license to do here, Terry? He's letting you write a one-act play for Christ's sake." Terry Louise Fisher slowly nodded her head, and the meeting was over.

It is no coincidence that the only time I played a speaking role in *Cagney & Lacey* was in this episode. It was a vignette I wrote as an introduction to the final drunk scene. I played a stereotypical Broadway producer who storms past the two drunken detectives, irked at his show's poor notices to the point of exasperation: "Doesn't anyone know what a producer does?" my character wailed.

Well, hardly anyone.

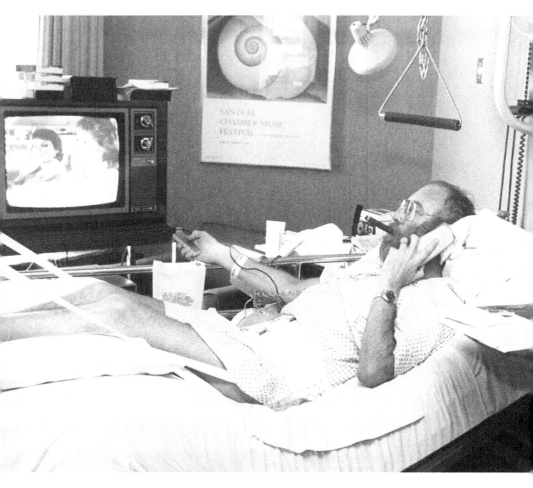

On my back, in traction, and on the job. Not sure how I got away with smoking a cigar at Cedars-Sinai Hospital.

Photo: Rosenzweig Personal Collection

CHAPTER 26

CHOCOLATE AND VANILLA

I was beginning my second week of traction and back treatments at Cedars-Sinai, when Terry Louise Fisher called with the news that CBS hated the script on the biological clock episode. We were within two weeks of shooting this material, and the network wanted major changes. They were even willing to go back to the original idea they had once rejected—let Cagney be pregnant and miscarry. At least, they said, that had some action and drama.

Terry, Peter, and I had all come to love the compromise we had been forced into and did not want to return to the original notion. Peter indicated to me that Terry was in a funk about all this, and so I told them both not to despair. They didn't even have to meet with Barr or anyone else at the network; I would handle it and call for a meeting at the hospital. Tony agreed to meet with me in my room at Cedars and even brought his assistant, Karen Cooper.

After the amenities were over, I asked to hear their notes on Terry's script. I was attentive as they recited every predictable complaint you could possibly imagine. The bottom line was that the picture was, in that pre-*Seinfeld* era, "about nothing," that it had "no action," was "talky," and, as if that were not enough, a "major bore." They felt there would be no one left in America to watch the less-than-stirring conclusion I had all but dictated.

I acknowledged their concerns, conceded the possibility that they might be right, and disarmed them with the news that I had a solution. Having said that, I then went on to state that I did not *believe* they were right and that, while they were presenting a unified front on their side, I had Lefcourt, Fisher, Gless, Daly, and Corday on my side.

"We all love the script," I said. I went on, "Here, then, is the problem. You say it's vanilla, and I say it's chocolate. I can do a lot of things to this, but I can't make it vanilla. I will never be able to satisfy you or your notes on this script."

I think they assumed my solution was that I therefore had another script we could get ready in time for production. Nope. The solution was that they pull the plug on this, the last of our contracted-for seven episodes.

"Let's make six," I said. "I'm sure I can get Orion to come around. The six should be more than enough for Shephard to make his pickup decision one way or the other, so no hard feelings." This was a major bluff. The cost to Orion of one less episode into which they could divide all the costs of doing business on our series would have been in the tens, possibly hundreds, of thousands. I wouldn't have flinched even if I wasn't in traction.

"We're not going to pull any plug," said Mr. Barr. "You've made too many good episodes and done too much good work for us not to honor your desire to make this one your way."

They understood that I could not accomplish their notes. They got it that they would never like this episode and could only hope that there would be a next season and that I would then see eye to eye with them, based on what—they were totally convinced—would be a learning experience for me.

I thanked them, and we parted pals. Well, they parted. I was still in traction.

A week later, I was finally released from the hospital and, against the doctor's advice, immediately went back to work. Sharon was basically content with our biological clock episode and seemed most concerned with the two scenes involving Ron, the new confidante created for her by Terry Louise, as the Cagney counterpart to Harvey Lacey. Ron was a new neighbor, and he would be single, good-looking, but gay. He and Cagney were to become pals.

Why gay? Our thinking was, if Cagney needed someone to talk to other than Lacey, we did not want this person to be another woman; that would just compete with what we already had. If he were a heterosexual male, then the romantic possibilities clogged things up for us. The character of her father (played by Dick O'Neill) really didn't work that well for us in certain areas, so, quite naturally, we came up with this. Terry had written him wonderfully well.

Meanwhile, broadcast standards continued to plague us on language concerning the pregnancy test stuff in the script, among other things Cagney's line where she needed to excuse herself from a conversation with her new neighbor because it was time for her to "pee in a bottle."

I met and read several actors for the part of Ron, the new neighbor, and Sharon participated in the process. One Saturday (so selected because Ms. Gless's shooting schedule didn't give us time on a weekday), Sharon and Terry Louise came to my house for a script conference, mostly on the Ron scenes. That same afternoon, the new *Ms.* magazine arrived, and we were featured nicely. I was feeling good, as it was my only day (thus far) sans back brace. Sunday, I spent at Lacy Street preparing for Monday night's presentation for the National Organization for Women's fund-raising event for the L.A. chapter, which amounted to putting together film clips from all of our—as yet to be broadcast—new season's work.

The following day, I met with Harvey Shephard. I wanted to push him for more promotion money and more publicity for the show, but, almost before my pitch began, Shephard interrupted. He wanted to know if we had cast our seventh episode yet. I thought it a strange question on such a minor issue (considering it was coming from the head of network programming). When I said we hoped to be fully cast that same afternoon and that we would start shooting in forty-four hours, he lowered the boom.

It was a major mistake, he believed, for Cagney's new confidante to be gay. He pointed out how much resistance the show already had in small-town America, how "they" had yet to accept mature, working women as leads.

"Please," he begged me, "win that fight before you take on another."

He felt that I might be undoing all the hard work that had been, and was being, done to save this show. I was not prepared for this broadside.

I told Shephard I would do what I could, but I was in turmoil inside. What would I tell the writers? What would I tell Sharon, who had already registered her enthusiasm for, at last, getting her own version of a Harvey Lacey? I didn't have a clue. Following this, Mr. Shephard went on to assure me of his good will toward the series and of his intention to do even more to promote the show. I staggered out of this meeting in which I got all I could have asked for, but there was no joy due to this new wrinkle.

I canceled my public speaking engagement at my step-daughter's school,[43] telephoned the writers to alert them, returned to Lacy Street to tell Sharon and confront my then-despondent writing staff.

---

[43]   Barbara's only child, Evan Corday, was then entering adolescence and attending a private high school in Los Angeles. Today she is a successful literary agent in Hollywood.

I improvised. "Let it be the brother!" (Cagney's long-estranged California-based brother who she has this confab with.) Terry and Peter were glassy-eyed, as they knew few of the jokes in the script worked with the brother. Still, they would try to make my fix work.

Sharon was terrific. She saw how difficult this was for me and immediately shifted into her team-player mode. If I had asked her to help me fight CBS on this, she would have—I am sure—gone to the wall with me. Both of us realized this was no time to make such a stand. We wanted to live to fight another day.

All afternoon was spent polishing the reels for that night's presentation to a hundred-plus paying guests. I could not, in the time allowed and with my back aching, and with my mind on this script problem, get this down to less than an hour. Too long—too bad.

The evening began as I was being driven to the screening room. (I could not drive due to my back injury.) As we left Lacy Street, I was handed the new *TV Guide* with a "Welcome Back *Cagney & Lacey*" article by Erich Segal. The essay was a three-page love letter to the series. I had never imagined anything like this. It was a glowing commentary by a respected writer, published in a magazine with more viewers interested in television than any other in the world, and all on the eve of our premiere. It was staggering. Then the screening, which was greeted by cheers, tears, and a standing ovation! It is what most people would consider a triumphant day. I only mention this with any hedge at all to indicate how distracted I was by the morning's meeting with Shephard.

I retired at 11 PM with a sleeping pill, a new addition to my life due to the back injury. At 4 AM, I awoke with a start. The brother solution would not work. I had given the writers an impossible fix. I went to my den and began writing, completing the two requisite scenes by 7:30 AM.

At 9:30, Lefcourt arrived at my house to discuss Terry's new pages. I presented him with mine, and Terry's went into the dumper. My solution worked and survived (with minor modifications) that afternoon's reading and that evening's meeting with Sharon. I then went to approve the dub on the first episode and concluded my twenty-hour day at 11:40 PM.

I slept well, despite a horrific nightmare, and awoke to discover we were in the *New York Times* with an interview with me and a reminder that production on the much-maligned biological clock episode was finally under way. A good start to a good day.

Oh, yes, there is more. The broadcast standards notes on language also came to a head (no pun intended). In trying to make some "horse trades" with them, I pointed out the good news that Ron was no longer gay. "Oh no," they moaned. "We felt he was a good image for the gay community." Sometimes it is very hard to keep up in this business.

A digression or two is in order for those who keep score on such things:

My fix turned out to be, at best, a band-aid. I converted Ron to a heterosexual recently out of a long and (he thought) loving marriage; he was, thus, too damaged to be fair game for Ms. Cagney. We cast it, shot it, but I eventually excised the entire subplot, along with most references to the new neighbor from the finished filmed product. (Among other things this meant losing the hard-won line about peeing in a bottle.) Terry Louise Fisher's creation of the gay neighbor would finally appear in our last two seasons on the air (86–87 and 87–88) with nary a whimper from CBS. Barry Sattels played the part, and Ms. Fisher, then with *L.A. Law*, objected to our use of this character she had created until we reminded her that she had fashioned this work while on the *Cagney & Lacey* payroll, specifically for *Cagney & Lacey*, and that the character was, therefore, owned by Orion and *Cagney & Lacey*. We also pointed out that she had been cashing her character reuse fees on a regular basis without mentioning any kind of problem. The objection was quickly dropped.

The day of our opening night arrived, and with it excellent to out-and-out rave reviews for our episode of "Matinee." The biggest cloud on my horizon—the almost all-consuming concern as to what I would do or say if reactions were a yawn and the response was "What was all the fuss about?"—was lifted. I had, it seemed, been living under that shadow forever.

The next day's overnight ratings were incredible—high 30s and low 40s. We were all (me, Shephard, Rosenbloom, Corday) in disbelief. How amazing this would all work so well. The world was calling, commenting on the quality and content of the episode, and now the numbers as well.

The national numbers, revealed twenty-four hours after the overnights, fulfilled the promise of the earlier ratings: A 21.9 rating and a 38 share. It was a truly phenomenal set of numbers for CBS on a Monday night. My feelings were strange: first, exhilaration; next, concern (how big would next week's almost-certain drop-off be?); then, excitement again. The primary reaction was tiredness. I felt like the only wrestler left standing in the ring after a "Louisiana Death Match." The previous day I had had plenty of energy. Perhaps, I speculated, it was simply the rarified atmosphere of success to which I was having trouble adjusting.

Everyone was buzzing about us. *Donahue* wanted the women to fly to Chicago and be on his show. We'd been trying to get on his program for a year, and now he was asking us. I do love to win!

Tony Barr, of course, was the one who called with the numbers initially. He was quite pleased but noted that the blue[44] pages on "Choices" (our biological clock episode) hadn't helped him at all. I reminded him that I had once told him I could not satisfy his notes and that it was silly for us to argue now as the episode was in the final stages of production. He agreed but just wanted to log a reminder for next season. We were all beginning to assume there would be one.

The ensuing week we scored again: a 35 share. We were actually rated ahead of *60 Minutes*, an unbelievable coup for CBS on a Monday. If Shephard's months-ago statement held, that only March numbers would count, then our pickup for next season seemed assured.

On April 5, I attended my final rough-cut screening of the season at CBS; it was "Choices." Though I was steadfast in my approval of the episode, I was now steeled for the worst. My best-case scenario was that perhaps I would get a "not bad" from Tony Barr or a "not as bad as I feared" kind of comment.

As the film came to a close and with the lights not quite yet fully illuminated in the CBS projection room, Tony Barr got to his feet. "It's an Emmy show," he exclaimed. He went on to state that this episode would bring Sharon her Emmy.[45] Barr then extolled the direction (Karen Arthur) and closed by admitting he was completely wrong; he said he could not visualize from the script how perfectly this would play.

---

[44]   Each set of script changes is put out in a different color. Blue is the first set of changes, pink the second, and on and on through goldenrod. The original script—or first draft—is on white paper.

[45]   Mr. Barr's prediction aside, Tyne Daly would win again, this time for her work in our episode "The Baby Broker." I agreed with Mr. Barr's assessment, however, and made "Choices" our official entry with the Academy for Best Series over Lefcourt's urgings to submit "Baby Broker." To this day, Lefcourt claims we would have won had I followed his advice. To imply that I would listen to Barr over Lefcourt is to ignore my earlier statement: "Choices" was always a strong personal favorite of mine.

I finally interrupted this onslaught of praise with thanks, disbelief, and a warning. "Tony, you are giving me a loaded gun for next season."

"I know it," he said. "God help me."

Our pickup for the following season was all but confirmed, or was it? Shephard did not promote or advertise the show during its two weeks of pre-emptions, and we went on the air cold in mid-April against opposition that had full-page ads in *TV Guide*. We got a 28 share and took the hour. Normally this would be cause to celebrate. I wondered how much weight Shephard would give to the 7-share drop-off since our last outing. I think it was former MGM's TV chief, David Gerber, who labeled the term "paranoid producer" a redundancy.

Corday was positive a pickup was imminent and tried to reassure me. "You are renewed with a 35 share or with a 28," she said. "The only difference is that with a 35, CBS meets you at the airport with a band."

She was right, of course. My problem was I wanted the band.

CHAPTER 27

FORGET IT, JAKE, IT'S LACY STREET

With the news of a pickup, we began our preparations for the fall. It would be our first time at Lacy Street with a full season order of twenty-two episodes. It is odd to reflect on just how natural it seemed—to be going back to this place that none of us ever believed could serve as anything like a realistic home base for an ongoing television series.

The concept for a Lacy Street–like place dated back to Toronto and to the original *Cagney & Lacey* M.O.W. Although our budgetary savings in that northern city were more than compensatory for what was then a shallow talent pool in a community not then fully attuned to the needs of the film industry, one of our biggest problems with the move was that stage space, in that municipality, was severely limited. As a consequence, a real building (with enough space and high enough ceilings) was sought. What was ultimately found, a three-story abandoned brick edifice owned by the city, had been the dog pound. The structure had then been recently gutted, preparatory to being torn down. We prevailed on the city fathers to delay their demolition, and, for one month in April of 1981, the Torontonian home for wayward dogs became Manhattan's mythical 14th Precinct.

Later that year, when CBS unexpectedly ordered *Cagney & Lacey* to series, we fretted about where to actually make the show. Our Toronto dog pound had since been destroyed. Besides, we felt it would be difficult to try to produce this hurry-up, short-order series by long distance. To some extent that also ruled out actually going to New York, but we never even got to that debate because of the prohibitive cost factor of production in and around Manhattan in that cost-conscious era.

The natural thought was to film the series in Hollywood, but at such late notice it would be difficult (read expensive) to find proper stage space. There was also the matter of construction costs of our requisite number of permanent sets, including, in addition to the various elements of the 14th precinct—squad room, desk sergeant area, Samuel's office, locker rooms, the ladies' room—the Lacey household and the Cagney loft.

The one-time furniture/mattress factory that was found, suitably enough on Lacy Street, provided ample space for everything we would need and was (ironically) across the street from the proposed site of the new Los Angeles dog pound. It seemed fated to be ours, but only a Bette Davis reading could have done the place justice: "What a dump."

We were only going to be there, we thought, for six episodes. We would have to move eventually; the eighty-one-year-old structure could not be properly air-conditioned in the summer nor could the drafty, cavernous interiors be adequately heated in the winter. It leaked. The plumbing was problematic. It was damp and had a significant population of rodents. As soon as we became successful, we said, we would move. Success wasn't so easy to come by.

Our next order was for thirteen episodes; too few for any sense of permanence. All right, we'd try another season in the hellhole. (Besides, at that time, the writers and producers all worked out of decent offices in West Los Angeles.)

We then received an order for nine episodes to fill out the season. (No time to move now; besides, I had just forced Orion to build cubicles at the old factory for the editors and writers to save me driving time.) Cancellation came next, and with it our return of Lacy Street to the rats. CBS then was to admit their mistake, resulting in a seven-show order and making a homecoming to Lacy Street the only plausible solution. Now, finally, and at last, a full order of twenty-two shows.

Robert Towne's famous line from *Chinatown* was paraphrased on a large sign put up on the premises by Peter Lefcourt: "Forget it, Jake, it's Lacy Street." The idea of finally leaving our (by then) beloved mattress factory was never again seriously discussed.

"Lacy Street" had become a synonym for camaraderie. It reminded me of an observation I had made for the first time as a teenager in the 1950s. The Morris Garage people of Britain had begun to export their classic MG Roadster to Los Angeles in relatively large numbers. It had a rubberized convertible top with isinglass side curtains. On a rainy California night you would be dryer walking to your destination without hat or umbrella than you would be driving in that MG. Those who owned them would touch their horn with a friendly honk when coming upon another of their fraternity; it was in the best tradition of the Knights of the Road.

Years later, when I lived in Malibu and became one of those community activists who fought the real estate developers (by constantly voting against the installation of sewers and extolling the virtues of our country cesspools), I felt a similar comradeship. Neighbors—brothers in adversity—that's what we were at Lacy Street.

Fifty thousand square feet and everyone who worked there was working on *Cagney & Lacey*; conversely, virtually everyone who worked on *Cagney & Lacey* was—by 1982—there. Unlike a conventional studio operation, there were no extra bodies, no extraneous personnel, no "suits," no members of other crews (who might stir a pot or two by comparing payroll checks or overtime chores). We were a solid, and solitary, unit.

Since there were no restaurants in the immediate area, we catered meals—breakfast and lunch every day, and many evenings we served dinner as well: twelve-hour minimum days, at least five days per week, working together, eating together, and sharing the adversity of our terribly outmoded facility together.

There was synergy to the place as well in terms of how our pictures were made. If an editor needed a line of dialogue to bridge a cut, it was a short walk to the filming area where he could sidle up to our sound man, Mo Harris, make the request, wait a bit while the line was recorded on the spot, and return to his editing room with the requisite material in hand.

My editorial acumen was enhanced by Lacy Street as the facility, and its proximity to the stages and the actors allowed me not simply to cut a film but rather to rough it in and then, as in the old studio days gone by, order an additional close-up, or a retake, or a new scene entirely with actors who we had under contract on sets that were always ready, and right next door.

There was a popcorn machine outside my office that operated nearly around the clock. Grips, technicians, teamsters, actors, editors, writers, and secretarial staff would come by for a snack. Most would stick their head in my office's open door to greet me with a "Hi, Boss." There was no Universal tower, no executive suite.

Director Alex Singer was always one of my favorites. It was more than the luck of the draw on scripts that many of our best episodes bore his credit as director. He is a voracious reader, an intellectual, a bit of a philosopher, and a student of offbeat human behavior. I was, therefore, not surprised when he entered my office one morning—popcorn box in hand—and said, "I want you to describe to me, if you will, the essence of the graffiti in the men's toilets at Universal Studios."

This was typical Alex. Why settle for hello when a polemic can be posed? I did not wait long before answering: "Racist. Sexist. Homophobic and … pornographic."

"Excellent," came Mr. Singer's response. "And what about Paramount Studios?"

I pondered for only a moment; was this a trick question? I thought not. "The same," I speculated.

"Correct." Singer was clearly delighted. "Now," he asked, "what about the graffiti here at Lacy Street?"

I took a moment. I tried to visualize the walls in the men's room some three hundred feet from my office. My brow furrowed, and Singer's patience faded. He made his point as he leaned over my desk, putting his face close to mine and whispered, "There isn't any."

He was right.

It didn't say so much about the crew we had hired—many of whom had probably contributed to the decor of men's rooms at studios all over town—but what it did address was the way these men felt about the place at which they now worked. It was not a faceless or anonymous monolith. It was ours. It was Lacy Street.

Some months later, I was standing next to Director Singer at our graffiti-less urinals. As we each relieved ourselves, I spoke of how I missed having my own private toilet. It wasn't something personal against him, or anyone in the company, I quickly added. It wasn't for sanitary reasons or even my penchant for enjoying some quiet reading time while ensconced on the commode. The real reason I wanted my own toilet was to avoid the walk from my office to the facilities Mr. Singer and I were then occupying. (Not only was the near-football field length a considerable distance from my office; it also meant my having to pass in front of several actors' dressing rooms, the wardrobe department, the property master's office, three editing rooms, Dick Reilly's post-production cubicle, and our screening room. Invariably, as I would attempt to make a beeline from my desk to the head, any number of people would stop me "just for a second," to see this costume, fabric, prop, piece of film, or just to chat or discuss a dubbing date.)

Singer cut me off. "Barney, you're a big success now. Do it. There's that storage space next to your office. It's on the street side of the building, so tying into the sewer lines will be no big deal. The whole thing could be done quite luxuriously for maybe $10,000. Just do it."

He was right. I was a success, and, if I wanted this perquisite, I should have it.

A week or so later, Director Singer asked about the progress of my plans for a restroom retreat. I had to tell him I had decided against it. "It smacks of elitism," I said. "Very un-Lacy Street."

One did not need to elaborate on such thoughts with Alex Singer.

Gloria Steinem, a great friend of our series, on the left and Sharon on the right. Am I a lucky guy or what?

Photo: Rosenzweig Personal Collection

CHAPTER 28

NO ONE CAN WRITE THIS SHOW BUT ME

The summer of 1984 has to go down as one of the very best of my entire life. The elation and joy of it all coming together so beautifully in the spring of that year did not subside. Letters of thanks and congratulations poured in from all over the world for, by this time, the series had made its debut in Canada, Australia, and England—where it became an instant smash hit. The summer was one of the very best, but not without its challenges.

My concerns about the staff—Lefcourt, Fisher, and newcomer (to us) E. Arthur Kean—were somewhat allayed by the return of Steve Brown. Steve's organizational skills are substantive, and this became all the more important to me as I increasingly occupied my time with the fringe benefits of my new celebrity.

Both of Corday's pilot projects for Columbia failed to get picked up, and she found to her dismay that she was not even allowed proper mourning time. After all, how many hits did any married couple need? The assumption that my wife and I had now joined an elite echelon of the super rich, with a syndicatable show, was given voice in our social circle. There was open speculation that we were now millionaires with perhaps $30,000 to $50,000 per episode in retroactive guaranteed advances. If they only knew the truth of our deals, Corday might have received a sympathetic condolence or two on the demise of her pilots.

Meanwhile an old cloud came back on the horizon. CBS miscounted and gave Sharon top billing over Tyne in the ads for one of our episodes for which it was Tyne's turn. Ms. Daly was on the rampage again, but that summer at the fiftieth birthday party for Gloria Steinem at the grand ballroom of the Waldorf-Astoria in New York, I took a few minutes to talk to her, and she seemed to understand the plausibility of human error on the part of CBS. For a while, anyway, she dismissed her latest conspiracy theory.

Near the start of production for 1984–85, only weeks after ending our short seven-show season, Tyne was in a curiously ebullient mood while Sharon was tired and in a terrible funk. Lefcourt had referred to it as the cuckoo clock syndrome: when one bird was out, the other would be in; they were never in the same place emotionally at the same time.

In the midst of this and while preparing other projects for her own Can't Sing, Can't Dance Company at Columbia, Corday phoned to say that, for old time's sake, she and her erstwhile partner, Barbara Avedon, would like to do a script for the show, actually, two scripts.

What they visualized was a two-part episode dealing with Mary Beth Lacey's discovery that she had a cancerous tumor in her breast. Avedon's ex-husband, Mel, was a well-known oncologist, and I was pitched by Corday that there was much new information for women that was not getting out about the virtues of lumpectomy over mastectomy.

I have my own, at best, questioning views of the efficacy of western medicine, so I was excited about the idea from the outset and bought the concept over the phone.

Peter Lefcourt was displeased. The acquisition of new material was his department. He felt that I had breached our arrangement by buying an idea without consulting him.

I tried to assuage his feelings. I acknowledged the correctness of his position, while still holding to my prerogatives, especially when the pitch not only came from my wife but involved the co-creators of the series itself.

"What would you say," I asked, "if I was Marsha Mason and we were working on *The Odd Couple* series together, and my spouse—Neil Simon—called and said he wanted to write an episode?"

"You should still check with me," was his response. I shook my head. These kinds of territorial disputes were things I could not take seriously. Uncharacteristically, Peter stewed. I had not heard the end of this.

There were other objections. Terry Louise Fisher did not want to do a medical show; Steve Brown quickly aligned with his former partner, while new writing staff member E. Arthur Kean's only concern was that the women authors would not know what it would be like to have breast cancer. Really? As if *he* would and *they* wouldn't? I was getting annoyed.

Avedon and Corday made an appointment to come to the office to break down the story for the writing staff. I elected to attend this conference (something I did not normally do when outside writers were meeting with the staff) and was horrified by what I witnessed.

"If this is the way you treat freelance writers who come to us with their ideas," I said—primarily to Steve and Terry in the post-mortem that followed the departure of Avedon and Corday, "then I am amazed we have not yet been brought up on charges by the Guild."

I went on. "Forget the fact that one of these women is your boss's wife, or that the team that was just in here are the only writers who ever faced a truly blank page on this project. You may even dismiss the fact that because of them you all have jobs paying you well into six figures. But what I don't get is how you could be that rude or that hostile to ordinary, everyday, fellow professionals."

They were hardly contrite. I guess you don't reach their level of success as writers in Hollywood without developing very thick skins. There are a lot of jokes at the Writers Guild of America (WGA) dinners about those insensitive, clod-like producers and prima donna directors. The entertainment committee of the WGA might consider an update of their routines by looking a little closer to home.

Maybe it was a defense mechanism. Maybe, after years of note-taking from producers, directors, stars, and networks, the writer on a television staff gets territorial and really begins to believe the oldest cliché in their handbook, namely, "No one can write this show but me." Season after season, show after show, it always remains the same: "No one can write this show but me." Those were the exact words spoken to me by Paul King in 1967 when, at the age of twenty-nine, I took over the *Daniel Boone* series. It was the same phrase said to me by Rick Husky, as he had turned over the reins on *Charlie's Angels,* and now, though unspoken, it was essentially what was being said by the *Cagney & Lacey* writing staff. And they believed it! They believed it as individuals and as a group. It is one of the things wrong with television.

"Staffthink," the belief that "no-one can write this show but me," leads to the homogenization of a series and of television in general while discouraging the freelance writer, the artist with a singular story to tell, that he or she might be able to reveal better and with more passion than anyone. Most staffs are horrified at the thought of opening the doors to outside writers, whom they consider unguideable and less talented than themselves. Because they are writers and not producers (regardless of what credit they may negotiate for themselves), they are, as are most of their fellows in the Writers Guild of America, compulsive rewriters.

And then there is the matter of economics: hiring a freelancer cuts into the staff writer's income as individual script money, over and above their weekly salaries, now would go to the freelancer instead of them. As a result, a very insular, if not incestuous, situation exists. At its worst, it is repetitive in spirit, in character, and in dialogue. At its best, it is the same, with only good stylistic achievement as a cover. Worst of all, if, as in the early days of television, there are any budding Paddy Chayefskys out there—wonderful, talented, young writers who need encouragement—they will have a hard time getting that from any of those staffing a current TV series.

Obviously this is a Jones[46] for me, going way back in my career from the early days of the creation of the so-called hyphenate. For the most part I maintain a certain amount of equilibrium with the staffs I have hired (forced to hire, really, since the almost-total demise of the freelancer), but there are days when my button on this subject gets pushed. This was one of those days.

---

[46]   Black/jazz slang meaning "issue" or "problem."

CHAPTER 29

HIGH-CLASS PROBLEMS

The fight with the writing staff was over, for the time being. Their attitude seemed to be "we'll wait and see what comes in from the freelance writers Barney has hired."

We'll never know because Corday had to pull out almost before she started. She had been offered the presidency of Columbia Pictures Television under chairman Herman Rush. It would involve many sacrifices, but the opportunity of becoming the then-ranking female in the entire industry was a tough one for anyone to pass up. (It was pointed out at the time that this would make me the first gentleman of Columbia; I was delighted.) Avedon, thus abandoned by Corday a second time, would press on with the two-parter alone.

We returned from New York City and the Columbia party at 21 for Corday in late June. Along with everyone else, I was excited for her, with my ebullience only tempered by my seeming inability to get my energy level back into high gear for *Cagney & Lacey*. I wondered if this was a complication brought on by the new economic facts of life in the Rosenzweig/Corday household.

Our financial future was now virtually assured. It was a "high-class problem," as Corday said, but one I would have to deal with in terms of motivation. It's sort of like being paid for a job in advance, or what a professional ballplayer must go through after he's negotiated a monster deal for himself and then finds he is in a batting slump. I suppose if one has to have a problem, then this is a good one.

The billing thing would not go away. Because of the CBS advertising mistake earlier in the summer, Tyne had once again become crazed on the subject. The work continued to be good on the screen, but backstage a war was about to break out.

Tyne asked for alternating billing on the scripts, and Lefcourt, without discussing this with me, caved. Sharon was pissed. These were on scripts—something seen only by our staff, crew, and a handful of CBS executives. I overruled Lefcourt's order and awaited Ms. Daly's reaction; it didn't surface—not directly, anyway. I then met with Gless, who confessed that she was unhappy at work for the first time in her life.

The scar tissue from those difficult weeks of renegotiation all those months before had not healed, not for any of us. Sharon was different from Tyne Daly or me. She was not an experienced or calloused infighter. The process was exhausting to her, while it seemed as if Tyne used her anger as an energy source. Just whom she might be trying to punish remained unclear. It might be me, but, then again, it might be herself. By alienating and exhausting Gless, she could punish us all. I knew a confrontation was coming and that it would be soon; I began to consider precipitating it.

Meanwhile, Tony Barr was back. Both he and Karen Cooper called from CBS yet again with major problems. This time it was on our script for "The Taxicab Murders," written by Ronnie Wenker-Konner and directed by Karen Arthur. Both of the CBS current programming executives had come to accept the fact that *Cagney & Lacey* did not always catch the bad guy; they even acknowledged that it was the very thing *TV Guide* chose to highlight in their headline for the Erich Segal article. But now, they said, we had gone too far. Not only did Cagney and Lacey not catch the bad guy, they arrest and interrogate the wrong guy!

That tore it for Mr. Barr. The good news was I had my loaded gun, and Tony remembered he had handed it to me just a few months before in that CBS screening room following our "Choices" episode. These arguments now had a lighter tone, a sort of passion check by the network, just to make sure I was still there and still caring.

I had fended off every objection they could come up with when Karen Cooper spoke up. "Look, Barney, you're always telling us about the moral victories at the end of your shows. What's the victory here, for God's sake? They are wrong."

"I'm glad you asked that, Karen." I fairly leaped onto the phone speaker box on my desk and—truth to tell—it helped my performance immeasurably to have (unknown to Barr or Ms. Cooper) the entire writing staff there in my office as an audience.

"Cagney and Lacey arrest the wrong guy. They make a mistake. And what do they do?" I was positively evangelical as I went on. "Do they commit suicide? Do they resign their posts? Do they writhe about on the floor in self-loathing? No. They go to lunch. They tell a couple of jokes, and they go to lunch; and that's the victory. They are indefatigable. They are *not* their jobs. They are human beings who occasionally make mistakes. And it's OK. That's an important thing to say to an audience, don't you agree?"

Tony Barr was laughing on the other end of the phone. The major problem was over. "Do it your way, Barney."

We did.

Heyday on the Hollywood dais circuit. From left: TV producer extraordinaire Steven Bochco, Fox TV president Harris Katleman, me, NBC chief Brandon Tartikoff, *Dynasty* executive producer Esther Shapiro, and Paul Witt of the highly successful Witt/Thomas production team.

Photo: Rosenzweig Personal Collection

Success was grand, but it, too, had an underbelly. For the past fifteen years or so of my life, I had developed a persona—an attitude—that had served me well. I had cast myself as a victim of sorts. I wanted to do something, and *they* (the studios, the networks, or the system) would not let me. That was in the long ago; for now I was being allowed to do pretty much what I wanted. I had been proven right, and I was a success.

But all that energy, which in the past had been channeled and focused in a battle to survive, now had no place to go. It was rattling around and somehow making me tired and irritable. It was distressing. I wanted to stop fighting. Who, after all, does not want peace? I wanted to relax and enjoy my victories. It wasn't happening. I was like the soldier who, returning home from battle, finds the horror of war a dim memory and now misses the adrenaline rush and his comrades in arms. There had to be, I thought, more to success than this.

It was confusing, for I was not longing for new conquests. I simply wanted to take time to enjoy things the way they were. I found my Hollywood community particularly intolerant of this. (Only in success do they persist in asking what your next project is. The idea that one might want to savor the current one—after working for years to get it right—is as rare as a gambler walking away with his winnings in Las Vegas.)

I sensed my inability to recognize that I was now at the time of life where I was reaping benefits for all that I had fought for in the past.

It reminded me of the quip Dr. Jonah Perlmutter (older brother to my friend and lawyer, Sam) had made about a dozen years before. I had been unemployed for some time, *Daniel Boone* was behind me, and, as a result of my dream to finance, produce, and distribute my indy project (*Who Fears the Devil*) all on my own, I had become a walking financial disaster. Still I was tan and lean from tennis games and enjoying my life on the beach in Malibu. On this particular occasion, I was holding court with a group of hardworking friends who were curious as to how I was able to manage so well without employment.

"I no longer have a neurotic need to succeed," I explained.

At which point, psychiatrist Perlmutter joined the group and countered my glibness with speculation. "Perhaps you have a neurotic need to fail."

To this day, I worry that he might have been right.

I was not the only one going through the success blahs. The entire crew seemed different. That June of 1984, the general mood among staff, writers, secretaries, assistants—everyone it seemed—was somehow discordant, less unified in purpose. I began to worry that with success might come a form of lethargy that I would not be able to handle.

I felt there was a real danger of things falling apart. In adversity—in those earlier, difficult days of short orders—temporary alliances had been made; truces had been effectuated. Now, no one seemed to realize that the real war was far from over. We would not be against summer programming for long. I had to find a way to communicate all this to all parties, including my own inner psyche.

I started with Tyne Daly. I told her it was time for us to repair, that I had had enough of our war. She took my hand and nodded. We agreed to get together as soon as our mutual schedules allowed so that we could deal with all this.

My next move was to include Gless in on the meeting with Tyne. I was determined that all our hidden agendas were going to be brought to the fore.

At week's end, with the phone call informing me of the wrap of that evening's production schedule around 10:30 PM, I excused myself from my dinner guests at home to return to Lacy Street for this meeting, which ended around 3:30 Saturday morning.

The meeting was good—not great. The women had their complaints, but I was determined to deal with the (for me) more real issues of pain and hurt we had caused each other. To do it properly, I said, required probably a week's retreat, but at least some hurts and misconceptions were dealt with in the four-plus hours we had.

There was some yelling, some tears, and some tremulous voices. At one point, I pushed Sharon to confront Tyne with her anger over the billing thing, and she finally let Tyne know she had seen the (infamous) telegram sent from Yugoslavia about "honour." For a minute or so, I joined this part of the fray as we sort of ganged up on Tyne. She was reduced to tears as she apologized for her past behavior. We wound up hugging each other.

I then explained, as best I could, my philosophy (borrowed from the venerable Howard Strickling, my first boss in show business, and not Governor Dukakis, who would popularize it years afterward) that "a fish stinks from the head." I told them that I alone was no longer the head; that we were a troika. To only a very small extent did they accept that responsibility; still the idea was introduced.

They had a litany of complaints; most were reasonable, some based on misinformation. I promised to begin the very next Monday to deal with what I could to the best of my ability. It would have been lovely to say all this was now settled, but we were a long, long way from that.

Over the weekend, as they had done once before in a time of trouble, Tyne Daly and Sharon Gless convened with champagne on Sharon's living room floor, where they set out to—and basically did—repair. On the following Monday, I gave a speech (as opposed to *pep talk*) to the cast and crew. Everyone seemed most impressed, including Tyne and Sharon, who had their share of nitpicks, but basically agreed it was a B+.

A few days later, an incredulous Dick Rosenbloom called. He heard I had made a speech, but now wanted to know what it was I had said to Tyne and Sharon. Over the weekend he had received a phone call from Sharon thanking him for the ads in the trades, and today he had received a personal note from Tyne Daly to the same effect. He was in disbelief. Repair was in the air.

CHAPTER 30

THE SUBJECT IS MONEY

The summer numbers against ABC's reruns and NBC's baseball had *Cagney & Lacey* constantly in the top five—usually number one or two. *Advertising Age* predicted a 28-share average for the show against football and first-run movies in the fall, and I hoped they were right. That summer also brought six Emmy nominations—two more than the previous year and a gaggle more than year one, when the only nomination garnered was for hair dressing. (Evidently, Academy members, not unlike the American viewing public in general, had ignored our premiere episodes, but apparently did assume that any show featuring two females must have them well coifed.)

Nominations this time were for Sharon and Tyne (of course), the show itself, film editing for both "Choices" and "Baby Broker," and sound mixing for "Bounty Hunter."

The odds of success, at least through 1984–85 and into one more season, seemed good. The syndication marketplace for one-hour dramatic series was at an all-time high and growing. My gambler's instinct began to take hold. It was time, I felt, to make a play.

I was not predicting the syndication market collapse of 1986, which would cause investors in hour-long dramatic shows to lose fortunes and totally turn the television industry on its ear. I'm not prescient; I'm not even particularly clever. I'm also not greedy. I simply felt it was time to walk away from the tables and not look back (or care) what the guy who took my spot was making.

All I wanted was to get mine. I also had little or no faith in the Orion team, who perceived the universe quite differently. The sky was apparently going to continue to expand, if not be limitless, as far as Orion's Jamie Kellner was concerned. The man, who I first knew as Dr. No when I needed an ally at Orion, was now Dr. Know. I thought his position was no more than bluff and bluster.

Orion was a movie-driven company. The partners at this company cared little for television, but the movies they had been making in 1983 were losing money—a lot of money. Out socially with Herman Rush, Corday's boss at Columbia, I told him of what I thought was an interesting window of opportunity. He listened avidly and followed my suggestion by going to the top brass at Orion with a firm cash offer, cash they could use to shore up their movie division: over $800,000 per episode, retroactive to episode one, with a guarantee to keep us in production for another full year past our current order, even in the event the network was to cancel the show. If we failed at the network, the deal was worth fifty to sixty million dollars; in success, over twice that amount. Tens of millions net to Orion and millions for me, plus at least one more year of working on the show I loved.

The men of Orion turned it down.

This was not funny money they were rejecting. Mr. Rush was the chairman of the television division of Columbia Pictures Corporation—then a wholly owned subsidiary of the Coca-Cola Company. This was a guaranteed payday of monumental proportions, backed by one of America's great companies.

They turned it down.

Their argument was that if they sold to Columbia they might as well go out of the television business. (My sentiments exactly, and who, I asked, would have noticed?) I countered with the suggestion that if they didn't want to sell to Columbia, then they should market the show themselves into syndication and do so immediately while we were hot.

I wanted to get away from those tables a winner. Kellner said his predictable no. He felt the show was going to be worth $1,100,000 per episode, maybe more. Why sell now for $800,000? In all the time we were on the air, these guys could not even launch a *Cagney & Lacey* calendar or a T-shirt. I had no reason to believe they could successfully merchandise the series, despite Kellner's bravado.

I even tried to convince Mace to join me in an effort at selling out our position to Orion. I felt the company would never buy out as small a profit participant as myself but hoped they might go for a larger package. Mace apparently thought I was trying to pull a fast one.

A little over a year later, the collapse of 1986 was a reality. It was brought about by many forces in the marketplace, all easily predictable with hindsight: President

Ronald Reagan's deregulation led to an explosion in the number of independent television stations, and almost overnight there were too many to be supported by advertising revenues. Some would go under, and heavy debt—owed to program suppliers such as Orion—was seen as one of the reasons. Technology was also a factor; when *Cagney & Lacey* started production in Toronto in 1981, there were perhaps a million VCR units in the United States. By the time we closed up shop in 1988, there were over fifty million. That, too, had its impact on free television, as did the proliferation of cable.

The bottom line was that in 1987, less than two and a half years after Herman Rush's offer of $800,000 per episode, Orion would sell the series to Lifetime Cable for $100,000 per episode. Instead of looking at a hundred million dollars, Orion would gross (even including ever-expanding foreign revenues) less than a quarter of that amount. Not chicken feed to be sure—especially on an initial investment of under $30,000—but to the profit participants, the difference between a twenty million dollar and a hundred million dollar gross is the difference between getting something substantial and receiving very little, if anything, at all.

All I knew in the summer of 1984 was that I had a severe case of opening-night jitters, pre-Emmy anxiety, and a motivational problem for myself, the staff, the crew, and the stars. I would have felt better, I thought, with a lot of cash in my pockets.

While it is true that the next ten to twelve months were exceptionally rewarding, there were, as referred to earlier, "challenges."

For the record, Barbara Avedon did eventually turn in part of the much-argued-about two-parter. Because Corday was unable to work with her, Ms. Avedon took on another partner (an element not approved by us). The gossip was that Avedon, in fact, handed over the assignment to the Corday surrogate and turned in the resultant first draft without even reading the work herself. We were told her intention was to address herself to this draft when she had our comments in hand. Whether she had read it or not, she had, by her own admission, not really contributed to its writing. I felt this was unprofessional and disloyal to me and to the show she had helped create.

I was embarrassed. Worse yet, the script was awful, but more than any of this—from my perspective—was the position taken by the writing staff: This was Barney's folly, and they weren't about to rewrite a script they hadn't ordered and never wanted. I was outraged and stayed away from the office for days while trying to cool off enough so as not to have to fire all of them. This "lovers' quarrel," as Peter Lefcourt termed it, was ultimately resolved through compromise by both sides.

Writer Patricia Green was brought in to begin—virtually from scratch—what would be our two-part episode on breast cancer. I did my part by promising Rosenbloom that my days of trying to bring Avedon back to *Cagney & Lacey* were now history.

I had learned from my business manager that I either had to spend less or make more. This news again focused my attention on the lack of fairness inherent in my *Cagney & Lacey* deal. My settlement with Orion required my involvement with other projects for the company. They had refused to alter my antiquated deal on *Cagney & Lacey* or to open the coffers of the series itself in any substantive way.

The fact that, at that time of the 1984 World Series, Orion would not trade *Cagney & Lacey* for ownership of the San Diego Padres and that I was more important to the former than Steve Garvey to the latter had me getting more and more agitated on the subject.

My old deal remained in place while Orion simultaneously paid me under the terms of my new contract. I would have to continue developing other projects under this arrangement, but it was acknowledged that the bulk of my time would be spent on *Cagney & Lacey*. What was not being addressed was the fact that with so much time being spent on the series, the upside of my overall deal—the potential for great gain by developing new projects during a time when I had some heat—was substantially reduced.

I was now making over $500,000 per year, a lot of money for a kid from Montebello but a fraction of what peers such as Bochco on *Hill Street Blues* or Gary David Goldberg on *Family Ties* were bringing down. Their fees and ownership positions in their series amounted to tens of millions, way out of the realm of possibility for me due to my antiquated deal with Mace, the unfairness of which was now being fully exploited by Orion.

Jamie Kellner finally presented me with a compromise worthy of the term. Orion would recognize that my involvement in the series was so time-consuming for me—while being important enough to them—that my chances of creating and/or following through on new ventures were at least somewhat curtailed. In exchange for this potential loss of upside revenue, Orion would settle me out on that issue by granting me a small percentage of their gross sales on the series. This would have no impact on other profit participants, coming, as it did, totally out of Orion's share, and, to my satisfaction, potentially meaningful with the production of enough episodes. My requests, that I share in the fruits of success and that Orion leave Mace alone, were thus honored. Of course this would come back to bite me in the ass in the future, as Mace would interpret this as an illegal conspiracy against him, but I didn't know that, or anticipate it, in 1984.

The subject of money is an awkward one. Many of us in show business (which in this era includes not just television, movies, and the theater but athletics and certain kinds of journalism as well) are extremely well paid. To the average person, it must seem out of all proportional reason, but oftentimes we are dealing with exceedingly short life spans and incredibly long odds. To be a success, to be associated with a once-in-a-lifetime hit, is tantamount to winning the lottery, and every bit as rare.

"Once in a lifetime": often that is exactly what it is—only once. The demands of time and stress on one's lifestyle are enormous; the monies made by the corporations who employ us, phenomenal.

The people who pay Oprah Winfrey over $60,000,000 per year are, themselves, making a substantial profit. So are the employers of the fabulously successful and highly paid Katie Couric and Shaquille O'Neal. That *Cagney & Lacey* brought to me less money than the 10 percent received by the agent for Gary David Goldberg on *Family Ties* remains a bit of a sore spot.

By the end of the third season (which in the summer of 1984 was just commencing production), we would have fifty-seven episodes. They would all be made at or near the license fee. With the foreign revenues already then pledged or in hand, *Cagney & Lacey* was in profit at its initial network run—virtually unheard of for a one-hour filmed show on network television.[47]

The summer came to an end with all of us awaiting a late (mid-October) premiere date on CBS. We had never before had such a long stretch of production without any kind of feedback. The pressures of working in this kind of vacuum while awaiting the results of our six Emmy nominations only added to our pre-opening night jitters.

---

[47]   Exceptions might have been *Dynasty, Dallas,* and some of the soaps, which had extremely high license fees and few production requirements outside of studio control. Since soaps have never had much residual value, due to their serialized nature, they had always commanded top dollars from the networks, hence lower or nonexistent deficits. For the rest of us, it was not uncommon for programs such as *Hill Street Blues* to be running at a six-figure per episode deficit while a year later *Miami Vice* would rack up deficits of over a quarter million *per* episode—more than five million dollars per year.

On the set, a pre-Emmy cake is about to be dismantled by the two women, who are each odds-on favorites to win. That year Ms. Gless took the prize, but more often it was Tyne Daly. For the entire six-year run of *Cagney & Lacey,* no other actress could take the award from one of these two.

Photo: Rosenzweig Personal Collection

That fall, I hired executive assistant Carole R. Smith, who still works for me all these years later and is pretty much a member of the Rosenzweig family household. I also brought in my discovery, Georgia Jeffries, to write for *Cagney & Lacey*. Actually, it would be more factual to state Ms. Jeffries had been discovered by others as well, and even had one or two scripts commissioned. I knew none of that when my then-secretary Niki Marvin brought a spec script by Ms. Jeffries to my attention. Based on my read of that material, we commissioned a script from her for "Unusual Occurrence," making it the first project of hers ever produced (thus my claim of discovery). Her second script for us ("Rules of the Game") led to her being asked to join our staff. She went on to be the recipient of two Writers Guild Awards and one Emmy nomination for her work on *Cagney & Lacey*. Ms. Marvin, whose career with me was not particularly pleasant for either of us, went on to produce Stephen King's *The Shawshank Redemption* as a feature motion picture. Clearly she was "miscast" in the role of secretary.

I was becoming more convinced that we were doing better work than ever before and that we had some excellent episodes completed and in preparation. Finally, on October 17, 1984, opening-night ratings were in: 21.6/34 share: the highest-rated show of the night on all three networks. It was a good beginning.

Our second episode that season took the hour against a Sophia Loren movie-for-television and was the highest-rated show of the night on any network. The previous week's numbers had us fifth in the nation. All over town we were referred to as the success story of the season on CBS—a blue-chip show.

On week three the competition got stiffer in the form of a very exploitable M.O.W. on NBC, which clobbered our show, resulting in our worst ratings since the disasters of the spring of 1983. I was not at all sure how to interpret this in light of the previous two weeks and our incredible summer numbers but came to realize that, unlike most series, we would never face regular competition (but rather football, specials, and movies) and that we would always be living under this particular pressure-sharpened sword. It was also one of the ironies of having such an intelligent and well-educated audience, an audience aware of its options and quite capable of exercising its right to choice on a regular basis. They were not (couch-potato-like) glued to the CBS network on a Monday night, or any night for that matter.

"Sister" Christine Cagney made a brief appearance in our episode of "Burnout." Prayer didn't help. Ms. Daly won her second Emmy for that very episode.

Photo: Courtesy of MGM

CHAPTER 31

MONEY AND GLORY

In the fall of 1984, we were enjoying our first twenty-two show order. By the end of November, even with very stiff competition, *Cagney & Lacey* was regularly ensconced in the Nielsen's list of top-twenty shows. I began looking forward to the future with thoughts of preparation for yet another pickup, and the fall of 1985. This was more than compulsive behavior on my part. I had a number of projects under development for Orion, and if any of these were to become a practical reality, I would have to find someone(s) who could, while I moved on, truly take over the reins at Lacy Street. Better, I thought, to get that settled sooner than later.

Individual meetings with Peter Lefcourt, Terry Louise Fisher, and Steve Brown indicated that the former would probably not want to return but that Terry and Steve would. I was not overjoyed at having them back without the very talented and invariably affable Lefcourt as a balance.

The writing team of Jonathan Estrin and Shelley List continued to show interest in coming on board, a not uninteresting alternative given Lefcourt's pronouncement. Then—for reasons unclear to me—Terry Louise Fisher added a wrinkle, saying she would only return *with* Steve Brown who, incidentally, was characterized as pissed because I would not commit to him for a new season. There was no way I could afford to hire Estrin, List, Fisher, *and* Brown. I would not be able to eat my cake and have it; I needed to confront that and simply make a decision between the two teams: continuity versus perceived higher talent, the familiar versus new blood, experience versus inexperience—the romance of the only slightly known. It was a tougher decision than it looks on paper, and I took my time making it.

By December we had been filming for nearly 150 days without a hiatus. It was the longest stretch of production I had ever experienced, due to the near overlap of our earlier short order of seven, merging almost immediately into this first full order for twenty-two episodes. Everyone was tired and, as a consequence, irritable.

I had produced more episodes per season in my youth on *Daniel Boone*, but those were six-day shoots with reasonable start dates, sensible hours, and plenty of breaks along the way for rest and recuperation. *Boone* was from another era of television and, in fact, a better time in which to toil in the world of corporate Hollywood.

In the late sixties, networks ordered their fall schedule no later than early spring, months before they would later do during the 1980s or even today. This long, accepted delay of at least three months forces producers into longer shooting days, fewer hiatuses, and resultant heavy overtime payments to the crews and their suppliers to have a chance at making air dates. Nothing is done about it because everyone is making more money as a result of this policy: more money from the networks to the studios to compensate for the additional costs this late decision-making incurs; more overtime money for labor to put into divorce settlements because workers don't get home to their families; and more money for medical problems that result from accidents and injuries that too often occur to an exhausted work force.

It is to the eternal discredit of the various guilds and unions that they continually pander to this system, as well as the greed of their members, by negotiating ever greater overtime payments while disregarding the quality of life of their members. All that aside, at Lacy Street we were all counting the days until the Christmas break.

One evening on the set, Tyne apologized for not having a year-end gift for me and asked me to settle for her gratitude. She also apologized for being grumpy in the early going of the episode we were currently shooting (which had her character contracting breast cancer). As one might surmise from the foregoing, she was quite pleased with herself, her partner (as each of the women referred to the other), the episode's director (Ray Danton), and her own work. Sharon, too, was in very high spirits. It was a big difference from the previous week, but then so was every week.

The cancer episodes, "Who Said It's Fair" Parts I and II, were special, precipitating this digression. Pat Green's two scripts (I thought) were extraordinary, and my restraint at not doing an "I told you so" to the staff was something of which I was (I think) understandably proud. The cast, as usual, was nothing less than sterling; the information we were imparting was substantive, relatively new, and potentially life-saving. The episode gave me the opportunity to string some semi-subtle beads of my own: taking a piece of music we had used in an episode from the previous season ("Burnout") and reprising it, sans comment, months later in this story. It is the sort of tactic that is of no import to the casual viewer and a major reward to the zealous fan.

The norm in *Cagney & Lacey* was for positions of authority (judges, medical examiners, school principals, bank presidents) to be cast with female actors. We were, after all, a show about women, and we felt it was important to show successful women in the workplace as often as possible. I rescinded my own rule about this sort of casting for this episode. Mary Beth Lacey's doctor would be male, and not only male, but an actor with the least amount of sexual chemistry we could find. Millions of women would be watching this episode, and a measurable percentage of them would have similar medical concerns. We were advocating getting a second opinion, seeing more than one doctor, and ultimately exploring lumpectomy over mastectomy. I did not want Mary Beth's on-camera visit to be in some glamorized setting or to be some rarified experience made easier by consultation with an attractive feminine role model or a *Dr. Kildare* wannabe. Most women in America did not then have access to a female physician or a handsome oncologist, and I didn't want them using that as an excuse for not taking such a necessary visit.

Estrin & List continued to play reluctant brides in terms of accepting my proposal to come to work on *Cagney & Lacey*, and I was getting very bored with that courtship. I, therefore, began renegotiations with Terry Louise, worked on trying to snare the very talented Patricia Green, and next—to placate them both—Steve Brown. Terry's one-time lover/sometime writing partner, Pat Green's new mentor, and my sometime pain-in-the-ass Brown continued to be a major asset to the story department, while too often forgetting his early admission to me that he was not a producer. That was, in those days, heavy understatement. He continually had a "bull in a china shop" effect on actors, directors, and various department heads. I respected him but felt I had to carefully define and limit his areas of responsibility.

On another front, I lost my big battle with broadcast standards over the "screw him" line in Georgia Jeffries's teleplay on sexual harassment ("Rules of the Game," directed by Sharron Miller). In a coffee shop scene between the two women, Cagney is encouraged by Lacey to do the right thing and charge a superior officer in the NYPD with sexual harassment. The blonde detective gives a litany of things her tormentor can charge her with if she makes such an accusation.

"Screw him," says Lacey, in uncharacteristically raunchy fashion, to which Cagney dryly replies, "I've already ruled that out." Seems mild today, but I couldn't win that one at CBS in the mid-1980s.

Heavy editing chores prior to the holiday and a hectic PR schedule (as I did thirty or forty "phoners," plugging our January-February product, a long interview for a *People* magazine cover story and also one for a possible *TV Guide* cover) kept me busy.

For the second week in a row, we garnered a 34 share. The big news of the month, however, was the three-hour lunch with Kellner and Rosenbloom.

That was when they gave me their presentation of what my position in *Cagney & Lacey* was worth. Despite my deal (even by their definition) being a "C-minus"— assuming the virtual certainty of one more pickup by CBS—the conservative estimate of dollars to be paid to me (most of it within the next three years) was from three to five million dollars!

OK.

I thanked the two gents, told them that my anger was diffused and that I would go off to mull their request that I review and extend my overall deal at Orion another two years.

But why should I? With that kind of money coming to me, why, I asked myself, should I ever do development again? Why not just keep working on my "little" show for as long as it would last, and as long as I was having fun? I would, I theorized, hold myself out as available for any sure-fire project that came along and caught my fancy. With a little caution I was in that enviable position of not ever having to work again. It was no less than amazing, the salutary effect this had on me all week.

I kept my true feelings from Orion, telling them I would mull their offer over the holidays so that I could, while they were in a negotiating mode with me, get as much as possible for my Lacy Street group. It should be pointed out that while I was projected to get from 3 to 5 million dollars, Orion was (off a Filmways speculation of $27,500 in 1974) now the owner of a 60 to 100 million dollar property. Mace, who inherited the project from my old deal, who had never been in an editing room or on a dubbing stage for the series, who had never been to Lacy Street or had anything to do with the network sale or with casting (and, for all I know, had never even seen an episode on television), was—according to these selfsame projections, going to receive probably 10 million dollars.

(The Kellner/Rosenbloom projections on future profits, given me in 1984, were a guess-timate, made before the collapse of the syndication market. As of this writing, neither Mace nor I have received a penny for our profit points, as first Orion, then subsequent owner MGM, claim there aren't any profits. Perhaps the "C-minus" nature of my deal and the feelings about that may now be clearer. To be fair, monies that were settled on

me [a small percentage of Orion's end or gross] for giving up my opportunities under my 1983–85 Orion deal have been, and continue to be, paid.)

Christmas and my Caribbean cruise with Corday came and went. I was back at work and began setting the staff for the (still at that time hoped-for) next season. All I had to do now was get CBS to pick us up.

Meanwhile the network had agreed to fund nine scripts. We had Terry, Steve, Pat Green, and Georgia Jeffries; they were pleasant to work with, understood the terrain, and were not afraid to work hard. "If it ain't broke, don't fix it," but I feared we would never realize our potential with this group.

I am, in this arena, somewhat less than even-handed, tending toward being a bit hypercritical of these people who I liked very much. Some facts: We did win one Emmy award for writing: Pat Green ("Who Said It's Fair" Part II), and two nominations (Deborah Arakelian, "Child Witness," and Georgia Jeffries, "Turn, Turn, Turn" Part I). We did collect two Writers Guild awards (both by Georgia Jeffries for "Unusual Occurrence" and "Turn, Turn, Turn" Part I). But these awards paled next to the accolades collected by the writing staffs of *St. Elsewhere*, *Hill Street Blues*, *L.A. Law*, and *thirtysomething*. I believed (perhaps somewhat unfairly) we were making very substantial bricks with—at best—very ordinary straw.

CHAPTER 32

SURPRISE AT THE GOLDEN GLOBES

The weeks of Christmas rest had hardly made a dent in the fatigue factor. We had about another month of filming and then some post-production work and hopefully a good long period of time off. I was not the only one who needed it. Tyne Daly was showing all the worst signs of exhaustion. Although she and I were getting along very well, I was receiving reports from many in the company as to her mood swings and her flares of temperament, ranging from attitudes about publicity, to references to her family life (or lack of same), to attacks aimed at co-workers. In true cuckoo clock fashion, Sharon had been in very good spirits but was very tired as well.

Cagney & Lacey had entered the language. In January 1985, our title served as a punch line for a *New Yorker* cartoon; more and more we were being acknowledged as a staple, a standard. Still, given my experience with this venture almost from day one, I remained nervous, not believing we could relax at all.

I found it necessary to push CBS advertising for a change in approach. I also pressured myself and everyone else on the publicity front. The continuing high-powered assaults we were getting from NBC and ABC, with strong female-oriented M.O.W.s aimed at our core audience, made our ratings, at best, inconsistent.

There was also my own desire never to be in development again and my growing belief that it would be very unusual if anything else in my professional life ever came along that would challenge, satisfy, or offer me anything compared to *Cagney & Lacey*. I wanted to enjoy it, to keep it going as long as possible, and then—to something completely different. Whatever the option, I resolved not to spend my life attempting to duplicate this satisfying experience.

Most of the time I worried about our performance in the Nielsen's, but I also acknowledged that it just might be that, ultimately, the thing that would take us off the air would be Tyne's unwillingness to continue. I hoped I could stall that a year or two, but only time and Ms. Daly would tell. Lest it go unsaid, at that time I was *not* worried about Sharon's departing the show. Unlike Tyne, Sharon had reiterated over and over again that she was happy, would honor her deal, and would stay with the series as long as I wanted her. Ms. Daly, on the other hand, would make a positive reference to our future one day and very shortly thereafter ask what I was going to do for a replacement for her whether for the next day, the next week, or the following season. It could be unsettling.

I lunched with Tyne's husband, Georg Stanford Brown, to discuss his directing for us in the hoped-for coming season. This was very important to Tyne, and I did not feel I could finesse this any longer. (Although Georg is a respected director and one with whom I had worked before, the conflict of interest between his role as director of our show and as husband of our star was difficult for me, if not for him.) The meeting was a bit strained (probably because of the obvious fact that so many episodes had been now made without his help), but, in the overall, it went well.

Later in the afternoon I saw Tyne. She had been in a fairly foul humor for two weeks and I kept waiting for it to reach a boil, but once again she was quite pleasant with me. We even had a few laughs together as she recounted her mild tantrums with staff, crew, and directors. She really hadn't (at least from my point of view) been that bad.

Then, as if on cue, the cuckoo clock cooed, as Sharon Gless appeared in tears and quite distraught. She had learned from Monique that, although she was brilliant in our sexual harassment show ("Fair Game," written by Georgia Jeffries and directed by Sharron Miller), that I had, in editorial, juxtaposed a scene so that her big moment did not end the picture as it had in the script. Gless wanted it changed back, and I told her that I did not reedit pictures based on notes from the cast. (I also gave her my reasoning and my feelings about this, and, although she understood, she still wanted her way.)

She saw it as a slap at her acting (it wasn't) and as a comment on Tyne's popularity and importance (also incorrect). It didn't seem to matter that Sharon was then arguably the bigger television star—or that she had (by far) the most fan mail; Tyne Daly had seniority on our series, had been there first, and it took a long time for Sharon to get over her feeling of being considered second to Tyne Daly. In those days, the accolades for Ms. Daly by the TV Academy only exacerbated this.

None of it was discussed openly. The bottom line here was Sharon's unhappiness and how much I was hurting her by not surrendering to her demand.

Potentially, it opened a real Pandora's box to do what she wanted; it also would not be a simple thing to accomplish, as the episode's negative had already been cut. Still, it was not impossible. (Once, on our "Burnout" episode, I made a change I didn't agree with at Tyne's request. That one had been easier, as it had come before we had finalized, or "locked," the film by cutting negative.)

Maybe I should bend on this one, I thought. Maybe I should just do this and say to hell with it. It really was vintage Gless. I hadn't seen her so distraught or insecure in a long time.

I did not agree with her and felt strongly that this would weaken the episode, but it was, after all, only an episode. Sharon's feelings were more important to me than that. I guesstimated that the change would cost $2,000 and was dismayed to learn it would be closer to $6,500. What the hell!

After putting some final editorial touches on Part I of the two-parter and finishing a concept meeting with director Allen Baron on the season's penultimate episode, I whizzed out to the company's location to see Ms. Gless and to tell her of my decision to capitulate to her request.

She looked particularly radiant that evening as she began our meeting with a thank-you for the flowers I had sent that morning and my note, which tried to express how I hated seeing her upset. I then told her I wanted her to win, but that I also wanted her to know I still did not agree. I was only going to do this to please her, I said, even if it was at the expense of one of our episodes. She appreciated the offer but (almost predictably) declined. She even said that she understood my explanation for why I edited the show as I did and was simply concerned that I did not think she was enough of an actress to hold the audience's attention for the finale. It was her insecurity, not modesty, but still she presented it sweetly. I remember thinking what a quality person she was and how grateful I was to know her. As stated, so often before in this tome, a class act.

The following evening were the Golden Globe Awards. Sharon, Tyne, and the show were nominated. I asked Sharon if she had prepared an acceptance speech. She harrumphed at my perceived sarcasm.

"Me neither," I said. "I'll join you at the bar."

At the Golden Globes, we lost again, and I got more into my cups than usual. At the table were Tyne and Georg, Peter and Donna Lefcourt (still then a couple), PK, Terry Louise, Steve (mentioned here together, but no longer an item), Michael Fuchs, Corday, me, Hector Figueroa, and Sharon (our cinematographer and star were then a duo). Angela Lansbury won the actress award, surprising no one very much, nor did it seem to displease Sharon or Tyne (who appeared to be steeled for that, while sharing the conviction that our show would win).

Then a few minutes later, Angela Lansbury's producer, Peter Fischer, was accepting the Best Series award for *Murder, She Wrote*. All of us were at least slightly stunned. The modest Golden Globe recipient said something about how surprised he was, and I, in an aside too loud to be discreet, added, "*He's* surprised?"

I'd gotten used to losing to *Hill Street Blues*, but this was too much. Everyone agreed it was time to get me out of the hall, and so we adjourned to the then-famed Beverly Hills Bistro for more bubbly and chocolate soufflés. As I nursed the next day's severe hangover, I focused on the reality that it was getting harder and harder to attend these functions and lose.

CHAPTER 33

MILLION DOLLAR BABY

Tyne Daly was eight-weeks pregnant. She told me this in the strictest confidence after a full day's location work, less than a week after the aforementioned Golden Globe debacle. We were in her motor home as she asked me to be happy for her and added that Sharon did not know yet, nor did her children. The amniocentesis (which should be done on pregnant women Tyne's age—then thirty-nine) would not be done until she was four months along. I had to assume this would go to term and figure out an accommodating production plan.

Tyne asked that I keep her secret until February 15, when the season's work would be completed, for then there would be time for her to sit down with her two teen-age girls to present them with the news. She did not want them to read about it in the tabloids. I agreed.

The smart thing to do here, I reasoned, would be to go right back into production and make as many shows as we could before late June, when, to use Tyne's words, she would be "looking like the Queen Mary." How did I do that without alerting the people I'd pledged not to tell? How would I keep the walking wounded going? Tyne and I hugged on parting and said nice things to each other.

The prospect, due to Tyne's pregnancy, of going almost immediately back to work without much of a break had me concerned. The alternative was even worse. This was bound to become a production nightmare of additional cost factors, with the child truly becoming a "million dollar baby." On the other hand, if I could get my strength up and keep going, the newsworthiness of all this and the story material it would give us—yes, Mary Beth Lacey would have a child in midlife—could all be very beneficial to our series.

That same week, Sharon and Tyne were on the covers of both *TV Guide* and *People*. Tom Brocato looked like the hottest press agent in town. I diary-noted then that he should pay us for giving him permission to claim he actually did this work. Peter, PK, and Carole had been out all week with what we would refer to as the "Lacy Street crud." (Our furniture factory/television studio was drafty and damp; mildew was a fact of everyday life, and, with the hours we were keeping and food being served communally, it was like kindergarten in terms of when one got sick, all came down with some version of whatever it was that was going around.) As a result of this particular siege, in addition to my own work, I had been doing theirs. A truly hectic, but (God help me) fun week. What wasn't fun was the realization that my worst fears regarding Steve and Terry and their lack of producing acumen might be true.

Sharon had some script problems that week and so did I. Peter, in a phasing-out mode and sick, did not do a good job on the revisions, and so, first Terry and then Steve were sent to Sharon to solve her problems. Each of them then, in conversations with the actress, made it worse, and I was needed to put out the fire.

The above barely tells the story. Not only was the script made worse and Sharon driven to frustration and near hysteria, but Steve and Terry's hyper-emotional report of the situation further magnified and misrepresented the issue. I easily rewrote what had to be done and quickly converted Sharon's mood to one of easy, good humor.

What, I wondered, did this mean for next year? Probably that Steve and Terry did not have the weight for this job even though my entire budget had been expended on them. Would I now have to do this work myself? That was the prophecy I saw being realized.

Things were not getting easier. The last week of production for the season was simply awful.

Ralph Singleton was a very good production manager, and, as a reward for services beyond the call of duty (or his salary)—he had occasionally, sans credit, served as line producer and always as head of maintenance for Lacy Street—we had rewarded him with the privilege of directing our twenty-second, and final, episode of the season, even though he lacked experience, especially in the area of communicating with actors. Tyne bitterly resented this. It was, as she (correctly) said, "beneath her talent." She reminded me (again, accurately) that she "deserves better." I agreed with all this, acknowledged the mistake, and I apologized for my error in judgment.

"Let him work for *Air Wolf*," a reference to a not-too-successful but then-current TV action show. Ms. Daly went on. The more I attempted to mollify her, the greater was her anger.

Of course, the stupidest mistake was one of those by-the-numbers, traditional television producer faux pas: save the worst for last, never do now what you can put off, and so forth. It resulted in Ralph's directing commitment being fulfilled on the last show—the show when our actors were their most tired.

"I am on empty," Tyne said. She stared at me with dead, shark-like eyes.

I was totally empathetic for I, myself, was so tired, so stressed out due to the work that season, the short order that preceded it, the months of horrific negotiations before that, and the whole Orion–CBS–Mace Neufeld emotional roller coaster, that I was physically weak. Tyne's method of getting herself to work those days was to manufacture energy through antipathy (most of it focused on Ralph, with plenty left for me).

Earlier in the week, at the end of a shooting day, Tyne, John Karlen, Corday, and I shared drinks and laughs in her trailer; all at the expense of poor Ralph.

There was a minor upset revolving around Sharon and the fact that, with no hiatus at all, this also-exhausted star of mine would have to postpone vacation plans to travel to Tahiti because she was being sold into *Letting Go*, an M.O.W. for ABC costarring John Ritter. She was in tears as she told me this, but her tiredness and attendant despair were quickly surpassed by her desire to do this new film.

She thought she would still get plenty of rest after that in the South Seas, not knowing that I might well order the company back in April due to Tyne's yet-to-be-announced pregnancy. ("Not knowing" because of my pledge to Tyne not to reveal anything to anyone until February 15.)

On the next-to-last day of production, Tyne's enmity for Ralph had reached the stage where everyone, save for Ralph, was talking about it. Ms. Daly had foresworn subtlety for caustic sneers and public derision. To what end? This was what I asked her in her trailer. "You have made your point, Tyne." I apologized again for my grievous error. I told her the barbs were wasted on Ralph. "He is having the time of his life."

Tyne was aghast at this.

"Just one more day and a half," I pleaded. "Let's try and be nice to each other and have pleasant memories."

"I want him to die," she snarled. She alluded to enjoying seeing the gophers in her backyard perish, having ingested her carefully distributed poison. That was her fantasy for Ralph. I got to my feet in the trailer,

"You want a director?" I asked rhetorically. "Here's an 'actable' for you. For the day and a half that remains of this shoot, you be *Little Mary Sunshine*. Let's see if you're enough of an actress to pull that off."

The meeting ended in a hug, some laughter, and an agreement by her to try.

The work in Tyne's trailer had a good effect. Our assistant director, Paula Marcus, called me later and thanked me for the obvious change in disposition. Ms. Marcus claimed we would never have made it through the day without this help.

Oh, I nearly forgot. Earlier in Tyne's trailer she spit out her opinion of that week's on the air episode (Part I of our two-parter on cancer). Predictably, she hated it: all of it, her scene work, my editing, the script, the camera work, the direction. She couldn't have been more wrong. The episode was sensational. Months later my opinion would be substantiated by the Academy of Television Arts and Sciences.

Part of the conversation was her question whether Sharon knew that following this new job with John Ritter the blonde must come immediately back to work at Lacy Street due to the pregnancy. Tyne enjoyed my discomfort of having to live all alone with my burden of knowledge on that score, not being able to consult with writers, lawyers, agents, production managers, accountants, or anyone for fear the story would get out before Tyne had a chance to tell her daughters.

Finally, our last day of the season: I was called to the set, where, rumor had it, our indecisive-now-turned-democratic director was holding a debate on how to stage the episode's finale. Something snapped. I came to the fore and, in front of everyone, dictated the ending—beat for beat, shot for shot.[48] Not good form, not my style, and not to Ms. Daly's liking (since she had a whole different scenario she had decided to invent at this eleventh hour). Tyne and I quarreled in front of almost the entire company and then huddled. She agreed to do it my way for this "last and final time," for she would "not return to this series anymore." She closed with the statement that she "had been a whore for me for the last time"—then she exited. Shades of 1982–83.

---

[48]   I take some pride that without any push from me—in fact without any foreknowledge on my part at all—the Museum of Television & Radio used this brief sequence of my shots in their collage of television moments of the past fifty years.

I followed her to her trailer to attempt reconciliation. She drew herself up in a regal pose and calmly asked me please not to enter her domicile on wheels. I did not. Sometimes when a woman says no that is what she means. There was no doubt Tyne was serious, and my belief in settling things as quickly as possible would just have to be put in abeyance this time. It would be interesting, I speculated to no one in particular, to see our performance at that night's wrap party.

The evening of our wrap party for the season was a success. Tyne and I exchanged kisses and hugs, and she even delivered a semi-apology for the outbursts of the past week.

We had wrapped on the fifteenth of February, the same day I ostensibly "learned" of Ms. Daly's pregnancy. I went to Harvey Shephard and asked for an early pickup so that we could quickly go back into production, in order to have some episodes on the air prior to our announcement and portrayal of Mary Beth Lacey's pregnancy (which would, of necessity, run on screen several months behind the pregnancy of the actress who played her). He told me he would have to consult with his management in New York.

It was all slightly complicated and made all the more so by everyone's being tired and now facing little or no vacation; the prospect of a writer's strike, which loomed in the near (within two weeks from then) future; and (would you believe it was still there?) Orion's penny-pinching act.

There was, at that chintzy little company, no understanding of the impossibility of our going on as we had. I felt we deserved some amenities, some concession that—now that we were successful—a portion of the company's harvest might accrue to those who actually did the labor. I was not pushing Marxist doctrine, or even pay raises. This was about getting decent toilet facilities, a reasonable lunch break, better air-conditioning, an eleven-hour workday.

Ball clubs win the pennant, and the bleachers get painted. What I wanted amounted to little more than that: some kind of reinvestment and demonstration of interest by the company. Nothing came without twisting arms.

I remembered my negotiations with these people—remembered the ten weeks of emotional chaos prior to the seven episodes that saved the series. I remembered, and I did not want to go through anything like that again.

I tried to explain to the powers that were that the penurious, "let's do it again for *poor* old Orion," would no longer be effective; that everyone was aware of the company's windfall with *Cagney & Lacey,* and that we all knew that each new pickup on the series meant millions to the company. I speculated that pregnancy or no, the people at Lacy Street were simply not going to function under the same impossible conditions. I went on to state that Orion should figure on paying a 10 percent commission on their new wealth and anticipate a two million dollar deficit for 1985–86 against their minimum sixty to one hundred million dollars in projected profits on the series.

An automatic no came from Orion management: that same anti-labor, anti-talent, blindly pro-corporate tone I remembered so well from the days of negotiation with them—those days that were more exhausting than making any of three series.

"You mean," I rejoined, "that Orion would risk twenty million dollars in order not to spend two million dollars? What kind of business decision is that?"

Orion, I was told, was quite capable of that kind of decision, and that "shoot the deal" was a major philosophy, with the partnership headed up by Arthur Krim. I felt these bosses were like the Van der Veer folks in New York; we were the diamond mine, and they simply could not conceive of our shutting down or not sending our allotment of gems, from which they would profit.

I had, some time ago, decided I didn't want to be in development anymore. Now I didn't want to do any of it. I hate notes. I didn't want to explain to people what it was I was doing: *"Just watch the magic and enjoy the results."*

This, of course, was unrealistic. Where could I work and not have notes? I thought it was at Lacy Street. I thought because I had pulled something off that was miraculous, because, over and over again, I had been proved right (and that I charged so little for this service) that I would not—at least there—need to suffer fools; but it was never ending. I was depressed to learn that this was still the dark at the beginning of the tunnel.

What if, I speculated, I told Orion I would not deal with their shit any longer? "Find a producer for *Cagney & Lacey* and pay me my non-exclusive fees," I could say. I would move from Lacy Street, the writers' strike would hit, and Orion would put my overall development deal (due to expire seven months after that February date, in September 1985) on force majeure.[49] I felt this strike, should it happen, could go on for months. Without me at Lacy Street, crossing the picket lines, could they make the show? Doubtful. Therefore, I would have to go back,

---

[49]   Literally means "major force," such as war or labor strike or other things prohibiting a firm from conducting business. What it comes down to is giving the company the right to suspend and extend contracts and make no payment on them.

without leverage, to protect my syndication payoff of two or three million dollars plus. Or would I? I can be a pretty self-destructive asshole when I get righteous.

With the possibility of no income from Orion and none from *Cagney & Lacey* and the industry shut down due to a strike, I figured I'd better spend the weekend going over our accounts to see just how we could operate on Corday's salary alone. I was digging myself into a very deep emotional hole.

I was cheered somewhat by the news delivered to me on Monday morning that our pickup from CBS was official. We were renewed for twenty-two more episodes—even before *Dallas*. Admittedly, we did have to go to extraordinary lengths (Tyne's pregnancy) to get it. *All* we had to do now was make the shows.

At a birthday bash for La Gless, hosted by yours truly, at the very original Chasen's in Beverly Hills. Sharon is flanked by her first leading man (RJ Wagner) and her [at that time] last leading man, John Ritter. From left: the then Mrs. John Ritter (Nancy Morgan), RJ, La Gless, Ritter, Barbara Corday, Robert Walker (agent and Ms. James' escort), and Monique James. Standing between Hector Figueroa (right) and me is Jill St. John (the then soon-to-be Mrs. RJ Wagner). Tyne was out of the country on a holiday and not able to attend.

Photo: Rosenzweig Personal Collection

CHAPTER 34

BUSINESS AND JUSTICE

The "impossible" conditions to which I have referred were primarily the hours and how our format required Tyne and Sharon be in virtually every scene. Since we could not change the latter without doing a major revamp of the show, what I was attempting to do was change the former. We were working at least fourteen hours per day with only half-hour lunch breaks. It was inhumane, even without factoring in Tyne's pregnancy.

Much of this is about these two, very hardworking women, but, as long and hard as Sharon and Tyne worked, when they arrived at our factory in the morning, people were already there to greet them, to clothe them, and to apply makeup and dress their hair. Electricians and grips, assistant directors, caterers, and drivers were already well into their day. When our stars left for the evening, many workers still remained to clean and wrap the equipment and the wardrobe and prepare for the next day. The workload was truly insane and fueled by greed (both of the rank and file and the bosses).

At this point, it seemed to me, with the benefit of a rare early go-ahead from the network, we could make some adjustments, returning our work schedule to some semblance of sanity, reminiscent of the way it was in the 1960s.

Singleton, Stan, Rosenbloom, biz affairs maven Robert Mirisch, and I met to discuss plans. Rosenbloom was presidential, and I was semi-calm, but not very. I had come down (or was it up?) a bit from my mood(s) of the weekend, but I was not in the best of shape. Still, I was somewhat effective, and I believed I would get the tools I needed. Rosenbloom and Stan voiced genuine concern whether we could continue with Tyne pregnant. I was tired of being second-guessed, and my latest ploy was to analogize myself with Patton: "Just give me the gas, and I will get us to Berlin."

I had offered a producer post on the series to Ann Daniel of ABC. She was flattered and now mulling the career change. She couldn't come to work until summer, but I wanted to keep that possibility open. I believed she would be terrific. I had, at that time, no second choice. I needed someone I could respect and trust, and who had communication and leadership skills. This was not a job for any of the types who had worked under me in the past. I would be better off, I reasoned, having no one than spending bucks for that kind of "talent."

A week of these interminable conferences with Rosenbloom and his staff had now elapsed. Rosenbloom had yet to capitulate on several points, but I believed I would win, though I knew there would be fights and waste ahead. Despite a great deal of underlying mutual affection, we really were from very different camps—and this was often illustrated in the peculiar Lacy Street idiom of the time.

There was the question/answer used by the staff, department heads, and writers, known as ABC. It stood for "At Barney's Convenience" (as in, "When's lunch?" "ABC." Or, "When are dailies?" Again, "ABC" would be the answer. The second was chiefly used by the crew. SSN stood for "Stan Says No" (as in, "Can we have another (a) set of lights, (b) camera, (c) roll of toilet paper?" The answer was invariably "SSN").

Stan Neufeld (I reiterate, no relation to Mace) was known as the White Rat even before his tenure on the groundbreaking *Naked City* New York series in the early days of episodic TV. He reportedly once answered a crew member's request for water on the set with the admonition that the worker should bring a canteen from home. At Orion, while his bosses flew nothing but first class from L.A. to New York and back again, Stan would likely book himself on some obscure airline with a layover in some place such as Fargo, North Dakota, for two hours or longer, saving the company $130 on his airfare. If it were my money, I think he'd be my first choice to handle it, but only after being assured he would attend several seminars on the dangers of tripping over dollars to pick up nickels. That, in a very real way, is what we were now meeting about.

Meanwhile, on a happier note, Pulitzer Prize–winning critic Howard Rosenberg had become a born-again *Cagney & Lacey* fan. He now wrote a rave for the series and for our cancer two-parter in the *Los Angeles Times*.

I continued to press on in a most manic way. These phases were noteworthy in that my moods were high, as was my energy, until day's end, when I collapsed into sleep. There was so much to do that, even without the Orion stumbling block, it would have been a Herculean task. With them, fumbling along, it was all the more arduous.

By week's end, as promised, Steve and Terry delivered nine scripts of *Cagney & Lacey* for the new season. God bless them, they *did* work hard. My lawyer and agent suggested a meeting to discuss the future. It was hard for me to see beyond this current mass of work. Corday was also inundated in her presidential post at Columbia Studios, largely due to the pending WGA strike. Our marriage was literally on hold.

On Saturday morning, March 2, 1985, I was awakened by a phone call from Steve Brown. He informed me that the writers had voted to strike. It would become official at midnight the following Monday. My natural instinct was to want to escape to avoid the depression I was feeling.

This strike had nothing to do with me. None of the issues really touched me. I had run a model shop, employing women, minorities, and freelancers. The irony was that this strike would have a greater negative impact on me than on anyone else. Others could shut down: the season might start a little late, but everyone would be in the same boat—everyone, except this producer and his pregnant star. A delay was disastrous and probably put us into a situation where we could not deliver to the network. In that event, cancellation was more than just a possibility.

My come to me/go from me fortune was getting on my nerves. The stress factor was such that I felt I might not live to see (let alone enjoy) the damn money anyway. What I had to do, I theorized, was to forget about the fucking millions and just do what I wanted—easier said than done.

What did I want? To go on strike with everyone else and have a holiday of sorts and possibly see the show canceled? To work? To go for the gold, cross the picket lines, and tell the Guild to go screw? Each had appealing aspects. Each had disastrous potential. The obstacles placed in my path and that of this show had truly been Homeric. That's why it's such a good story. "Without conflict, it's just two white chicks sittin' Around talkin'."[50]

Abe Somer was also back in my life. My old college chum had resurfaced—this time as Tyne Daly's attorney. He was on the phone delivering a not-so-veiled threat

---

[50]   This last sentence was a phrase used regularly in meetings with the writing staff and alludes to the title of the John Ford Noonan play *A Couple of White Chicks Sitting Around Talking*.

that Tyne Daly might not return to the series because I would not defend her claim against CBS concerning her personal contract with them for TV movies.

(Ms. Daly apparently wanted to enforce the pay-or-play provision of her deal, and CBS, understandably, wanted the commitment rolled over due to the short *Cagney & Lacey* hiatus, which was not their fault but rather a direct result of *her* pregnancy.)

I reminded Abe that his client was pregnant, and "on empty" just days before; did she really want to go right into work again? Then, in a more menacing tone, Abe reiterated the threat that his client would withhold services. I was so tired and beaten down that I honestly didn't care. I said the equivalent of "do me something." And the conversation was over.

Of all the bad news that week (Abe, the strike, Tyne Daly), by far the most debilitating was that delivered by the men of Orion. I felt they were so blind and unappreciative. Just for publicity, or as an entree to talent and networks alone, any company would gladly sustain a flagship like *Cagney & Lacey*, even if it was only a break-even proposition. At this time, It was at least a fifty million dollar–plus bonanza, and still Orion kept up their miserly, pessimistic, poor-boy gloom-and-doom mentality.

I felt betrayed by them. It felt as though they not only failed to help but added to my burden. They did not pay me well. They did not appreciate what I had done. They only seemed to question me and get in my way, forcing me to use up precious energy, which I needed for other battles.

I do not believe this was only my singular point of view; of all of the writers, directors, and actors to which—thanks to *Cagney & Lacey*—Orion had access during the 1980s, none of them, although many were asked, chose to make any kind of overall deal with that company. Compare that simple fact to the long-standing relationships that existed between talent and MTM, Paramount, or even the oft-times maligned Universal Studios, and some idea can be gleaned of how this company was then being perceived by the industry.

I would have liked strokes. They seemed incapable of strokes. OK, I didn't need them. The money? Well, I was paid in other ways: glory, fan mail, peer accolades, prestige, celebrity, the illusion of power. I would plead with them to give me what I needed to do, what I had to do, and to stop questioning and examining everything ad nauseam!

I had proven that I knew what I was doing: two revivals after cancellations, no deficit after fifty-seven episodes, a public relations and critical blockbuster, and a totally independent operation requiring virtually no draining of their capital, overhead, or manpower—plus an industry hit—for whatever that meant in relations with all three networks! Jesus, it aggravated me!

I was beside myself as I thought about the future, post–*Cagney & Lacey*. My growing inability to tolerate notes would not serve me too well in the marketplace. I remembered how frustrating unemployment was and how embittered I felt. I tried to think positively. Unemployment, as I had experienced it, probably wouldn't happen again: I wouldn't be dead broke so quickly for openers, my children were grown, and I had had the satisfaction of having pulled off my miracle in *Cagney & Lacey*. Lastly, I was nearly twenty years older; I did not have to worry about filling up as much time as I had when I was a youth of thirty. No, this time I did not foresee having to flip a coin, as I nearly did in the mid-1970s, between bartending and driving a taxicab. Despite this interlude of positive thinking, I was feeling totally frazzled in 1985 and remember getting a big laugh from the then-hospitalized Sidney Clute, when I paraphrased famed comic writer Hal Kanter, that I did not actually have a beard; it was my face that was unraveling.

I stated earlier that I genuinely like Dick Rosenbloom. Whatever our differences, we had (and I believe still maintain) an underlying affection for one another. He is a nice man. Because of these feelings, I took the time, in mid-March of 1985 while the writers' strike was still stumbling toward a conclusion, to tell him the truth of how I was feeling about our relationship.

He took it fairly well but didn't really get it. He told me it was all a result of my paranoia about Mace and my understandable physical exhaustion—not a bad couple of guesses on his part. This was followed by a typically long Rosenbloom-led meeting on next season's plans, in which I finally won—I thought—my plan for an eight-day schedule.[51]

They wanted to drop the annual New York shoot, and they were planning an unrealistically short break for Tyne's baby to be born. These both concerned me. I reasoned that these things could be confronted later. I was on my game in the meeting and behaved myself as well. I did not believe any real damage had been done twixt Rosenbloom and me.

Rosenbloom seemed to be softening on his hard line, vis-à-vis our additional production costs for the season. I was working at being patient and tolerant. The veneer on my shield was very thin.

---

[51]   It was always part of my plan to expand from our unrealistic seven-day shoot to an eight-day. Now the Daly pregnancy made that a virtual necessity.

Tyne was seething. She was angered that I would not take up her cause with CBS over her pay-or-play commitment. She had now aligned me completely with the bosses. She was "disgraced," her honour (my spelling, not hers) demeaned. She was seeking justice—as usual, by her definition and to her specifications. It was all so childish and petulant, and yet, somehow, eloquent.

That I did not agree with her position was greeted with derision. When I suggested that perhaps she'd prefer having another producer to talk to, she accused me of deserting her. It was complicated by my understanding her pain and my empathy for her search for justice and fairness.

It wasn't money that Tyne wanted. She longed desperately to win—to beat the bosses. She forced them to sign a pay-or-play commitment, and now they were using her unborn child to "punish" her by reneging. She just could not let go of the pain of her past. And I did—and do—relate to all of this; did—and do—understand it. And I also heard how crazed she sounded. No wonder my attorney, Stu Glickman, had been avoiding my phone calls that week—to him I probably sounded every bit as distraught as Ms. Daly.

"They"(the bosses) get to us because it is their nature and because it is our fate to be gotten. The trick here, I think, is to recognize that we play just as big a part in this as they do. I was ruminating on something very much like the above, sitting poolside in my beautifully manicured yard (which was adjacent to my very own tennis court and all-tile swimming pool), having just received the news that the writers' strike was officially over, and realizing—if you can believe it—that I was depressed. It was partially a postproduction malaise, but only to a degree. The confrontation with Tyne, my ongoing, not necessarily realistic, concerns for my financial future, my vain obsession with my fifteen-pound weight gain over that past year, all of it had me wallowing in a syndrome that at best could be described as unattractive. I needed to make some decisions, and I seemed unable to do so. I was feeling lost and overwhelmed.

It was silly, for compared to the past, there was not that much to do. I was just wallowing in this, consumed by my sense of "overwhelm." I had to do something. I decided on the frontal approach and invited Tyne Daly to lunch. She accepted. I talked to her about business and justice and related it to the ABC takeover that was on the front pages that week.[52] I was pretty good with the "camel and

---

[52]   By Cap-Cities. The men at ABC who had made so many bad decisions that had resulted in the stock being devalued (which allowed this takeover to happen) were now each rewarded with millions as part of their buyout. Justice indeed.

the scorpion" tale of the Middle East,[53] but I almost blew it when we got on the subject of Abe Somer. At one point I thought I had lost her. One of the mistakes I often make with Tyne—as we talk and I like her and her brilliant mind—is that I forget she is an actor and one must always be careful what one says to someone of that persuasion. Anyway, in my diary I graded the meeting B.

Tyne had gone on the wagon, quit smoking, and given up coffee—all for the baby. She seemed very aware that her behavior in the waning days/weeks of our last shoot had not been so hot and wanted to improve that. She conceded to having a black belt in mouth karate and recognized she was therefore dangerous. She told me she had started therapy and "hoped to be well by April 15."[54]

---

[53]   A scorpion asks a camel for a ride on its back so as to cross the Nile. "No," says the camel, "you are poisonous, and if I let you ride on my back, you will sting me and I will die." "Nonsense," says the scorpion, "then I, too, would also die when you sink in the Nile." That made sense to the camel, and so a bargain was struck. Midway across the river, much to the camel's surprise, the scorpion stings him. Immediately the poison rushes through his veins, and, as he is dying, the camel asks why. Why this betrayal, especially since it will only result in both their deaths? "It's my nature," says the scorpion. Just for the record, I know of one other rejoinder from the scorpion, which is again delivered after a shrug: "It's the Middle East," he says.

[54]   The date of our unusually early start, necessitated by Tyne's condition.

CHAPTER 35

BATTLES ON THE HOME FRONT

I had won the right from Rosenbloom for an eight-day schedule (up from the original budget for seven days of production). How I used most of that time was to limit our shooting day to eleven hours, expand lunch from a half hour to an hour (Tyne appreciated this; Sharon did not. Ms. Gless said she got sleepy with such a long break), and set aside three hours per episode for my new idea of an elongated cast reading and script discussion with the writers and actors (Sharon liked this; Tyne did not. Ms. Daly believed she was giving away too many of her secrets and that her performance would thus lose spontaneity). Victories did not come easy at Lacy Street and were rarely complete.

My wars now were all on the home front, with Rosenbloom, the staff, and the cast. I no longer had to battle with CBS. By 1985 and our 85–86 season, the people at the network had come to acknowledge what the show was, and pretty much left me alone to do it.

Some will argue that the season of 1984–85 was our best. It did receive ten Emmy nominations, and there were wins for Tyne (her then-precedent-setting third victory in succession), for editing (Jim Gross), for sound (Mo Harris), for direction (Karen Arthur), for writing (Pat Green), and myself for Best Dramatic Series.[55] For those who keep track of these things, such qualitative episodes as "Heat," "Unusual Occurrence," "Stress," "Happily Ever After," "Rules of the Game," and "Who Said It's Fair I and II" (our cancer two-parter) headed up the list of episodes that were absolutely top drawer.

---

[55]   Besides the aforementioned winners, Sharon Gless, writer Deborah Arakelian, composer Nan Schwartz, and supporting actor John Karlen were also nominated.

Some days before that awards night, a phone call from Tyne at 12:30 AM interrupted what had been a deep sleep. Ms. Daly was incensed over the writing of her character in "On the Street," our projected third episode of the new season.[56] It was the script we would be reading later that afternoon. I thanked her for sharing and went back to sleep. As stated so often before, Tyne Daly is a piece of work, but (truth to tell) I would always take her caring and custodianship over ambivalence any day or, for that matter, in the middle of the night.

At 9:30 that morning, I was at CBS for what was billed as a major battle over "The Clinic,"[57] our script dealing with the bombing of abortion clinics. We had received three pages of single-spaced notes from Gil "Stainless" Steele, the CBS rep on our series from the network's broadcast standards department, and, besides the usual language and cautionary notes, there was the very ominous, and (to me) onerous "suggestion" that our two leads should be on opposite sides of the abortion issue, thus giving the episode better "balance."

"Marshal your forces," I said to the minor exec. "I will have one meeting and one meeting only with your department on this subject." I went on to clue him in to the fact that, although there was much on which the two detectives might disagree, neither Cagney nor Lacey would *ever* betray the 67 percent of working women in America who believed in a woman's right to choose. I warned Gilbert Steele to "steel" himself for this battle, for I would certainly be ready.

I was, in fact, well prepped for a colossal fight but found myself preempted by West Coast standards and practices director Carol Altieri at the morning conference. "Understand something, Barney," she said. "You are among fans. Tell us what is non-negotiable for you."

The air went out of my contentious balloon with that welcome. "Stainless" Steele's memo was relegated to the files. To this day, I believe that had the fight taken place, as advertised, the episode would have been a better one. I was so disarmed by the trust and warmth of that meeting that, in letting down my guard, I actually gave away more than I would have in conflict. Regardless of my susceptibility to flattery, Cagney and Lacey did remain pro-choice.

---

[56] It was good enough to become our season's premier episode, directed by Alex Singer and written by Cynthia Darnell.

[57] "The Clinic," written by Judy Merl & Paul Eric Myers and directed by Alex Singer.

A short meeting with Georgia Jeffries followed, in which I shared some of my continuing concerns about our staff; then a meet with Harvey Shephard where I got a sympathetic ear to my release plans for next season; followed by a "money and justice" quickie with CBS business affairs chief Bill Klein, regarding dollars for a New York shoot. Lunch with Meta Rosenberg was next.

Ann Daniel had yet to commit to the job of being my trusted producer on the series, and so I discussed the possibility with Meta, whom I had long admired, of coming to Lacy Street and producing the series for me. Besides being my one-time aunt-in-law (widow to Aaron's brother, George "Rosy" Rosenberg), Meta was—among other things—a top-notch photographer, a top literary agent, the executive producer and sometime director of *The Rockford Files*, and a very talented and super-smart lady. I left the luncheon feeling good about this prospect. Meta's qualifications, coupled with my lack of enthusiasm for that afternoon's reading (due to Tyne's middle-of-the-night phoner), had me whistling as I pulled into my parking space. "Do your worst," I thought. "You won't have me to kick around very long."

The reading was a rough one. Steve Brown was out of his chair more than once, and—if he weren't then in escrow on a new house—might have been out the door. Ultimately, we spent nearly three hours and did not get through the entire script. We sent the actors home around 7 PM and adjourned to my office for discussions and notes. By 10 PM I was—as in the past with so many scripts—acting all the parts and spewing out dialogue as Georgia Jeffries and Pat Green took copious notes. Even Steve Brown was smiling. As our meeting concluded around midnight, I announced what a good time I'd had. I drove home with the realization (re: Meta Rosenberg/Ann Daniel and leaving Lacy Street), that I had better be careful what I ask for lest I get it.

I called Tyne to tell her how excited I was over the changes that were in work and about this new reading-rehearsal process that was helping to bring it all about. Although pleased with my enthusiasm, she found the three-hour session exhausting. She also registered concern for the pain her "mouth karate" might inflict. I encouraged her to keep fighting, believing better material would result, but—if possible—to try avoiding buzz words like *dumb* and *stupid*.

That same mid-May of 1985, Dick Rosenbloom, the Orion TV production gang, and I were still in conflict with one another. We had been in production over a month on the new season, and there was yet to be an agreement on a budget or an operating plan for that year. The eight-day shooting plan was once again under attack because of its potential violation of the actor's "span,"[58] as was the New York shoot (which, if we did it at all, CBS and not Orion would pay for, thanks to my annual "money and justice" meet with the network's Bill Klein).

Stan came up with his annual suggestion for saving money, which amounted to a mid-stream change in the format of the show by giving more work to Kove, Lumbly, and Waxman. Why not? He didn't have to make the show or defend the change to the network. I suggested that such an alteration of our successful format was possible. All they had to do was fire me—please!

I alluded to the favor MTM did Steven Bochco by firing him off of *Hill Street,* but there were no takers.[59]

I pushed their man, Ralph Singleton, into the limelight as on-the-set line-producer (a good idea from PK the night before). This was met with a delayed, albeit excellent, reception. "Delayed," I think, because they weren't sure what I was up to. I believe they were trying to ascertain if they were being set up, and, in a way, they were. Ralph was a known commodity where the women were concerned, and, although it was true his first loyalty was to Stan, he was not disloyal to me.

Besides, Ralph was there in the meeting; he therefore knew I was the one offering him the credentials he had always coveted. I reasoned his constant presence on the set should relieve Orion a bit and just might diffuse some of the minor day-to-day problems with the women, thus making my job easier.

---

[58]   Refers to the span of time or number of calendar days during which a series may be shot without incurring penalty payments to the actors. By going eight days per episode, instead of seven, we were automatically adding twenty-two extra shooting days to the overall schedule. The possibility of violating "the span," therefore, became a real economic issue.

[59]   MTM shows, always among the most expensive to produce thanks to an almost-exclusive policy of hiring hyphenates to run their shows, had *Hill Street* listed as their most expensive. Cost issues came to a head in 1983 when NBC bought another show from Bochco, *Bay City Blues.* That was canceled after four low-rated episodes and, coupled with increased costs on that series plus *Hill Street* (which Bochco resisted efforts to reduce), proved to be the last straw for MTM. Bochco was fired soon after the hundredth episode was filmed. No need to mourn; Bochco had another series commitment from NBC, so all that was needed was a new studio. Fox and Harris Katleman to the rescue, and *L.A. Law* was born. It might have given Rosenbloom, et al., pause that *Hill Street* was soon canceled after the Bochco departure.

Rosenbloom correctly got that, since I was promoting Ralph, I was no longer seeking a high-priced producer and that more and more of my time would be spent on *Cagney & Lacey* and less and less on future development for Orion.

It had been six months since I had learned of my pending multi-millionaire status from Rosenbloom and Kellner. I had made my decision. I would stay with *Cagney & Lacey* but not re-up with Orion. This would hurt Rosenbloom's feelings, which I could only hope would be somewhat mollified by the $250,000 per year savings his company would now receive, since they would no longer have to pay me for my exclusivity or for development. I was coming to—though not yet arrived at—the place where I would not resent the $250,000 annual loss in exclusivity money from the company. It was my choice, and I was doing what I wanted. Orion's risk was that I might—upon hearing an interesting offer—take it, and leave them to find a replacement for me on *Cagney & Lacey* at (perhaps) multiples of that $250,000 figure. Given my emotional history/attachment with this show, Orion's management would have to figure their risk was small in that regard.

CHAPTER 36

JUST LIKE BEFORE ... ONLY DIFFERENT

The season of 1985–86 was not far behind its immediate predecessor in quality: a real accomplishment considering the loss of Peter Lefcourt and Terry Louise Fisher. (Ms. Fisher asked for, and was granted, release from her contract on the first day of production on the new season, stating she was burned out and near collapse because of no real hiatus as a result of the Daly pregnancy. It had always been a given that Lefcourt would not return.)

In looking over my diary for that period, it is, in the overall, not unlike the previous year, except a lot was different. For the second time in succession, I picked up the Emmy for Best Dramatic Series, Sharon Gless—at long last—brought home her first statue, as did John Karlen (Best Supporting Actor), along with Georg Stanford Brown (direction). For the record keepers, our best episodes included such individual shows as "Ordinary Hero," "On the Street," "Mothers & Sons," "Power," "DWI," "The Gimp," and "Parting Shots." Nominees who did not win that year were Tyne Daly, along with Outstanding Guest Performers in a Series, Peggy McCay and James Stacy.

I would make a monster deal while creating The Rosenzweig Company, find myself back in production with old friend Ronald M. Cohen (for the first time since our successful pilot of *American Dream*); add two new running characters to *Cagney & Lacey* (Detective Jonah Newman, played by Dan Shor, and Cagney's new lover, an ACLU attorney played by my former *American Dream* leading man, Stephen Macht).

I also created a terrific but pressure-filled campaign regarding our abortion clinic episode—which had even Corday conceding I was the best press agent in the family.

Sharon and James Stacy in character for our multiple-award-winning episode, "The Gimp." It is, I think, noteworthy that Mr. Stacy received more favorable fan mail as the Cagney love interest than all other male leads we cast during the life of the series combined.

Photo: Sharon Gless Personal Collection

Sharon Gless on the night, in 1987, of her second Emmy win. Also at my Hancock Park front door are Carole R. Smith (left) and Monique James.

Photo: Rosenzweig Personal Collection

Stephen Macht, who played ACLU attorney David Keeler in *Cagney & Lacey* as well as Danny Novak, the male lead of my *American Dream* series, and Sharon in a CBS publicity shot.

Photo: Courtesy of MGM

We were not the only series to take on the issue. *Spencer, For Hire* followed us by only a week or so and actually made a better episode on the subject. They slipped by, without attack from the right-to-lifers and, as a result, went basically unnoticed. My tactic was quite different. I not only notified the media that we were tackling the subject, I also contacted such natural allies for our series as the National Organization for Women (NOW) and the National Abortion Rights Action League (NARAL), asking for their support in the very likely event the so-called right-to-life forces attempted to picket CBS affiliates, urging them not to air the episode. There was no indication that they would do this, of course, or that the country's abortion foes even knew of our episode's story line, but I played the censorship card nevertheless, and the other side fortunately complied by attempting to do just what I said they would in the first place.

I did not make this up entirely out of paranoia. In our first season (the one with Meg Foster's Cagney, spring of 1982), the forces of the political right took exception to an episode they hadn't even seen ("Better Than Equal," with script by Bud Freeman and directed by Ray Danton). The story featured a strong anti-feminist, Phyllis Schlafly-like character, played by Julie Adams, and CBS affiliates were picketed by her supporters and other right-wingers to not air the episode. I do not know how many stations actually folded under this kind of pressure, but I do know that the affiliate in Chicago did capitulate and refused to air the episode. It cost us valued rating points in a key market at a critical time in the life of the series, and I resolved, in 1982, not to let that happen to me again.

"The Clinic" campaign that fall of 1985 was a sensation. Major articles in the *New York Times, USA Today,* the *Los Angeles Times,* the *Washington Post,* and interviews with me on the *CBS Evening News with Dan Rather, Entertainment Tonight,* and *MacNeil/Lehrer* followed. Only Corday asked, "What do you call this campaign? Please ban me, or ban me, please?" Our ratings stunk, the competition was getting tougher and tougher, and I thought we needed the juice. Harvey Shephard agreed. It was amazing how I could continually stir the pot on this then-four-year-old show.

That season, because of Terry Louise Fisher's unanticipated absence, I would also add to the staff supervising writer-producer Liz Coe, as I more and more acquiesced to the industry reality of hyphenates in title if not in function; and, finally, although I had long ago stopped wooing, was turned down by Meta Rosenberg, who "didn't want to work that hard," and then also by Ann Daniel, whose stock options at ABC had simply become too valuable (due to the Cap-Cities takeover of that network) to do anything but remain at ABC for her option rights to fully vest. The cuckoo clock accords would end (at least temporarily) as both Tyne and

Sharon simultaneously attacked the same issue: the publication of a novelization of *Cagney & Lacey*.

(Shortly after returning to work to start the season in the spring of 1985, the women discovered that Dell would be publishing a novelization of *Cagney & Lacey*. Both of my stars chose to believe that I had somehow conspired with Orion to keep this a secret from them. It was simply a matter of not thinking it important enough to share, but it was an underestimation on my part and was, as interpreted by the two women, a matter of me "pissing in *their* tomato juice.")

The book was part of Orion's general merchandising campaign (such as it was) and authored by a writer I had never heard of (before or since). It was presented to me as an accomplished fact the previous January. I remember not being happy about it at the time and insisting on having some input. I volunteered Corday, PK, publicist Eileen Peterson, and myself to the task, so that at least our fans would not be totally nonplussed by what they read. I spent several days, without compensation, reading, editing, and commenting on this enterprise, proving the theory that no good deed goes unpunished.

I tried to tell the women that their beef was with Orion, with their agents and lawyers, and asked to be removed from the middle of this (I had enough troubles just trying to make the show; I didn't need to take on the grief of corporate Orion), but no dice. I'm the one they saw every day, I'm the "daddy," and I got it in the ear. (At this stage of the game, Tyne and Sharon took their custodianship of the characters they played so seriously they believed they should be allowed control over such matters. I don't know what book they read on American capitalism, but it was not one with which I was familiar.)

Bottom line, here's how bad it was: If I thought, in May of 1985, that Dell or Orion would have accepted my check to cover their $20,000 out-of-pocket expenses and simply burned the manuscript, forgetting the whole thing, I would have personally delivered the $20,000 with thanks.

Mace Neufeld would name me as codefendant (with Orion) in a 25 million-dollar lawsuit. Mace wanted, among other things, "his share" of my exclusivity money from Orion, and charged me with co-conspiring with that company to defraud him of those monies. Had I taken the deal at Columbia that Orion simply matched comma for comma, there would have been no possibility of such a claim, but because I had allowed Orion to equal the original Columbia offer, I suppose Mace felt he had his opportunity to include me as a codefendant in the suit that was primarily, it seemed, aimed at Orion.

My innovation of special screenings of *Cagney & Lacey* episodes in motion picture theaters (ostensibly to help us select which episode to submit for Emmy consideration) became a highly successful public relations stroke, and, on the negative side, there was a major crisis involving me and the two stars over a cover story in *TV Guide* (August 10, 1985), which had Gless not speaking to me for over two weeks.

There was the ill-fated *Fortune Dane* series, starring Carl Weathers. I also produced a tribute to Corday, as a result of her being named "Humanitarian of the Year" by a major Jewish charity (the show starred Sharon Gless, Tyne Daly, and Michele Lee, while featuring a young and then-relatively unknown comic, Jay Leno, along with Robert Stack, RJ Wagner, Carl Weathers, William Shatner, Joe Bologna, and Robert Culp as the Columbia Boys Choir, singing "Anything Goes" and "You're the Top," with special lyrics by Marilyn & Alan Bergman).[60]

Gless won the Golden Globe (the only time anyone associated with *Cagney & Lacey* got this prize, despite many nominations), and Harvey Shephard decided to leave CBS for indy-prod at Warner Brothers to be replaced by Kim LeMasters: *Ave, Caesar, morituri te salutant!*

Exhausted, debilitated, and just plain *tired* are words I continued to use a lot in my journal. It's not just that I have a limited vocabulary—that's the way it was. The work was not getting easier. On the contrary, it was getting more and more difficult. Stress, both physical and emotional, the hours, and the minimal vacation time were some of the contributing factors.

The Orion team had taken their toll. They typically withheld the necessary tools, or delivered them so late, after lengthy and tiring arguments, that my victories were often pyrrhic.

There was my own tendency to hire people I liked or trusted but who did not necessarily do the job well enough to be left alone to do it. My susceptibility to Sharon and Tyne's demands, which caused an extra workload for me and all those with me, cannot be minimized, and, finally, there was an industry-wide problem: the entertainment explosion of that time, the resultant geometric progression of the dollar worth of any film or television package, was—via the trickle-down theory—having an effect on me as well.

---

[60]   The Bergmans' lyrics include the songs from *Yentl, The Way We Were* and "Windmills of Your Mind" (the theme from *The Thomas Crown Affair*), to name only a few. The evening for Barbara was a smash, with *Variety* stating it was "produced perfectly."

The Columbia Boys Choir I assembled to pay tribute to the 1985 "woman of the year," Barbara Corday. From left: RJ Wagner, Robert Stack, Joe Bologna, Carl Weathers, William Shatner, and Robert Culp.

Photo: Rosenzweig Personal Collection

The good news was my meager percentage of profits would be greater. The bad? Each show or potential show on television was worth so much more (practically with each passing day) that the various individual film and television companies were grabbing up every piece of writing talent with any kind of credits at all and putting them under exclusive contracts at exorbitant sums of money, in the hope that those people would create and produce even more such product for their corporate vaults.

The result was that we were no longer playing musical chairs the way we had, for now the rules were reversed. Instead of removing a chair, each turn we were removing a player.

Staff writers would leave shows for overall development deals, effectively exiting the series marketplace to become entrepreneur-developers, regardless of their lack of expertise or suitability in this arena. Existing shows would, as a consequence, have to go deeper and deeper into the talent barrel to find workers.

The best television writers left series television years before the mid-1980s. Now the industry would make millionaires out of the less-than-brilliant ones who remained, leaving only the most minimal talents and beginners to do the work.

It wasn't just that writers were being put under exclusive contract and therefore generally unavailable for hire. It was my reluctance (read refusal) to grant producer credit to some kids in their early twenties with something like only two episodes as a writer of a *Wonder Years* to their credit.

I also resisted the packaging fee as immoral and a form of extortion. These agent add-ons had their beginnings in the long-ago of television, in the days when, for example, a network would place a direct call to the William Morris Agency or the Music Corporation of America in New York. The network would call one of these major agencies because what they perceived they needed was a new variety series, starring someone such as (again, only a potential example) that agency's client, singer Perry Como.

The agency would package the show, providing from its roster of clients not only Mr. Como, but the producer, director, the musical coordinator, choreographer, costar, et al. For presenting the network with this very neat package, the agency would require a fee: usually 10 percent of the show's entire budget, over and above the contractual commissions charged their clients for getting them work and negotiating their deals.

There was so much money involved that it was not unusual for the Morris office to be making more than their own client(s), including Perry Como, the guy whose talent had precipitated the whole thing in the first place. To soften that blow, the talent agents would (after some pressure from the client and, ultimately, the justice department) eventually agree not to commission the client personally but to be content with only the packaging fee. This kept Como and other such talents sanguine, as it appeared, at least on the surface, as if they were saving money by not having to pay commissions. No one seemed to calculate what those hundreds of thousands per week being paid to the packager were truly costing Mr. Como in the form of reduced profits or in monies not expended on making the show better. And who would do that anyway? Certainly not William Morris or the accountants they hired to calculate such things for the producer/star.

Bad as all this was, at least the Morris office or the Music Corporation of America did, in those days, provide a service. But by the 1970s, right up until the present, the concept of the packaging fee had finally been subverted to the point where one single element created a so-called package; if an agency had a star, a producer, or anyone who was of the essence to the deal, that would (in this modern era) constitute a package.

By insisting on—and getting—a packaging commission, Zeigler/Diskant, the literary agency that in the late 1970s represented the Steinbeck estate, would actually reap a greater fee on my *East of Eden* miniseries than would their client, the estate of author John Steinbeck. The affordable $400,000 then paid by BNB in total for the rights would, instead of going to the Steinbeck heirs (who would then pay the normal 10 percent commission of $40,000 on the sale) be allocated as follows: $150,000 to the Steinbeck estate and $250,000 to the agent for "packaging" the project, which, by the way, they didn't do.

The conflicts of interest are obvious and abhorrent. The very people who have a fiduciary responsibility to represent and protect their clients are, in a very real way, taking the food from their mouths.

There was no need for such fees on *Cagney & Lacey*, and I would not pay them. Ronnie Meyer, who I believed liked and respected me well enough personally, nevertheless once told his client, Sharon Gless: "Barney is not a friend of the agency." The agency in this case was the super powerful and ubiquitous CAA. To be labeled "not a friend" could mean that many doors might be closed in the very tough struggle to buy/lease/rent the writing and directing talent necessary to make a quality show.

The final freeze-frame from our Emmy Award-winning episode of "Heat."
Photo: Courtesy of MGM

To work on such a show as mine might be good for the client, but the test since the 1980s has been, is it good for the agency? True as this was at CAA, it was just as much or more so at the other of the then-big-three talent agencies, William Morris, and ICM.

Good for the client was old-time thinking. That was from the days of the client being number one, someone to be served by the agent. Now it was all about the agency, and all any self-respecting agency cared about were those lucrative packaging fees paid directly to them, usually at the expense of their very own client.

A writer cannot be packaged, but a writer-producer, a hyphenate, can, and more often than not, is. That, then, was the goal. That is why Steve and Terry wanted to be "in the club," and that is why—since they were truly qualified to be producers in name only—it fell to me to somehow take up the slack. I was, as a consequence, working harder than ever.

With all these contrarian forces, why then was *Cagney & Lacey* so good? One must not underestimate the contributions of Tyne Daly and Sharon Gless, nor the determination and professionalism of the staff—including the writers—that supported them and me. Very essential to this mix was our attention to character, attitude, and detail.

Mary Beth Lacey and Christine Cagney came from different worlds; their perceptions of the universe were different. If they had never met and one day were to find they were sharing an elevator, they would not speak.

There was always, therefore, the potential for conflict, the quintessential ingredient in any good drama. Is conflict all by itself enough? Of course not.

My friend Jack Klugman had a show called *Quincy, M.E.* He played the title role, a forensic specialist and medical examiner for a large city. In a typical episode, a body would be brought into the coroner's laboratories. It was an obvious suicide—except it wasn't. Quincy's expertise and his facile mind made it clear that the suicide was bogus and that death was the result of murder. He would then take his findings to the police.

"For God's sake, Quincy," the detective sergeant would say, "will you quit playing cops and robbers and just stick to your job?" Quincy argued, but to no avail. Conflict, see?

Our hero next went to his boss with his findings. This guy was so buried in the bureaucracy of his job that he had no patience with Quincy's findings and would tell him just to do his job and "bury the stiff." Even more conflict. To top it off, Quincy would be ultimately proven right. The hero wins!

It's good stuff, but here's the problem: the next week the same thing, or a slight variation, happens again. That's true for the following week as well, and the weeks and months after that. Plenty of conflict, but it's all so predictable and—let's face it—implausible. I mean, after this sort of thing occurred three or four times in succession, wouldn't the boss and the cops begin to assume that this guy Quincy just might know what he is talking about?

It's a major burden for even the fabulous Jack Klugman to carry, and it's what used to happen in television—a lot. It was one of the things wrong in the series' cosmos.

With *Cagney & Lacey,* we had an advantage. We created a Cagney from a well-to-do family with a college education (including some study abroad). She was single, lived in a loft in Soho, and loved New York, the theater, concerts, and the excitement of her job, to which she brought ambition, hubris, and a sense of family tradition.

Lacey was married with children. She was blue-collar. She was sick of the city with its noise and pollution, and she was tired: physically tired of holding down the job at the 14th Precinct, keeping up with her ambitious partner, being a homemaker, wife, and mother, and trying to make up for her lack of self-esteem by attending night school classes in literature near her home at Queens College.

The two women saw the world differently and brought something of themselves and their backgrounds to their work. Conflict was the result—and not necessarily predictable conflict. Sitting on a 1989 panel for the National Association of Social Workers, award-winning producer Dorothea Petrie[61] asked me, "How did you do it? How did you make it socially relevant and entertaining at the same time?" That answer can be found in this same "formula."

In our abortion clinic episode, women going to abortion clinics are being harassed. Cagney and Lacey are assigned the case. The two women have feelings about abortion, and, naturally, those attitudes are in conflict with each other. But, it's not what you might think.

They are both in favor of a woman's right to have a choice in this regard; Cagney, however, is a Roman Catholic. Her father prods her with the reminder that "Abortion is a mortal sin, and besides," he adds, "there's a lotta Irish up top," referring to the potential prejudice of the ambitious Cagney's Catholic superiors in the police department on such matters.

---

[61]   Producer of *Love Is Never Silent* and other classy projects.

Cagney is further upset at the implied sexism of the assignment, and, until the harassment turns to bombing, the blonde detective is annoyed about the perceived low-esteem social-work aspects of such a case in terms of career advancement.

At that time, Lacey is the mother of two and visibly pregnant with a midlife baby (her "choice"). What is driving her to stand up to her partner, to help women with this clearly difficult decision? What, besides her own humanity? We tell the audience, by way of a Lacey monologue, that at age nineteen, before meeting her loving and wonderful Harvey, Mary Beth was herself in need of an abortion and that at that time such procedures were illegal in the United States. We discover that is why our heroine did not finish her education; she needed the money, her second semester tuition money, to fly to Puerto Rico and to pay the abortionist. He did not speak English and indicated, as if she were a dog, that she was to lie atop his "operating table." Harvey Lacey, of course, knows the story, but once started—Ancient Mariner–like—his wife must tell it through its completion. She ends on a political note: "There's people who want us to go back to that, Harvey."

"It's OK, honey," he says, "its OK. It'll never be that way again."

She nods, remaining steadfast about her prediction. "It'll be exactly like that," she says.

This is good material, strong, emotional stuff, tying in the police work of our principals with their characters' own emotional fabric. As noted earlier, "The Clinic" was by the writing team of Judy Merl & Paul Eric Myers, although to be accurate, they did not create the scene I just described. It was dictated by Barbara Corday, pretty much as she recalled it from her own life's experience. Merl and Myers did some fine freelance work on our show, as well as other series; I do not single them out here as criticism but more to illustrate the intensity of how our team worked together, how we made it relevant and entertaining. It was involving and unpredictable as well.

Where did we get off? This wasn't brain surgery or treating cancer. Not quite—though our multi-award-winning cancer two-parter did emphasize the importance of early detection and the preference for lumpectomy (over the more radical and disfiguring mastectomy) weeks before the *New England Journal of Medicine* came out with headlines saying exactly the same thing. We did treat cigarette smoking as an addiction years prior to Surgeon General Koop coming forward with the news that it was one.

We had Mary Beth Lacey abstain from drinking alcohol and coffee during her pregnancy over a year before our government made the same recommendations. We advocated safe sex and the use of condoms (first time on prime-time TV in the United States), attempted to expose the virulent malignancy of racism in all aspects of our society (including our own series' regulars), and regularly dealt with sexism and—most graphically—with the heartbreak of substance abuse. Film clips from our episodes were used to illustrate segments of *Nightline, MacNeil-Lehrer, CBS Evening News with Dan Rather, The Today Show*, and many other local and syndicated news broadcasts and informational shows.

Our awards came from many sources in addition to the Emmys and included citations, plaques, and trophies from such diverse sources as the National Commission on Clean Air, the National Organization for Women and other women's groups, the Scott Newman Foundation, the National Council on Alcohol Abuse, the Media Office of the Governor of California, Women in Film, Humanitas, the National Conference of Christians and Jews, the Center for Population Options, New York City and State citations, as well as several from our hometown, Los Angeles.

We were touching people's lives, effecting change both in behavior and laws. We were lauded in the nation's *Congressional Record*.

The conceit came to us quite naturally. We believed we were doing something important and the Mace Neufeld phrase that "it's only television" never occurred to a single one of us.

A Washington DC speaking engagement when I was NARAL's "Man of the Year." That's Gloria Steinem with the gorgeous profile.

Photo: Rosenzweig Personal Collection

Barbara Corday and I were the recipients of Couple of the Year Awards from the ACLU on this festive night in Los Angeles. Georg Stanford Brown is on the left, then Barbara, me, Sharon, Tyne, and John Karlen.

Photo: Rosenzweig Personal Collection

Many, besides the aforementioned Ms. Petrie, wanted to know how we did it. More recently, the British, now in the days of the economic unification of Europe and all that it will mean to their exploding television industry, have asked how many writers we used on staff. Wrong question. We did it with two, and we did it with five—and all the numbers in between. We did it with men only and with a staff made up of a majority of women. It didn't matter. Were they superstars? None of the writers or directors have gone on to great individual success, as have the alumni of many other hit series.[62]

First-time directors didn't get spirited away to success as they have on other shows. Some of the writers went on to make big time/big money deals in development, only to disappoint.

I believe that with *Cagney & Lacey*, their devotion, their energy, and their time (to the exclusion of nearly all else) was a much bigger factor than their talent, no matter how considerable.

"Series nun," Ms. Fisher would call herself. It also referred to the other females on my staff. Why not? Lacy Street was our church, and we were all devoted to what it was we were doing there.

---

[62]   None of our writing staff could possibly lay claim to the accolades that have come to their then-competitors: John Wells, Steven Bochco, David Kelley, David Milch, Michael Kozell, Marshall Hershkovitz, Ed Zwick, Winnie Holtzman, Glenn Gordon Caron, Linda Bloodworth, Barbara and Karen Hall. I salivate at the thought of what it might have been like to work with such talents. True as that is—as great as this list of writers was and is—none of them, in my obviously biased view, have a greater television series credit to their dossier than *Cagney & Lacey*.

CHAPTER 37

HERMAN, THE REACHER

Annual writers meetings were held at the close of every season to discuss the character arcs of Cagney and Lacey for the coming year and the direction the series would take in the event of renewal. The meeting in 1985 was different for many reasons, not the least of which was the exhaustion factor, made even more acute by the announcement of Tyne's pregnancy and the realization by the writers that—having just completed a season's work—they were now being asked to immediately go right back in harness on yet another season without a break.

Tyne was due to deliver in the fall (October 1, 1985, to be precise), near the time of our season opener. Since we were photographing months ahead and were not on the air with first-run programming in the summer to track the pregnancy, Mary Beth would have to give birth months after the woman who portrayed her.

I opted for a February 1986 delivery. That was a Nielsen sweeps month, and such a noteworthy occurrence, I reasoned, couldn't hurt our ratings. Keeping Lacey pregnant longer than the actress who played her created more challenges than simply having to order an inordinate amount of bird seed to fill the pouch Ms. Daly would wear to simulate her actual pregnancy. It would further require that, only months after delivering her own very healthy child, Tyne Daly would have to reenact labor pains and the birthing process all over again.

Back at our dining room table meeting, it was quickly decided that the baby would be healthy and that it would be a girl. (What else?) The bad news was it would force us to put the episodes on the air in pretty much the same order in which they were made (to properly follow the pregnancy and Tyne's anticipated growing corpulence). This would not allow me to creatively readjust our release schedule to put strong episodes up front or against perceived weak competition. It meant I could not bury faulty segments, which I would normally try to place opposite some blockbuster M.O.W., and it also forced the staff to be a bit more careful where the stringing of story and character beads was concerned.

To protect ourselves during the latter part of Tyne's pregnancy—and her time of delivery and recovery—we had to design a period of block shooting (a couple of weeks in this case toward the end of summer, where we would consolidate all the Tyne Daly material we had left and film it—without regard for continuity—in order to bank this material for inclusion in episodes we would subsequently complete when Ms. Daly's pregnancy made her no longer available to us. This, too, put an additional burden on the staff, as we needed material well in advance of the norm to accommodate this accelerated production schedule.

A similar period of maternity leave would have to be invented for Mrs. Lacey, and that would necessitate a change in the modus operandi for a Lacey-less Christine Cagney. This would then require quite a format adjustment, the possible invention of some new characters to temporarily fill the void, and the expansion of already-existing roles.

Uppermost in all of our minds was how long we could conceal Tyne's girth. Corday felt we were kidding ourselves, in that she believed Tyne was going to begin showing very fast. Just how realistic was it to think we could photograph her behind desks or sofas and not have the audience be distracted by this obvious device? "Obvious," in that by airtime our fans would already know of the pregnancy, courtesy of the tabloid press.

We debated over the so-called obligatory scenes that we had all seen hundreds of times before: The telling of "the news" to the husband, to the adolescent children. We discussed when Cagney would find out (before Harvey or after?). Even if we had these scenes play as early in the season as possible (say, October 1), how could she deliver as early as February? Wouldn't Lacey therefore have to remain pregnant throughout the entire season? (That's Tyne Daly carrying around pounds of bird seed for nearly seven months!) Even if we wanted to have her pregnant throughout the better part of the year, it was quickly conceded that this was a fantasy. There was no way Tyne would not be showing by the earliest date we could start filming.

"You know," I said to the assemblage of writers gathered around the dining room of Barbara's and my Hancock Park home, located in the heart of one of the oldest residential neighborhoods in Los Angeles, "if I really had the courage of my convictions, we wouldn't do any of this obvious stuff."

All heads were turned toward me. "Let's stay with Lacey giving birth in February," I began. "That means at season's start Lacey is four to five months pregnant.

Harvey already knows; the kids know; Cagney knows; so does the whole damn precinct. We shoot Tyne as she is, with no attempt to hide anything." I went on:

"The first episode of the season opens with Coleman" (our desk sergeant who was known to "make book" on almost anything). "He is preparing the Lacey Baby Quinella—odds on boy, girl, weight, color of hair, eyes. Lacey doesn't like it, but it's the talk of the precinct. That's how we open; that's how we tell everyone Lacey's pregnant. All the so-called obligatory scenes will have been played during the summer—off-stage. All those familiar scenes are missed 'cause we're not gonna tell 'em. America would quickly get it and say, 'Ain't that just perfect *Cagney & Lacey?*'"

I can't recall if there was applause or not. There should have been. It was a terrific save.

Over a year later, with Jonathan Estrin and Shelley List now leading the writing staff and in attendance, we had another such meeting—again around that same large dining room table. This time there was no pregnancy. The Lacey's, cramped in their apartment, would move at long last to their own home and that—plus the new baby—would provide us with plenty of stuff for them. But what about Cagney?

"Let me give you the last line of dialogue from the last scene of the forthcoming season's final episode," I began. It was admittedly an odd and dramatic way for such a meeting to convene.

"We are in a tight two-shot of our stars, and they are seated. We don't know where they are. Finally, after a long beat, Cagney stands and says, 'My name is Christine, and I'm an alcoholic.' We pull back into a wide shot revealing we're at an AA meeting: freeze-frame, the end."

This time I did get my applause.

"Now," I said, beaming at the writing staff, "your job is to backtrack over the twenty-one episodes that will precede this and figure out a way to get us to that moment."

The idea for all this had its germination quite by accident in the season that had just ended—the one focusing on Lacey's pregnancy. Originally we had, in creating Cagney's father, descended to stereotype. He was written as a retired Irish cop, and naturally he liked to drink. It provided us with some good material over the years, usually of a comic or sometimes-poignant nature. We never dealt with it as a serious problem. Then, in 1985, we made an episode called "Filial Duty" (written by Richard Gollance and directed by Sharron Miller) in which, as a subplot, Charlie Cagney was hospitalized with pneumonia.

As the title of the episode implies, we were going to introduce the problem, so prevalent in our society today, of adults having to deal with their aging parents. This issue had been on my mind, as my own Grandmother Fanny was deteriorating rapidly and—in the process—heavily impacting the quality of the lives of my parents. Such a thing would now become Cagney's burden and, we hoped—in addition to her problems in the workplace or her adventures as a healthy, heterosexual, single female in a major urban environment—humanize her in a recognizably dramatic way.

Pneumonia, of course, doesn't last indefinitely, and we were looking for something that would not go away—a problem that Cagney could see herself having to deal with for the rest of her father's life. We had already done a show on cancer, and we didn't necessarily want Charlie bedridden.

"Y'know," I said one day sort of casually, "he sure drinks a lot." That was it. A touch of cirrhosis and the news that nearly floored our heroine:

"Your father is an alcoholic."

The two Cagneys did all the classic things, beginning with denial, but eventually Christine saw the truth of the doctor's diagnosis.

Many weeks later, we were in production on yet another episode, "DWI," ("Driving While Intoxicated," written by Les Carter and Susan Sisko, directed by Al Waxman). Within the body of the show was an argument between Cagney and her partner who was—by then—on maternity leave.

It was a good script and a good episode, but this particular scene was not—as I read it anyway—one of the high points of the hour. The day it was shot, I had heard from several of the noncombatants that the juices were really flowing on the stage that day and the two women were definitely showing off their acting chops. I drifted by the set, and Tyne cornered me.

"Good stuff today," she said. "Are we really gonna get into this alcoholism thing with Cagney?"

I believe I covered my surprise at the question. The script was about a homebound, very pregnant Lacey, who was witness to a hit-and-run accident perpetuated by a drunk driver. Nero Wolfe–like, Lacey tries to solve the case from the confines of her apartment and, out of necessity, enlists the aid of her partner. Cagney thus finds herself working night shift for the city and for Lacey by day.

As a consequence of the disruption of her sleep habits and her time off, Cagney—in the story—is understandably irritable, leading to an argument or two with her partner. I wasn't sure what Tyne was talking about, but it didn't stop me from responding positively to my star's obvious enthusiasm.

"Of course," I countered. "Whaddaya think, this stuff happens by accident?"

I avoided any other contact with the set until the next day when I could view the film of the scene under discussion so as to get a better handle on what was being talked about.

Sure enough, the viewing of dailies made it clear. Sharon and Tyne had brought a dimension to the scene that I had not realized was there. They had not altered the dialogue (you just don't do that on one of my shows without permission); the change was achieved with intensity of performance and emphasis, and the results were there for anyone to see: Cagney's defensiveness on the subject of her own drinking and that of her father's, in an episode ostensibly about something else entirely, convinced me we were onto something that would ultimately be more fully explored in the following season.

That season began in New York, where we picked up shots with our principals all over Manhattan. As had become our practice, these would be used to pepper throughout several episodes to be filmed at our home base in Los Angeles. The New York crowds loved Sharon and Tyne, recognizing them wherever we went. It was hard to believe that only a few years earlier, when we would tell folks on the Manhattan streets we were filming *Cagney & Lacey*, all anyone wanted to know was where was the *Yankee Doodle Dandy*? [63]

It was a heady time, a time where others in my peer group opportunistically franchised themselves by becoming involved with other ventures. I, on the other hand, remained on the course I had set for myself of concentrating only on *Cagney & Lacey*. Not an easy (or particularly astute) decision, as Steve Brown, Tyne, Sharon, and the Orion penny-pinchers kept driving me more than a little nuts. Still, I remember being in basically a good mood. Do you think the six-figure check I received in late May of that year as the first of several guaranteed advances against foreign income on *Cagney & Lacey* had anything to do with this? Bet your ass!

---

[63]   Reference is to classic (1942) award-winning film, *Yankee Doodle Dandy*, directed by Michael Curtiz, written by Robert Buckner and Edmund Joseph, with uncredited writing by Julius and Philip Epstein. Actor James Cagney received the Oscar in a career-defining role as George M. Cohan.

In the midst of all this, Herman Rush came back into my life. The chairman of Columbia Pictures Television leaned across the narrow breakfast table close to my oatmeal and asked, "What do you want?"

What a tough question. My goals have always been short-term—my answer always the same as the Jack Lemmon character in *Save The Tiger*[64]: "One more season."

I had been trained from childhood to dream small. It was the Cabots, Rockefellers, Vanderbilts, Kennedys, and Bushes who talked to their children about running corporate empires or the country. That didn't happen in any Montebello, California, household I had ever been around.

What did I want? Herman Rush was a reacher, a creative deal-maker. He helped me think about what I might want by structuring an unheard-of (by me anyway) and fabulous deal. What really put it over was *TV Guide*.

In August, we received ten Emmy nominations—our most ever—but there was no joy at Lacy Street. The *TV Guide* piece on Sharon referenced earlier came out the same day as the Academy announcement (August 1985), and both La Gless and Ms. Daly saw it as a disaster and me as the villain of the piece. The facts were that our ladies and, in fact our show had, over the years, a very checkered relationship with *TV Guide*, and so my two stars had a tendency to be super sensitive about that particular publication (as opposed to being just *very* sensitive as they were with every other outlet). I came from the school of "if you spell my name right, there is no such thing as bad publicity."

When we were new, this most popular TV publication practiced a tougher kind of journalism than it does today. Over the years, we had been treated relatively well by the *Guide,* but more than once they had crossed the line and published something gratuitously hurtful or nasty. As a consequence, Tyne refused to cooperate with them—ever—and Sharon was a bit leery of them as well. I was probably less than smart to have been as open and candid with their reporter as I was.

At first, I was somewhat relieved by the article, as I feared—and predicted—a hatchet job. From the perspective of fearing the worst, it was not so bad. Rereading the article today reinforces that and even introduces the thought that the piece was (is) fairly benign, but that was not Sharon's view—not then. The day the article came out, so did the word that Ms. Gless was not even speaking to me. *That* was a

---

[64]   Starring Jack Lemmon (for which he won the Best Actor Oscar) and Jack Gilford, written by Steve Shagen, directed by John Avildsen, and produced by my old pal and Filmways alum Ed Feldman.

first, and it cast sort of a pall over the entire company. I had no idea how long this would continue, and I began to wonder if I had lived by the sword of publicity too long. Maybe this would be the very thing that would do me in. Tyne was pissed, too, but I was used to that (and it's a very different kind of thing anyway).

"Too bad," I remember saying to no one in particular, "until now, the last two weeks had been pretty terrific."

The incident put me in a more responsive mode to my attorney, Stu Glickman, and my longtime friend and sometime agent, Lee Rosenberg. They were pushing the Herman Rush offer for Columbia; they felt it would work out and that it would be an extremely lucrative deal. If I was successful, and prudent, I could make a major bundle of money. If not, I still would do pretty well. Of prime importance was the fact that it was a benchmark.

The lexiphanic Lee Rosenberg said, I had "reached the apogee of phase one" of my career. It was now time to move on.

The unreconciled fight with Gless had made this decision easier. I was now moving on to other (multiple) stuff. The hands-on phase of my career was, I thought, drawing to a close. I was sad about the Gless thing. Normally it might be patched up, but, when she discovered that I was "leaving" the series (or at least handing a great deal of it over to other parties), she would add this "betrayal" to the *TV Guide* thing, and that would be that.

It was ironic that this unpleasantness had motivated me—for once in my life—to make the "sensible" business decision that my advisors had been promoting for so long.

I felt as though I had been forced to leave the nest and test my wings as a more mature being than I was before. This new phase had potential, but it would not be the same for me ever again. This was, I believed, close to a closing chapter for *Cagney & Lacey* and me. Although I would be involved in some aspect of the show for a long time to come (and fairly heavily so for the remainder of the episodes we were currently filming), it would, I reasoned, *never* be the same.

It was good for me. It was the right thing, but it was sad, too. The show had brought me so much—virtually everything I could have hoped for—but it was not smart, not economically or emotionally, for me to stay any longer. What else could be expected? Should I remain on the show at 25 percent of my fees and a smaller fraction of my deserved ownership position until the very end—declining lucrative, multiple opportunities—only later to attempt my next project, phoenix-like, from the ashes of a canceled series?

Who said yes?

I think many had come to expect that. Maybe I had, too. This was all going to require a readjustment on my part.

I might appear to be a daddy to a lot of my cohorts, but this was really gonna demand my growing up—and fast. I had miles to go. I wondered what happened to all that talk of early retirement. It was on hold for at least two years while I tried my hand at moguldom.

I expected at least two series, and quite possibly a lot more would come out of this new phase. If they were good, and/or smartly produced, there was no telling what the next move might be. It would all surely be bigger and richer, but probably not so personally satisfying as what I had just come through. How could it be?

The phenomenon of *Cagney & Lacey* was one of those all-too-rare occurrences. Many things were now possible for me, but I would never be young again. *Cagney & Lacey* was my first bona fide hit. There might be others, but there would never be another first.

How would the women respond? How would I tell them? I didn't know. It was complicated by the current tenseness in our relationship. They might want to keep on as if to spite me, to show me what a minor role I played in their success. That would be to my advantage.

They might use this as an excuse to break up (as noted before, they could be slightly self-destructive). Or they might just say thanks and go on, continuing to strive for "deeper, richer, fuller, better" without me. If so, I would be on the sidelines rooting them on. It was conceivable that they had been expecting me to do something like this all along.

CHAPTER 38

NO GOOD DEED GOES UNPUNISHED

My first decision as president of The Rosenzweig Company would have to be where I would office. I would try to remain at Lacy Street until pre-production started on project number one, then move to new headquarters. The key would be how the cast and staff of *Cagney & Lacey* would handle my being there but not really being theirs.

Project number one was the Carl Weathers commitment Lee Rosenberg had spoken to me about some time before; it was the one I had, when first asked, declined the opportunity to produce, and now it had found a home at Columbia Pictures Television. In the intervening time since what I thought was our final meeting, Weathers had interviewed several writers under contract to the studio and selected the guy I had recommended, my old pal from *American Dream*, Ronald M. Cohen.

The teaming of Cohen and Weathers lacked an element, as far as ABC was concerned. They wanted an experienced executive producer to be over Ronald. He, in turn, announced that there were only two who were acceptable to him: Eddie Milkis *or* Barney Rosenzweig. He did not know when he made that remark that I just might be dealing with his studio employers for the formation of The Rosenzweig Company.

TRC (The Rosenzweig Company) was largely the creation of Herman Rush's fertile mind. It was controlled by me and co-owned by Columbia Pictures Corporation, which acted as bank and distributor. The new company would function as its own entity, subject to only the slightest of economic restraints by Columbia. Naturally, all creative controls resided with me.

The Weathers project was really folded in at the eleventh hour, as I agreed to do this favor for my friend Ronald, for my new bank, for Herman Rush, as well as Corday (Rush's president of the Columbia television division of Columbia Studios), and even agent Lee Rosenberg (who, besides representing me, had Carl Weathers for a client).

It was the late summer of 1985, and I had been led to believe we would not have to be in production until January 1986 for a March air date. I soon learned that wasn't so and that January would be the targeted debut of the series. That necessitated a November start of production. It was the madness of the original *Cagney & Lacey* schedule all over again, only here we had a star but no M.O.W. (as I did on *C&L*), meaning there was no visual blueprint (no pilot film) to show to a new writing staff.

Fortune Dane was Ronald Cohen's idea (and, God forgive him, his title). He had suffered fools for most of his career, but now he had his chance—a commitment from a network, a star in Carl Weathers, with whom he could communicate, and a friend for an executive producer who precluded the need of a studio and who could fend off the network in his defense.

I was cognizant that the ABC commitment came to us from Carl Weathers in the first place and that he was the star of the show. I was determined that this man would not be forced to go down in flames, flying a banner he could not endorse, or on a project to which he could not relate. This attitude led me to foolishly cave to Carl's urgings that we film the series away from Hollywood (locating our operation nearly 500 miles to the north in Oakland, California). I also erred in believing the network's lip service to Weathers being a crossover star.[65] When our show debuted, it was on Saturday night, following the new Redd Foxx series and *Benson*. (Hey, folks, it's Saturday Night Noir on ABC.)

Too quickly, I tried to imbue this project with the same spirit of troika I had only recently introduced on *Cagney & Lacey*. It was a mistake. At Lacy Street, Sharon and Tyne might have been flattered, but in reality they declined the mantle of co-leaders. On *Dane*, Ronald and Carl all too readily accepted. The bottom line result: too many bosses, a show that wasn't any good, and it was my fault. I was

---

[65]   In this context, a show business term referring to a black actor who also has appeal to white audiences. There are more and more notable examples every day, and far too many to mention. A very nice contrast to my early days in the business when the only one who would come to mind was Sidney Poitier.

spending too much time on renting hammers and buying nails and not enough time on those creative, political, and leadership things I do well.

"You have approached the apogee of phase one of your career," Lee Rosenberg has said. Too bad. I liked phase one.

I was stuck, the deal said, for years. Maybe I could negotiate out, but still I felt I was bound for at least the Weathers project. I was not miserable, simply pissed I had allowed myself to get conned into this at a time when I should have been, and could have been, having a better time of things.

My old employee, Peter Lefcourt, was living my fantasy. He was then a series "doctor" on *Our Family Honor*, and pulling down $45,000 per episode. That's the way to be an employee; come to work when they're desperate, charge an arm and a leg, do it your way, and, if they don't like it, let 'em pay you off. I'd dreamed of it for years, could have had it, and passed it for this "offer I couldn't refuse."

Meanwhile, the work with Ronald Cohen was not going well. Brilliant, indefatigable, and so intimidating to virtually everyone, Ronald would inadvertently and invariably distract coworkers from their real chores. To those workers, everyday tasks were mundane compared to the web Ronald spun. I had gotten used to working with lesser talents who simply did what I told them. I found that I had come to prefer that to the constant tension of this relationship with my old, very talented pal.

In the early days of *Cagney & Lacey*, I had said to Tyne and Sharon, "Give me one minute a day: one minute in dailies where I laugh, cry, or am surprised. If you do that," I would say, "at the end of the episode, I'll have seven good minutes. That's all I need to make a terrific episode. Hell, it's all America deserves."

The women laughed, but more often than not would ask if I'd gotten my minute that day.

Director Ray Danton, in a losing argument for an extra day's shooting on an episode, once quoted Robert Browning to me: "Ah, but a man's reach should exceed his grasp, or what's a heaven for?"

I didn't miss a beat as I replied, "Ah, but 'tis better to aim for San Diego and hit it, than shoot for the moon and fall on your ass."

Danton loved it, had the two quotes framed, and presented them to me for my office.

I tried to communicate this concept to Ronald. After commercials and titles there are approximately forty-six minutes of picture in any hour-long television episode. I admonished Ronald to get that "one minute a day." He wouldn't listen. He would not aim for that plausible target, nor settle for a realistic and achievable seven good minutes per show. In his pursuit of his definition of excellence, he fought for all forty-six, sans priorities. He would, as a consequence, wind up with no good minutes at all. His goals might be admirable, but they were not possible—not on a television schedule—and not on a television series, where it is absolutely essential to set one's priorities, and to give every moment relative (as opposed to absolute) value or weight.

I wanted him to listen to me, to take advantage of the hard-won lessons of my experience. I reminded him of our biggest fight on *American Dream*. It was in 1979, on an early draft of that pilot script. In our story, after the Novaks had moved to the inner city, their youngest son became the victim of a schoolyard mugging. Ronald, with his sense of verisimilitude, had the boy brought home in an ambulance. When the kid's father came home, he was confronted by the school's security guard, who assured the older Novak that in the future he would keep an eye on the boy; that he had some empathy for the beating the twelve-year-old took, because only a year earlier his daughter was gang-raped at the same school.

Personally, I had thought the kid should have a bloody nose, a black eye and some minor scrapes—no ambulance, no security guard, and no gang-rape.

"How in hell can you justify the family staying in that Chicago neighborhood after your version?" I had asked my talented friend. He had yelled at me, called me a fathead, and disparaged my humble beginnings on the Fess Parker/*Daniel Boone* series. As our argument intensified, I had seen my check, payable to him for $10,000, on his desk. I had grabbed it and moved toward the door.

"Where are you going with my money?" he hollered.

"Listen, asshole, you want to be an author," I yelled back, "go to it. You want to be paid by me; you're going to have to listen!"

Ronald sat back down in his chair. "Tell me again what you want," he said.

"I want a father-son scene in the kid's room," I began. "He's in bed with a black eye, a large bandage across his nose, and a nasty scrape on his forehead. No ambulance or security guard. Our hero learns that his son was robbed of his lunch money and that was what the fight was about. Danny Novak tells his son, 'You fight for your life. You fight for your sister, but not for money, not ever!' It's a warm scene, a *Daniel Boone* scene, and it ends with the kid asking his dad for boxing lessons."

I followed Ronald's instructions that I return in an hour and that I return the check to his desk. When I came back, Ronald was lying on his couch, one arm draped across his eyes. With the other he pointed toward his typewriter. I crossed to it and leaned over it to read the new scene.

"Do you remember what I did then?" I asked the author who, now more than six years later, sat in the den of my Hancock Park home.

"Yeah," he said, looking at his shoes. "You walked across the room, leaned over, and kissed me on the mouth. First time I've ever been kissed by anyone with a beard."

I smiled at my friend, the owner of this extraordinary talent, and said, "Ronald, I'm too old and too rich—too spoiled by the past few years. The fights used to be fun. Not now. I can't do it anymore."

Ronald looked up at me. "You want me to change my behavior," he said.

I nodded.

His glance now went to my mantle and the statuary that was there. "What the hell," he said. "You're the one with the fucking Emmys. You deserve it."

We embraced. I believe he was sincere. Ronald wanted to cooperate. He wanted to change. He just couldn't do it.

Of course there was also the matter of my own miscalculations. I had been locked in combat for so long with *Cagney & Lacey* that I was unaware of an industry-wide freeze that had been imposed by all three networks on the amount of money they would pay for any new program. (The freezing of these license fees had amounted to a major rollback, since costs of labor, materials, and rent continued to escalate on almost a daily basis.)

Then, within a short time of the signing of this deal, came the first indicators of the economic collapse of the syndication market—especially impacting my specialty, the hour-long dramas. "Too difficult to program," they said, "too quickly dated," and "too expensive."

In terms of efficiency, I must add that, on top of all this, I had also minimized the very real contributions of the loyal and professional help and advice I had received on *Cagney & Lacey* from Mick McAfee, Stan Neufeld, and Dick Rosenbloom. These talented men would not be available to me on *Fortune Dane*.

As if that wasn't enough, Lee Rosenberg's agency, Triad, was to receive a packaging commission of over $20,000 per one-hour episode in up-front commissions alone (a cost we didn't have on *Cagney & Lacey*). Finally, I had to start up from scratch, rent office space that would expand or contract depending on a fluid production schedule, and I had to do so in a highly inflated California real estate market.

All my calculations were a joke. I was angry at my advisors for not being more help, for not bringing me up-to-date or keeping me current. I was also angry at myself, for it was all my responsibility.

There was also the discovery, which involved a friend and, relatively new-to-me at the time business manager, costing me hundreds of thousands in a real estate venture he had put together that went sour. And as if that wasn't enough, while attempting to save that sinking ship, he would turn over my account to an underling who misfiled the governmental form for the investment tax credit application on *Fortune Dane,* making it forever null and void and costing me over $500,000 in after-tax dollars. This clerical error would bring my losses to over a million dollars and, with it, the realization that I would be working all those sixteen- to eighteen-hour days on *Fortune Dane* for nothing. (Did I hear someone say, "Easy come, easy go"?)

There is something very disquieting about being twenty-five pounds overweight and forty-eight years old at 2:30 in the morning, when you lie in bed wondering if that minor chest pain you feel is only gas. I was not holding up well. The pressure of the past few months, of simultaneously producing two television series in two different cities, plus the genuine dissatisfaction with the results of my labors (coupled with a true loss of touch with the reward system), had me buckling.

I was exhausted, discouraged, and disillusioned. I loved my house; I was rarely ever in it any more. I now was taking less and less advantage of its tennis court and pool, and I found myself thinking of selling it—beginning to equate it with a money pit. My God, it was one: nearly $30,000 a month of mortgage, taxes, insurance, and maintenance. Thirty thousand 1986 dollars at that!

I was feeling on the edge. The bad news was constant and dribbled in from all sides.

My communication skills seemed to be failing me as one employee after another screwed up one assignment after the other. It would have been laughable were it not having such an awful cumulative effect on everything I was doing and, as a consequence, on me. The Howard Strickling phrase, "a fish stinks from the head," continued to resonate.

Ronald continued to publicly flail about, blaming our production team, me, the directors, Carl, ABC—you name it. I imagine, in private, he even blamed himself. Everyone was crumbling, beginning to seek out targets to blame. Everyone, save for Carl Weathers. He seemed to not see problems, only opportunities. Mr. Weathers, at least in public, kept his game face on. One had to admire him.

CHAPTER 39

LET THE GOOD TIMES ROLL!

"Bigamist," Tyne Daly was screaming at me from the toilet in Sharon's motor home. Sharon, more than a little drunk, was trying to comfort me over the collapse of *Fortune Dane*.

Tyne, every bit as inebriated as her partner, yelled out the "bigamist" line again. I had gotten what I deserved, she bellowed. "Your place is with us!"

They went on about how it was important that my services be exclusively theirs. *Now* they needed me. Five minutes before they were turning shit into Shinola with help from no one. The conversation would bounce all over the place.

"If you're saying you're better than the material," I countered, "no one will argue. You are the best at what you do on the planet. Everyone knows it, but it is very unnecessary to say so yourselves, and not particularly attractive."

We were at the beginning of what would prove to be our penultimate season; Estrin and List were now leading the writing staff. The material was not great, but certainly up to the norm for that time in a season. Tyne and Sharon were very critical, despite protestations that they "liked the new team as people." Sharon began building a real jack story about the "unplayability" of the scenes, and both had forgotten (or didn't care) that they had always felt this way about the scripts— whether authored by April Smith, Terry Fisher, Peter Lefcourt, or Liz Coe. Now they longed for those "great" writers from our past—and if it weren't so sorely felt by them it would have been funny.

The women were bridling about the responsibility of having to go over and over the scenes before they would become "playable." I strongly urged them to act. "Say the words, and don't bump into the furniture," I would add, paraphrasing the late, great Spencer Tracy.

"Try just serving the material and don't take on the job or responsibility of the entire entity. Let me do my job, and I'll have the writers do theirs."

Tyne and Sharon agreed to try. I remained sober throughout that three-hour session, taking the women's abuse for a time, trying to insert an idea here or there, but mostly (and this was the best part) just watching them. The friendship, the guarded compliments or criticism, the occasional touched bruise, the recounting of (for what, the thousandth time?) their history together and how it came to be; the genuine affection, the lack of total honesty (out of fear of where that might take them), the miscommunications (as first one, then the other, missed a compliment or a moment of tenderness—and too bad because the moment was gone fast) it was my privilege to witness it all.

I remember considering staying sober at those sessions more often. The disadvantage to that was one felt not quite as included. I also recall considering taping those meetings of the troika but dismissing the idea as impractical.

We would finally part, hugging all around; no one wanted to be the first to leave (possibly out of fear of what might be said behind the back that wasn't there). It was another rare evening with the ladies, one of many in my memory.

It was June 1986. Sharon, Tyne, and I were obviously on speaking terms again, but it did not come easily. The silent treatment I received as a result of the previous summer's *TV Guide* article lasted several weeks, with Sharon finally breaking the hush by asking for a meeting in which she told me she wanted the dispute to end but that she needed an apology from me. When I asked why she would believe the apology when she did not give credence to anything else I had to say on this matter, Ms. Gless simply replied, "Because I want to." I capitulated.

Months earlier, Steve Brown somehow, and very prematurely, learned of my plans to do *Dane*. He wasted no time in giving me his ultimatum that he would quit if I turned *Cagney & Lacey* over to Liz Coe. He managed to stir up a little hysteria at the time; first Rosenbloom called in a panic, then Gless (another nail in the Steve Brown coffin).

"You are who I act for," Sharon had said. The good news was that this led to the subsequent talk of apology over the *TV Guide* thing. I assured both her and Rosenbloom that I was not leaving the series but merely pulling back a bit. Steve Brown was to depart with my blessings. Liz Coe would now lead the staff of Georgia Jeffries, Pat Green, and Kathy Ford. All this took a backseat to the arrival of fall and the festivities of the Academy of Television Arts and Sciences.

In 1985 (for the 1984–85 season), I received the first of my two Emmy statuettes as executive producer of the year's Best Dramatic Series. I had been nominated twice before for *Cagney & Lacey*; in 1983, for the 1982–83 season, and 1984, for work in that shortened seven-show order year. This third time was definitely the charm. I won again in 1986 (for the 1985–86 season) and was then nominated for the fifth time in a row in 1987 (for the 1986–87 season).[66]

I personally thought we would win in 1984 for that season of the seven-show order, not just because the episodes were among our best but because of the stir we had created by being canceled and then brought back. Steven Bochco's *Hill Street Blues* was just too formidable, and I began to believe that if we couldn't win then—with all that industry sentiment on our side—then we might just never prevail.

I resolved to stop preparing speeches, and not because I'm superstitious (I am), but because all that rehearsing only added to the disappointment of losing. I remember being in that auditorium when the announcement came:

"And the winner is—*Cagney & Lacey!*"

I remember it, not only because it was an important event—a biography-name-changing event (instead of Barney Rosenzweig or Producer Barney Rosenzweig, I became for all time—at least in the trade press—Emmy Award–winner Barney Rosenzweig), but I remember it because of something I felt midst that throng. There was something I felt, and there was something else that was absent.

For the first time in all my years of attending these occasions, I felt consensus, without a trace of envy from my peers. What was absent was the sound of the gnashing of teeth. I strode down that aisle to collect my reward, and the feeling I had from every one of those people applauding was:

"That guy worked hard for this," or, "you can't begrudge anyone who pulled off what he did" or maybe—just maybe—a sense that there could be justice in Hollywood.

Corny? It was my moment. My stroll down that aisle, and that's how I remember it. I was one happy guy!

Weeks after that first win, our 1985 opening night garnered a rave review from the *New York Times*. We got a 34 share and easily took the hour. Harvey Shephard was delighted and called me with the good news. That same fall, Tyne had her baby and Sid Clute finally succumbed to cancer.

---

66   My first Emmy nomination was in 1982 for the eight-hour miniseries *John Steinbeck's East of Eden*, but I lost that year to *Shogun*.

The Emmy excitement had not worn off. Mail congratulating me continued to pour in, and it was all very gratifying. People stopped me in elevators and on the street, recognizing me from the award show on TV, and congratulating me. Celebrity was something I was enjoying.

The view from Brooklyn. On location in New York, Sharon and Tyne give me arms full of talent in one of my favorite photos.

Photo: Rosenzweig Personal Collection

Our annual New York shoot for *Cagney & Lacey* was upon us, and I was looking forward to that—ten days in the Big Apple with Sharon and Tyne. I had to laugh as I found myself viewing this as an escape from Ronald Cohen and Carl Weathers. My female stars would, I was sure, present me with plenty of *mishigas*[67] on their own.

The week in New York was excellent. It was true quality time with the women, plus some good footage shot, culminating with the storied Stage Deli asking the women to create a *Cagney & Lacey* sandwich. The two women had now entered the realm of such legends of the past fifty years as Joe DiMaggio and Frank Sinatra. (Typically, Sharon and Tyne, without regard for things commercial, created some awful combination that could not possibly remain on any menu for long.)

Tyne and I then went on to Washington DC as part of the promotion on our abortion show: Eight solid hours of public speaking and meetings. Ms. Daly was tired but in her element. I attended the National Conference of Working Women luncheon in DC, where the show was to be among several honored. A full house of nearly a thousand heard speeches and saw a tape montage of the year's award winners and runners-up. The format then called for each of the recipients to stand at the appointed time at their respective tables, introduce themselves and their project, and say a word or two. This went on for some time to a polite, if unenthusiastic, audience. Finally it was my turn.

"Hello," I began. "I'm Barney Rosenzweig, executive producer of *Cagney & Lacey.*"

The room erupted into applause. I was standing there a long time drinking it in. This was nice. This was better than smelling the flowers.

Back in L.A., I lunched with Peter Lefcourt. He was tempted to return to *Cagney & Lacey* and would let me know the following week. My day continued, ending at Lacy Street around 2 AM, another in a series of late nighters. In Sharon's dressing room around midnight, I remember attempting to explain why, as a director, Ray Danton was unique.

I pointed out, as I have so often before, that "he has no life, no friends. He just lives for the work." The irony of making that fairly disparaging statement about someone else near the end of my own seventeen-hour day did not escape either Ms. Gless or me.

Liz Coe was getting closer to becoming a memory on *Cagney & Lacey,* as she was less and less able to inspire anyone's confidence, except mine, and that was no

---

[67] Yiddishism meaning craziness, aggravation, or tumult. Pronounced mish e goss.

longer good enough. Lefcourt would finally decide against a return, so my court-ship of the writing team of Jonathan Estrin & Shelley List thus went into full gear with positive results; Liz would elect to leave the series, rather than "serve" under the new team.

After our read-through of the season's penultimate *Cagney & Lacey* script, I took Dan Shor aside and let him know his character (Jonah Newman) would be killed in that season's final chapter. He said he understood.

I had a nice half hour on the set with Sharon. She had just turned down a million-dollar offer to star in the twelve-hour miniseries *Amerika*, despite her feeling that it was the best script she had ever read. The problem was that it could not be done during the *Cagney & Lacey* hiatus. It was clear that the gossip of her trying to hold up Orion by not returning to the series was overstated. She pointedly expected me to return full-time next season, and I was able to hedge an answer long enough to allow her to be called back to the set. It is what I wanted to do, but I was not sure it was possible.

Could I simply stop the deal with Columbia? Tell them to keep their $800,000 per year? Could I ask them to suspend and extend? Would ABC roll over the six-show commitment to me for another year? I doubted it. Should I return to *Cagney & Lacey* because I love it, playing the fool to Orion and Mace Neufeld once more? To hell with them, you say. "Do what you want." But how would I react months later, having possibly given up all the above? How would I react to one of those "lovers' quarrels" between Tyne and/or Sharon and myself? I needed to make some very hard decisions.

Late one evening in February of 1986, even as *Fortune Dane* was winding down, John Karlen, Al Waxman, Marty Kove, Harvey Atkin, Carole Smith, Sharon, and I all gathered in my Lacy Street office after the day's work. It was a minor laugh riot. Sharon called later to say that we had to make it a weekly event. It was great to feel my head on the pillow at day's end and to think how much I enjoyed the respite from *Fortune Dane* and the evening's interval with the folks from *Cagney & Lacey*. Then—at 12:40 AM—the phone. It was Tyne Daly. She had just read Liz Coe's "Parting Shots" script, and hated it. She couldn't sleep after finishing it and didn't want me to either.

It was almost as bad a reaction as she had to our scripts on "Date Rape," "Burnout," the breast cancer two-parter, and the return of Lacey's father (coincidentally, some of our best). Ms. Daly's call, damning the writers, came on the same day (although, admittedly, hours before) *Cagney & Lacey* received three of the seven

1986 Writers Guild nominations for Best Series Teleplay (Deborah Arakelian for "Child Witness," Patricia Green for "Who Said It's Fair" Part II, and Georgia Jeffries, who won for "Unusual Occurrence").

The reading for Liz Coe's script was attended by everyone in our regular cast plus our entire staff. Tyne was rude during her presentation, and I interrupted the reading to tell her so in front of all assembled. She apologized on the spot, and I accepted. There was talk that the writing staff might actually get together and erect a special monument memorializing the event. It was a good moment.

"Parting Shots," our final *Cagney & Lacey* episode for the season, was aptly named. My worries about everyone's emotional concerns for a departing colleague (Dan Shor) were misplaced. The script, strongly favoring Sharon, came under heavy attack, first by Tyne Daly and then our director—her husband, Georg Stanford Brown.

Tyne saw Cagney's behavior in the teleplay as reprehensible—so much so that it would end the partnership. Georg conceded the importance of the episode but was (it seemed to me) concerned that such a benchmark did not feature his spouse. At this point in our mutual history, I had come to believe it was more than a little coincidental that the times of greatest difficulty with Ms. Daly, vis-à-vis Lacey in juxtaposition with Cagney, seemed to occur primarily on episodes directed by her consort.

(It should be noted that this kind of behavior from either of the women was unusual in that neither of the two stars, competitive though they might be, were ever what I would have classified as line counters. Neither would ever display concerns about whose part was being featured in any particular episode. It just was not who they were—or are. They were invariably supportive of one another, more than willing to pick up the slack for the other, and constantly looking out for each other if fatigue or some other factor distracted from the work. It is the very uniqueness of this particular conflict that brings it to this volume and leads me to suspect a third party's influence—Mr. GS Brown.)

Liz Coe feared sabotage of her very good script. Sharon, meanwhile, felt all alone, without a caring or supportive director, and wanting, desperately, to do justice to this material. (La Gless had moved past paranoia and with good reason, for "they" really were out to get her this time.) My blonde leading lady took a recognizable defense posture of appearing not to care. She did care, of course, and on closing out the week she was unnecessarily apologetic for not having the ability to measure up to Liz's script.

Meanwhile, Tyne, seemingly oblivious to her partner's needs, relentlessly pursued first me, then Liz, then me again. She would have her half of the scene. (It had,

I was to learn, boiled down to the last scene in the film, which, coincidentally, would be shot last.) We made adjustments for her, but I insisted on maintaining the final moment—the clear indication of affection between the two partners regardless of what had gone on in the drama prior to this final moment. Five full working days before this, Tyne called me from her mobile home in tears, unable to continue this "demeaning" work. I was in the middle of a meeting with my new head writing team, Jonathan Estrin and Shelley List (now called "Listrin" by me) but took the call, which lasted a few minutes and ended with her slamming down the receiver. In the old days I would have been out of my office (meeting or no) and on the way to the set, but because this was being directed by her husband, I did not go. He could handle her, I reasoned, and so he did.

The scene she was then complaining about was viewed the next day in dailies, and it was excellent. Liz phoned. She was once again under siege by Tyne on the subject of that final scene and believed that Georg would not direct Tyne's final moment. I returned to Lacy Street after a dinner party with Corday and waited for the 1:30 AM wrap to discuss this with our director.

I opened with a compliment on dailies—specifically the controversial scene that Tyne had resisted so heavily the day before. Instead of acknowledging the compliment, as he usually would, Georg began to demonstrate his own frustrations over failing to win earlier arguments on the script. He spoke of being forced to "badger" and "manipulate" his wife and that (I presumed referring to the upcoming last day's work and that final scene) he would never do so again.

I reminded him that I was not talking to the star's husband but rather to *my* employee, and I asked if he was going to direct the final scene to the specifications of the producer or not. He would try, I remember him saying, but there were no guarantees "as to the actress's ability to play the scene." He suggested I talk to her, and I assured him I would. The conversation was not a violent or nasty argument, rather it was low-key and intense. Well, anyway, low volume. I was, I thought, firm and on my game.

The following shooting day, I was in Tyne's motor home. As always, she was brilliantly articulate. Ostensibly, her point was that, as written, Cagney's behavior was so despicable that Lacey would find it intolerable: something from which the partnership could not recover.

I told her that if she was counting on Sharon Gless's Cagney being "unlikable," in this or any episode, that she was making a bad bet and an unfortunate choice.

Her decision to play anger was one thing, but the alternative she advocated was loveless and would not serve her character or our series well.

"I don't know how to play what you're asking for," she stated. She wanted me to tell her how to do it. I reminded her that she "was the lady with the three fucking Emmys" and that she should figure it out. Once again—it seemed for the hundredth time—she requested that I let her out of her contract so that she could leave this series that was so damaging to her "honour." This time I was ready for her: "Be careful what you ask for lest you get it, lady."

She insisted she wanted her release.

"OK," I said. "If you are serious, I'll get you out. Give me five episodes next season at scale, and you're a free woman." She lifted those tired lids off her cheeks.

"At scale?" she asked incredulously.

"How bad do you want out, pal? Put up or shut up."

There was a long pause. The subject was changed. Finally, she wanted to be assured we would do good work next year. I smiled in the affirmative.

The next day (our last of the season), she performed the scene as I asked her to and at one point appeared in my office with three questions to be answered yes or no:

1. Did I understand that what it was she did for a living comes from so painful a place that she would never be fun to work with?

    "Yes," I answered.

2. Would I support her stand vis-à-vis *Cagney & Lacey* and stopping its distribution in South Africa?[68]

    "Absolutely," I replied.

3. Would I be back next season?

    "I don't know," I said.

"If you're back then I'm back," she rejoined.

---

[68] At that time, South Africa was still in the grip of apartheid, and many artists were asked to support boycotts of the offensive regime. Orion would authorize my promise to Tyne not to distribute the series in South Africa as long as the country continued its policy of apartheid.

I asked if I could ask three questions—yes or no answers only. She nodded.

"Can I have a hug?

"Yes."

"Do you know that I love you?"

"No."

"Do you know that I admire and respect you?"

"Yes."

At week's end, I escorted Ms. Gless to the WGA Awards. Our own Georgia Jeffries was the winner, and Sharon announced that she would not return to the series if I was not on board.

"Parting Shots," indeed.

What I had learned was that I could not—and did not want to—produce two series simultaneously. What to do was the dilemma. Columbia was paying me $800,000 per annum, in guaranteed advances and reimbursed overhead, in antici- pation of my fulfilling my role on my six-episode, blind commitment with ABC. In addition, they were (naturally) hopeful I would produce other things as well. Sharon and Tyne were demanding I return to *Cagney & Lacey* and were threaten- ing to walk if I did not.

I felt the happiest solution for me would be to roll over the ABC commitment for another year and to suspend/extend the Columbia deal—thus allowing me to stay with *Cagney & Lacey*. That was not a slam dunk. I would have to appeal to Columbia and ABC for relief on my contract.

Herman Rush was terrific in allowing me to suspend and extend until the comple- tion of *Cagney & Lacey;* so was ABC's Brandon Stoddard in giving me permission to roll over my commitment to his network. Both men seemed to understand my passion for *Cagney & Lacey* and extracted nothing for this favor.

History indicated that Rosenbloom and Orion would not be as generous, but that proved not to be true. Apparently my full-time presence at Lacy Street was also missed by the Orion brass, for they agreed to raise my per episode fee from the then-ridiculously low point of $13,000 per episode to something close to my then-current deal of $40,000 per segment, for a guaranteed $880,000 per season. (When I asked why now and not before, it was explained that a loophole in Mace's contract had been discovered and that they now felt comfortable with breaking away from the original—and admittedly antiquated—deal.)

I was the industry's reigning Emmy Award-winning producer. I was finally content that I was being compensated properly, and my two stars were unreservedly pleased to have me exclusively back with them. Let the good times roll.

CHAPTER 40

IF YOU CAN PAINT, I CAN WALK

"June 12, 1986, only 19 6/8 more shows to go."

My favorite diary entry midway through the third episode of our twenty-two-show season. Another favorite recollection that year was the note director Ray Danton left for Jim Frawley, the man who would immediately follow him in the episodic progression of the six to ten directors we would use in a season. First of all, it began: "Dear Bill" (sic). Danton then went on to wish Jim luck saying "It's been tough, but I've finally whipped the crew into shape for you." The troika of Gless, Daly, and Rosenzweig were not the only egos occupying Lacy Street.

The season of 1986–87 was my very best with Tyne. She seemed happy, even admitted to still being amused by the job and me. She would tease and taunt me, and I kept forgetting it was all an act, that there might not even be a Tyne Daly. With her, all was illusion; everything a performance. As to her toughness on directors: few people in our industry are as bright, talented, or experienced as Tyne Daly, and even fewer of them are directing episodic television.

It had come to pass that Sharon, by this time—at least in terms of results—was as good a performer as Tyne. Some would say maybe better, if nothing else because of her authenticity. The qualification (in terms of results) is because it cost Sharon more. She didn't then (and still does not) have Tyne's technique or experience on which to draw. Sharon could rarely do it by the numbers. Each time, each day, on each scene, Ms. Gless had to conjure it all up from below ground zero.

It was like working with two great opera singers, when only one sang from the diaphragm; there was always the concern that the other would injure herself.

Our seven Emmy nominations[69] that season included one for Georg Stanford Brown's direction on "Parting Shots," ironic after how unhappy he was throughout the process.

In September, I repeated as Emmy winner for Best Dramatic Series, Sharon and John Karlen also won, as did Mr. Brown for directing. We collected 80 percent of the statues we could possibly get, as our two other nominees, Peggy McKay and James Stacy, were competing against each other (for Best Performance by a Guest Star in an episode). Stacy went on to win several other prizes for his performance as "The Gimp" (which particularly pleased me since I had so many fights with our network liaisons over the decision to cast a genuinely handicapped person in this episode that not only brought us more fan mail than any other in our history but proved to be Cagney's greatest romance). There were also wars with Stacy himself over the interpretation of just how his handicap would be portrayed.[70]

I had just about gotten to the place where I had stopped waiting for the other shoe to drop. The Listrin team was very pleasant for me to work with, and I would, despite the minor complaints of my starring dynamic duo, bring this writing team back for what would be our final year on the series.

I felt the women were a bit unreasonable about the writing. The material was different for a lot of reasons, but the most important loss was that we were no longer doing the late-night erasing sessions in their trailers as we had before. That important process had really all but stopped with the advent of Tyne's pregnancy. More and more now, Ms. Daly was understandably eager to get home once she had completed her twelve- to fourteen-hour day. No one could quarrel with that, but it was costing us that 5–10 percent edge that had always made such a special difference. We had also been on the air a long time.

---

[69]   Our seven nominees: Tyne, Sharon, the show itself, Karlen, guest stars Peggy McCay and James Stacy (first time the category of Performance by a Guest Star in a Dramatic Episode was established, and the only coed acting category in the Emmy award structure), and Georg Stanford Brown.

[70]   Episode referenced is "The Gimp," written by Cynthia Darnell, story by Norm Chandler Fox, directed by Sharron Miller. Since Stacy himself was an amputee and not a paraplegic, once cast he balked at playing the part from a wheelchair. That the character be "wheelchair bound" was an important story point, and I was very forceful in advising James that we had hired his talent and whatever empathic feelings he might access, not his particular/unique handicap.

The war against complacency required constant vigilance. Quality control was the business in which I now found myself. We were slipping, but it was not by much. We were certainly not faltering in the eyes of our public.

The acclaim and the awards kept piling up, even from as far away as the United Kingdom, where *Cagney & Lacey* for quite some time stayed on the top of their ratings as the highest-ranking imported show in all of Britain. It resulted in the formation there of CLASS (the Cagney and Lacey Appreciation of the Series Society), with a membership totaling in the thousands, plus a command performance for Tyne and Sharon to appear for the queen mother at the fiftieth anniversary celebration of the BBC. They were the only stars of a then-current American series who were invited, and they accepted, contingent on my accompanying them, which I did. The flowers smelled sweeter and sweeter.

"I bet you don't make as many entries in your diary as you used to." Sharon Gless was right in the late fall of 1986 as she reminisced over our past fights. She missed them, she said, and was disappointed that I did not. There were still flashes—a bit of anger over a script, a scene, a line, a stage direction—but for the most part things had become peaceful and downright pleasurable. We were all maturing nicely, and, when the slightly paranoid, very insecure Sharon Gless looks at you and simply says, "I trust you," well, you know it is the highest form of praise and the finest thing she could ever possibly say about a fellow human being.

By now, it may be clear to the reader that I was falling for my blonde star. If so, in the fall of 1986, it was still not entirely clear to me.

In October of that year, shortly after the Academy Emmy wins, Sharon, along with multi-award-winning writer Fay Kanin, received the Genii Award from the American Women in Radio & Television. Norman Lear, introduced as "King" Lear, gave the introductory remarks for Kanin (the behind-the-camera winner) while I was brought forward as "the heir apparent" to the aforementioned king, so that I could speak for Sharon, the in-front-of-the-camera recipient. I did not give a speech. What I did was present a small film I had made to speak for me and to serve to introduce my star.

The film lasted just under eleven minutes. It was made up of clips of Sharon's work (initially short trailer-like snippets from most of the TV shows and movies she had done from *Marcus Welby*, to *Rockford, Switch, Star Chamber, Airport, The Immigrants, Turnabout, The Last Convertible, Movieola*, and then *Cagney & Lacey*). There was one scene with Tyne, and then an optical dissolve to a plethora of moments, sans dialogue, musically scored with Joe Cocker singing, "You Are So Beautiful to Me." As the film was coming to an end, I leaned over to Sharon, seated next to me on the dais, where, in the dark, we had held hands throughout most of the film's eleven minutes and whispered, "I wish the lights would never come up."

The lights, of course, did. And there was hardly a dry eye in the house. My filmic tribute to Ms. Gless was a hit. It was also a learning experience for me, for, as I was busy over several nights constructing this homage to my friend and star, I began to notice feelings for her that were—in my experience—quite unique and overwhelming.

It was not long after that—basking in the reflections of that afternoon at the Genii Awards—when Sharon and I began making love. It was unexpected, spontaneous, and very passionate. It was also not very circumspect or prudent, being that the locale for this surprising tryst was Sharon's motor home at Lacy Street.

The next day when I first saw her, again in the motor home, Sharon smiled as I entered, then asked: "Any regrets?"

There were too many to list, so I simply said, "Yes."

My response was not all together expected by my beautiful leading lady, so I went on to explain that this was not a good idea for either of us. First of all, I was married—and married to Barbara Corday at that. My Mrs. was known—and respected—by almost all in our tiny company. Second, Ms. Gless was then romantically involved with the captain of our film crew, cinematographer Hector Figueroa. There was also the lack of professionalism, coupled with the not-very-bright decision of a man running a show involving two stars of equal stature, especially if my objectivity were to come under question as a result of our having an affair.

There was the very real danger of having all that I had worked for come crashing down, as some Hollywood wag might well say, "Oh, I get it. It wasn't about feminism or women's rights at all; the guy just wanted to fuck the blonde."

It was a painful conversation as we agreed that what had happened between us the day before would not recur.

Weeks passed. Sharon and I were good at our word. No one was the wiser, and another bullet seemed to have been dodged. Then the invitation from the BBC to come to London for that vaunted network's fiftieth anniversary celebration. The women would not go without me, and I urged Barbara to break away during this week in late November to make the trip and share in the accolades; a good time would surely be had by all. Barbara was busy. Mid-season replacements and preparation for another pilot season at Columbia Studios would have to take precedence for my executive spouse.

And so we were a foursome: Mr. and Mrs. Georg Stanford Brown, Sharon Gless, and me. Ten hours in the first-class section of an overnight flight to London sitting next to one of the most beautiful women in the world, with whom I had—only weeks before—a memorable rendezvous. We were all over each other before the plane began to traverse the Atlantic. On arriving at the Ritz Hotel early in the morning and after a bit of an old-fashioned English breakfast, we all repaired to our respective rooms to clean up and to enjoy the free time that was ours until the following day. It wasn't long before I was up the back stairs of the Ritz and being admitted to the fabulous suite that had been reserved for La Gless.

It was a volatile afternoon and evening. We made love, fought, made love, then argued and made love some more. Mostly I remember that the tempest we were creating on our own was being matched by Mother Nature as the French windows of that suite kept blowing open in the midst of a terrific rain storm, causing the diaphanous curtains to eerily dance into the room. Lights and shadows—just like in the movies.

We were in London for days, the most exciting and romantic days of my life. It is different making love to a star you have been watching for years on screen than performing the same act with a mere mortal. There are moments—many moments—where you feel as if you have transcended reality, somehow finding yourself costarring in your own incredibly sensuous movie. It set in motion a surfeit of feelings and emotions; guilt was not one of them. I do not do drugs, but I could imagine that what I was experiencing might well become my drug of choice.

If all that weren't turn-on enough, there was the action going on outside the bedroom: the accolades and response to the two women I had joined together and to the show they so ably would represent. Backstage at the Drury Lane Theatre, Paul McCartney stopped to ask Sharon for her autograph. The Beatles were still very much a presence in my frame of reference, so it impressed the hell out of me, but once again, it demonstrated (if, indeed, the BBC invitation had not) that *Cagney & Lacey* was a far bigger success in the United Kingdom than it ever was (or would ever be) in the United States.[71] (It should be noted as this book goes to print in the spring of 2007, that the entire series has been sold—yet again—in the United Kingdom, a full quarter century after its initial release.)

---

[71]   Not only were the BBC ratings on the show huge, that network would rerun the entire series three separate times in prime time. At that time such a thing had never happened before in the UK.

Tyne Daly, about to go on stage in front of the Queen Mother, the Duchess of York (Fergie in those days), and a full house of tuxedo-clad Brits representing their who's who of English show business, threw me an off-stage, whispered aside: "Barney, I forgive you everything. You got me on stage at the Drury Lane."

At the fiftieth anniversary bash for the BBC at London's Drury Lane Theatre, a backstage reception line for her highness, the queen mother. Sharon and Tyne were as smitten as everyone else.

Photo: Sharon Gless Personal Collection

The next day, we were a foursome again, as Sharon and I took a respite from destroying her suite. Ms. Gless had a plan to leave for L.A. earlier than the rest of us, as Hector was waiting in L.A. to take her to her mother's house in Carmel, California, for Thanksgiving. Georg and Tyne unwittingly helped my cause by joining me in urging Sharon to stay another couple of days, pointing out she would then still have time to make a connection to Carmel in time for the holiday feast.

Our chauffeur, Martin Lewis, handed over his touring car's mobile phone, and in minutes Gless had explained to Hector (although only in part) that she would be taking her return flight a couple of days later than planned. I remember marveling at the new-to-me technology that made this trans-Atlantic call possible from a moving car and have been grateful to cell phones ever since.

On the dais of CLASS (*Cagney & Lacey* Appreciation of the Series Society) in London, England: Sharon Gless (the blonde) and the author.

Photo: Rosenzweig Personal Collection

That night, the four of us attended a show in London's West End that had world premiered only days before: Andrew Lloyd Webber's *Phantom of the Opera*. That then-newly minted musical, presented in the very theater for which it was designed, has (I am sure), over the years, impacted many couples; still, I cannot imagine Mr. Webber ever had two more perfect members of an audience than he had that London night in the personages of Sharon Gless and Barney Rosenzweig. The flawed hero, the heroine, torn 'twixt a romance with her Svengali and her more conventional fiancé, the opera and showmanship as a backdrop, the high melodrama of it all. I was in sensory and emotional overload. Sharon held herself together better than I, but not much.

We were far from discreet on that flight over the Atlantic en route to the States, and I believed we had been spotted by someone I was pretty certain I knew back in Hollywood. The good news was that Tyne and Georg remained clueless.

On landing at LAX, Sharon was met by Hector. He had packed her bags for Carmel and was prepared to make their connecting flight. Barbara was there with a limo to take me home. We were all too quickly returned to reality. Sharon came running over to my car to say good-bye, tapping on the window for me to open, which, with tears running down my cheeks, I did. Barbara either didn't notice this moment or chose not to ask what it meant. I volunteered no information on this or anything else relevant to it as we drove home.

There would be no agreement this time between Sharon and myself, save that we would each do our best to keep our affair ongoing and clandestine. She was not asking me to break up my marriage, although she did voluntarily end her long-standing relationship with Hector. Then, after a few weeks had passed, I was asked to visit her motor home, where, upon opening the door, I was confronted by a stuffed monkey, sitting atop a music box, playing "Masquerade" from *Phantom of the Opera*.

It was the back-up prop from the production in London, which Sharon, unbeknownst to me, had pleaded to purchase for her unnamed lover. Her unusual request was granted; it seems, in the theater, even prop masters can be hopeless romantics. The monkey and his music box are—to this day—among my most prized possessions.

Photo: Sharon Gless Personal Collection

Sharon Gless at a special reception in London. That is Brian Connolly, a fabulously talented English performer, on the far right of the frame and Barry Manilow, one person removed down the line to the left. Oh yes, that is Princess Diana, who is offering her hand to La Gless.

Photo: Sharon Gless Personal Collection

Sharon with two of London's finest.
Photo: Sharon Gless Personal Collection

One of my favorite photos of Sharon and me. Occasion was the celebration of our hundredth episode of *Cagney & Lacey,* and the photographer was ironically Sharon's beau at that time, cinematographer Hector Figueroa.

Photo: Rosenzweig Personal Collection

CHAPTER 41

QUALITY CONTROL

On the Lacy Street front, Sharon and Tyne were closer now than ever; it is, they say, "the best year of our marriage." The growth patterns for all of us were apparent, and the work continued to be good, if uninspired. The lack of soaring had Sharon and Tyne critical, but I thought they failed to see just what an accomplishment there was in maintaining a level of quality.

Miami Vice slipped badly its second year and its third was worse; *Moonlighting* was not nearly the show it was in its first season. *Hill Street Blues* was stumbling as well (though not so much as the other two). Our show was—on balance—doing some of its best work, missing some of the highs of the past, it was true, but also dodging the lows. We were maintaining a high standard of quality, and I felt we three should learn to take more pleasure in that—the getting on base with each time at bat—and learning that was now our game. The emotional extremes of the home run batter, clearing the fence or striking out, were part of our past. We were fine. It had been a great year for *Cagney & Lacey*, and so all the other bad news fell into the background.

Writer Joel Oliansky once said that I "was a born producer." I have always elected to believe this was meant as a compliment; still, you never know. That I am no futurist is made evident by the facts of 1987, particularly when juxtaposed beside my diary entry of December 26, 1986. It was not to be, as I had predicted, *"One of the best years yet."*

It *was* the year of some extraordinary good work on *Cagney & Lacey*—especially our two-part, award-winning episodes on alcoholism ("Turn, Turn, Turn" Parts I and II[72])—which rivaled our previous two-parter on breast cancer for topicality, relevance, and for being credited as a potential life saver.

Another rollover by Stoddard at ABC and a suspension/extension by an equally sympathetic Herman Rush was put forth in anticipation of yet another season for *Cagney & Lacey*. That order for yet another semester of the series was not so easy in coming.

CBS had preempted us for the month of April, saving our two-parter for May sweeps. The chances of us doing well in any sweeps period (against typical block-buster competition) were slim. Coming after five weeks of preemptions and the subsequent loss of audience flow, the odds were reduced substantially. Instead of having CBS making their decision based on March numbers (two of three were already in and excellent) and our two-parter following in April (when we are on a roll against relatively weak competition), this piece of scheduling "genius" was put forward, clouding my horizon.

I had three choices:

(1) Do nothing

(2) Get on the bandwagon and use the CBS line that the two-parter was so superior it was being saved for May sweeps

(3) Raise a stink through the press, the National Organization for Women, and all my other pro-feminist contacts

If I did either 1 or 2 and May 15 came and we were not on the schedule, I would never forgive myself. Acting on 3, however, was not without its problems. Not only would a national press campaign be a lot of work, it could cause plenty of trouble with CBS (for the only way to do this, at that point in the series' history, was to personalize the battle. The issue of May sweeps and a five-week hiatus was, I believed, a little too technical for our lay audience; besides, after five years, it would be tough to pull out the same old tactics used in the past). This time it could get nasty. I would have to give interviews about a post–Harvey Shephard CBS and be quoted on Kim LeMasters' disdain for the series from the outset. I wouldn't make many friends at CBS with that tactic.

An evening's discussion with Corday, Ann Daniel, and Len Hill (by this time, Mr. and Mrs.) regarding the CBS situation resulted in my first sleepless night

---

[72]   "Turn, Turn, Turn" Part I, written by Georgia Jeffries; "Turn, Turn, Turn" Part II, written by Shelley List & Jonathan Estrin. Both episodes directed by Sharron Miller.

since *Fortune Dane*, one year before. I found myself regressing emotionally into the pre–*Cagney & Lacey* period of my life—feeling angry, bitter, and powerless. I thought I had put those victim feelings behind me, and it frightened me to see how short a distance I had actually come.

Sitting at a dinner table with those three network executives—for that's what they were at the nadir of my life in the early eighties—had me breaking into a cold sweat and fearing for my future. It was just like the bad old days all over again.

My sense of anticipated loss was acute. The power of being on the air with a series that provided me an opportunity to say whatever I wished endured only through the life of the show itself. It was nontransferable. The true power (over the life and death of that program) was not mine.

I would begin to mourn. I knew, as did Shakespeare's Mark Antony, that such a Caesar would not come my way again. It was not the fear of being able to come up with another hit; the chances, I felt, of doing that—now with *Cagney & Lacey* as a springboard—were greater than ever. It was the loss of this particular franchise that I could not tolerate, the unique confluence of events of my own power and abilities, the women's movement, the synergy with Corday, added to the equal wizardry of Tyne and Lacey, then multiplied by the affinity of Sharon for Cagney, Cagney for Lacey/Lacey for Cagney—and increased by the congruence of Sharon and Tyne themselves. There was the uniqueness of the Lacy Street experience and of my first true, authentic hit. These things could not be put back together again, and the terrible sickness is that I began this lament far sooner than necessary.

Our ratings in March continued to be good-to-excellent. We took the time period every week in the month. Still there was no word from CBS. I requested a meeting with LeMasters and Bud Grant. I was calm and seemingly in control of my emotions. I asked for an early pickup to be announced at our April 2 special screening of the two-parter;[73] they would "reflect on it." I requested that they be straight with me and tell me if they were considering canceling the show.

"We're considering picking it up," Mr. Grant said. It was sort of a glass half full/half empty condition. The next day, the *New York Times* revealed that Gene Jankowski[74] had termed *Cagney & Lacey* "marginal." I was being urged by the press to respond to this assault. I decided to keep a low profile. Discretion truly

---

[73]   "Turn, Turn, Turn" Parts I and II for the National Council on Alcoholism.

[74]   Gene Jankowski, then head of the entire CBS network and ranked over Bud Grant and Kim LeMasters.

became a better choice than valor, but even in my agitated state I was not bereft of ideas.

A planned promotional screening for the National Commission on Alcoholism, to be attended by various civic and political leaders, would feature the organization honoring those of us connected to the production. I asked them to give the laurel to Kim LeMasters of CBS instead, reasoning that it would be more than a little difficult for him to accept such an honor with one hand while canceling the series with the other. It had become a game of centimeters, and I would grab territory wherever I could.

LeMasters called. My plan of having him receive an award at our special screening was working. Kim wanted to announce something but conceded he did not have authority to grant an early pickup. It was political, he said; Jankowski didn't wish to appear to be undermining the news division or *West 57th Street*. The whole mess was over the unscheduled five-week break *Cagney & Lacey* was being asked to take. *West 57th Street* would replace us, and, according to Jankowski, one or the other would then make the fall schedule.

It seemed patently unfair to us since the stats that *West 57th Street* might rack up would be against the semi-weak competition of the month of April, while we (on the other hand) would be judged by our ratings against the formidable counter-programming inherent in May sweeps.

At this point, what seemed to matter to LeMasters was that I not "call out the press." He wanted to know if I would be satisfied with a CBS commitment for twenty-two scripts, scripts that CBS would guarantee to fund even though they could not yet confirm a new season of production. It amounted to a $600,000 show of good faith (the dollars required of the network for us to commission those twenty-two scripts), and it enabled us to prepare for a new year well in advance of the announcement of the next season's schedule. I felt it was a good start and told LeMasters we would be happy to accept the offer.

The Beverly Hills screening of our two-parter at the Fine Arts Theatre played better than any film with which I have ever been associated. Sharon's riveting, powerful performance swept all of us (audience, director, writers, myself) to a triumphant conclusion. We packed the several-hundred-seat movie house, and the film received a standing ovation. Even the self-critical, often insecure Gless was moved to tears.

LeMasters was gracious and announced the script order and, in a—for him—unusual display of emotion, enthused that a pickup was a virtual certainty. Even the always taciturn Ronnie Meyer, Sharon's longtime agent, had to exclaim, "I didn't know she was that good." The evening was a resounding smash.

A few weeks later, the two-parter was also screened for NOW at the Kennedy Center in Washington DC. There, too, it was greeted with standing applause and rave reviews from, among others, the *New York Times* and the Pulitzer Prize–winning Howard Rosenberg of the *Los Angeles Times*. The ratings were terrific, and, frankly, *West 57th Street*'s were not. We got our pickup for year six.

My love affair with Sharon had gone through some very rocky times and was more off than on, as I found it difficult-to-impossible to be lover and executive producer and married to another all at the same time. We had pretty much stopped seeing one another, but now in DC, we were most definitely on again—something to do with geographical monogamy. Only my assistant, Carole R. Smith, whom we had dubbed the "mother of the couple," had any idea as to what was really going on. Tyne Daly remained in the dark, as did my spouse and everyone else.

The "thing" with Sharon was, to understate it all, an explosive relationship, fueled by sex and alcohol. One or the other of us would end it, then long for it to resume. I could hardly bear her not being a part of my life, to not have her with me. Movies I would attend were now distorted by the affair; Sharon's image would (in my mind's eye) be super-imposed over the face of whatever leading lady was then on screen. It was bordering on obsession. Sharon's emotional state, so far as I could tell, was not that disparate from my own, but added to that was her own natural insecurity whereby she would voice concern that perhaps I had fallen for my muse—remembering the Rita Hayworth quote about men going to bed with Gilda but waking up with her. Was it, she wanted to know, Christine Cagney I loved or her? My assurances for the real girl over the reel one were not always believed.

Our constant breakups were terribly painful. My desire for Sharon, a growing sense of guilt over my marriage, my concerns over both of our images in light of the work we had created and all that it meant to us were burdens I could not always handle with equilibrium.

This would be the year that Sharon would win her second Emmy.[75] There was a second Writers Guild nomination for Georgia Jeffries and a Director's Guild nomination for Sharron Miller, both for their work on the two-parter. Sharon and Tyne were named "Women of the Year" by *Ms.* magazine (our second, albeit

---

[75]   1987 Emmy nominees were the show, Sharon, Tyne, John Karlen, editing (Jeanene Ambler for "Turn, Turn, Turn" Part and Georgia Jeffries for "Turn, Turn, Turn" Part II).

shared, cover). There was the Governor's Award from the National Commission of Working Women (a first) when, in Washington DC they took *Cagney & Lacey* out of competition forever, dubbing the series "the quintessential show for working women."

The Museum of Broadcasting (now called the Museum of Television & Radio) honored our series with a special tribute screening, and I received a "good guy" plaque from the National Women's Political Caucus and the *Channels* magazine Award of Excellence. The roses were plentiful, but my olfactory system had been damaged by the heavy economic losses I had taken and by the recurrence of those feelings of powerlessness I thought I had put behind me. On the surface, my life was ideal, but I was—more and more—being gripped by the darkness I perceived on my horizon.

I had been led to believe that if you produced enough episodes and did so efficiently then that was all that would be required. I was like one of the chicanos in Jaime Escalante's calculus class at Garfield High School.[76] I had worked hard, played fair, won according to the rules in place; now I was being asked by the power establishment to take the test again. I wasn't up to it.

Our final season moved on. Bob Hegyes was added to the cast as Detective Manny Esposito; Merry Clayton would replace Carl Lumbly as Isbecki's partner and become the third woman detective at the 14th Precinct. My baby brother, Joel, finally got his directorial shot and did fine.[77]

Al Waxman would need to undergo heart bypass surgery and be lost to us for from six to eight weeks. This called for yet another of those difficult-on-the-actors-staff-and-crew block shoots, where for two weeks we shot nothing but squad room material involving the corpulent Lieutenant Samuels in order to bank enough material for several episodes.[78] Al Waxman never performed better. It was as if he

---

[76] Reference is to the true story portrayed in the film *Stand and Deliver*.

[77] Joel was finally given the opportunity to make his film directorial debut, over the objections of Dick Rosenbloom, who by that time probably felt one Rosenzweig in this business was more than sufficient. I put up a financial bond to assuage Orion's concerns by paying director Reza Badiyi to stand by if Joel faltered. My brother, I am pleased to note, came through, with flying colors. Episodes were "Ahead of the Game" (actually made for the 1986–87 season and written by Allison Hock) and "You've Come a Long Way, Baby" (written by Fred Rappaport).

[78] For insertion in yet-to-be made episodes in an effort to minimize the absence of such a key character.

was, on some subconscious level, leaving a memorial to himself in the event he would be unable to return.[79]

---

[79]   Al Waxman did return and, thirty-five pounds lighter, completed the season, but died several years later after completing yet another series I would supervise, *Twice in a Lifetime*, for the Pax network. There Al played Othneil, a character I created for him.

CHAPTER 42

CHANGE EQUALS PSYCHOLOGICAL LOSS

Arguably our last season was our weakest, although even here we had two of our most powerful episodes: the acquaintance rape segment ("Don't I Know You")[80] and our payoff to young Harvey Junior's hero worship of Oliver North ("Friendly Smoke").[81]

The women were under contract for one more year, and the ratings were good enough for renewal if anyone was willing to fight for same. I gave Orion more than one opportunity to have me do so, and, as usual, they mishandled the situation.

Tyne and Sharon were bone weary. The whole venture had been a monumental test of their endurance and their psyches. Considering only half of what they'd been through, both women had behaved admirably. This had not been a guest star format or, even with all due respect to the male members of the cast, an ensemble show. These women had carried all the weight and had done so under unbelievably difficult circumstances.

They had, for a few seasons, been paid just about as much money as anyone could reasonably want, and they were realistic enough to know that the kind of creature comforts even their housekeepers might demand were impractical at the pace we were working, or undeliverable at the facility we occupied.

The only thing, then, they wished for that they didn't have was a piece of the action—a rooting interest in the afterlife of the series they had done so much to shape. There were no boycotts or work stoppages by these two. They did not put

---

[80]   Written by Kathryn Ford, directed by Sharron Miller. An Emmy nomination for Ms. Gless.

[81]   Written by Shelley List & Jonathan Estrin, directed by Reza Badiyi. An Emmy nomination and win for Ms. Daly.

that proverbial negotiating gun to their corporate masters' heads as so many stars had done over the years. All they could hope for now was justice. That is in short supply in Hollywood; still, I took their case to Larry Hilford, who had just succeeded Jamie Kellner at Orion.

By this time the news from the syndication market was bleak. Orion salesmen in the field were coming up empty.

"Y'know," I began, "I've sold this show not once but three times, and in New York and L.A., the toughest markets in the world. I find it hard to believe I couldn't sell it in Des Moines."

I pointed out that I could be like a fanatical dervish where this series was concerned, and that I was willing to supply this service gratis, since I already had a percentage of the show and it was to my benefit to see this package sold; all Orion had to do was to pay my airfare and hotel bills. Hilford wanted to know how I'd do it.

"Same as always," I replied. "By sheer force of will."

I thought by now I deserved to be trusted on that score. Hilford, who impressed me as a man who didn't want anyone playing in his sandbox, said he'd think on it.

"One more thing," I added. "I'll need a sales tool. I want Tyne and Sharon to be involved, to make appearances all over the world, to have their photos taken with station managers and their kids." I could, I told Hilford, deliver the two Award-winning actresses if they were given a tiny piece of the profits. "Call it sales commission if you want," I added. The answer was no.

"Give them a bad definition of profits. Christ, you say the show isn't worth anything, that you can't sell it; what's wrong with giving them each 5 percent of nothing?"

"Principle," was his reply.

"Principle?" I shrieked. "These gals are killing themselves. The Orion management team inherited this series, has never put a speculative quarter into it, and now does nothing to sustain it while reaping a multi-million dollar bonanza and you talk to me about principle? I have to ask, Mr. Hilford, what kind of principle is that?"

Hilford pointed out that the women were paid a high salary for that.

"They are paid, Mr. Hilford, to put in twelve-hour days as actors; no more, no less. You haven't got a clue what these women do or what they have brought to this company; you wouldn't have a job without them, and I dare say if it weren't for them, Orion wouldn't have a television division."

Hilford countered with the view that help was not needed, which I thought was curious in light of his own admissions of failure in the marketplace. He then expressed the view that it was of no particular interest to him or his company if this very expensive show continued into its seventh and final season. The 125 episodes they would have at the end of the current season were more than sufficient for their purposes, he claimed.

I believed this was rank stupidity. I pointed out that Orion was grandfathered under the old tax laws and still had the investment tax credit on *Cagney & Lacey*, that foreign sales on the series were escalating at an amazing rate, and, with our minor deficits and assuming only the bare minimum in U.S. sales, it would still pay Orion millions annually to keep the show in production.

"Forget the money," I went on. "Are you saying your company has no use for this flagship and all that it means—or at least should—to your television division?"

Hilford had enough. The meeting was over. We never spoke again.

Months later he would make the very questionable decision to sell the *Cagney & Lacey* series to Lifetime Cable at a fraction of the figure we had all been talking of for some years. He had an underling call to explain that this was "a very good deal," for it only involved "basic cable" in relatively "small markets." That Lifetime Cable then played in New York, Boston, and Los Angeles, to name only three not-so-small markets, and that the cable service would run our episodes both day and night (until even the most ardent *Cagney & Lacey* fan was satiated), would not, according to the Orion mavens, "adversely affect future sales." Hilford was new at Orion, but he was the perfect match for the management team he had joined.

Days after the Lifetime sale, I was asked if Sharon and Tyne would be willing to do promotional spots for this new customer. I reminded them of Hilford's earlier statements that no help was needed from the stars. Orion came back the next day with an offer to pay the women $10,000 each for what would be no more than one hour's work.

"Why don't you give them a percentage of profits—which you keep saying are worthless—and save the $20,000?" I queried. No takers. To their credit, Sharon and Tyne held to their principles and refused to do the promos.

Tyne and Sharon were appreciative of my efforts but were genuinely pissed at Hilford's turndown. Tyne begged me to end the show. It was not within my power to do so. What I could do was promise that for the first time I would do nothing to promote or sell the idea of a pickup with CBS and that I would let Kim LeMasters know of my decision to leave. The absence of a key creative element would probably provide the network chief with more than enough of an excuse to end the life of a series he never cared for in the first place.

I had finally had it with Orion. Larry Hilford was probably as big a factor in my decision to depart at season's end, as was Jerry Weintraub's persistent offer for me to leave production and join him as executive vice president and chairman of the television division of the Weintraub Entertainment Group.

"I'm going to make you very rich, very fast," said Weintraub, the charismatic dynamo. He had my attention.

The decision to join Weintraub—leaving production to become a suit—was, in fact, as motivated by Kim LeMasters' actions as it was by Hilford's or Weintraub's.

Georgia Jeffries had left *Cagney & Lacey* at the end of the previous season. She then accepted my offer to join The Rosenzweig Company as its senior development VP. Her job was to find or write the series that would fulfill the six-show commitment I had with ABC and to creatively develop other writers and material for future projects to be produced by the company.

A screenplay came our way: *Sisters* by Jill Gordon. It was one of those rare finds: a script fully realized that required little or no input from either Ms. Jeffries or myself. We liked it just the way it was. It had been developed by ABC; they had passed on the property and put it in turnaround to the supplier, Columbia Pictures Television. It had nearly gotten made, but another so-called non-franchise property developed at the same time at ABC got the nod instead. That show was called *thirtysomething*.

The Columbia executives had done their homework. With ABC no longer a possibility and with no chance of selling anything to NBC's Brandon Tartikoff that had not originated with him, it left—in that pre-cable era—only CBS. Although Columbia's deal with The Rosenzweig Company was then in hiatus, it wouldn't hurt, they reasoned, to run the project by two such hot CBS properties as Ms. Jeffries and myself. After all, CBS was our home network.

Leaving even less to chance, Columbia executive Steve Berman got the script to actresses Marilu Henner and Kristy McNichol. They agreed to come on board, subject to having the man who produced *Cagney & Lacey* as executive producer.

There I was, the only CBS Emmy Award-winning drama producer of that decade, sitting in LeMasters' office, script in hand; Jill Gordon, the writer of that script, contractually committed to stay with the show for the life of the series, and WGA Award–winning writer Georgia Jeffries, enthusiastically agreeing to supervise Ms. Gordon and the writing staff under my direction. In addition we had Marilu Henner, making her first commitment to a television series since *Taxi,* and Kristy McNichol, obligating herself to series television for the first time since the very successful Spelling/Goldberg series *Family.*

"In a more perfect world," I said, "*Cagney & Lacey* would have worked in the post office. This is *that* show, that possibility. This transcends *Cagney & Lacey;* it is its logical successor."

LeMasters turned it down. The man who would lead CBS to the ratings cellar was unmoved by the material, the assembled team, or my spiel. I became reflective. This was not my script. I had not influenced even one comma. Jill Gordon was not my discovery. Kristy McNichol and Marilu Henner were not even my idea. All I had been asked to do was be the iron man running back and "punch it in from the three." Someone else had slugged it out for the previous ninety-seven yards; all I had to do was get it into the end zone and score the touchdown.

Instead, I found myself on the one-yard line with eleven guys piled on top of me and lye invading my nostrils. I speculated that I was getting too old for this; perhaps I should try coaching. Enter Jerry Weintraub.

I was grateful for his giving me the opportunity to move gracefully to the relative safety of the sidelines but also could not get over how sad the whole thing was. I was caught in a dilemma. I loved making a show but could no longer go through what was necessary to get there. It had all been rather like crawling naked over razor blades: once you've done it, you can't forget the experience, and you are not likely to willingly go through it again.

Artists like to think of themselves as victims, according to author Joseph Epstein. He claims that best-selling novelists are driven in limousines to give lectures whose main message is that the artist in America has no place to rest his head; that painters with serious real estate holdings rant against a vile and philistine country. HL Menken's solution for the complaints of writers about the loneliness of their work was to prescribe a few days on the assembly line. Menken may have been right about a lot of things, but I don't think that was my problem.

I had succeeded in a way few of my generation could imagine. It was more than a hit television show—it was the cancellation and the subsequent renewal. It was the monolithic CBS having to say to the *New York Times* and the world, "We have made a mistake. We were wrong. Barney Rosenzweig was right." It was the vindication of all those years of rejection and rebuff that enlarged my ego to the point that my skin had to be metaphorically stretched thin to provide cover for a goiter-sized, self-important lump, located very close to the surface of my persona.

Larry Hilford and Kim LeMasters merely reminded me of what I already knew: that I was powerless. After all I had been through, I no longer had the energy to argue the point or the ability to summon the strength to fight back. I would close down The Rosenzweig Company.

Overwhelming all of this was the decision to move out of my home, to end my nearly ten-year marriage to Barbara Corday, and to effectively change nearly every aspect of my life.

I once wrote a line for Christine Cagney to say to her partner (then in a slight depression over the move from her apartment of over fifteen years). "Change," Cagney pontificated, "equals psychological loss." For me, at that moment, the truth of my own dialogue was profound.

Hollywood divorces are legendary, in their abundance if nothing else. Somehow, this one was a shocker. It wasn't the breakup of Brad Pitt and Jennifer Aniston, but it tore at the fabric of our tiny community nonetheless. Corday and I *were* a most visible power couple; she, then arguably, one of the most popular women in all of Hollywood, I—at the time—the producer of a show that everyone in our town admired, if for no other reason than its sensitivity to women.

My decision to break off the marriage seemed to disconcert nearly everyone in my tiny circle. My sense of isolation was, therefore, more than imaginary, and all the more conflicted by my ongoing feelings of friendship for Corday and concern for her obvious pain at being left behind. I was all over the emotional map, but mostly I was floundering. Barbara didn't get it and thought that the whole thing was about my affair with the blonde who was playing Cagney.

"So you're fucking her," she would say. "What's that got to do with us?"

It was more complex than that. In fact, when I finally told Corday of the affair in the fall of 1987 (nearly a year after it had begun), the thing with Sharon was all but over. The news of my moving out of our home had everyone we knew abuzz. People, who were supposed to be Barbara's or our friends, seemed to delight in spreading whatever gossip they could conjure. Sharon and I had kept a very low profile, but it didn't matter what anyone knew. *The National Enquirer* was out in force, and, of course, Sharon—the single one—became the target of all the specu-lators as the most likely culprit in the destruction of my one-time happy home. It was mostly guesswork, but the fact was, we *were* having an affair.

This was all complicated by the second merger in a year involving Columbia Studios, one that Barbara would not survive. In the midst of her personal upheaval came a professional crisis as well.

Barbara and I had an incredibly synergistic relationship. We were best friends. As times got rougher and rougher for me in those last days of the seventies and the early months of 1980, Corday would lend emotional support and endorse my dreams of retirement.

"Tell me about the rabbits," she would say, and I would follow the *Of Mice and Men* Steinbeck reference with a veritable catalogue of what we would do with the rest of our lives and how we would do it. My goal was always to get out of show business; it became hers in support. We constantly assessed and reassessed what we would need to make our escape from Los Angeles and the business. Both of us felt that we could not stay in the City of Angels without being part of the entertainment industry, and so various alternative places and lifestyles came under scrutiny.

When I became, as indeed did she, successful beyond either of our dreams, she remained focused and, as best she could, kept me so. Few couples have so well managed each other's careers or their respective images. It was one of the most profound relationships of my life. It was, with the possible exception of my mother, the only time in my life I have been loved unconditionally. Sometimes love isn't enough.

At the end of 1987, I was turning fifty, becoming a grandfather for the first time, losing a ton of money through inexpert management (and some say fraud), and nearing the end of my beloved television series, *Cagney & Lacey* (then the single most important thing in my life). I was cracking. Corday held on tenaciously, believing this would be over the day I awoke to discover I was fifty-one and that the trauma of a birthday ending in a zero was over. I was in more trouble than that. The plethora of feelings that were assaulting me put me into overwhelm. I all but short-circuited. I forced an end to the marriage and the sale of our home. I was like Shakespeare's Macbeth: *"In blood stepp'd in so far, that, should I wade no more, returning were as tedious as go o'er."*

For years, as if a nurturing parent, Corday protected me and took on—as her personal assignment—the task of making me feel good. Despite her own heavy workload, she drove herself to make our home a showplace and to attempt to satisfy my every whim. She constructed our social calendar and filled our lives with peers, family, and activity. Regardless of my raised consciousness, or avowed position as one of Hollywood's leading feminists, I was a fairly stereotypical male around the house. Corday would often paraphrase actress Lee Grant's now famous line by saying: "I've been married to a chauvinist and I've been married to a feminist; neither would take out the garbage."[82]

More than my marriage was in trouble. There was no minimizing the shock I felt at that crucial accounting error and the subsequent venture mistake by my former business manager that would set me back over one million dollars. The collapse of the syndication market, costing me additional millions and causing me to virtually lose touch with any semblance of a reward system, coupled with my stressed-out state at finding myself powerless—particularly at Orion and at CBS, two places to which I had devoted an uncommon amount of time and energy—was just about more than I could bear.

That benchmark fiftieth birthday loomed; more important still was the irrefutable fact that sooner or later I would lose my show—my voice. Even Barbara Corday couldn't make me feel good anymore.

---

[82]   Lee Grant's line is the same, only Communist and Fascist replace chauvinist and feminist. The line was made famous by her during a guest appearance on *The Tonight Show* with Johnny Carson.

CHAPTER 43

TRIAL BY JURY

My life was in turmoil, but nearly 200 years ago some circus ringmaster said, "The show must go on," and ours certainly did. I refer the reader to the Museum of Television & Radio's archival department, where it is possible to view the 1987–88 Los Angeles tribute to *Cagney & Lacey* on videotape. For one hour of questions and answers from the audience that overflowed the auditorium of the L.A. County Museum that evening, Barbara Avedon, Barbara Corday, Sharon Gless, Tyne Daly, and I are all on stage, sitting side by side.

I was then newly separated from Corday, who was either in limbo, emotionally fried, or both; Gless and I were (once again) on the cusp of ending our romance, and no one—save for a pharmacist—could ever guess where Avedon might be coming from. The irony is that with all the potential drama at hand, the *only* person *any* of us seemed worried about that night was Avedon, who—it might be remembered—had been "abandoned" by erstwhile partner Corday not once, but twice, and fired by me, not once, but twice.

Watching the tapes of that evening, one would never know that anything was amiss. Avedon, indeed all of us, were up to the task. Still, if you ever want to see some real acting, I commend you to those archival tapes.

My affair with Sharon was all but over, as was my life with Barbara. I took temporary digs at a small house in the Hollywood hills. It was a bit of a bachelor pad, but it got much too little wear and tear from this now on-the-loose producer.

At my on-the-set fiftieth birthday celebration in 1987, I got a hug from my terrific associate producer, PK Knelman (now Candaux).

Photo: Rosenzweig Personal Collection

Barbara dined out on her "woman betrayed by a sister" story, giving public speeches alluding to her former friend/now home-wrecker Sharon Gless. It wasn't true, of course. Sharon and Barbara were never friends; they barely knew one another. In the six years of the series we made together, Sharon had only been to our home twice: once for a script conference with Terry Louise Fisher and me that did not involve Barbara, and the other time for a post-Emmy party Barbara and I hosted for the entire *Cagney & Lacey* company. Truth did not stop my estranged spouse from creating a real sister-like history, now (of course) desecrated by the blonde backstabber.

What was I supposed to do—attend the awards banquet for Women in Film and call out from the audience that Barbara was not telling the truth? I left her to her fantasy. Sharon had no other choice but to do that as well, and, in the Academy of Television Arts and Sciences' blue ribbon panel system, where, in those days, less than twenty votes were tabulated for the final winner, I have always believed that Barbara's oft-repeated story cost Sharon her third Emmy.[83]

In a way, and for the longest time, I was the beneficiary of this fabrication; for as long as Barbara chose to believe that it was all Sharon's fault, there wasn't much anger left over for me. I was invited, weeks after the separation began, to the family Thanksgiving feast, and, nearly a year after that (in her then-new position as VP of development of the CBS network, under Kim LeMasters of all people) Corday was heard to tell Mace Neufeld, then visiting the network to discuss some potential project: "I don't do business with people who are suing *me* (sic)." Since Barbara had never been named as a codefendant in Mace's suit against me, clearly, our disconnect was not as real from her end as it was from mine.

---

[83]   Won by Tyne Daly for "Friendly Smoke." No one is a bigger fan of Ms. Daly's than this author, but this particular entry was not Tyne's best work, whereas Sharon's performance in our episode "Don't I Know You" was among her very best. The reference to the Academy's blue ribbon panel is pure speculation on my part. The Emmys were, at that time, in my judgment, the fairest of all the major awards, in that once nominated, all the contenders were screened by a panel of judges on the same television monitor at the same time. Each of the performances was therefore guaranteed to be seen by the judges. That is not necessarily true for the Oscars or the Tonys. At any rate, feelings in our community against Sharon and myself were running so high that it is not a stretch to imagine that one or two members of that finite panel found themselves influenced. One or two votes would, in this setting, most definitely affect the outcome. For the record, the TV Academy no longer uses this blue ribbon panel system.

Tyne Daly was going through her own marital debacle, although it was then not known to most of us. Ms. Daly would make the move from our series to critical acclaim for her role as Rose in *Gypsy*, but by the time she collected the Tony for that outstanding performance, her long-standing marriage to Georg Stanford Brown would be over.

Sharon went into rehab at the strong urging of Ronnie Meyer, who had deduced that his client was either a very bad drunk, an alcoholic, or both. Meyer's diagnosis aside, according to Sharon and her counselor at Hazelden, if La Gless was addicted to anything, it wasn't booze, it was me.

It *was* a strong thing between us. Every part of my intellect told me to flee that scene. Comedian Mort Sahl admonishes all men to "never fall in love with an actress or any other female impersonator."

All who knew me (and I am sure it was also true for Sharon) advised strongly against continuing the relationship. Even the venerable Chinese zodiac gave out strong advisories against our pairing. It was continually on and then off. It was beyond capricious.

"Some experiences so possess you," John Fowles wrote in his novel *The Magus*, "that the one thing you cannot tolerate is the thought of their not being in someway forever present."

Sharon's birthday in 1989 at the Music Center in Los Angeles for *Phantom of the Opera*. Perhaps the third or fourth time we attended this show, having also seen it in London and New York.

Photo: Rosenzweig Personal Collection

At the time that was true for me with *Cagney & Lacey*, it is still true of my relationship with Sharon Gless. She has always been my "big deal." Ms. Gless and I are approaching our sixteenth wedding anniversary. *Ozzie & Harriet* it ain't, but it *has* been a fabulous adventure.

Marriage is, I think, probably always best defined by the people who are in it, and Sharon's and mine is a case in point. It has been through many permutations. Neither of us are the people who recited vows to one another at her Malibu Beach home back in May of 1991 with helicopters from the *National Enquirer* looming overhead. I am no longer her Svengali-like knight in shining armor; I am not the powerful producer she fell in love with, and Sharon is no longer a size-eight beauty, earning a veritable fortune on an annual basis. Somehow we have survived life's changes and come to care about each other as much or more than ever, although (admittedly) we live several miles south of *The Enchanted Cottage*.[84]

---

[84]   Reference is to the heavily romantic MGM fantasy film of the 1940s, starring Robert Young and Dorothy McGuire.

Sharon and me, flanked by her brother, Michael Gless, and her first cousin, Liz Springer (the former Elizabeth Bauer of Raymond Burr's *Ironside* series), on the occasion of wedding number one on May 1, 1991, at Sharon's Malibu Beach home.

Photo: Rosenzweig Personal Collection

The Rosenzweig clan on the beach at Malibu on the occasion of wedding number two, May 4, 1991. Sharon celebrates the first; I celebrate them both (or else). The gals in the silk suits are my "best men," daughters Allyn Rosenzweig, Erika Handman (next to Sharon), and Torrie Rosenzweig. Granddaughter Hailey Laws, our flower girl, stands in front of my mother, Myrtle, and on her right is my father, Aaron, who was then about the same age as I am now. Granddaughters Greer Rose Glassman and Zoey B Rosenzweig are not pictured, as they were, at this time, yet to make their appearance on the planet.

Photo: Rosenzweig Personal Collection

More than once our arguments have become heated enough that the D word has been uttered. Divorce should be easy for us. I have had practice at it (twice), our business managers keep most of our money separate, we have no offspring, and there is zero community debt. The last such time we lurched toward such a final solution, just before our tenth anniversary, Sharon stopped screaming at me just long enough to gather up her dignity and to tearfully pronounce, "All right. You can have a divorce. But *you* tell the children."

"The children" (Erika, Allyn, and Torrie) are mine, two marriages removed, and all in their forties. The other child is niece Bridget Gless, and she is nearly the age of my daughters. All I could do was laugh, and then hold her in my arms. We have never mentioned the D word since. What, never? Well (with acknowledgment to WS Gilbert), "hardly ever."

Many years before all this, on the afternoon of May 25, 1988, I received a phone call at the villa I was occupying all by my lonesome[85] that overlooked Acapulco Bay. Richard M. Rosenbloom, president of Orion Pictures television division, was calling from Los Angeles with news of the third—and final—CBS cancellation of *Cagney & Lacey.*

"An era has ended," he said.

I placed international calls to my estranged wife, to Sharon, to Tyne, and to my worthy assistant, Carole R. Smith. Only the first two were initially reachable. Sharon said she was glad she heard the news from me rather than someone else. Barbara, whose life for the last six months had been one of total displacement, sounded strained and a bit bitter on the phone. "An era has ended," Rosenbloom had said. He didn't know the half of it.

I did go to work for Weintraub before realizing that there was really very little "there," there. The corporation Jerry had put together was not a sham, but most of the promised financing never came through—or at least found a quick exit, once the quality of the films produced before my arrival were screened. It was not a great gig after all, but I found Jerry truly fascinating as have so many before and after me. He is a great show business character, worthy of his own biography.

Mace's lawsuit did come to fruition. I hired my friend and the previous year's California Trial Lawyer of the Year recipient, Marshal Morgan, to defend me. He

---

[85]   Alone by virtue of my marriage being over and my "thing" with Gless then very much in abeyance. The locale was the Villa Vera, made famous in the days of Errol Flynn's stardom in Hollywood.

readily agreed to handle this case that he deemed a "slam dunk." There were early storm warnings on this lawsuit, first from my then-new business manager, Jess Morgan (no relation to lawyer Marshal Morgan). We were not, he relayed, getting billings of any size from Marshal's law firm. I attributed this to my very friendly relationship with Marshal, but Jess was more than skeptical; to him, no billings meant no work was being done.

Then there was the unofficial call from Mr. Neufeld's attorney asking my pal and sometime lawyer, Sam Perlmutter, if—since Mace was not really "after Barney"— I would be willing to join his client in the lawsuit against Orion and kick in $25,000 toward attorney's fees? Sam thought it interesting enough to pass along; my response was quick and vituperative. "I wouldn't give that asshole twenty-five cents! Tell him to go fuck himself."

Barbara took off from work to attend the trial on a daily basis. Mace, of course, was also there, always in the company of his hand-holding spouse, Helen. The idea that it had probably been at least twenty years since either of these two had actually held hands anywhere was noted by this storyteller along with the observation that the normally natty Mr. Neufeld was attending each day of the two full weeks of trial seemingly in the same suit, which looked as if it came off some low-end department store rack. The Neufelds, it seemed from this seat in the bleachers, were in full performance for the jury.

Neufeld's lawyers finally rested, and the judge had us all break for lunch before hearing from the defense. It was late morning on a Friday; Loeb & Loeb (the Orion lawyers), along with Marshal and me, made a beeline for the nearest coffee shop. The two lawyers were debating whether to present a defense. They felt that Mace had not made his case and that all they had to do was ask for a summary judgment; Neufeld's claim would be thrown out, and that would be it. By presenting a defense, they maintained, we couldn't possibly be any better off and just might "step in something."

I interjected. "Fellas, I know very little about the law, but I know something about audiences, and let me tell you what I believe that jury (our audience) has heard and what they didn't hear. They didn't hear that the plaintiff, the guy in the $100 suit, has 'his' and 'her' Rolls Royces in his Beverly Hills garage, and a two million dollar African art collection in the attached mansion where he lives when he is not flying his private plane.

"They didn't hear," I went on, "just how much of his net worth has been 'earned' by this selfsame, ongoing sort of litigious behavior against any number of former associates, and I am not so sure they understand that his whole involvement in this project is a legal fiction, or that I only took additional fees when Orion's business affairs department sold me on their judgment that what was being done was not only perfectly legal but, for all I knew, might have come about as some sort of a tit-for-tat arrangement between Mace and Medavoy to which I wasn't privy.

"You guys," I continued, "might be right technically, you might be right legally, but if this testimony isn't heard and it is up to that jury, we are dead meat."

Both sets of lawyers were convinced I was wrong. I would not overrule the venerable men of Loeb & Loeb or my own counsel, despite my growing belief during the trial that Marshal was winging this whole thing. The lawyers' plan was followed; no defense was presented. The motion for summary judgment was carefully listened to by the judge, and, as I watched his body language, I began to be convinced that my team was right after all. Then, just (I believed) on the verge of deciding to rid his courtroom of all of us, to end the thing right there, the old guy in the robes spoke. "I think the jury, which has been here for nine days hearing this case, should have the opportunity to make the decision here."

Marshal leaned over to me. "No problem," he said. "We're in great shape. It's Friday afternoon, and this jury is gonna want to get out of here in time to beat the traffic. This will be over in an hour."

He was wrong by two and a half days. The following Tuesday afternoon the jury found for Mace Neufeld against Orion Pictures Corporation and its codefendant, Barney Rosenzweig. My part of the judgment was $1,300,000.

A meeting was held between all the combatants in the judge's chambers; the defense attorneys pleaded for a lessening of the amount awarded. The judge wasn't having that. The guy from Loeb & Loeb then surprised me, asking that, at the very least, the judge let Mr. Rosenzweig out of this as, at worst, he was truly an innocent bystander who could have no idea what Orion might or might not be paying Neufeld in the deal that precipitated this lawsuit. The judge wouldn't allow that either.

I was referred to a top-notch law firm in San Francisco that specialized in appellate work. I learned no new evidence could be put forward in an appeal and no new testimony. The lawyer's task would be to find, within the context of what was already on the record (by having been presented in court) where an error had been made and then to show that it would be unjust if that error were not corrected by this appeal process.

The San Francisco lawyers were not so sure they could be effective doing that but would try the case against their better judgment for a whole lot of money. The case they wanted, after reading all the transcripts, was the malpractice suit they said I should file against my friend, attorney Marshal Morgan. I couldn't bring myself to follow that advice.

I had been paid a lot of money by Orion, a few million in advances against my ownership position. Now Mace had been awarded a large share of that: $1,300,000. One problem was I didn't have the millions that had been paid on those advances; it hadn't been spent exactly, it had been expensed out to my *partners*: 10 percent to the William Morris Agency, 5 percent to my business managers, and 50 percent of what remained, as part of the community property settlement, to my ex-wife, Barbara Corday.

I went to each of them for their share of the judgment. The Morris office squealed; Jess didn't like it at all (he never believed Marshal was doing the work and might have asked for better counsel if he knew he, too, was at risk). Barbara wasn't at all happy with this request either.

This money was received by me after Mace's lawsuit had been filed. The aforementioned threesome wanted their share as soon as it came in—even though it should have been clear to all that there was a cloud on the horizon. It had to be acknowledged that they all knew—no matter how remote the chance—that Neufeld might prevail. I did not hold the money back against the trial date or place it in escrow; I paid it out to them. Now that we lost at trial, it was time that all returned that proportionate share of the monies they had received in order to satisfy the judgment.

Each finally came through ($130,000 from the Morris men, $65,000 from Jess Morgan's company, $455,000 from Corday).

CHAPTER 44

THE BEGINNING OF THE END

Author-barrister John Mortimer admonishes his readers never to learn to swim. His reasoning for spurning this aquatic skill is that while sailing, should one capsize, there might be the temptation, if one were a swimmer, to strike out for the shore and, invariably, drown. "Better," he says, "to cling to the wreckage" and await rescue.

That is what I did and, in very short order, came up with the CBS series *The Trials of Rosie O'Neill*, as well as *Christy*, along with four *Cagney & Lacey* reunion movies. This was all made possible by the firing/resignation of Kim LeMasters and the ascension to power at the network of Jeff Sagansky.

Sagansky was my kind of executive. Unlike LeMasters, who I felt had a need to prove he was the smartest man in the room (and, indeed, the only human being I have ever met who actually had read Machiavelli's *The Prince*), Jeff Sagansky believed in hiring good people and letting them do what it was they were being paid to do. That is not to say he didn't occasionally get into micromanaging a script, and he was plenty smart and good at it as well; but when he did, it was somehow acceptable (at least to me) because his method was steeped in boyish enthusiasm. He has an infectious charm about him.

Jeff was supportive, not competitive, but for me, as a storyteller, dealing with a buyer who would always be my most important audience, the quintessential difference between Sagansky and LeMasters was that the former understood what the latter seemingly could not—or would not: That the fundamental synergy between the two opposing forces of the storyteller and his audience (in this case the seller and the buyer) is the willingness and ability to suspend disbelief.

There are only lights and shadows on that screen. The audience must bring something to the party; that essential "thing" is the willingness to sit back and be entertained, to be disarmed. My perception was that Kim LeMasters simply would not do that and that he had to prove—at a script meeting or a screening—that he was smarter. To do that he had to keep his faculties very alert, never letting down his guard or allowing himself to be seduced. The gal from *The Arabian Nights* would have been boiled in oil long before Ali Baba met those more than three dozen thieves if LeMasters had been her captor.

I remember a particular note-taking session, following a screening for LeMasters. His comments were precise *and,* the argument could be made, technically correct. However, to effectuate what he was asking would have—*in my opinion*—damaged the larger issues of the film itself.

"There are twenty-four frames per second[86] that run through a projection machine in order for us to perceive natural human-like movement on the screen," I began my part of the LeMasters meet. "I have read where a highly intelligent individual can, by concentrating very hard, actually perceive the lines been each and every frame." The reference to the capability of a highly intelligent individual had, I thought, captured LeMasters' attention.

"It's possible," I nodded, "but, Kim—why would you want to do that?" I gave him a bit more on the willingness to suspend disbelief and then added, "Y'know, if you are looking for mistakes, there are twenty-four per second." Sagansky might smile gleefully at this point, but not LeMasters—at least not in my experience.

It was Sagansky who wanted to revisit *Cagney & Lacey* via the reunion movie format. I had never wanted to do this in the five-plus years that had passed since those bygone days on the series. By then, Sharon and I were married.[87] Tyne (now post-Broadway and starring for me in the CBS series *Christy*) was very much a close friend of us both. There was never a doubt that I could deliver the two women to the roles they had made famous. I had other reasons for not pitching this as something I wanted to do.

---

86   Run more than 24 frames per second through a motion picture projector or camera and a slow motion effect is produced. The more frames, the slower the images appear to move. Run less than 24, and the images seem faster. That herky-jerky movement you see today in the old-time silent films is because in those days the standard was to film and project at 18 frames per second. If one projects, at 24fps, a film shot at 18fps, you get those funny-looking movements, which we have come to accept as natural for that kind of movie from those early days.

87   At California's Malibu Beach: May 1 and/or May 4, 1991, depending on whom you talk to.

First off, I had no desire to make Mace—or Orion—richer. Secondly, I wasn't at all sure that we should compromise the memories people had of our show. We would revisit this terrain, I reasoned, at our peril, for we would not only be compared with other movies on TV, but with memory—and a memory that had probably received some coloration that would be difficult, or impossible, to live up to with any new incarnation.

I told Sagansky I would think about it, but not all that much. The movie-for-television business was an OK business, but not my specialty. My forte was series television, and one could make a whole lot more money in that arena than in the TV movie field. Then it occurred to me that I might be able to eat my cake and have it as well.

I went to Orion with the proposition that I would make these movies (at least two—for that was my minimum guarantee from Sagansky) on the condition that Orion would sell me the *Cagney & Lacey* library: all 125 episodes, plus the original Loretta Swit film.

Len White was now Orion's president during their period of then-recently announced bankruptcy; he was caretaker over what he hoped would be a takeover (or sale) of the entire company—including their fairly substantial library of films and some TV shows.

My theory was that I could use these yet-to-be-made movies as the locomotive that would pull the train: the collection that was my erstwhile series. White was sympathetic to my emotional attachment to the show, happy to have some action, plus the possibility of an influx of some dollars, which—at least—might justify some of his salary and expenses.

The price he would have me pay for the right to make the movies was an outrageous $250,000 per film, way too high for rights on any movie-for-television of the time. But that figure would, he added, be applicable to my overall purchase of the entire series library, the price of which he set at $6,000,000. It was a lot of money for a series that had already had the sprocket holes run off of it and had been handled badly in the field to boot. There was also the fact that I didn't have six million dollars. That didn't matter so much if you subscribed to the Jerry Weintraub philosophy that "If you live long enough, you cannot overpay for a film library."

Canal Plus, the French TV and film distribution company, was prepared to front the six million on my behalf. Betsy Frank, then of the Saatchi & Saatchi advertising agency in New York and always a big *Cagney & Lacey* fan, indicated there might be millions available from one of her clients, if the women would be available for product identification ads. I was ready to cut Sharon and Tyne in on this new action and was confident I could deliver them for that kind of campaign.

A tiny wrinkle in the deal was that President White did not want it perceived as a sale or as someone cherry-picking the Orion library. This, therefore, had to be presented as a partnership between myself and Orion, with the latter receiving 10 percent of the profits. White needed this, he said, for appearances and told me he never expected there would be any profits. Clearly he had experience with bookkeeping in the film and television business and assumed my guys would keep books the same as his guys.

Unfortunately, "my guys" are scrupulously honest, and the current holders of this copyright regularly receive profit distributions from the movies while there have never been any on the series itself coming to me from the other side. (Whoever said "What goes around, comes around" clearly has never been in my end of show business.)

In order to effectuate the purchase, a phase of "due diligence" was begun. I went on, preparing to make the two *Cagney & Lacey* films back-to-back that late spring and summer in Los Angeles. Steve Brown & Terry Louise Fisher were set to write both scripts. James Frawley would direct the first; Reza Badiyi would helm the second. My youngest daughter, Torrie, was the associate producer; my middle daughter, Allyn, would serve as costumer; my oldest, Erika, as well as niece, Bridget, would both have small acting roles; and my son-in-law David Handman was one of our film editors. It was like old home week.

(The films were individually called *Cagney & Lacey: The Return* and *Cagney & Lacey: Together Again*, but collectively—along with the two other reunion films we would eventually make—were all lovingly known as *Cagney & Lacey: The Menopause Years*.)

I told Steve and Terry we should treat the six intervening years since our series had ended as if our fictional characters had continued to have a life during that time and to establish this early, as we had all those years before, with the Lacey baby quinella. Both Sharon and Tyne had aged and put on some weight in the process, and so we would play that.[88] Lacey would have taken her retirement, and

---

[88]   The previous year, Sharon had made her London stage debut at the Criterion Theatre opposite Bill Paterson in Stephen King's thriller *Misery*, creating the role on stage made famous by Kathy Bates on film. For artistic reasons, Ms. Gless decided to bulk up for the role, gaining sixty pounds, and was now finding it difficult to shed same. I am not married to Ms. Daly, so I haven't heard her reasons, but it never seemed to matter as much to Tyne as it did to Sharon.

a menopausal Cagney would have been promoted to the district attorney's office and—since series' end—gotten married!

Sharon hated this idea and not even the casting of old pal and Tony Award–winning actor James Naughton in the role of her husband would change her view. I stuck to my guns, as I hoped the marriage would give us some stuff to work with and show some growth or change in our characters.

The argument over this is barely worth mentioning, but, in fairness to my spouse, I will admit for the record that fan reaction to the marriage was (at best) mixed to negative.

Tony Award–winning actor James Naughton, as the man who would be married to Christine Cagney in the first of our reunion films and then be divorced by her in the second. This portrait was on display at their home for the reunion party scene that took place in the early going of *Cagney & Lacey: The Return.* This twosome had met and costarred at Universal Studios in the early 1970s in *Faraday and Company* along with Dan Dailey and Geraldine Brooks.

A happy reunion of the cast for our first reunion movie, *Cagney & Lacey: The Return*. Terrace is on the set of the fictional Cagney NY Park Avenue manse. Front row, from left: Al Waxman, Ms. Gless and Ms. Daly, John Karlen, and, in the rear, Robert Hegyes, Merry Clayton, Marty Kove, and Paul Mantee. Carl Lumbly was (somewhat reluctantly) in the film and in this sequence but somehow did not get into this shot.

The irrepressible Carole R. Smith, flanked by *Menopause Years* pals and stars, Tyne Daly and Sharon Gless, circa 1994.

Photo: Carole R. Smith Collection

David Paymer, as ADA Feldberg, "introduces" Cagney and Lacey in a scene from our first *Menopause Years* reunion film. Paymer's appearance in the first two of this quartet of films merits a special comment: in the years that had passed since he began his career, first as a hapless street character on *Cagney & Lacey* in 1982 and then graduating to his recurring role as our assistant district attorney, the actor had become a star in his own right working with the likes of Robert Redford and Billy Crystal and, eventually, having his own series. He had truly grown beyond this tiny (but memorable) part and/or our ability to pay him. He "showed up" anyway for old time's sake, and for a lot less than his market price, demonstrating a class and a sense of gratitude not very often expressed in the film and television industry.

The overall reaction to the reunification of Sharon and Tyne and to the films themselves was excellent from all quarters. The first movie got outstanding reviews and was rated the number-one film on all networks for that week, the top-rated show of any kind on the CBS network, and ultimately the number-two movie on all of television for the entire 1994–95 season, subsequently being edged out (by an eighth of a rating point) by the *Rockford Files* reunion movie.

With that kind of success one could argue that the network might have called with—oh, I don't know—say, a couple of simple questions, such as "How many more can we have, and how fast can you deliver?" In fact, the only calls were from the trade press, wanting to know just how large an order I had received from CBS as a result of our precedent-setting numbers. Lisa DeMores, of the *Hollywood Reporter*, agreed with my tongue-in-cheek supposition that perhaps the broadcasters had lost my phone number. I asked her to publish it, which she did, the very next day on the *Reporter*'s front page. I got my phone call that afternoon.

I argued successfully to save the second film for May sweeps rather than February as originally planned because I thought it best that there be a bit more waiting time between the two outings and because some of our promised publicity coverage, namely a *Ms.* magazine cover (it would have been our third) and a few other such breaks could not be ready for publishing in the time between the smash October release and the initially scheduled February air date. CBS programmers warned that granting my request might cause us to lose our Sunday night slot, but I wasn't concerned—only because I didn't anticipate the full ramifications of an upcoming changing of the guard at CBS.

This changeover was made official in the late spring of 1995; Jeff Sagansky announced he was leaving CBS, with power being turned over to Peter Tortorici, his lieutenant of the past few years. I had survived many battles with Tortorici during the creation of *The Trials of Rosie O'Neill* and would win most, if not all. These would prove to be pyrrhic, as time and time again (as he became more and more powerful) I was to realize what a long memory he possessed. I have often wished I had allowed this adversary to win some of those earlier fights on my public defender series.

Along with *Cagney & Lacey*, the *Rockford* reunion movie had done so well, I was told that CBS was now considering setting up a Mystery Movie Night that would play once a week through the month of May sweeps. This would, Tortorici said, be heavily promoted and designated as appointment television by the network, with a *Cagney & Lacey* one week, a *Rockford* the next, and a special *Murder, She Wrote* two-parter to make up three spokes of the wheel.

Then, without letting us know, Tortorici acquiesced to pressure from Universal Studios (home to both *Rockford* and the Lansbury show) to keep those two shows on Sunday nights in May while programming *Cagney & Lacey* all on its lonesome on Tuesday night. I thought this was absolutely ridiculous; Tuesday was traditionally a non-movie night for CBS and, at that time, a black hole for ratings on the network. It also meant we would be placed right opposite the very successful *Home Improvement* series and Steven Bochco's *NYPD Blue* (usually referred to by me as *Cagney & Lacey* in drag). Bochco's show was then at the height of its popularity, drawing a huge, urban, educated audience, the same target group coveted by my own series.

We did OK, not great, but great enough. CBS management sent flowers to both Sharon and Tyne with thank-yous. The second-place numbers on that tough night were apparently greatly appreciated by the CBS brass, and the proof of that was an order to production on the two additional *Cagney & Lacey* scripts previously commissioned during the Sagansky years: *Cagney & Lacey: The View through the Glass Ceiling* and *Cagney & Lacey: True Convictions*.

We would, for economic reasons, make these in Canada, heading back to the city where it all began for two months of back-to-back production in Toronto on scripts by Michele Gallery (one of those very fine *Lou Grant* writers I had been unable to hire all those years ago for my series) and directed by John Patterson and then Lynn Littman.

In these last two films, Cagney would now be divorced, and Lacey back at work on a regular basis. Multi-award-winning actor Michael Moriarty would provide Christine's romantic connection in film number four.

Between these films, due diligence regarding my purchase of the *C&L* library droned on. The Orion files were a "rat's nest," and each of those file drawers contained some sort of bad news with nary a moment of "bank error in your favor." A cursory look at the Canal Plus deal revealed that, although they would put up the money, I would be (again) an employee and without a very good contract at that.

My attorneys were becoming exasperated with this process. At this point in show business history, so many deals have been made, so much—so-called—new ground broken, that most of the work for an entertainment lawyer is, in reality, hand-holding, agenting, and minor amendments to boiler plate contracts. That was not the case here. This was tough slogging through international deals, contracts, residuals (some paid, some maybe not), bankruptcy filings, and handwritten receipts, often in a foreign language. I became exhausted with the procedure, as did my attorneys.

It was then I realized, as I had so many years before, that at this point in my life, I longed for a partner. I simply could not do all I needed to do alone, could not bounce back quickly enough from the daily disappointments and the hourly calls about another piece of negative information from the Orion archival files and still do the real work that was required of me. I tried more than once to merge with someone with whom I thought I might be able to work or with whom there might be some synergy. One was simply not interested; the other was flattered but frightened of the independent game. Who could blame them?

CHAPTER 45

ON THE ROAD AGAIN

That spring in the mid-1990s I would hit the road again with Sharon and Tyne, doing our best to promote our (by then) virtually unpromotable one-time-only Tuesday night movie. We felt tossed away by CBS against the very formidable (and firmly established in their time slots) *NYPD Blue* and *Home Improvement* and so moved quickly on to Toronto and production on the third and fourth *Cagney & Lacey* reunion movies.

On the way we moved to center stage in front of hundreds of thousands of women, all gathered on a Sunday in April for a rally of the National Organization for Women, at the Mall of our nation's capital. Sharon and Tyne were both thrilled to be featured at the event, and the audience could not have been more receptive. Tyne, harkening back to that time in London at the Drury Lane Theatre, turned to me and stated gratefully, and graciously, "Barney, you do get me onto the best stages."

Sharon and Tyne acknowledge the crowd from the outdoor stage of a Washington DC women's march at which they were featured.

Photo: Rosenzweig Personal Collection

It came to pass that sending the women flowers and a thank-you for giving CBS respectability on that spring Tuesday night was one of Peter Tortorici's final acts as network programming chief. It had been three years since *The Trials of Rosie O'Neill* had been canceled, largely due to this executive's altering the show's time slot so often that even the most ardent fan could not find the show. Likewise, he had all but precluded any future for *Christy*, despite the show's critical acclaim, Tyne's Emmy, and the terrific job MTM president Bill Allen had done attempting to get the network to pay some attention to this series.

Tyne Daly as Miss Alice with Kellie Martin, who played the title role in *Christy*, on the set of our location in Tennessee.

Both shows were caught in the switches of the new demographic needs now expressed by Sagansky's immediate successor. It was all so wasteful and so stupid.

Mr. Sagansky had become inordinately successful, in a very short time frame, by rescuing CBS from the ratings cellar simply by doing all he could—as quickly as he could—to appeal to the audience that was the CBS base. Before that was Kim LeMasters' futile search for the so-called fountain of youth, the audience ranging in age from teenagers to folks in their forties.

Sagansky, knowing the CBS audience had traditionally skewed older and less urban, immediately turned LeMasters's strategy on its head. He successfully catered to those viewers over forty in his quest for a quick turnaround for the network, achieving his goal, but not without some cost. Advertisers pay more for younger audiences than they do for old, and it irked Larry Tisch and the corporate power elite in New York that a higher-rated CBS show would make less money than a lower-rated but younger appealing show on ABC. It may have irked them, but they were making money—a whole lot more money than they were when LeMasters led them to the number-three spot among the three major networks.

Sagansky would eventually depart for greener pastures. His replacement, in an attempt to impress the bosses and their desire for even higher advertising revenues, all but abandoned Sagansky's successful philosophy and (almost inexplicably) returned to the same ideas that had brought Kim LeMasters to failure. This time it would not take Larry Tisch and his crew at CBS corporate so long to react. Within weeks of our Tuesday night showing and the accompanying flowers of 1995, Mr. Tortorici found himself out of work and replaced by one of the industry's shining stars, Lorimar's studio head, Leslie Moonves.

The announcement of the Moonves ascension in the nation's press boosted CBS stock several percentage points (the only ratings that *really* matter to management), increased the sales price of the network in their dealings with Westinghouse (preceding the eventual sale to Sumner Redstone's Viacom Corporation some months later), and added to Mr. Tisch's already substantial fortune by tens of millions of dollars.

I didn't own any CBS stock, but I remember feeling at the time that, poor as things were with Peter Tortorici, this announcement did represent another one of those moments of "change equals psychological loss."

Peter T. was less than forthcoming, a gent who played his cards very close to the vest. Worse, from my perspective, his learning curve seemed inordinately flat. All that aside, in the brief time-frame he was ensconced at CBS, I produced the final season of *Cagney & Lacey*, two seasons each of *The Trials of Rosie O'Neill* and

Christy, as well as the *Cagney & Lacey* reunion movies. At the very least Tortorici knew me as a producer who could deliver a pretty decent product on time and on budget. Most important, for better or for worse, he was a network chief to whom I had access.

I had never met Mr. Moonves. If he knew me at all it was only by reputation, not altogether a bad thing, I thought, but it did put me into a larger kettle with a whole lot more fish.

The Moonves announcement was in early June. By then I was more than midway through production in Toronto on both the third and fourth *Menopause Years* reunion flicks. Sharon and Tyne had a great time, and both films had gone well and were made a lot more economically than the two I had done the previous year in Los Angeles. The efficiency and hard work of my long-time associate Paula Marcus (not available on films 1 and 2), the exchange rate of the Canadian dollar vis-à-vis American currency at that time, and the incentives put forward by the governments in Ontario (local) and Canada (national), brought in several hundreds of thousands of additional dollars to my production company.

By the time of the Moonves announcement, it was clear that *Christy* would not return to the network, Bill Allen had been unceremoniously dumped by his new management team at MTM, and I had come to think of The Rosenzweig Company as a business that was at a point of diminishing returns in more ways than one.

It had been less than a year since my mother had passed away, my father was in failing health, and a cursory check of my corporate books caused me to realize that, despite a great deal of production activity and a fairly efficient operation, my little company was barely treading water.

There were major economic forces at work in the film and television industry at this time, and my tiny corporation was being buffeted about by the gravitational pull of the opposing powers that were. The battle over the government's financial interest and syndication rules as applied to the television industry was moving from the boardrooms of the major studios and networks to the FCC and the U.S. Congress. Determined to make independent production less attractive (so that key issues being negotiated would be ceded by the production companies and studios), the networks had begun to engage in a form of price fixing and restraint of trade that in better times would have brought out the forces of the justice department.

Or maybe not; where, after all, is the congressman who would stand up and challenge a network's business dealings (something arguably more tangible than being critical of Janet Jackson's wardrobe malfunction at a football telecast)? Who is the politician that would risk not being on the evening news back home when running for reelection?

Like someone in a small boat, tossed at sea by the wakes of major vessels, I would either have to get a whole lot larger (investing whatever saved capital I had in the process), merge with another entity, become a publicly held corporation, or fold most of my tents and reduce the size of my company, my profile, and, of course, my overhead. Orion's decision, in the final stages of the due diligence process, to re-license *Cagney & Lacey* to Lifetime Cable for a few million—thus dramatically reducing its value to me as a potential buyer—would pretty much make the decision for me.

Orion's Len White must have been as tired of due diligence as I. (Either that, or, once again, his company needed to make a rent payment or keep the utility bill current.) It was all right with me. I was sick of the whole process and found myself saying, more often than not, that I would rather talk about *Cagney & Lacey* than actually make it. In reality, that is true for me of just about anything having to do with show business.

I had decided that what I would like to do is what I had always wanted to do, which was to get out—out of show business and definitely out of Los Angeles. There was the concern that I did not have enough of a stash to live life as elegantly as I would like. I thought (then at fifty-eight years of age) I could work a few more years to achieve whatever financial cushion I might need. The accumulation of capital was never my thing; still, I resolved to work toward that, provided I could do so on my terms.

It is a tricky thing to write, in a book for general consumption, about personal finances. There will be readers (hopefully) from varied economic stratum with multiple definitions of when "enough" is just that. What is a lot to one individual is not so much to another. Certainly, if one were to live by the standard of 99.5 percent of the Americas, I was doing great. But to Michael Eisner, Brad Grey, Steven Bochco, or any of the truly successful people in Hollywood, my cache of cash was chump change, to be sure.

From Toronto and our wrap party for cast and crew, I flew into New York for a meeting with CBS president Peter Lund and a subsequent dinner with Larry Tisch and his extraordinary lifetime spouse, Billie.

The Lund meeting took place at his New York office within hours of the official Moonves announcement and continued on as we took a friendly walk through the streets of Manhattan toward whatever it was that constituted his final appointment of that June afternoon in 1995.

Talking with Lund was easy and affable. How I began was to state what I believed was then absolutely true and with which Lund said he agreed: that *Cagney & Lacey* was a CBS asset at least as valuable (and less expensive to maintain) than Dan Rather. (This was 1995—nearly ten years before Rather would run afoul of the Bush bloggers who would seek his head and did succeed in getting him to resign his post as network anchor.)

What I proposed was that I be allowed to continue making two *Cagney & Lacey* movies per year for the next five years. I would promise to make them for a competitive license fee and to deliver Sharon Gless and Tyne Daly in the title roles. Furthermore, if at any time the movies failed to perform up to a pre-negotiated ratings level, the network then would have the right to cut back or cancel whatever movies had not yet been committed to production. Simple.

Lund thought it all had merit but was (understandably) clear that such commitments would now have to come from Moonves. I understood that, of course, but spoke of my apprehensiveness about this since, not only didn't I know Moonves, but worse, he didn't know me. Lund promised he would pave the way for that, referring to me as "First Family" at CBS.

Sharon and I dined that evening with the Tisches, and business was never discussed. It wasn't (I thought) necessary.

I had been in business a long time with the Eye network. It was virtually an exclusive relationship from 1981 through 1995. In relationship to the network, The Rosenzweig Company was not unlike an independent family farm in Middle America. For fourteen years, I had labored in the fields, brought my produce to the main road, and waited for the big company's truck and trailer to come along and pick up my goods. From Peter Frankovich to Bill Self, to Harvey Shephard, Bob Silberling, Tony Barr, Jeff Sagansky, Howard Stringer, David Poltrak, Tony Malara—the best collection of network executives I have ever met—to Kim LeMasters, Peter Tortorici, and Steve Werner, who (as far as I was concerned) could have just as well worked at ABC (where they might have soared), plus all the many I have not named who fall somewhere in between these two extremes, the whole CBS experience was by far the best of my professional life. Nothing, not my early days at MGM or at 20th Century Fox, or my start as Hollywood's wunderkind on *Daniel Boone*, or all the time devoted to being a true independent out in the field, could compare with the creative and financial rewards I had during that time frame. I had risen from something of a brash upstart in Harvey Shephard's office to (as Peter Lund had phrased it) "First Family."

The perception of my status at CBS probably accounts for why I was able, near the end of 1994, to (months before the "First Family" meet with Lund) sit down at the Bel-Air Hotel with Peter Tortorici. He was then still very much in his job as head of programming and still, at that time, understandably impressed with the astounding numbers on the first *Cagney & Lacey* reunion film and the critical achievement and resiliency of my series *Christy*.

Peter wanted to demonstrate his enthusiasm; to do something tangible that I would appreciate. Why? Perhaps that is better understood when it is explained that this near exclusivity I had granted for so many years to CBS was done without financial remuneration. What I was being paid was for what I made and delivered. There were no holding monies exchanged, no exclusivity money paid; therefore, a little schmoozing or hand-holding by a network executive toward one of his suppliers not only couldn't hurt, it was partially a job description.

Tortorici offered to augment the Sagansky commitment of a third *Cagney & Lacey* movie to a fourth. I shook my head. You didn't need good lighting, which the bar in the Bel-Air Hotel did not provide in any case, to see that this offer wasn't going to carry the day for CBS. What I wanted was something very special. What I did was to tell Mr. Tortorici the opening two minutes, beat-by-beat, shot-by-shot, of a new television series. Peter liked what he heard. He hadn't expected a pitch meeting, but that is what he got, and I defer to no one in terms of craft at this particular aspect of the business.

What I wanted was for CBS to fund two scripts, each by a top writer, who would take the opening scene I had told Tortorici in that darkened bar and do their own take on what the series would look and sound like. I would, of course, supervise both writers and ultimately turn the scripts into no one but Mr. Tortorici, and he, in turn, would be the one to make the final decision on which of those two scripts would become the series we would make.

I pointed out that no pilot was necessary. We did not have one on *The Trials of Rosie O'Neill,* and there was no need to audition here either. He had approved the concept (which was not at all esoteric, but rather in the modern-day, private-eye mystery idiom), would have final say over each of the two top-tier writers I would hire, and was guaranteed that Sharon Gless would star and that I would produce. There was no one in this package that would need to audition for CBS. Tortorici agreed.

"One more thing," I added. "Whenever Angela Lansbury's show is over, that is the time slot I want. Sunday night at 8, right after *60 Minutes*." (There had been rumors that Ms. Lansbury was thinking of retirement, or at least ending her tenure on this show, but I presumed that was primarily a negotiating ploy by the agency mavens at William Morris.) Peter Tortorici did not even swallow hard.

He leaned closer so as not to be overheard. "I don't want to be known as the network executive who cancels *Murder, She Wrote*, but I also don't want to bankrupt the network to keep it," he whispered, going on to explain that William Morris was holding a gun to his head for a lot of money to continue on with Angela's show. Now, he happily explained, I was giving him a gun of his own: a series in the same genre with a top producer and a genuine CBS star in the lead.

I smiled but understood that the chances were slim and none that Angela Lansbury would depart this very lucrative operation, employing not only herself, but her son and her husband as well.

"Use the gun or don't use it," I answered back in equally hushed tones. "Someday *Murder, She Wrote* will move from that Sunday night time slot, and, when it does—for whatever reason—I want it understood it is mine."

Peter Tortorici shook my hand. The meeting was over. I think he picked up the check. Some months later, he also picked up *Murder, She Wrote*.

And then, he moved it, away from that coveted Sunday night slot, scheduling in its place some easily forgotten comedy programming and apparently forgetting his pledge to reward Sharon and me for years of exclusivity to CBS. He didn't even make a phone call; that, as they say, is show business. I read about it in the trade press. He was fired ten days later. I wished at the time that I could have taken credit for his demise.

It was all blood under the bridge. After all, why should I worry? The New York meeting with Lund had gone well; I would contact Moonves, get him the two scripts commissioned by Tortorici (*McQue* by Ann Donahue, later of *CSI* fame, and *Maguire for Hire*, by Chris Abbott, who had headed up *Magnum, P.I.*, both for CBS). I referred to these as *Whatever Happened to Nancy Drew?*—since Sharon would be playing a private-eye some forty years older than the famed teenage sleuth and could, I thought, have had an audience imagining what might have happened to the Carolyn Keene creation if life had occurred in a realistic, albeit less than idyllic, fashion. If nothing else, I hoped to walk away with what I really wanted: the commitment for two *Cagney & Lacey* reunion movies per annum.

The women get their stars on Hollywood Boulevard. A well-deserved tribute.

Photo: Rosenzweig Personal Collection

Helping Tyne and Sharon celebrate the announcement of their stars on Hollywood Boulevard are from left: Ed Asner (Sharon's costar in *The Trials of Rosie O'Neill*, to mention one of his myriad of credits), Michele Lee (a close friend of both women and a near miss for the role of Mary Beth Lacey), Eddie Albert (like Asner, too many credits to mention except that he starred with Sharon and RJ Wagner in *Switch* long before *C&L*), Sharon, Hollywood's honorary mayor, Johnny Grant, John Karlen, Tyne, Tyne's brother, Tim Daly, and Tyne's *Christy* costar, Tess Harper.

Photo: Rosenzweig Personal Collection

Postproduction and delivery of both *Menopause Years* movies 3 and 4 happened that summer in Los Angeles; still there was no indication as to when I might meet Moonves. Word was all over town that the new CBS chief was in a buying mode, and I wasn't getting even an appointment to be introduced. I had to face a very significant fact: Les Moonves had attained incredible success in the television business, and he had done so with absolutely no help from me. I was, in other words, not on his list of good guys or people to whom he might be indebted or could depend on, and, because of my relative exclusivity to CBS for over a decade, I was not strongly connected anywhere else.

The sale of CBS to Westinghouse hurt even more. I had finally had a lovely social dinner with an owner of a network, and, within weeks of that meal, the guy sells the company! The sale of Cap-Cities (ABC) to Disney was another clincher. ABC was tough before, but now they would be so vertically integrated as to preclude any action for an independent.

All this and more was on my mind as I finally sat in the CBS waiting room that August morning in 1995, awaiting my summons to the inner sanctùm, anticipating my first appointment and my first meeting with the new CBS chief.

Moonves must have smelled my pique at being asked to cool my heels, not only for the minutes outside his office, but for the weeks I had waited since his ascension to that powerful throne. Possibly it was the adrenalin or my clenched fists on entering his office, as—only moments before hearing "Mr. Moonves will see you now"—I had had a hostile encounter (one of many) with CBS mini-exec Steve Werner.

The very bright son of a pal of Larry Tisch, Mr. Werner was the only network executive I had ever met who gave nepotism a bad name. The kid had an unfortunate way of dealing with what little power he was given by his superiors, coupled with (at best) a modicum of communication skills. It all came together in him as my model for a nightmare network executive.

"*I* have scheduled the next *Cagney* for October," he said, almost gratuitously, as he passed me sitting at Television City's second floor reception area.

"What happened to November?" I asked, as if I gave a shit (or as if it were my business, but this pipsqueak saying "I *have scheduled*" simply took my pre-Moonves meeting nerves over the top).

"We were the second highest-rated movie of the year last November on a Sunday and with little or no help from CBS!" I had to project a bit as he had not paused before or after his opening salvo. "Yeah," he countered over his shoulder, "but your next outing was a flop."

That did it. I was out of my chair and would have tackled him in the hall had not the summons to the Moonves meeting intervened.

It is hard to quarrel with the success of Leslie Moonves since his anointment by the CBS powers of yore. I suppose, if one were to be negative, the case could be made that he has reached the pinnacle he is on during a very different era with smaller, more fractionalized audiences, that standards of success are lower than they were, and that the vertical integration of the entire industry has changed the relationship between talent and network, but I won't do that. I give this devil his due, and it is only right that I do so. I never thought he would make it this far, or for this long, if for no other reason than I have always believed there is a difference between what it takes to be a studio head and to be a network chief that transcends even the divergence between seller and buyer.

You can be a tough guy and a bully and a control freak as a studio head (as was my personal favorite, Gary Nardino), but as a network topper, I think it is advantageous to be a nurturer and a diplomat. A good-guy, cheerleading, Sagansky-type Moonves is not. That was immediately apparent as he sat with his back to a large window in that familiar CBS corner office, totally back-lit by the California haze that streamed through the glass. I commented that I could not see his face; he made no effort to correct that situation. My mind wandered as we spoke. Is this Bob Daly? Is it Bud Grant? Harvey Shephard? Kim LeMasters? Jeff Sagansky? Peter Tortorici? What difference did it really make? It was another forty-year-old white guy. "Nothing ever happens at the Grand Hotel."

CHAPTER 46

"KID" ROSENZWEIG

The meeting with Moonves was a disaster. If Peter Lund had, indeed, paved the way, then Moonves had taken exception to having an executive from the New York office encroaching on his turf.

The paving might not have mattered in any event. The fact is, I was not good at the meeting. Was it the Werner confrontation in the hall just moments before, or the long wait throughout the summer for some kind of sign from the new management team that a track record such as mine would be respected? Whatever it was, I simply felt blindsided and was having a tough time recovering in that room.

Moonves had not read the scripts for *Whatever Happened to Nancy Drew?* nor did he seem even remotely interested in them. He let me know that he didn't want to be bothered with this kind of development stuff and that I should deal with his lieutenants (or even lesser executives much farther down the network food chain). It also became clear that my projects were on the wrong side of the demographic pool to be of real interest to Mr. Moonves.

For someone such as myself, the playing field would now, I was told, be a level one; I would have to get in line, along with everyone else in Hollywood. So much for "First Family" and eleven years of my relationship with the network.

Prior to the Moonves meet, I had been informed by a couple of trusted CBS executives that I had scored on the two private-eye scripts (two for two, it was said). As a result, the Moonves disinterest shocked even more than usual. "Shocked," perhaps, but not rocked as I would be by the Moonves flat-out statement that he had no interest in a multiple picture deal for *Cagney & Lacey*, gratuitously adding, "The first one was a fluke, and the second was a flop."

I gathered that, since I had just heard the same phrase from young Werner, precipitating our altercation in the hall outside the Moonves office, this was now the official CBS line. I was reeling, finding myself in full retreat from my original position of a ten-movie order over a five-year period.

Backpedaling, I asked for script money for two new *Cagney & Lacey* movies and holding money for the women. Moonves said he would wait to see how the two *Cagney & Lacey* films I had just completed would perform before making that decision.

"If you wait that long, I cannot guarantee delivery," I said.

The backlighting of his countenance kept me from seeing the narrowing of eyes, but, from the tone of the response, one would have to guess that narrowing is what they must have done as he spoke in the manner of Tony Soprano: "Are you telling me if I call you in January with an order for the fall, you're not going to be able to deliver?"

"That's exactly what I am telling you," I said, regaining some of my equilibrium. "My deal with the women is to hold themselves available to me for May and June, when any other show they might do would be in hiatus." I continued on quickly, so as to counter what I perceived as mounting incredulity that I would have a plan so far in advance of any production date. "This very morning—Tyne Daly called, saying she has an offer to do *Gypsy* in London in May, and she asked, 'What do I do, Boss?'"

Moonves was not impressed. He simply shrugged and said he would not put up any script or holding monies.

"Look," I said, "it is clear you have no interest in this material, which is certainly your prerogative; so, even though I am not contractually obligated to notify you of my intentions, I feel it only fair to let you know that I have to look for another home for this franchise."

The words from the backlit executive were clear and deadly on point: "If I even hear of your talking to another network about *Cagney & Lacey*, I will bury the two films I now have in our vaults."

There was a pregnant silence in the room. There was no question such an action by the CBS chief would irreparably damage the viability of the show. Moonves knew that—and more to the point—he knew that I knew it. It would seem that Leslie Moonves was bringing to television what Tonya Harding had brought to ice skating.

I got up from the couch, which, I was sure (based on common industry gossip regarding the diminutive network chief), would witness more pleasurable conquests for Moonves in the near future. Anita Addison, then recently installed as a network development executive, accompanied me out of the office. I probably looked as though I needed someone on whom to lean.

There is no question I was intimidated. I believed Moonves would make good on his threat to bury my show; I was also somewhat disoriented, not fully understanding how I had (so quickly) gone from "First Family" to this moment. At the outer door of the Moonves suite, connecting us to the reception area, I paused long enough to observe Ms. Addison's one-time (during my now long-ago Paramount days) friendly face. "That may be the worst network meeting I have ever been to in my life."

Ms. Addison, ever cheerful, smiled at me and said, "Oh, I have been in a lot of meetings with Mr. Moonves. That one wasn't bad at all."

"It was bad enough for me," I said. "I am not a rich man, but I am too rich for this. I will not be coming back."

I walked away, not expecting or waiting for a response. It has been over ten years since that meeting, and I have continued to honor that pledge of not returning to that, or any other, network. I did, however, continue in business with CBS for several months as they still had two of my films to release.

"Business" is heavy overstatement. It implies some kind of give and take. That was hardly the case. It was a very one-sided affair. I did take the Moonves threat seriously. I was sufficiently cowed that I made no attempt to approach his competitors at the other networks.

September 11, 1995: *It has been over a month since that awful meet in the Moonves lair. Today's special edition of the* Hollywood Reporter *on the fall schedule lists the CBS movies, and there is no mention of* Cagney & Lacey. *Would Les Moonves really bury us, simply to prove his point that young is where it's at? Do I know?*

My diary would go on and on, date after date, week in, week out, well into the following January, noting my many dilemmas, including, but not limited to, how to properly promote my two films without a cooperative CBS or, at the very least, publishable air dates. I knew, from past experience, that in order to be effective, to have a chance at the Sunday TV supplement covers, we had to have a minimum six weeks' lead time. What I got, on the first of the two films Moonves was holding hostage, was nineteen and a half days

While waiting those two months for some word from CBS, I met regularly with publicist Joan Carrey on designing a nationwide publicity tour for Sharon and Tyne, one that could be put together with very little advance notice and—

obviously—at my own expense. Work also included trying to find a tenant to sublease my expensive Hollywood office space (to help stop the bleeding) while I also toiled at effectuating my forever disappearance from the film and television scene by finalizing plans with our decorator for Sharon's and my new digs at Miami's Fisher Island.

Why Florida? I had always believed that one could not retire from show business and hang around the L.A. area. I had seen others being given the fish eye, because, whether by choice or not, they were not working; the supposition invariably being that the person not working was unable to get a job. That was not my idea of a happy retirement. Besides, Florida was probably the only place in North America where people might still call me "kid."

Deep into the second week of October of 1995, we got the word from the network; the first of our two air dates would be October 25, and against the World Series. The CBS failure to officially notify *TV Guide* in a timely fashion of when we would air cost us that publication's valuable close-up feature and, also due to time constraints, effectively killed the piece scheduled by *In Style* magazine. Barbara Salztman, of the *L.A. Times,* and Gail Pennington, of the *St. Louis Post-Dispatch,* both confirmed that, had they been given any reasonable notice at all, there was little that would have competed with *Cagney & Lacey* for a cover of their Sunday TV supplements for that last week of October.

A week later, from Minneapolis, where the Tyne Daly/Sharon Gless/Barney Rosenzweig troika was doing its eighteen-hour-a-day road tour for *C&L III,* I called Leslie Moonves to tell him of those lost opportunities. I added that the $10,000 his network had spent on producing by-the-numbers color art (still photos) and mailing those to editors across the country was totally wasted, since there was so little time between when the announcement of the air date was made and the air date itself. As a result, I said, none of this material could, or would, be used.

Moonves seemed nonplussed, saying he had been told that the six weeks I had asked for was unnecessary. My response to that was, "Fire whomever the asshole was that doesn't know this simple fact of Sunday supplement deadlines." I don't believe Moonves followed this advice, but he did promise me sufficient notice in the future for *C&L IV.*

Our road show was a happy and exhausting time: the three of us, doing our act, singing show tunes to one another between appearances, betting money as to who had which lyric right during our private moments, and venting our displeasure with CBS, in front of live audiences. We were on the radio or TV, or on the phone with journalists in cities we could not visit. From guest lecturing at Brandeis University to joining a Lily Tomlin fund raiser in Boston, from St. Louis, to Pittsburgh, to Minneapolis/St. Paul, Chicago, New York, Boston, and DC, we did our best to make folks aware that a new *Cagney & Lacey* reunion film was coming their way.

It was the Johnny Appleseed approach. We were out there tossing our seeds and hoping that some day it would all bear fruit. On the road, mornings usually began with a 5:30 AM leave from the hotel for the local CBS affiliate, time with hair and makeup for the two women, and then a morning talk show segment at about 8 AM. From there we would continue on with whatever radio talk shows there were in the vicinity, perhaps a lunch with the area's print media, more radio, and then the afternoon local TV spots. Dinner would, more often than not, be with a top local TV editor representing the area's biggest newspaper. It was rare when our efforts ended before 10 PM, for we most often got a flight at that point to our next destination.

From my diary: **October 25, 1995:** *This show may fail, but it will be through little or no fault of this duo. I'm proud to be in their company. Yesterday, a very good review in* Daily Variety, *today the biggest rave I have ever seen in the* Hollywood Reporter. *No reviews published anywhere else of consequence. Tonight's the night!*

The ratings for *C&L III* were, by my standards, less than stellar (something like a 10 rating and a 15 or 16 share), but apparently there was enthusiasm for this performance at CBS, where the ratings were over half again what they had previously garnered on a Wednesday night for the season; if one considers we did that while taking on the World Series, it was a bit more impressive.

The day following this news, word from a source at the network was, that in a staff meeting, Les Moonves referred to me as his new best friend, going on to say that I was right and he was wrong. He did phone me and was complimentary, reiterating his promise for more lead time in the future for promotion. I was apparently unimpressed as I noted in my diary:

October 27, 1995: *All I want to do is pack up my offices and stuff here in L.A. and get the apartment in Florida ready for occupancy so that I can move the hell out of here.*

Just about this time Sharon accepted an offer to star opposite Tom Conti in Neil Simon's *Chapter II* in London. She would be in the UK for six months. It was a great thing for Sharon, coming as it did at a terrific time in terms of her own self-esteem issues. I had overheard her on the phone turning down some inquiry for her services with regret because of our upcoming move to Florida and all that would entail. After the phone call, I asked what was going on, and, when she told me, I suggested that, all things considered (she being a far better actress than a packer) she would probably be a lot better off doing something she did well. I told her I would "produce" the move, getting us into and onto Fisher Island, and that she should go to London and act on the stage in a work by one of America's great playwrights opposite an award-winning leading man. My wife could not have been more relieved.

It was a quiet Christmas holiday that year with my father in and out of the hospital and Sharon off to London for rehearsals.

January 7, 1996: *The move from Malibu to Miami's Fisher Island goes on. We are on, or slightly ahead, of schedule. On Friday last (1-5-96), Tom Nunan passed on my inquiry regarding NBC's level of interest, if any, in MAGUIRE FOR HIRE, or MCQUE (the Nancy Drew projects for Sharon). The rejection from this friend who thinks of me as a mini-father figure could not have been—all things considered—an easier let down. It still hurt. More than I could have imagined it would. I am no longer suited for this. If I had any doubts (which I don't really think I did) today's phone call could only reinforce the decision to get away from these people who give me too little and who hurt me too much.*

January 8, 1996: *At 12 noon, Steve Werner calls from CBS with the news that our air date will be January 29. A Monday, and against the Country Music Awards special, which is always a monster hit. I made no comment about Leslie Moonves and his promise of at least six-weeks notice instead of the three we were getting. Curiously, I am not in much of a fighting mode. It isn't as it used to be—my "David" to their "Goliath." I just feel as if I've passed all this. I am, let's face it, now too old to play "David." Tomorrow I will take most of the day off from packing to think on this and to, hopefully, come up with a plan. Right now it (the plan) is to do some campaigning, but to spend very little money on this and to deal with the show as if it were the last (probably is) and to go out with the dignity I think we deserve. Since CBS isn't giving it to us, then I will.*

I wrote a short press release. I was careful in the story not to be too overt, only obliquely referring to the lack of synergism between my own goals and those of the network. I massaged the story carefully so as not to sound like a victim and, in fact, did not feel like one. I phoned the Moonves office, saying to his secretary, "Tell him it is not what he thinks," and "I believe he will be pleasantly surprised." A few minutes later he returned the call.

I told him that, contrary to what he might have guessed, I actually thought that returning *Cagney & Lacey* to a Monday night against the Country Music Awards was an interesting idea and possibly a great counter-programming move. The only problem was the short time-frame. He immediately broke in, wanting to apologize about breaking his word.

I interrupted. "Not important," I said. "With this short a period of time, and with Gless in England, there is a distinct limit as to what I can accomplish with publicity," I told him. "Without Gless and Daly to play off each other on the road, the only way I can get in the paper, to be the lead item in Liz Smith, or wherever, is to do and say things that are confrontational and somewhat controversial." I added that I could appreciate the fact that he didn't seem to like that.

"No," he confessed he didn't, but he wanted me to be out there plugging. He just "didn't want to be mentioned or have CBS criticized in anyway."

"Can't be done," I said. "I only know one campaign for this show, and it is always guaranteed to work. It's the gal show against the all-male establishment that runs the network. It is David versus Goliath. That's all I did last time, and it is all I've ever done. This time, it would just be me, so, although fundamentally it would be the same thing, I don't have the star power of the women, so it would have to be a bit rougher to find its way into print."

I didn't want to do that, I said, and here was my solution: "We can't do it with publicity, unless it is the very kind of publicity that you (Moonves) hate, so let's do it with advertising, which you control!"

I went on to say I thought we could win, that I thought it was fate that he chose January 29 to air the show, because that's the day I leave for Miami and I'm happy to have this be a going-away present from CBS.

The best campaign, I told him, would be for CBS to call it the last *Cagney & Lacey* ever—unfortunately, they couldn't do that without risking a lawsuit for damaging the franchise. But, I added, "I could put out a press release: 'Cagney & Lacey Cancels CBS.' The press will eat it up with a spoon."

I pushed forward. "It will in no way mention you, Les, or in any way bad-mouth the network. We are just going our separate ways."

Moonves liked the idea, saying he would get right into it with his promo people but couldn't promise a specific number of on-air promos.[89]

I interrupted. "Promises don't mean much to me anyway, Les," I said with hardly an edge. "All I care about right now is that the final chapter in this quartet of films I have made is treated with the respect my work, and the work of my stars, deserves."

He agreed. He told me that none of this was personal; he wanted to assure me of that. I told him I couldn't give less of a shit if it were. Just "Do all that can be done for this show, and we might scare the hell out of those music awards." He thanked me several times for my attitude and for the ideas and said he'd get right on them.

January 12, 1996: *My press release, canceling the CBS network, went out today. I will be surprised if the press doesn't have fun with this. Joan Carry, knowing that the TV press are all in town at the same hotel on a TV junket, had the release slipped under the door of each of their rooms this afternoon. I'll keep my fingers crossed that this doesn't backfire. I don't think it will, though it is possible that if it generates heat on Moonves he will forget that he is part of this plot and will turn on me again. It's worth the shot.*

Moonves did turn. The story broke in the Morning Report section of the *L.A. Times*' Calendar section under the headline, "Take That, CBS." They printed a good portion of the story and got a quote from Moonves that I had "demanded" a commitment of ten *Cagney & Lacey* movies and that he would not make such a commitment. He would say no more, effectively letting the air out of our mutual publicity balloon. We managed to get good space in *The Milwaukee Journal* and the *New York Daily News*, but that was pretty much it. The way these things work is to have fun with it, to keep this sort of thing going between the two parties. But Moonves trumped me at my own game by simply refusing to enter the fray; so much for synergy. "*Everybody,*" I noted in my diary, "*has an asshole. Leslie Moonves is mine.*"

By months end, our ratings on *C&L IV* would be published, and they were unacceptable. A 15 share—our lowest ever. I had stayed an extra day in L.A. in the hope that the ratings would be good enough to allow for some gloating time. No such luck; barely third in a four-horse race.

---

[89] Slightly shorter version of on-air promotions or point of sale advertising, which is what an ad for a TV show, seen on TV, is—an ad for people who are watchers of that network (they are at the "point of sale").

January 31, 1996: *I will limp out of town this morning and look forward to a better life in Florida. Our Planet Hollywood party and screening just for us (no press) was great fun. Tyne cried a bit. John Karlen was quite pleased with the film, as were the fans that bothered to call and most of the reviewers who went to print. It was a good little movie. Whatever, I'm out of here.*

My best productions: from left, *Menopause Years* associate producer and award-winning filmmaker in her own right, youngest daughter, Torrie Rosenzweig; eldest daughter, Erika, who was featured in a small part in one of our reunion films and is married to David Handman, one of my favorite film editors; and Allyn, who worked as a costumer on the original series out of Lacy Street before becoming a full-time mom. The photo by famed photographer Greg Gorman was a gift from Sharon for my sixtieth birthday. The gift of my beautiful children was courtesy of first wife, JoAnne Benickes.

Photo: Rosenzweig Personal Collection

CHAPTER 47

MIAMI NICE

I had happily set up housekeeping at our new digs on Miami's Fisher Island, commuting that first year between Florida and London to visit Sharon (who had, while costarring with Tom Conti in Neil Simon's *Chapter II,* justifiably become the darling of the English critics). My wife then went on to a five-year stint as Debbie, the PFLAG Mom, on Showtime's groundbreaking series *Queer as Folk,* while Tyne Daly parlayed her Tony Award-winning performance in *Gypsy* into a long-term Emmy-winning role on the CBS series *Judging Amy.* With a few brief interruptions, I have been enjoying life in general without work and with no dark clouds on my horizon.

No dark clouds. This is largely because my horizon is now seen from a small island off the coast of Miami Beach—as far as one can get from Hollywood and the film industry while still residing in the continental United States.

The industry in which I grew up has, coincidental with my departure, been in the throes of apocalyptic events. Besides the sometimes in and sometimes out of the business, MGM, what was Columbia Pictures Corporation, Tri-Star, and Embassy are now divisions or offshoots of the Sony Corporation. RCA Victor is no more; the image of the happy canine looking into his master's gramophone is now nothing but a collector's item.

The studios conceived by the Warner Brothers and Lorimar (a one-time giant of the television industry) are now merged with the Time Publishing Empire (HBO) and, for a while, Ted Turner. Rupert Murdoch owns both the Fox Studios and the Fox network and enough television outlets and newspapers and satellites to be scary. Universal Studios, NBC, and Telemundo are a division of General Electric, and Disney has taken over ABC and ESPN and more. CBS, the Tiffany network of William Paley, is now merely a division of Viacom, which also owns Paramount Pictures Corporation, to be cut loose or brought back into the fold seemingly at Sumner Redstone's whim, or (I presume) in order to vie for more corporate shelf space.

My fabulous longtime assistant, Carole R. Smith, at Miami's famous Joe's Stone Crab, to help me celebrate my sixtieth birthday.

Photo: Rosenzweig Personal Collection

Three in a million: 2004 with Carole King, Sharon, and me at the March for Women's Lives in Washington DC, where I made the crack about all those women and not one of them remembering to raise the lid on the toilet seat.

Photo: Rosenzweig Personal Collection

We are at the time Brandon Tartikoff predicted in the 1990s of only a half dozen sequoias standing in the Hollywood forest—and not all of these are of domestic national origin.[90]

In some ways we are only at the beginning of this cycle. If what has just passed has been the American century, then it is in no small way thanks to the entertainment industry. It wasn't so many decades ago that French, the language of diplomacy, was considered the international means of communication; today, it is English. That is not thanks to Margaret Thatcher or any American politician. Teenagers in the Soviet Union who wear Levis and know the lyrics to Bruce Springsteen songs are responding to what they see and hear in the media, and most of that from the entertainment capital of the world.

Since the advent of World War I—and the subsequent need in Europe to use nitrate for gunpowder rather than motion picture film stock—that capital has been in my old hometown.

America may no longer make the best automobiles, steel, or even computers, but it still manufactures the best filmed entertainment in the world. That's not a birthright; only Europe's past mistakes made it possible in the first place. Now it is the United States that is making the mistake of underestimating the value of the export of the American dream, and it is difficult to judge just where we will go from here.

Approaching my seventieth year on the planet, I confess to being less interested in what is to come than what has transpired. My past, the mistakes and the tri-

---

[90]   Sony, of course, is a Japanese company. Rupert Murdoch is a transplant from Australia, and General Electric is about as multinational as any company can get.

umphs, the wins and all the other stuff, is my legacy. It is, I suppose, the hope of any purveyor of autobiographical material that their not-so-recent past will resonate for others besides themselves, and so, in conclusion, I submit what follows:

In the seven years between 1981 and 1988, I produced 127 hours of *Cagney & Lacey*. One hundred twenty-five hour-long episodes and a two-hour movie-for-television—all broadcast on the CBS network—and all for a then-publicly held company known as Orion Pictures Corporation. Later, in 1990 and into 1992, I produced another television series, *The Trials of Rosie O'Neill*, also broadcast on CBS, but this time for The Rosenzweig Company. (The Rosenzweig Company production of the four *Cagney & Lacey* reunion films would come about in the mid-1990s.)

On the air for six years, *Cagney & Lacey* was an authentic hit, grandfathered under the Department of Internal Revenue's then-existing and generous investment tax credit rules. It was produced (I mention yet again) at or near the network's license fee. There seemed to be almost unlimited opportunities for profit: the distribution of the production itself (both foreign and domestic), the prospect of substantial merchandising and commercial tie-ins, plus the eventual marketing of various video packages. It was all in the realm of the possible for that series.

The Trials of Rosie O'Neill, although celebrated as the highest-rated, best reviewed new dramatic series of 1990, had only thirty-four hour-long episodes during its two-season run on CBS. In the time that had passed since *Cagney & Lacey*, Ronald Reagan had deregulated the television industry, with the resultant collapse of the syndication market for hour-long dramas; the investment tax credit had been rescinded by Congress; and, with only two seasons on the air, *Rosie O'Neill* had virtually no chance of any kind of merchandising or marketing tie-ins.

For a thirty-four episode series, there is little or no afterlife; certainly no syndication, no cable sale, no demand for videos. Despite all that, in those two years, I made nearly as much money as I had in the over seven years I had been involved with the two most renowned women law enforcers in the history of television. It was, for a brief time, almost a license to print money. It was the difference between being an owner (as I was on *Rosie*) and an employee, however well thought of, as I was on *Cagney & Lacey*.

The religion of the television producer has always preached one primary doctrine:

Make 125 episodes of anything—reasonably close to the license fee—and you may spend the rest of your days (should you so desire) floating aboard your own yacht on the Aegean.

I didn't get the boat. The promised dollars weren't there.

The TV producer's religion, however, isn't always about money. After all is said, done, and dealt with, regardless of the changes of rules by governments, the lawsuits, the wrecked marriages, the greed, stupidity, and downright dishonesty by former partners and self-proclaimed allies, the perceived unfairness of the system—there is one undeniable truth:

Had God, all those years ago, visited my office, and said:

"Barney Rosenzweig, there will be a television series. It will be called *Cagney & Lacey*, and you will make that show. It will be canceled and you will save it … more than once, and everyone will know it was you who did so. The network will tell the *New York Times* and the world that it has made a mistake and that you, Barney, were right and they were wrong. Your peers will honor you. There will be Emmys, Golden Globes, and many other honors. You will be celebrated by your university, your community, and your industry. Women's groups throughout the nation will name you their 'man of the year.' You and your show will be written of in virtually every television history book for the remainder of the millennium.

"But … there will be no money."

I would have filled the briefest moment of silence following all of that with one simple question:

"God, where do I sign?"

On the set (Times Square, New York City) for the finale of the first of our quartet of *Cagney & Lacey: The Menopause Years* reunion films.

© CBS Broadcasting Inc. John Seakwood/CBS

BARNEY ROSENZWEIG

Began his show business career as an MGM office boy in 1959, and rose to become one of television's most honored producers, winning two Emmys from the Academy of Television Arts and Sciences for Outstanding Dramatic Series (*Cagney & Lacey*), and a Golden Globe from the Hollywood Foreign Press Association for Best Miniseries (*John Steinbeck's East of Eden*). He is the recipient of citations from the Congress of the United States, the State of California, the cities of Los Angeles, Chicago and New York, multiple women's groups throughout the country, and, from the University of Southern California, where he now serves on the prestigious Board of Councilors of the School of Cinematic Arts.

Other honors awarded Rosenzweig's work include the ACLU "Bill of Rights Award," the Humanitas, Scott Newman and Christopher Awards, a special Luminas from Women in Film, as well as citations and salutes from the National Commission of Working Women, the Museum of Television & Radio, the National Organization for Women (NOW), the "Good Guy Award" from the National Women's Political Caucus, and the "Award of Merit" from USC as one of the university's "outstanding alumni."

Rosenzweig received his degree in political science at USC (1959), where he has established a Cagney & Lacey Scholarship. Other philanthropies include a two-year term in Los Angeles as chairman of the entertainment division of the United Jewish Fund, and as chairperson of the President's Council of the American Lung Association.

In 1991, Rosenzweig married his third wife, multi Emmy Award-winning actress Sharon Gless. They reside on Fisher Island in Florida, where Rosenzweig, quoting playwright Terrence McNally, says he "hasn't retired, he's stopped," conceding the difference to be subtle. The producer goes on to note that his "best productions" are daughters Erika, Allyn, and Torrie, and the "spin-offs," granddaughters Hailey Laws, Greer Rose Glassman, and Zoey B Rosenzweig.

Cagney & Lacey … and Me is Rosenzweig's first book.

BARNEY ROSENZWEIG FILMOGRAPHY

1999	Twice In A Lifetime (22 episodes)	TV Series	Executive Producer
1999	Smoke and Mirrors: A History of Denial	Documentary	Executive Producer
1996	Cagney & Lacey: True Convictions	M.O.W.	Producer (sole credit)
1995	Cagney & Lacey: The View Through The Glass Ceiling	M.O.W.	Producer (sole credit)
1995	Cagney & Lacey: Together Again	M.O.W.	Producer (sole credit)
1994	Cagney & Lacey: The Return	M.O.W.	Producer (sole credit)
1994–95	Christy (18 episodes)	TV Series	Executive Producer
1990–92	The Trials of Rosie O'Neill (34 episodes)	TV Series	Producer (sole credit)
1982–88	Cagney & Lacey (125 episodes)	TV Series	Executive Producer
1986	Fortune Dane (6 episodes)	TV Series	Executive Producer
1983	This Girl For Hire	M.O.W.	Producer (sole credit)
1982	Modesty Blaise	M.O.W.	Producer (sole credit)

1981	Cagney & Lacey (aka The Pilot Episode)	M.O.W.	Producer
1980	American Dream	Pilot	Producer (sole credit)
1980	John Steinbeck's East of Eden	Miniseries	Producer
1980	Angel On My Shoulder	M.O.W.	Producer
1976	Charlie's Angels (11 episodes)	TV Series	Producer
1976	One Of My Wives Is Missing	M.O.W.	Producer
1974	Men Of The Dragon	Pilot	Producer
1974	The Legend of Hillbilly John (aka Who Fears the Devil)	Theatrical Motion Picture	Producer
1967–70	Daniel Boone (78 episodes)	TV Series	Producer
1967	Tony Rome	Theatrical Motion Picture	Associate Producer
1966	Caprice	Theatrical Motion Picture	Associate Producer
1966	Smoky	Theatrical Motion Picture	Associate Producer
1965	Morituri	Theatrical Motion Picture	Associate Producer
1965	Do Not Disturb	Theatrical Motion Picture	Associate Producer

CAGNEY & LACEY EMMY AWARDS

1983	Tyne Daly	Outstanding Lead Actress in a Drama Series
1984	Tyne Daly	Outstanding Lead Actress in a Drama Series
1985	Tyne Daly	Outstanding Lead Actress in a Drama Series
1985	Barney Rosenzweig	Outstanding Drama Series
	Peter Lefcourt	
	Steve Brown	
	Terry Louise Fisher	
1985	Karen Arthur	Outstanding Directing in a Drama Series
1985	Jim Gross	Outstanding Film Editing for a Series
1985	Maury Harris	Outstanding Film Sound Mixing for a Series
1985	Patricia Green	Outstanding Writing in a Drama Series
1986	Barney Rosenzweig	Outstanding Drama Series
	Liz Coe	
	Steve Brown	
	Patricia Green	
	Ralph S. Singleton	
	P. K. Knelman	
1986	Georg Stanford Brown	Outstanding Directing in a Drama Series
1986	Sharon Gless	Outstanding Lead Actress in a Drama Series
1986	John Karlen	Outstanding Supporting Actor in a Drama Series

1987   Sharon Gless   Outstanding Lead Actress in a Drama Series

1988   Tyne Daly   Outstanding Lead Actress in Drama Series

GUEST STARS

Julie Adams

Jonelle Allen

Elizabeth Ashley

Lew Ayres

Talia Balsam

Jack Bannon

Kathy Bates

Bibi Besch

Peter Boyle

Georg Stanford Brown

Paul Burke

Betty Buckley

Jack Colvin

Carole Cook

Brian Dennehy

Charles S. Dutton

Peggy Feury

Geraldine Fitzgerald

Fionnula Flanagan

Robert Foxworth

Paul Freeman

Julie Fulton

Estelle Getty

Cliff Gorman

John Harkins

Anthony Holland

Judith Ivey

Peter Jason

Salome Jens

Marvin Kaplan

Noah Keen

William Lanteau

Dan Lauria

Stephen Macht

Janet MacLachlan

Dinah Manoff

Richard Masur

Ferdinand Mayne

Melanie Mayron

Mercedes McCambridge

Peggy McCay

Sidney Miller

Greg Mullavey

Lois Nettleton

Jeanette Nolan

Sandra Oh

Soon-Tek Oh

David Paymer

Barry Primus

Joe Regalbuto

Doris Roberts

Paul Sand

Barry Sattels

Milton Seltzer

Anne Seymour

Carolyn Seymour

Raymond St. Jacques

James Stacy

Susan Strasberg

Gail Strickland

Tom Troupe

Shannon Tweed

Amy Van Nostrand

Jennifer Warren

Carl Weintraub

Sam Weisman

Forest Whitaker

Lynn Whitfield

Gary Wood

Harris Yulin

Grace Zabriski

AWARD-WINNING ACTORS

Jonelle Allen	Tony (1)
Elizabeth Ashley	Tony (1)
Kathy Bates	Oscar (1), Golden Globe (1)
Peter Boyle	Emmy (1)
Betty Buckley	Tony (1)
Tyne Daly	Emmy (6), Tony (1)
Brian Dennehy	Tony (2), Golden Globe (1)
Charles S. Dutton	Emmy (3)
Fionnula Flanagan	Emmy (1)
Estelle Getty	Emmy (1), Golden Globe (1)
Sharon Gless	Emmy (2), Golden Globe (2)
Cliff Gorman	Tony (1)
Judith Ivey	Tony (2)
John Karlen	Emmy (1)
Dinah Manoff	Tony (1)
Mercedes McCambridge	Oscar (1), Golden Globe (1)
Peggy McCay	Emmy (1)
Michael Moriarty	Emmy (1)
Lois Nettleton	Emmy (1)
Sandra Oh	Golden Globe (1)
Doris Roberts	Emmy (4)
Paul Sand	Tony (1)
Forest Whitaker	Oscar (1), Golden Globe (1)
Lynn Whitfield	Emmy (1)

THE 14TH PRECINCT AND KEY LAW ENFORCEMENT

Tyne Daly	Det. Mary Beth Lacey
Sharon Gless	Sgt. Christine Cagney
Harvey Atkin	Desk Sgt. Ronald Coleman
Carl Lumbly	Detective Marcus Petrie
Martin Kove	Detective Victor Isbecki
Albert S. Waxman	Lieutenant Samuels
Sidney Clute	Det. LaGuardia
Robert Hegyes	Det. Manny Esposito
Merry Clayton	Det. Verna Dee Johnson
Paul Mantee	Det. Al Corassa
Michael Fairman	Dep. Inspector Knelman
Jason Bernard	Dep. Inspector Marquette
Dan Shor	Det. Jonah Newman
Beverley Faverty	Uniform officer
David Paymer	Todd Feldberg
Stanley Kamel	Mick Solomon
Jo Corday	Josie the bag lady
Edward Winter	Captain Jack Hennessy
Steward Coss	Squad room
Larry Da'Vol	Squad Room
Richard Minchenberg	Daniels

Vincent Schiavelli	Mongoose
Robert Costanzo	Monk
Michael Moriarty	Patrick Lowell
Richard Romanus	Det. Sal Caprio

FAMILY

Amanda Wyss	Bridget Cagney
David Ackroyd	Brian Cagney
Dick O'Neill	Charley Cagney
John Karlen	Harvey Lacey
Neva Patterson	Muriel Lacey (Harvey's mother)
Richard Bradford	Martin Zzbiski (Lacey's father)
Suzanne Stone	Claudia Petrie
Tony LaTorre	Harvey Lacey Jr.
Troy Slaten	Michael Lacey
Vonetta McGee	Claudia Petrie

THE MENOPAUSE YEARS
MOVIES

CAGNEY & LACEY: THE RETURN

Director: James Frawley

Writer: Terry Louise Fisher & Steve Brown

Editor: Geoffrey Rowland

Music: Dana Kaproff

Guest Stars: James Naughton, David Paymer, Susan Anspach, John Harkins, Bree Walker Lampley

CAGNEY & LACEY: TOGETHER AGAIN

Director: Reza Badiyi

Writer: Terry Louise Fisher & Steve Brown

Editor: Jim Gross

Music: Nan Mishkin

Guest Stars: James Naughton, David Paymer, Rose Marie

CAGNEY & LACEY: THE VIEW THROUGH THE GLASS CEILING

Director: John Patterson

Writer: Michele Gallery

Editor: David Handman

Music: Ron Ramin

Guest Stars: Lynne Thigpen, Chip Zien, Sandra Oh

CAGNEY & LACEY: TRUE CONVICTIONS

Director: Lynne Littman

Writer: Michele Gallery

Editor: Jim Gross

Music: Ron Ramin

Guest Stars: Michael Moriarty, Chip Zien

Cagney & Lacey

Barney Rosenzweig
Executive Producer

August 25, 1988

Dear Chris and Mary Beth:

You once said it better than I ever could: "We did it with our principles intact, which is not an easy thing to do in this job, in this city."

I choose to look on tonight's final broadcast, by CBS of our closing two-hour episode, as a tribute. It matters little if it is or not. Either way, they cannot honor you enough.

Vaya con Dios,

[signature]

**CAGNEY & LACEY
PRODUCTIONS
ORION T.V.**

P.O. Box 4718
Los Angeles, CA 90051
(213) 222-8160
(213) 222-0291

Full-page trade ad that I purchased in 1988 to call attention to our final
episode, since no one else would or did.

THE DIRECTORS

DIRECTOR	# OF EPISODES
Karen Arthur	7
Reza Badiyi	11
Allen Baron	1
Gabrielle Beaumont	1
Burt Brinkerhoff	1
Charlotte Brown	1
Georg Stanford Brown	5
Michael Caffey	1
Jackie Cooper	4
Ray Danton	10
Janet Davidson	1
Charles S. Dubin	1
Bill Duke	2
Jan Eliasberg	1
Jonathan Estrin	1
James Frawley	12
Harry Harris	1
Jeffrey Hayden	1
Helaine Head	3
Nessa Hyams	1
Stan Lathan	1
Peter Levin	2

DIRECTOR	# OF EPISODES
Victor Lobl	2
Stephen Macht	1
Nancy Malone	1
Sharron Miller	10
Christian I. Nyby, II	1
Joel Oliansky	1
Francine Parker	1
John Patterson	5
Leo Penn	1
Barbara Peters	1
Ted Post (pilot film)	1
Joel Rosenzweig	2
Nicholas Sgarro	1
James Sheldon	1
Alexander Singer	17
Ralph Singleton	2
Michael Vejar	1
Al Waxman	6
Claudia Weill	1
Don Weiss	1

THE SCRIPTWRITERS

Frank Abatemarco	Staff
Chris Abbott-Fish	Staff
David Abromowitz	Freelance
Claudia Adams	Freelance
Josef Anderson	Freelance
Leo A. Arthur	Staff
Michelle Ashford	Freelance
Barbara Avedon & Barbara Corday	Co-Creators
Gloria Banta	Staff
Larry Barber & Paul Barber	Freelance
Michael Berlin & Eric Estrin	Freelance
Robert Bielak	Freelance
Eric Blakeney & Gene Miller	Freelance
Harvey Brenner	Freelance
Steve Brown	Staff
Les Carter & Susan Sisko	Freelance
Norm Chandler Fox	Freelance
Liz Coe	Staff
Robert Crais	Staff
Cynthia Darnell	Freelance
Sharon Elizabeth Doyle	Freelance

Paul Ehrmann	Freelance
Robert Eisele	Freelance
Kathryn Ford	Staff
Debra Frank & Scott Rubenstein	Freelance
Bud Freeman	Freelance
Fred Freiberger	Staff
Dan Freudenberger	Freelance
Marshall Goldberg	Freelance
Richard Gollance	Freelance
Patricia Green	Staff
Jack R. Guss	Staff
Allison Hock	Staff
Max Jack	Freelance
Georgia Jeffries	Staff
Steve Johnson	Freelance
E. Arthur Kean	Staff
P.K. Knelman	Staff
Larry Konner & Ronnie Wenker-Konner	Freelance
Jeffrey Lane	Freelance
Peter Lefcourt	Staff
Shelley List & Jonathan Estrin	Staff
Terry Louise Fisher	Staff
Brian McKay	Freelance
Judy Merl & Paul Eric Myers	Freelance
Chelsea Nickerson	Staff
Michael Piller	Freelance
Wayne Powers & Donna Dottley Powers	Freelance

Frederick Rappaport	Freelance
Del Reisman	Freelance
Barney Rosenzweig	Executive Producer
Lisa Seidman	Freelance
Hannah Louise Shearer	Freelance
Lee Sheldon	Freelance
April Smith	Staff
Aubrey Solomon & Steve Greenberg	Freelance
Frank South	Staff
Douglas Steinberg	Freelance
Kevin Sullivan	Freelance
Bill Taub	Freelance
Rogers Turrentine	Freelance
Joe Viola	Staff
Marcy Vosburgh & Sandy Sprung	Freelance
Samm-Art Williams	Freelance

978-0-595-41193-1
0-595-41193-2

Made in the USA
Monee, IL
17 April 2021